THE MANY FACES OF EVIL

The Many Faces of Evil traces transformations of conceptions of evil – malevolence, sin, vice, willful destruction, wanton cruelty – in the Western tradition. It is a collection of stellar primary sources – presented in rough chronological order – drawn from sacred texts and works by theologians, philosophers, historians, political theorists, poets, novelists as well as contemporary psychologists and legal theorists. Amélie Rorty's introductions accompany the selections.

Amélie Oksenberg Rorty is the Director of the Program in History of Ideas at Brandeis University. She is the author of *Mind in Action*, and has edited many anthologies, including The *Identities of Persons*, *Essays on Aristotle's Ethics*, *Essays on Descartes' Meditations*, *Explaining Emotions*, *Perspectives on Self-Deception* and *Philosophers on Education*.

THE
MANY FACES
OF EVIL

Historical perspectives

Edited by
Amélie Oksenberg Rorty

Routledge
Taylor & Francis Group

LONDON AND NEW YORK

First published 2001
by Routledge
2 Park Square, Milton Park, Abingdon, Oxon, OX14 4RN

Simultaneously published in the USA and Canada
by Routledge
270 Madison Ave, New York, NY 10016

Routledge is an imprint of the Taylor & Francis Group

Transferred to Digital Printing 2005

© 2001 Amélie Oksenberg Rorty for selection and editorial matter

Typeset in Garamond by
Florence Production Ltd, Stoodleigh, Devon

British Library Cataloguing in Publication Data
A catalogue record for this book is available from the British Library

Library of Congress Cataloguing in Publication Data
The many faces of evil: historical perspectives / [compiled by]
Amélie Oksenberg Rorty.
p. cm.
Includes bibliographical references and index.
1. Good and evil. I. Rorty, Amélie.
BJ1401 .M26   2001
170 – dc21   00–067067

ISBN 0 – 415 – 24206 – 1 hbk
ISBN 0 – 415 – 24207 – X pbk

Printed and bound by Antony Rowe Ltd, Eastbourne

In gratitude to
M.F.B. and M.leD.
and the members of the Brandeis University
philosophy department

von denen man vieles lernen kann

CONTENTS

CONTENTS

CONTENTS

CONTENTS

PREFACE
Varieties of Evil

Ethics has recently taken the high road. Philosophers of all persuasions formulate moral ideals and principles. They chart conceptions of the good, of rights, of obligations; they offer a dazzling array of analyses of the virtues, of the norms of deliberation. Moving from theory to application, they advance criteria for the just distribution of basic goods like education and health care, discuss the conditions for the reparation of culpable wrongs and the limits of judicial authority. Even moral theory – philosophical reflection on the ontological and epistemological status of normative claims – has taken the high road: criteria for objectivity and grounds for the authority of morality are proposed. Discussions of the roles of reason and emotion in moral life and of the proper focus of moral evaluation (actions, intentions, character, or social institutions) abound. But although "the social formation of evaluative language" has received considerable attention from social theorists and philosophers of language, philosophers have on the whole paid little attention to the Dark Side.[1] We are told a great deal about virtues and ideals, but very little about vice and malevolence. Few ethical theorists have anatomized varieties of sheer wickedness or discussed the lures of sin, evil, immorality, cruelty. To be sure, weakness of will has received considerable attention from philosophers of mind interested in the conditions for voluntary actions; and some psychologically minded philosophers have discussed shame, guilt and agent regret. But with some exceptions, there is a division of labor between disciplines. Philosophers take the constructive viewpoint: they investigate the sources, authority and logical structure of moral obligation. Theorists in other disciplines analyze varieties of wrong-doing and varieties of corruption. Legal theorists formulate criteria for criminal liability; psychologists and psychiatrists speculate on the origins of sociopathology, aggression and violence; clergymen caution against greed or lust; committees of historians, theologians, political and legal theorists provide a forum for expiating war crimes and civic outrage by confession, reparation, reconciliation. Films and novels – science fiction, spy and detective stories – bring vicarious participation in the tones and moods of the Dark Side. Interestingly enough, all these explorations of the varieties of evil tend to be less technical, and (let's be frank) more readable, than elevating theology or careful moral philosophy.

This rather relentlessly upbeat turn is, in a way, surprising. After all, the morality of everyday life is largely conveyed in prohibitions. Negative commands can be given to children as guidelines for conduct without deep metaphysical or psychological elaboration. "Thou shalt not murder, steal, bear false witness . . ." are more focussed, clearer than "Love thy neighbor" or even "Be just." "Promote welfare" leaves even the wisest among us rather at loose ends. That's on the one hand. On the other hand, it should not be surprising that – with the interesting exception of the German Romantics – post-Enlightenment theorists have concentrated on defining human progress, including moral improvement, whatever that may be. These have been an unusually improvement-minded few centuries.

It has not always been so. Historically, ethics has given equal time to the Dark side, to prohibitions, vice, sanctions. Moral theorists attempted to formulate the principles that should guide censure and to locate the legitimate authority of condemnation and punishment. Until recently, philosophical analysis and moral indignation, even sometimes exhortation, went hand in hand. Nor was there so sharp a difference between charting the directions of ideal principles and mapping the pitfalls of waywardness. Augustine and Aquinas discussed original sin as well as courage and *caritas*; Butler and Kant discussed the suspect inclination to egoism as well as the morality of altruism and respect. More recently, James, Royce and Dewey in the United States, Mill, Jowett, Russell and Anscombe in Great Britain, and Einstein and Arendt as European émigrés found that their philosophic reflections brought them political commitments.

This book explores the dark side: it presents a history of Western conceptions of evil.[2] *The Many Faces of Evil* does not assume that there is *a* specific conception of moral waywardness, or that "evil" is a generic category with species and varieties. Quite on the contrary: like a family genealogy that discovers hidden adoptions and surprising genetic mutations, our chronicle disperses its subject. Nevertheless, merely for the sake of simplicity and convenience, let's refer to evil as an umbrella concept that has undergone dramatic transformations, marked by a rich vocabulary of distinctions: abomination, disobedience, vice, malevolence, willfulness, immorality, cruelty, aggression and crime. "Its" sources and analysis, "its" instances and characteristic scenarios have changed dramatically, in ways that indicate much larger changes in the conceptual worlds in which each of these notions functions.

Varieties of evil

The varieties of evil are semantically marked. The richness of the vocabulary – "abominations," "disobedience," "vice," "malevolence," "sin," "wanton cruelty," "immorality," "corruption," "criminality," "sociopathology" – indicates distinctive conceptual domains. Each has its primary place in a specific outlook, with a particular set of preoccupations and questions, a theory of agency and responsibility.

Nietzsche remarked that morality begins with primitive disgust and admiration. And indeed some of the earliest forms of our umbrella notion of evil demarcate *abominations* –

acts that, like incest, cannibalism, patricide and fratricide – elicit horror and disgust. Abominations are violations, disorders of nature that bring their own natural retribution in the form of plagues or expulsion from the social world. By contrast, the world in which evil is construed as a form of *disobedience* is a world defined by divine ruler who gives commands, exacts obedience, punishes or rewards (*Genesis* and *Exodus*). In that world, the domain of morality and immorality is marked in a space between divinity and humankind. A world focussed on virtue and *vice* is a naturalistic, social world (Theophrastus, Butler, Mandeville). Virtues are those character traits, which, like courage, justice, practical wisdom, preserve and enhance a community, a political system. The vices – character traits like greed, disloyalty, envy, self-indulgence, disrespect – threaten the social order. The origins and sanctions for vices are social: an unfortunate upbringing in a malformed polity can issue in the kind of corruption whose sanction is the loss of trust and cooperation. With *malevolence* (Pope Innocent III, Calvin), we enter a new world, a world of individual will and responsibility. While malevolence is normally a dispositional condition of a defective will, a person can knowingly and deliberately harm others in a rare flash of anger or revenge. *Sin* fuses disobedience with ill will (Aquinas, Jonathan Edwards). But while the earliest forms of disobedience can be relatively innocent or childish, sin presupposes that Everyman, in the full knowledge of the difference between good and evil, right and wrong, willfully violates the divine order by presuming the pride of judgment, to choose whatever it wills for itself (Milton's Satan, Goethe's Faust). When the disposition or proclivity to sin – construed as pride or egoism – is thought to be an inherently dominant motive (one that structures perception, emotion, desire, cognition), only divine grace can set aside divine punishment. Evil becomes less fraught when morality returns to the secular social order during the Renaissance and Enlightenment. Those who set aside the theology and metaphysics of sin turned to characterizing character traits that – like wanton cruelty – generate "man's inhumanity to man" (Montaigne, Voltaire). *Partiality*, *egoism* – the desire for glory, or self-interest – remain prime human motives, part of the inescapable human condition, but they are naturalized, judiciously tempered by practical reason (Machiavelli, Hobbes, Mandeville). So formed, they are no longer sins: they are thought to serve, rather than impede, the social virtues. Once a contrast has been drawn between individual interests and the comprehensive general or common good, rationality becomes the moral faculty. But it prompts the question: how is it possible for a rational being of good will to be immoral (Rousseau, Kant)? Following the Romantics' attack on the authority and the power of reason, the imagination is presented as fascinated by the sensuous lures of *corruption* (de Sade, Baudelaire). The traditional terms are entwined, sometimes radically reinterpreted (Blake, Nietzsche). The terminology shifts from theology and philosophy to law and psychopathology. Evil becomes *criminality* or *sociopathology*.

Metaphysics and the theological problem of evil

Within a theological context, "the problem of evil" mandates the task of reconciling the ways of God to man (Augustine, al-Ghazali, Milton). Lactantius formulated the problem:

> God either wishes to take away evils and cannot, or he can and does not wish to, or he neither wishes or is able, or he both wishes to and is able. If he wishes to and is not able, he is weak, which does not fall in with the notion of God. If he is able to and does not wish to, he is envious, which is equally foreign to God. If he neither wishes to nor is able, he is both envious and weak, and therefore not God. If he both wishes to and is able, which is alone fitting to God, whence, therefore, are there evils, and why does he not remove them?[3]

Hume, echoing Epicurus, critically formulates the theological problem elegantly and resolutely: "Is he [God] willing to prevent evil, but not able? Then he is impotent. Is he able but not willing? Then he is malevolent. Is he both able and willing? Whence, then, is evil?"[4]

Transposed to a metaphysical context, "evil" becomes chaos and disorder. Is the world is well-ordered? Does it form a coherent, harmonious, sustainable, intelligible system (Leibniz, Kant)? The moral version of the problem was most eloquently expressed in *Job*: Why do the just suffer? (Aquinas and Edwards offer a theological justification; Engels and Dostoevsky's Ivan express their outrage at the very attempt to rationalize or justify wrong-doing.)

Our chronicle gives roughly six generic answers – neither exhaustive nor mutually exclusive – to the metaphysical/theological problem of evil in all its variants:

1 Neo-Platonism (Augustine): There is nothing – no event, no entity, no action – that is, in and of itself, evil. What is thought to be "evil" seems so by comparison to a presumed greater good. It is a lesser degree – a privation – of something that is deemed better. For instance, while a despotic tyranny can be corrupt, unjust, inhumane, governance is in itself a human good. To be sure, tyranny can be, by comparison to a meritocratic republic, profoundly harmful, but it is a loss of something intrinsically good.

Many early neo-Platonists argued that all choice is *sub specie boni*: directed towards what is, and what is perceived as, good. No one voluntarily, knowingly chooses what they take to be bad or undesirable. Post-Christian neo-Platonists who, like Augustine, held that original sin perverts both judgment and desire were therefore faced with the problem of reconciling the inheritance of original sin – with its deviant effect on motivation – with divine benevolence. They standardly argued that a free will accords human beings with greater dignity – and thus the world with greater value – than correctly programmed "choice."

2 Theodicy and coherentism (al-Ghazali, Leibniz): Late neo-Platonists who held that even original sin and divine punishment express divine benevolence were moving towards what became a more general view about the order of the universe. As the arguments from theodicy had it, the world is as well-ordered as a complex system can be. It harmonizes apparently independent parts, each with its own trajectory. Metaphysical evils – violent upheavals and destruction in nature – play constructive roles in maintaining the ordered harmony of the cosmos. Earthquakes and volcanic eruptions, forest fires and tornadoes conserve the proper adjustment of natural elements and forces. When placed in the larger context of human history, even moral evils – human suffering and malevolence – conduce to the greater good. For example, Judas's betrayal of Jesus was an essential step towards the salvation of mankind.

Transposed to the social sphere, later secular versions of the coherentist view argued that when they were suitably regulated, vices like greed and envy spark the energy and productivity that make progressive civilization possible (Mandeville, Freud). All these "solutions" to the problem of evil issue heuristic promissory notes. Their guiding motto is: "Look for the benefits gained by harm and you will find they outweigh the damage."

3 Manichaeanism (some Gnostics): Good and evil are conflicting forces whose ongoing combat marks human history.

4 Pious rationalists (Kant): According to this view, human reason discovers its own limits: it posits the problem of evil and recognizes that it is incapable of solving it. Reason itself necessarily postulates the existence of a just and omnipotent divinity whose nature reason cannot itself comprehend. Critics of encompassing rationalism (Pascal, Kierkegaard) held that reason, itself recognizing its own limits, points to the necessity of distinctively different faculty, a leap of faith, a trust in divinity.

5 Pessimism (Schopenhauer): Evil is real; the world is not well-ordered, and may not even be rationally coherent.

6 There is no problem (Hobbes, Rousseau): The category of evil is not an objective ontological category. It involves projecting subjective or socially defined attitudes – approval or disapproval – onto the world.

The psychology of evil

Having dispersed the metaphysical–cosmological idea of evil, we are left with the fact that we find certain sorts of actions – wanton cruelty, mass murder, indifference to suffering, willful senseless destruction – monstrous, intolerable. Evil may not be an onto-logical category or natural kind, but it seems a fundamental feature of human psychology that (on the whole, normally, other things being equal, etc.) we are revolted by actions that we classify as "abominable," "evil," "inhuman." Indeed, we are often so horrified by such actions that we avert our eyes and minds from them . . . and yet, in truth, we are also fascinated, even lured by them. Why – despite our abhorrence of "evil" – are we also so attracted to it, in fantasy and in action? Do such actions have anything in common? Can actions (or motives) be classified as morally prohibited, obligatory, or permissible? What aspects of our ordinary psychology prompts us – lures us – to engage in 'evil'? Are there intolerable actions that are more common and subtle than the dramatic ones (genocide, holocausts, random murder) on which we focus? Are there motives or intentions that are in themselves evil, independently of whether they prompt evil actions? Do abominable actions have any redeeming features?

Some traditional answers to these questions are rooted in forms of life, in conceptual worlds that have become virtually incomprehensible to us: "Evil consists in disobedience of divine commands," "It is an expression of original sin," "It is prompted by the lure of the flesh," strike our contemporaries as more mysterious than the phenomena they purport to explain. In any case, they seem to open a regression of further questions: What is the rationale for the various divine prohibitions? What is the lure of disobedience? While contemporary discussions of these questions avoid the vocabulary of sin and divinity, they seem to come to similar fundamental stopping places: there are absolute prohibitions (Anscombe, Walzer); virtues and vices can nevertheless not be neatly separated into distinct classes (Rorty, Oz); humans can knowingly voluntarily desire what is wrong . . . precisely because it is wrong or forbidden (Stocker, Hampton); wrong-doing – and the movement towards wrong-doing – can be subtle, unnoticed, banal (Arendt, Rorty). Having dispersed some of the traditional ontological conceptions of evil, philosophers seem to have returned to the repressed . . . and to revisit the forms of some of the traditional discussions. Despite the enormous differences in experience and outlook, contemporary philosophers find themselves baffled at roughly the same places that perplexed their predecessors; and equally disconcerted by their inability to provide satisfactory solutions to the questions they feel obliged to continue posing. These are the sorts of issues that Kant and Wittgenstein would have characterized as hopelessly metaphysical.

Sources and witnesses

A historical chronicle of this kind calls on – depends on – witnesses of all kinds. Insight and testimony about evil is be found in mythology, theology, poetry, history, analytic philosophy, legal and political theory, medical textbooks. Explorers do not follow the artificial and accidental distinctions between academic disciplines; and they know that the distinctions between literary genres are themselves historically subject to the vicissitudes and accidents of fortune.

Our chronicle does not assume that there is a sharp distinction between philosophical analysis and moral rhetoric; nor does it differentiate the upbeat from the cautionary side of moral theory. Traditional philosophic arguments like those presented by Aquinas,

Leibniz and Kant are embedded within an entire world-view. Directed towards representing the most perspicuous well-reasoned account of what is true, they are implicitly also meant to elicit a specific set of attitudes towards the world. Narrowly construed, philosophic reasoning attempts to secure consent by constructing – and appealing to – interlocked, structured, presumptively valid inferential arguments from sound premises. Other literary modes – myths, metaphors and analogies, examples, thought-experiments – attempt to persuade by evocative narratives. Philosophers nevertheless frequently embed what have come to be classified as literary and rhetorical modes within their presumptively rigorous analyses and constructions. Augustine and Descartes wrote idealized autobiographical confessions and meditations; Hobbes, Rousseau, Mandeville and Nietzsche wrote historical thought-experiments that were driven by extended analogies and metaphors. On the other hand, the sermons, exhortations and biblical commentaries of many theologians depend on philosophical assumptions (Augustine, Luther, Calvin, Edwards). Poets and satirists presuppose and sometimes participate in theological disputes (Dante, Milton, Voltaire, Goethe, Blake). Because the sources of the conceptions of (what has historically roughly been categorized as) evil are so various, we have appealed to testimony from different historical eras and different literary genres. Because visual artists – painters and caricaturists – were also engaged in representing and interpreting conceptions of evil, we have included as many illustrations as we could (Ripa, Goya, Grosz).

Acknowledgements

In the nature of the case, a book of this kind is a cooperative enterprise. It began with a conversation with Moshe Halbertal about the banality of evil; it developed in the course of lively reflective exchanges with Myles Burnyeat and Michèle le Doeuff. It could not have been constructed without the counsel, erudition and support of many scholars and friends: Matthew Carmody, William Darrow, Georges Dreyfus, Ronald de Sousa, Cynthia Freeland, Steven Gerrard, Linda Hirschman, Jay Hullett, Natasha Judson, Aryeh Kosman, Genevieve Lloyd, Daniel O'Connor, Jennifer Radden, Deborah Roberts, William Ruddick, Elizabeth Spellman, Josef Stern, and colleagues and students who participated in seminars in the Program in the History of Ideas at Brandeis. My research assistants, Charles McKinley and Leah Long, generously and patiently provided indispensable help. Muna Khogali, my editor at Routledge, tolerated my repeated, "Look at what I have just found! We simply must include this amazing turn of thought." I am also grateful to anonymous reviewers for their comments and suggestions. Williams College and the members of its philosophy department offered hospitality and ideal conditions for study and writing.

A.O.R.

Notes

1 Of course there are exceptions. Interestingly enough, a disproportionate number of philosophers who have discussed the psychology of evil, immorality and forgiveness are women: G.E.M. Anscombe, Hannah Arendt, Cynthia Freeland, Jean Hampton, Mary Midgley, Martha Minow, Judith Shklar. The focus of men philosophers has been somewhat different: Peter Geach is a Catholic who analyzed the seven deadly sins, Michel Foucault and Ian Hacking were both interested in the linguistic construction of social practices, Philip Hallie, John Kekes, and Thomas Nagel analyzed moral issues implicated in war or extreme stress.

2 Perforce, we must ignore the fact that the distinction between "Western" and "Oriental" philosophy masks important and continuous cross-cultural continuities. There are strong Zoroastrian, Babylonian and Coptic influences on Judeo-Christian traditions. Hellenistic military and mercantile expeditions brought a flow of cultural and intellectual exchanges flowing East and West through Central Euro-Asia. When the sun never set on the British Empire, colonial enchantment with the exotic had its resonances in the moral world that Jowett and Kipling fashioned for the youth of England. Another book for another occasion.

3 Lactantius, *De Ira Dei* XIII.20:21. Translated Mary McDonald, *The Wrath of God* (Washington, DC, 1965), pp. 92–3.

4 Hume, *Dialogues Concerning Natural Religion*, ed. Nelson Pike (Indianapolis: Bobbs-Merrill, 1970), p. 88.

Part 1

FROM
DISOBEDIENCE
TO DISORDER

Francisco Goya, "Death Struggle."

The prohibitions of our earliest witnesses are remarkably direct and focussed: without metaphysical grounding or background explanations, they specify actions prohibited or abhorred by the gods. *The Egyptian Book of the Dead* consists of a large number of hymns, prayers and rituals compiled – as best scholars can determine – from about 2680 to 2345 BC. In "The Soul Meets Its Judges," a newly dead soul addresses the gods of the underworld, accounting for its life, specifying the deeds that it avoided. Assuring the gods that it respected the domain of the sacred, the soul protests that it did not steal food from the poor, did not malign servants, did not move boundary stones. The domain of the moral seems chartered by a humane and compassionate ethic, one that, besides giving due reverence to the gods, protected the weak and honored covenants.

Different as they are in tone and style, *Genesis* and *Exodus* (compiled from the ninth to the fifth centuries BC) both present themselves as familiar with the actions and commands of a divinity who demands absolute obedience and exclusive allegiance. His prohibitions are absolute and unqualified: do not eat from this tree; do not worship other gods; do not bear false witness against thy neighbor. Even the few positive commands – honor thy father and mother – are focussed. The scene and the sanctions of the original disobedience are vividly told, but its motive is obscure: the narrative is remarkably devoid of psychological explanation.

With Thucydides (460–408 BC) and Theophrastus (371–287 BC), we are brought to specifically civic evils, unmediated and undirected by divinities. Normally a sparse and restrained analytic historian, Thucydides cannot contain his horror at the massacres and blood lust of the excesses of war. As he describes the unbounded butchery of the Corcyrean civil war, he intimates that uncertainty, fear and deep enmity unleash chaos and carnage. In a wholly different vein, Theophrastus satirizes the absurdity of a variety of shameless self-serving rogues. They are presented as malformed grotesques rather than as demonic, monstrous forces.

Philosopher, moralist, politician and political theorist, Seneca (2/4 BC–AD 65) was suspicious of unregulated passions. Although anger is, like all emotions, part of the natural order, it is a prime example of the way that passions disrupt the harmony of both the soul and the social order. Like most passions, anger arises from limited and incomplete self-understanding. Mistakenly taking an insult or injury to be an onslaught on the core self, the angry person desires and plots revenge. In principle, he can correct the mistaken judgments that constitute the passions by identifying with the rationality that is his true nature. So informed, the true self realizes that it cannot be harmed by imprisonment or torture, let alone insults or slights. For Seneca, as for other Stoics, evil is not, as such, ontologically real. The Universe is, taken as a whole, rationally well-ordered. To be sure, there is pain and human suffering; but these are perspectival, partial, skewed judgments, by-products of the nexus of causes that constitute the cosmic order.

An ancient and continuous tradition, Gnosticism places evil within a cosmological setting. Its earliest texts – *Poimandres* and *Discourses*, attributed to a legendary figure "Hermes Trismegistus" (3rd–2nd century BC) – demarcate an armed domain of Darkness opposed to the harmonious Creative Light. Like much of the early Hermetic tradition, the Mandean Ginza texts were the work of many authors and editors, members of a community that was probably initially formed in the first century, that dispersed and flourished in the third and fourth centuries, and that can still be found in Iraq. It should not be surprising that it is difficult to determine whether the Mandeans who describe the anguish of the Fallen World were Manichaean: our sources for their beliefs come from such anti-heretical authors as Titus of Bostra (362–371), Theodoret of Cyrus (393–466) and Severus of Antioch (465–537). Much later, the Gnostic writings of Ezra ben Solomon in the Zohar (*c.* 1270–9) turn to Genesis to interpret the contrast – and the balance – between the World of Darkness and the World of Light as exemplified by the tensed mutual dependence of the Tree of Life and the Tree of Knowledge.

1

THE ANCIENT EGYPTIAN BOOK OF THE DEAD

The soul meets its judges

Hail to you, great god, Lord of Justice! I have come to you, my lord, that you may bring me so that I may see your beauty, for I know you and I know your name, and I know the names of the forty-two gods of those whose are with you in this Hall of Justice, who live on those who cherish evil and who gulp down their blood on that day of the reckoning of characters in the presence of Wennefer. Behold the double son of the Songstresses; Lord of Truth is your name. Behold, I have come to you, I have brought you truth, I have repelled falsehood for you. I have not done falsehood against men, I have not impoverished my associates, I have done no wrong in the Place of Truth, I have not learnt that which is not, I have done no evil, I have not daily made labour in excess of what was due to be done for me, my name has not reached the offices of those who control slaves, I have not deprived the orphan of his property, I have not done what the gods detest, I have not calumniated a servant to his master, I have not caused pain, I have not made hungry, I have not made to weep, I have not killed, I have not commanded to kill, I have not made suffering for anyone, I have not lessened the food-offerings in the temples, I have not destroyed the loaves of the gods, I have not taken away the food of the spirits, I have not copulated, I have not misbehaved, I have not lessened food-supplies, I have not diminished the aroura, I have not encroached upon fields, I have not laid anything upon the weights of the hand-balance, I have not taken anything from the plummet of the standing scales, I have not taken the milk from the mouths of children, I have not deprived the herds of their pastures, I have not trapped the birds from the preserves of the gods, I have not caught the fish of their marshlands, I have not diverted water at its season, I have not built a dam on flowing water, I have not quenched the fire when it

Source: *The Ancient Egyptian Book of the Dead*, trans. Raymond O. Faulkner, Austin, Tex.: University of Texas Press, 1972.

is burning, I have not neglected the dates for offering choice meats, I have not withheld cattle from the gods'-offerings, I have not opposed a god in his procession.

I am pure, pure, pure, pure! My purity is the purity of that great phoenix which is in Heracleopolis, because I am indeed the nose of the Lord of Wind who made all men live on that day of completing the Sacred Eye in Heliopolis *in the 2nd month of winter last day*, in the presence of the lord of this land. I am he who saw the completion of the Sacred Eye in Heliopolis, and nothing evil shall come into being against me in this land in this Hall of Justice, because I know the names of these gods who are in it.

The declaration of innocence before the gods of the tribunal

O Far-strider who came forth from Heliopolis, I have done no falsehood.

O Fire-embracer who came forth from Kheraha, I have not robbed.

O Nosey who came forth from Hermopolis, I have not been rapacious.

O Swallower of shades who came forth from the cavern, I have not stolen.

O Dangerous One who came forth from Rosetjau, I have not killed men.

O Double Lion who came forth from the sky, I have not destroyed food-supplies.

O Fiery Eyes who came forth from Letopolis, I have done no crookedness.

O Flame which came forth backwards, I have not stolen the god's-offerings.

O Bone-breaker who came forth from Heracleopolis, I have not told lies.

O Green of flame who came forth from Memphis, I have not taken food.

O You of the cavern who came forth from the West, I have not been sullen.

O White of teeth who came forth from the Faiyum, I have not transgressed.

O Blood-eater who came forth from the shambles, I have not killed a sacred bull.

O Eater of entrails who came forth from the House of Thirty, I have not committed perjury.

O Lord of Truth who came forth from Maaty, I have not stolen bread.

O Wanderer who came forth from Bubastis, I have not eavesdropped.

O Pale One who came forth from Heliopolis, I have not babbled.

O Doubly evil who came forth from Andjet, I have not disputed except as concerned my own property.

O Wememty-snake who came forth from the place of execution, I have not committed homosexuality.

O You who see whom you bring who came forth from the House of Min, I have not misbehaved.

O You who are over the Old One who came forth from Imau, I have not made terror.

O Demolisher who came forth from Xois, I have not transgressed.

O Disturber who came forth from Weryt, I have not been hot-tempered.

O Youth who came forth from the Heliopolitan nome, I have not been deaf to words
of truth.

O Foreteller who came forth from Wenes, I have not made disturbance.

O You of the altar who came forth from the secret place, I have not hoodwinked.

O You whose face is behind him who came forth from the Cavern of Wrong,
I have neither misconducted myself nor copulated with a boy.

O Hot-foot who came forth from the dusk, I have not been neglectful.

O You of the darkness who came forth from the darkness, I have not been
quarrelsome.

O Bringer of your offering who came forth from Sais, I have not been unduly active.

O Owner of faces who came forth from Nedjefet, I have not been impatient.

O Accuser who came forth from Wetjenet, I have not transgressed my nature,
I have not washed out (the picture of) a god.

O Owner of horns who came forth from Asyut, I have not been voluble in speech.

O Nefertum who came forth from Memphis, I have done no wrong, I have seen no
evil.

O Temsep who came forth from Busiris, I have not made conjuration against the
king.

O You who acted according to your will, who came forth from Tjebu, I have not
waded in water.

O Water-smiter who came forth from the Abyss, I have not been loud voiced.

O Commander of mankind who came forth from your house, I have not reviled God.

O Bestower of good who came forth from the Harpoon nome, I have not
done . . .

O Bestower of powers who came forth from the City, I have not made distinctions
for myself.

O Serpent with raised head who came forth from the cavern, I am not wealthy
except with my own property.

O Serpent who brings and gives, who came forth from the Silent Land, I have not
blasphemed God in my city.

2

THE BOOK OF
GENESIS/THE BOOK
OF EXODUS

Divine prohibitions

The fall of man

And the Lord God planted a garden eastward in Eden; and there he put the man whom he had formed. And out of the ground made the Lord God to grow every tree that is pleasant to the sight, and good for food; the tree of life also in the midst of the garden, and the tree of knowledge of good and evil. And a river went out of Eden to water the garden; and from thence it was parted, and became into four heads. The name of the first is Pison: that is it which compasseth the whole land of Havilah, where there is gold; and the gold of that land is good: there is bdellium and the onyx stone. And the name of the second river is Gihon: the same is it that compasseth the whole land of Ethiopia. And the name of the third river is Hiddekel: that is it which goeth toward the east of Assyria. And the fourth river is Euphrates.

And the Lord God took the man, and put him into the garden of Eden to dress it and to keep it. And the Lord God commanded the man, saying, "Of every tree of the garden thou mayest freely eat: but of the tree of the knowledge of good and evil, thou shalt not eat of it: for in the day that thou eatest thereof thou shalt surely die." . . .

Now the serpent was more subtil than any beast of the field which the Lord God had made.

And he said unto the woman,

"Yea, hath God said, 'Ye shall not eat of every tree of the garden'?"

And the woman said unto the serpent,

Sources: *The Book of Genesis*, 2:7–17; 3:1–24; 4:1–15; *The Book of Exodus*, 20:1–17 King James version.

"We may eat of the fruit of the trees of the garden: but of the fruit of the tree which is in the midst of the garden, God hath said, 'Ye shall not eat of it, neither shall ye touch it, lest ye die.'"

And the serpent said unto the woman,

"Ye shall not surely die: for God doth not know that in the day ye eat thereof, then your eyes shall be opened, and ye shall be as gods, knowing good and evil."

And when the woman saw that the tree was good for food, and that it was pleasant to the eyes, and a tree to be desired to make one wise, she took of the fruit thereof, and did eat, and gave also unto her husband with her; and he did eat. And the eyes of them both were opened, and they knew that they were naked; and they sewed fig leaves together, and made themselves aprons.

And they heard the voice of the Lord God walking in the garden in the cool of the day: and Adam and his wife hid themselves from the presence of the Lord God amongst the trees of the garden.

And the Lord God called unto Adam, and said unto him,

"Where art thou?"

And he said,

"I heard thy voice in the garden, and I was afraid, because I was naked; and I hid myself."

And he said,

"Who told thee that thou wast naked? Hast thou eaten of the tree, whereof I commanded thee that thou shouldest not eat?"

And the man said,

"The woman whom thou gavest to be with me, she gave me of the tree, and I did eat."

And the Lord God said unto the woman,

"What is this that thou hast done?"

And the woman said, "The serpent beguiled me, and I did eat."

And the Lord God said unto the serpent,

"Because thou hast done this,
Thou art cursed above all cattle,
And above every beast of the field;
Upon thy belly shalt thou go,
And dust shalt thou eat
All the days of thy life:
And I will put enmity between thee and the woman,
and between thy seed and her seed;
It shall bruise thy head,
And thou shalt bruise his heel."

Unto the woman he said,

"I will greatly multiply thy sorrow and thy conception;
In sorrow thou shalt bring forth children;
And thy desire shall be to thy husband,
And he shall rule over thee."

And unto Adam he said,
"Because thou hast hearkened unto the voice of thy wife, and hast eaten of the tree, of which I commanded thee, saying, 'Thou shalt not eat of it':

"Cursed is the ground for thy sake;
In sorrow shalt thou eat of it all the days of thy life.
Thorns also and thistles shall it bring forth to thee;
And thou shalt eat the herb of the field;
In the sweat of thy face shalt thou eat bread,
Till thou return unto the ground;
For out of it wast thou taken:
For dust thou art,
And unto dust shalt thou return."

And Adam called his wife's name Eve; because she was the mother of all living. Unto Adam also and to his wife did the Lord God make coats of skins, and clothed them.

And the Lord God said, "Behold, the man is become as one of us, to know good and evil: and now, lest he put forth his hand, and take also of the tree of life, and eat, and live for ever—" therefore the Lord God sent him forth from the garden of Eden, to till the ground from whence he was taken. So he drove out the man; and he placed at the east of the garden of Eden Cherubims, and a flaming sword which turned every way, to keep the way of the tree of life. . . .

And Adam knew Eve his wife; and she conceived, and bare Cain, and said, "I have gotten a man from the Lord."

And she again bare his brother Abel. And Abel was a keeper of sheep, but Cain was a tiller of the ground.

And in process of time it came to pass, that Cain brought of the fruit of the ground an offering unto the Lord. And Abel, he also brought of the firstlings of his flock and of the fat thereof. And the Lord had respect unto Abel and to his offering: but unto Cain and to his offering he had not respect. And Cain and to his offering he had not respect. And Cain was very wroth and his countenance fell.

And the Lord said unto Cain, "Why art thou wroth? And why is thy countenance fallen? If thou doest well, shalt thou not be accepted? and if thou doest not well, sin lieth at the door. And unto thee *shall be* his desire, and thou shalt rule over him."

And Cain talked with Abel his brother: and it came to pass, when they were in the field, that Cain rose up against Abel his brother, and slew him.

And the Lord said unto Cain, "Where *is* Abel thy brother?"

And he said, "I know not: *am* I my brother's keeper?"

And he said,

"What hast thou done? the voice of thy brother's blood crieth unto me from the ground. And now *art* thou cursed from the earth, which hath opened her mouth to receive thy brother's blood from thy hand; when thou tillest the ground, it shall not henceforth yield unto thee her strength; a fugitive and a vagabond shalt thou be in the earth."

And Cain said unto the Lord, "My punishment *is* greater than I can bear. Behold, thou has driven me out this day from the face of the earth; and from thy face shall I be hid; and I shall be a fugitive and a vagabond in the earth; and it shall come to pass, *that* every one that findeth me shall slay me."

And the Lord said unto him, "Therefore whosoever slayeth Cain, vengeance shall be taken on him seven-fold."

And the Lord set a mark upon Cain, lest any finding him should kill him.

The Commandments

And God spoke all these words, saying, "I am the Lord thy God, which have brought thee out of the land of Egypt, out of the house of bondage.

"Thou shalt have no other gods before me.

"Thou shalt not make unto thee any graven image, or any likeness of any thing that is in heaven above, or that is in the earth beneath, or that is in the water under the earth: thou shalt not bow down thyself to them, nor serve them: for I the Lord thy God am a jealous God, visiting the iniquity of the fathers upon the children unto the third and fourth generation of them that hate me; and showing mercy unto thousands of them that love me, and keep my commandments.

"Thou shalt not take the name of the Lord thy God in vain; for the Lord will not hold him guiltless that taketh his name in vain.

"Remember the sabbath day, to keep it holy. Six days shalt thou labour, and do all thy work: but the seventh day is the sabbath of the Lord thy God: in it thou shalt not do any work, thou, nor thy son, nor thy daughter, thy manservant, nor thy maid-servant, nor thy cattle, nor thy stranger that is within thy gates: for in six days the Lord made heaven and earth, the sea, and all that in them is, and rested the seventh day: wherefore the Lord blessed the sabbath day, and hallowed it.

"Honour thy father and thy mother: that thy days may be long upon the land which the Lord thy God giveth thee.

"Thou shalt not kill.

"Thou shalt not commit adultery.

"Thou shalt not steal.

"Thou shalt not bear false witness against thy neighbour.

"Thou shalt not covet thy neighbour's house, thou shalt not covet thy neighbour's wife, nor his manservant, nor his maidservant, nor his ox, nor his ass, nor any thing that is thy neighbour's . . .

3

THUCYDIDES

War and revolution

The Corcyraean Revolution

The Corcyraeans slew such of their enemies as they laid hands on, [also] dispatching those whom they had persuaded to go aboard the ships. Next they went to the sanctuary of Hera and persuaded about fifty men to stand trial and condemned them all to death. The mass of suppliants who had refused to do so, on seeing what took place, slew each other on consecrated ground. While some hanged themselves on trees, others destroyed themselves as they were able. The Corcyraeans were engaged in butchering those of their fellow citizens whom they regarded as their enemies. And although the crime imputed was that of attempting to put down the democracy, some were slain for private hatred, others by their debtors because of the monies owed to them. Death thus raged in every shape; and, as usually happens at such times, there was no length to which violence did not go; sons were killed by their fathers, and suppliants dragged from the altar or slain upon it; while some were even walled up in the temple of Dionysus and died there.

So bloody was the march of the revolution, and the impression which it made was the greater as it was one of the first to occur. Later on, one may say, the whole Hellenic world was convulsed; struggles being everywhere made by the popular chiefs to bring in the Athenians, and by the oligarchs to introduce the Lacedæmonians. In peace there would have been neither the pretext nor the wish to make such an invitation; but in war, with an alliance always at the command of either faction for the hurt of their adversaries and their own corresponding advantage, opportunities for bringing in the foreigner were never wanting to the revolutionary parties. The sufferings which revolution entailed upon the cities were many and terrible, such as have occurred and always will occur, as long as the nature of mankind remains the same; though in a severer or milder form, and varying in their symptoms, according to the variety of the particular cases. In peace and prosperity states and individuals have better sentiments, because they do not find

Source: *The Complete Writings of Thucydides: The Peloponnesian War*, Book 3, 81–5 New York: The Modern Library, 1951.

themselves suddenly confronted with imperious necessities; but war takes away the easy supply of daily wants, and so proves a rough master, that brings most men's characters to a level with their fortunes. Revolution thus ran its course from city to city, and the places which it arrived at last, from having heard what had been done before, carried to a still greater excess the refinement of their inventions, as manifested in the cunning of their enterprises and the atrocity of their reprisals. Words had to change their ordinary meaning and to take that which was now given them. Reckless audacity came to be considered the courage of a loyal ally; prudent hesitation, specious cowardice; moderation was held to be a cloak for unmanliness; ability to see all sides of a question inaptness to act on any. Frantic violence became the attribute of manliness; cautious plotting, a justifiable means of self-defence. The advocate of extreme measures was always trustworthy; his opponent a man to be suspected. To succeed in a plot was to have a shrewd head, to divine a plot a still shrewder; but to try to provide against having to do either was to break up your party and to be afraid of your adversaries. In fine, to forestall an intending criminal, or to suggest the idea of a crime where it was wanting, was equally commended, until even blood became a weaker tie than party, from the superior readiness of those united by the latter to dare everything without reserve; for such associations had not in view the blessings derivable from established institutions but were formed by ambition for their overthrow; and the confidence of their members in each other rested less on any religious sanction than upon complicity in crime. The fair proposals of an adversary were met with jealous precautions by the stronger of the two, and not with a generous confidence. Revenge also was held of more account than self-preservation. Oaths of reconciliation, being only proffered on either side to meet an immediate difficulty, only held good so long as no other weapon was at hand; but when opportunity offered, he who first ventured to seize it and to take his enemy off his guard, thought this perfidious vengeance sweeter than an open one, since, considerations of safety apart, success by treachery won him the palm of superior intelligence. Indeed it is generally the case that men are readier to call rogues clever than simpletons honest, and are as ashamed of being the second as they are proud of being the first. The cause of all these evils was the lust for power arising from greed and ambition; and from these passions proceeded the violence of parties once engaged in contention. The leaders in the cities, each provided with the fairest professions, on the one side with the cry of political equality of the people, on the other of a moderate aristocracy, sought prizes for themselves in those public interests which they pretended to cherish, and, recoiling from no means in their struggles for ascendancy, engaged in the direct excesses; in their acts of vengeance they went to even greater lengths, not stopping at what justice or the good of the state demanded, but making the party caprice of the moment their only standard, and invoking with equal readiness the condemnation of an unjust verdict or the authority of the strong arm to glut the animosities of the hour. Thus religion was in honour with neither party; but the use of fair phrases to arrive at guilty ends was in high reputation. Meanwhile the moderate part of the citizens perished between the two, either for not joining in the quarrel, or because envy would not suffer them to escape.

Thus every form of iniquity took root in the Hellenic countries by reason of the troubles. The ancient simplicity into which honour so largely entered was laughed down and disappeared; and society became divided into camps in which no man trusted his fellow. To put an end to this, there was neither promise to be depended upon, nor oath that could command respect; but all parties dwelling rather in their calculation upon the hopelessness of a permanent state of things, were more intent upon self-defence than capable of confidence. In this contest the blunter wits were most successful. Apprehensive of their own deficiencies and of the cleverness of their antagonists, they feared to be worsted in debate and to be surprised by the combinations of their more versatile opponents, and so at once boldly had recourse to action: while their adversaries, arrogantly thinking that they should know in time, and that it was unnecessary to secure by action what policy afforded, often fell victims to their want of precaution.

Meanwhile Corcyra gave the first example of most of the crimes alluded to; of the reprisals exacted by the governed who had never experienced equitable treatment or indeed aught but insolence from their rulers – when their hour came; of the iniquitous resolves of those who desired to get rid of their accustomed poverty, and ardently coveted their neighbours' goods; and lastly, of the savage and pitiless excesses into which men who had begun the struggle not in a class but in a party spirit, were hurried by their ungovernable passions. In the confusion into which life was now thrown in the cities, human nature, always rebelling against the law and now its master, gladly showed itself ungoverned in passion, above respect for justice, and the enemy of all superiority; since revenge would not have been set above religion, and gain above justice, had it not been for the fatal power of envy. Indeed men too often take upon themselves in the prosecution of their revenge to set the example of doing away with those general laws to which all alike can look for salvation in adversity, instead of allowing them to subsist against the day of danger when their aid may be required.

4
THEOPHRASTUS
Grotesque shamelessness

The Shameless man

Shamelessness may be defined as neglect of reputation for the sake of base gain.

The Shameless man is one who, in the first place, will go and borrow from the creditor whose money he is withholding. Then, when he has been sacrificing to the gods, he will put away the salted remains, and will himself dine out; and, calling up his attendant, will give him bread and meat taken from the table, saying in the hearing of all, 'Feast, most worshipful.' In marketing, again, he will remind the butcher of any service which he may have rendered him; and, standing near the scales, will throw in some meat, if he can, or else a bone for his soup: if he gets it, it is well; if not, he will snatch up a piece of tripe from the counter, and go off laughing. Again, when he has taken places at the theatre for his foreign visitors, he will see the performance without paying his own share; and will bring his sons, too, and their attendant the next day. When anyone secures a good bargain, he will ask to be given part in it. He will go to another man's house and borrow barley, or sometimes bran; and moreover will insist upon the lenders delivering it at his door. He is apt, also, to go up to the coppers in the baths, – to plunge the ladle in, amid the cries of the bath-man, – and to souse himself; saying that he has had his bath, and then, as he departs, – 'No thanks to you!'

The Patron of Rascals

The Patronising of Rascals is a form of the appetite for vice.

The Patron of Rascals is one who will throw himself into the company of those who have lost lawsuits and have been found guilty in criminal causes; conceiving that, if he associates with such persons, he will become more a man of the world, and will inspire the greater awe. Speaking of honest men he will add 'so-so,' and will remark that no one is honest, – all men are alike; indeed, one of his sarcasms is, 'What an honest fellow!' Again he will say that the rascal is 'a frank man, if one will look fairly at the matter.'

Source: *The Characters of Theophrastus*, London: Macmillan and Co., 1970.

'Most of the things that people say of him,' he admits, 'are true; but some things' (he adds) 'they do not know; namely that he is a clever fellow, and fond of his friends, and a man of tact'; and he will contend in his behalf that he has 'never met with an abler man.' He will show him favour, also, when he speaks in the Ecclesia or is at the bar of a court; he is fond, too, of remarking to the bench, 'The question is of the cause, not of the person.' 'The defendant,' he will say, 'is the watch-dog of the people, – he keeps an eye on evil-doers. We shall have nobody to take the public wrongs to heart, if we allow ourselves to lose such men.' Then he is apt to become the champion of worthless persons, and to form conspiracies in the law-courts in bad causes; and, when he is hearing a case, to take up the statements of the litigants in the worse sense.

[In short, sympathy with rascality is sister to rascality itself; and true is the proverb that 'Like moves towards like.']

5

SENECA

Anger as social disruption

Anger described; it is against nature, and only to be found in man

We are here to encounter the most outrageous, brutal, dangerous, and intractable of all passions; the most loathsome and unmannerly; nay, the most ridiculous too; and the subduing of this monster will do a great deal toward the establishment of human peace. It is the method of physicians to begin with a description of the disease, before they meddle with the cure: and I know not why this may not do as well in the distempers of the mind as in those of the body.

The Stoics will have anger to be a "desire of punishing another for some injury done." Against which it is objected that we are many times angry with those that never did hurt us, but possibly may, though the harm be not as yet done. But I say, that they hurt us already in conceit: and the very purpose of it is an injury in thought before it breaks out into act. It is opposed again, that if anger were a desire of punishing, mean people would not be angry with great ones that are out of their reach; for no man can be said to desire anything which he judges impossible to compass. But I answer to this, That anger is the desire, not the power and faculty of revenge: neither is any man so low, but that the greatest man alive may peradventure lie at his mercy.

Aristotle takes anger to be "a desire of paying sorrow for sorrow"; and of plaguing those that have plagued us. It is argued against both, that beasts are angry; though neither provoked by any injury, nor moved with a desire of anybody's grief or punishment. Nay, though they cause it, they do not design or seek it. Neither is anger (how unreasonable soever in itself) found anywhere but in reasonable creatures. It is true, the beasts have an impulse of rage and fierceness; as they are more affected also than men with some pleasures; but we may as well call them luxurious and ambitious as angry. And yet they are not without certain images of human affections. They have their likings and their loathings; but neither the passions of reasonable nature, nor their virtues, nor their vices. They are moved to fury by some objects; they are quieted by others; they

Source: *Seneca's Morals: By Way of Abstract*, Boston, Mass.: Estes and Lauriat, 1834.

18

have their terrors and their disappointments, but without reflection: and let them be never so much irritated or affrighted, so soon as ever the occasion is removed they fall to their meat again, and lie down and take their rest. Wisdom and thought are the goods of the mind, whereof brutes are wholly incapable; and we are as unlike them within as we are without: they have an odd kind of fancy, and they have a voice too: but inarticulate and confused, and incapable of those variations which are familiar to us.

Anger is not only a vice, but a vice point-blank against nature, for it divides instead of joining; and, in some measure, frustrates the end of Providence in human society. One man was born to help another: anger makes us destroy one another: the one unites, the other separates; the one is beneficial to us, the other mischievous; the one succors even strangers, the other destroys even the most intimate friends; the one ventures all to save another, the other ruins himself to undo another. Nature is bountiful: but anger is pernicious: for it is not fear, but mutual love that binds up mankind . . .

The rise of anger

The question will be here, whether anger takes its rise from impulse or judgment? that is, whether it be moved of its own accord, or, as many other things are, from within us, that arise we know not how? The clearing of this point will lead us to greater matters.

The first motion of anger is, in truth, involuntary, and only a kind of menacing preparation toward it. The second deliberates; as who should say, "This injury should not pass without revenge": and there it stops. The third is impotent; and, right or wrong, revolves upon vengeance. The first motion is not to be avoided, nor indeed the second, any more than yawning for company: custom and care may lessen it, but reason itself cannot overcome it. The third, as it rises upon consideration, it must fall so too; for that motion which proceeds with judgment may be taken away with judgment. A man thinks himself injured, and hath a mind to be revenged, but for some reason lets it rest. This is not properly anger, but an affection overruled by reason; a kind of proposal disapproved. And what are reason and affection, but only changes of the mind for the better or for the worse? Reason deliberates before it judges; but anger passes sentence without deliberation. Reason only attends the matter in hand; but anger is startled at every accident: it passes the bounds of reason, and carries it away with it. In short, "anger is an agitation of the mind that proceeds to the resolution of a revenge, the mind assenting to it." There is no doubt but anger is moved by the species of an injury, but whether that motion be voluntary or involuntary, is the point in debate; though it seems manifest to me that anger does nothing but where the mind goes along with it. For, first, to take an offence, and then to mediate a revenge, and after that, to lay both propositions together, and say to myself, "This injury ought not to have been done; but, as the case stands, I must do myself right." This discourse can never proceed without the concurrence of the will. The first motion, indeed, is single; but all the rest is deliberation and superstructure:

19

there is something understood and condemned: an indignation conceived, and a revenge propounded. This can never be without the agreement of the mind to the matter in deliberation. The end of this question is, to know the nature and quality of anger. It if be bred in us, it will never yield to reason, for all involuntary motions are inevitable and invincible; as a kind of horror and shrugging upon the sprinkling of cold water, the hair standing on end at ill news; giddiness at the sight of a precipice; blushing at lewd discourse. In these cases, reason can do no good; but anger may undoubtedly be overcome by caution and good counsel: for it is a voluntary vice, and not of the condition of those accidents that befall us as frailties of our humanity: among which must be reckoned the first motions of the mind, after the opinion of an injury received, which it is not in the power of human nature to avoid; and this is it that affects us upon the stage or in a story . . .

It is a short madness and a deformed vice

He was much in the right, whoever it was, that first called anger a short madness; for they have both of them the same symptoms; and there is so wonderful a resemblance betwixt the transports of choler and those of frenzy, that it is a hard matter to know the one from the other. A bold, fierce, and threatening countenance, as pale as ashes and, in the same moment, as red as blood; a glaring eye, a wrinkled brow, violent motions, the hands restless and perpetually in action, wringing and menacing, snapping of the joints, stamping with the feet, the hair starting, trembling lips, a forced and squeaking voice; the speech false and broken, deep and frequent sighs, and ghastly looks; the veins swell, the heart pants, the knees knock; with a hundred dismal accidents that are common to both distempers. Neither is anger a bare resemblance only of madness, but many times an irrevocable transition into the thing itself. How many persons have we known, read, and heard of that have lost their wits in a passion, and never came to themselves again? It is therefore to be avoided, not only for moderation's sake, but also for health. Now, if the outward appearance of anger be so foul and hideous, how deformed must that miserable mind be that is harassed with it? for it leaves no place either for counsel or friendship, honesty or good manners; no place either for the exercise of reason, or for the offices of life. If I were to describe it, I would draw a tiger bathed in blood, sharp set, and ready to take a leap at his prey; or dress it up as the poets represent the furies, with whips, snakes, and flames; it should be sour, livid, full of scars, and wallowing in gore, raging up and down, destroying, grinning, bellowing, and pursuing: sick of all other things, and most of all itself. It turns beauty into deformity, and the calmest counsels into fierceness: it disorders our very garments, and fills the mind with horror. How abominable is it in the soul then, when it appears so hideous even through the bones, the skin, and so many impediments! Is not he a madman that has lost the government of himself, and is tossed hither and thither by his fury as by a tempest – the executioner and the murderer of his nearest friends? The smallest matter moves it, and makes us unsociable and inaccessible. It does all things by violence, as well upon itself as others; and it is, in short, the master of all passions.

There is not any creature so terrible and dangerous by nature, but it becomes fiercer by anger. Not that beasts have human affections, but certain impulses they have which come very near them. The boar foams, champs, and whets his tusks; the bull tosses his horns in the air, bounds, and tears up the ground with his feet; the lion roars and swinges himself with his tail: the serpent swells; and there is a ghastly kind of fellness in the aspect of a mad dog. How great a wickedness is it now to indulge a violence, that does not only turn a man into a beast, but makes even the most outrageous of beasts themselves to be more dreadful and mischievous! A vice that carries along with it neither pleasure nor profit, neither honor nor security; but, on the contrary, destroys us to all the comfortable and glorious purposes of our reasonable being. Some there are, that will have the root of it to be the greatness of mind. And why may we not as well entitle impudence to courage, whereas the one is proud, the other brave; the one is gracious and gentle, the other rude and furious? At the same rate we may ascribe magnanimity to avarice, luxury, and ambition, which are all but splendid impotences, without measure and without foundation. There is nothing great but what is virtuous, nor indeed truly great, but what is also composed and quiet. Anger, alas! is but a wild impetuous blast, an empty tumor, the very infirmity of women and children; a brawling, clamorous evil: and the more noise the less courage; as we find it commonly, that the boldest tongues have the faintest hearts.

Anger is neither warrantable nor useful

In the first place, Anger is unwarrantable as it is unjust: for it falls many times upon the wrong person, and discharges itself upon the innocent instead of the guilty: besides the disproportion of making the most trivial offences to be capital, and punishing an inconsiderate word perhaps with torments, fetters, infamy, or death. It allows a man neither time nor means for defence, but judges a cause without hearing it, and admits of no mediation. It flies into the face of truth itself, if it be of the adverse party; and turns obstinacy in an error, into an argument of justice. It does everything with agitation and tumult; whereas reason and equity can destroy whole families, if there be occasion for it, even to the extinguishing of their names and memories, without any indecency, either of countenance or action.

Secondly, It is unsociable to the highest point; for it spares neither friend nor foe; but tears all to pieces, and casts human nature into a perpetual state of war. It dissolves the bond of mutual society, insomuch that our very companions and relations dare not come near us; it renders us unfit for the ordinary offices of life: for we can neither govern our tongues, our hands, nor any part of our body. It tramples upon the laws of hospitality, and of nations, leaves every man to be his own carver, and all things, public and private, sacred and profane, suffer violence.

Thirdly, It is to no purpose. "It is a sad thing," we cry, "to put up with these injuries, and we are not able to bear them"; as if any man that can bear anger could not bear an injury, which is much more supportable. You will say that anger does some good yet, for it keeps people in awe, and secures a man from contempt; never considering, that it is more dangerous to be feared than despised. Suppose that an angry man could do as much as he threatens; the more terrible, he is still the more odious; and on the other side, if he wants power, he is the more despicable for his anger; for there is nothing more wretched than a choleric huff, that makes a noise, and nobody cares for it. If anger would be valuable because men are afraid of it, why not an adder, a toad, or a scorpion as well? . . .

Of cruelty

There is so near an affinity betwixt anger and cruelty, that many people confound them; as if cruelty were only the execution of anger in the payment of a revenge: which holds in some cases, but not in others. There are a sort of men that take delight in the spilling of human blood, and in the death of those that never did them any injury, nor were ever so much as suspected for it . . . . For anger does necessarily presuppose an injury, either done, or conceived, or feared: but the other takes pleasure in tormenting, without so much as pretending any provocation to it, and kills merely for killing sake. The original of this cruelty perhaps was anger; which, by frequent exercise and custom, has lost all sense of humanity and mercy, and they that are thus affected are so far from the countenance and appearance of men in anger, that they will laugh, rejoice, and entertain themselves with the most horrid spectacles; as racks, jails, gibbets, several sorts of chains and punishments, dilaceration of members, stigmatizing, and wild beasts, with other exquisite inventions of torture: and yet at last the cruelty itself is more horrid and odious than the means by which it works. It is a bestial madness to love mischief; besides that, it is womanish to rage and fear. A generous beast will scorn to do it when he has anything at his mercy. It is a vice for wolves and tigers; and no less abominable to the world than dangerous to itself . . .

[The cruel man] can neither trust to the faith of his friends, nor to the piety of his children; he both dreads death and wishes it; and becomes a greater terror to himself than he is to his people. Nay, if there were nothing else to make cruelty detestable, it were enough that it passes all bounds, both of custom and humanity; and is followed upon the heel with sword or poison. A private malice indeed does not move whole cities; but that which extends to all is everybody's mark. One sick person gives no great disturbance in a family; but when it comes to a depopulating plague, all people fly from it. And why should a prince expect any man to be good whom he has taught to be wicked?

. . . [A] fierce and inexorable anger become the supreme magistrate; "Greatness of mind is always meek and humble; but cruelty is a note and an effect of weakness, and brings down a governor to the level of a competitor."

6
GNOSTICS
The war between Darkness and Light

(Ascribed to) Hermes Trismegistus, Letter II to Asclepius

You must not then, my pupils, speak as many do, who say that God ought by all means to have freed the world from evil. To those who speak thus, not a word ought to be said in answer; but for your sake I will pursue my argument, and therewith explain this. It was beyond God's power to put a stop to evil, and expel it from the universe; for evil is present in the world in such sort that it is manifestly an inseparable part thereof. But the supreme God provided and guarded against evil as far as he reasonably could, by deigning to endow the minds of men with intellect, knowledge, and intuition. It is in virtue of these gifts that we stand higher than the beasts; and by these, and these alone, are we enabled to shun the traps and deceptions and corruptions of evil. If a man shuns them when he sees them from afar, before he is entangled in them, it is by God's wisdom and forethought that he is protected from them; for man's knowledge is based on the supreme goodness of God.

(Ascribed to) Hermes Trismegistus, Letter III to Asclepius

The many are afraid of death, thinking it the greatest of evils, through ignorance of the truth. Death comes to pass through the dissolution of a worn-out body, and takes place at the completion of the number of years for which the bodily parts are coadjusted to form a single instrument for the discharge of the vital functions; for the body dies when it is no longer able to sustain the stress of human life. Death then is the dissolution of the body, and the cessation of bodily sense; and about this we have no cause to be troubled. But there is something else, which demands our anxious thought, though men in general disregard it through ignorance or unbelief... When the soul has quitted the

Hermes Trismegistus (source: *Hermetica*, trans. Walter Scott, Boston: Shambhala Publications, 1985); The Mandean text from Ginza (source: *Gnosis: A Selection of Gnostic Texts*, translated by Werner Foerster, Oxford: Clarendon Press, 1974); Compilations from Severus, Theodoret, Titus (source: *The Gnostic Religion*, ed. Hans Jonas, Boston: Beacon Press, 1958); R. Ezra ben Solomon (source: *On the Mystical Shape of the Godhead: Basic Concepts of the Kabbalah*, ed. Gershom Scholem, New York: Schocken Books, 1995).

body, there will be held a trial and investigation of its deserts. The soul will come under the power of the chief of the daemons. When he finds a soul to be devout and right-eous, he allows it to abide in the region which is suited to its character; but if he sees it to be marked with stains of sin, and defiled with (incurable) vices, he flings it down-ward, and delivers it to the storms and whirlwinds of that portion of the air which is in frequent conflict with fire and water, that the wicked soul may pay everlasting penalty, being ever swept and tossed hither and thither between sky and earth by the billows of cosmic matter. And so the everlasting existence of the soul is to its detriment in this respect, that its imperishable faculty of feeling makes it subject to everlasting punish-ment. Know then that we have good cause for fear and dread, and need to be on our guard, lest we should be involved in such a doom as this. Those who disbelieve will, after they have sinned, be forced to believe; they will be convinced, not by words, but by hard facts, not by mere threats, but by suffering the punishment in very deed. All things are known to God, and the punishments inflicted will vary in accordance with the character of men's offences. — *Ascl*. It is not true then, Trismegistus, that men's offences are punished only by human law? — *Trism*. Some parts of man, Asclepius, are mortal; that is to say, firstly, all those parts of him which are of earthy substance, and secondly, those parts of him also which live their life after the manner of the body, and likewise cease from life after the manner of the body. All these parts are liable to punish-ment in this life, so far as the man has deserved punishment by his offences. But man's immortal part is subject to punishment after death; and that punishment is all the more severe, if his offences chance to have escaped detection during his life on earth . . .

I say that there are daemons who dwell with us here on earth, and others who dwell above us in the lower air, and others again, whose abode is in the purest part of the air, where no mist or cloud can be, and where no disturbance is caused by the motion of any of the heavenly bodies.

And the souls which have transgressed the rule of piety, when they depart from the body, are handed over to these daemons, and are swept and hurled to and fro in those strata of the air which teem with fire and hail.

The one safeguard is piety. Over the pious man neither evil daemon nor destiny has dominion; for God saves the pious from every ill. Piety is the one and only good among men. The Father and Master of all, he who alone is all things, willingly reveals himself to all men. He does not indeed enable them to perceive him as situated in a certain place, or as having certain (sensible) qualities, or a certain magnitude; but he illuminates man with that knowledge alone which is the property of mind; whereby the darkness of error is dispelled from the soul, and truth is seen in all its brightness, and so man's consciousness is wholly absorbed in the knowledge of God; and being freed, by his ardent love of God, from that part of his being which makes him mortal, he is assured of his immortality in time to come. In this consists the difference between the good man and the bad. For in so far as a man is illumined by piety and devotion, by knowledge of

God, and worship and adoration of him, . . . he surpasses other men as much as the sun outshines the other lights of heaven.

The Mandean text

The world of darkness

In the name of the great Life! I cry to you, I instruct you, and I say: (you) true and believing men, (you) perceiving and separate ones: separate yourselves from the world of imperfection which is full of confusion and replete with error. First I gave you instruction about the King of Light, blessed be he in all eternity. And I told you about the blessed worlds of light in which there is nothing perishable, and about the uthras, jordans, and škinas, wonderful and brilliant. Now I will speak to you about the worlds of darkness and what is in them, hideous and terrible, whose form is faulty.

Beyond the earth of light downwards and beyond the earth Tibil southwards is that earth of darkness. It has a form which differs in kind and deviates from the earth of light, for they (both) deviate from each other in every characteristic and form. Darkness exists through its own evil nature, (is) a howling darkness, a desolate gloom which knows not the First or the Last. But the King of Light knows and perceives the First and the Last, that which is past and that which is to come. And he knew and perceived that evil was there, but he did not want to cause it harm, just as he said: "Harm not the wicked and the evil, until it has done harm itself." Its own evil nature exists from the beginning and to all eternity. The worlds of darkness are numerous and without end. He (the King of Light, or: one) said: "Broad and deep is the abode of evil, whose peoples showed no fidelity to the place which is their endless habitation, whose kingdom came into being from themselves. Their earth is black water and their heights gloomy darkness."

From the black water the King of Darkness was fashioned through his own evil nature and came forth. He waxed strong, mighty, and powerful, he called forth and spread abroad a thousand thousand evil generations without number and ten thousand times ten thousand ugly creations beyond count. Darkness waxed strong and multiplied through demons, dēvs, genii, spirits, hmurthas, liliths, temple- and chapel-spirits, idols, archons, angels, vampires, goblins, noxious spirits, demons of apoplexy(?), monsters, spirits of nets and locks, and Satans, all the detestable forms of darkness of every kind and type, male and female of darkness; gloomy, black, clumsy, rebellious, furious, raging, poisonous, stubborn, foolish, lazy, abominable, filthy, and stinking. Some among them are dumb, deaf, mute, stupid, stuttering, unhearing, speechless, deaf and dumb, perplexed, ignorant; some among them are insolent, hot-headed, violent, shrill, irascible, debauched, children of blood, of flashing fire, and devastating conflagration. Some among them are sorcerers, swindlers, liars, forgers, robbers, deceivers, exorcists, Chaldaeans, soothsayers. They are master-builders of every wickedness, instigators of oppression who commit murder and shed blood with no pity or compassion. They are artists of every hideous practice, they know countless languages and understand what meets the eye. They partake of every kind of form: some of them crawl on their bellies, some move about in water, some fly, some have many feet like the reptiles of the earth, and some carry a hundred . . . They have molars and incisors in their jaws. The taste of their trees is (like) poison and gall, their sap is (like) naphtha and pitch.

That King of Darkness assumed all the forms of earthly creatures: the head of the lion, the body of the dragon, the wings of the eagle, the back of the tortoise, the hands and feet of a monster. He walks, he crawls, creeps, flies, screams, is insolent, threatening, roars, groans, gives (impudent) winks, whistles, and knows all the languages of the world. But he is stupid, muddled, his ideas are confused, and he knows neither the First nor the Last, (albeit) he does know what happens in all the worlds. He has many qualities: he is mightier than all his worlds, stronger and more numerous than all of them and more powerful than all his creatures and stronger than they. When he so desires he conceals himself from them, so that they see him not, (but) he knows the heart of those who stand before him. When his generations take to flight before him he brings them back (again) by his word, and the dēvs whom he desires he makes to return and draws them up before him. When he pleases he magnifies his appearances, and when he pleases he makes himself small. He moves his membrum in and out (again) and possesses (the bodily parts of) men and women. And when he shakes all the mysteries, he rages with his voice, his word, his breath, his breathing, his eyes, his jaws, his hands, his feet, his strength, his poison, his wrath, his utterance, his fear, his dread, his terror, his roaring, (and) all the worlds of darkness are terrified. His form is hideous, his body stinks, and his face is disfigured. The thickness of his lips measures 144,000 parasangs. The breath of his jaws melts iron, and the rocks are scorched by his breath. He lifts up his eyes and the mountains quake, the whisper of his lips makes the plains shudder. He mused with himself, deliberated in his foolish heart, and plotted in his crafty mind. He rose up and beheld the worlds of darkness, which spread out without end. He became arrogant and exalted himself and said: "Is there anyone who is greater than I? Is there anyone whose power is equal to mine? Is there anyone who is greater than I, greater and more excellent than all the worlds? Is there anyone whose food is the mountains, in whose maw no blood can be found? Should there be anyone who is stronger than I, then I will raise myself to fight with him and will discover whence his strength comes."

He concealed himself and beheld the worlds of light from afar at the boundary of darkness and light: like fire on the summit of high mountains, like stars which shine in the firmament, like the radiance of the sun when it rises and comes from the east, and like the moon in its brightness. He beheld the lustre of that earth of light like burning lamps, which, protected by glass containers, shine forth.

He conferred with himself, flew into a temper, raged mightily, and spoke: "I looked at that world; what is this abode of darkness to me, whose 'magnificence' is hideous and frightful, whose food is black water and corruption? I will ascend to that shining earth and conduct a war with its king, I will take his crown from him, set it on my head, and I will be king of the heights and the depths." And he said: "If it is a garment, I will put it on, if it is food, I will eat it, if it is drink, I will drink it, if it is a house, I will destroy it, if it is an edifice I will make it a ruin, if it is a dwelling, I will live in it, if it is something that is stronger than I, I will pick a quarrel with it."

He was kindled with fire, he glowed in his mind, became hot with anger, and would have devoured all the world. But his ways are confused, his roads obstructed, and his paths tortuous. Notwithstanding he arrived above the earth in the moment as far as the lower frontier of darkness. In one day's travel he covered a distance of a hundred years.

When he beheld that resplendent form, he would have sprung up and risen from the howling, desolate darkness to that shining form, but he found no gate by which he could enter, no way to tread upon, and no ascent by which he might rise, because that form which he saw was in the heights, (whereas) he was in the depths, as were the human beings, the animals, and the cattle, which cannot ascend to the heights of heaven. He flew into a temper and was inflamed, like a greedy lion over his prey; and he did not rest or remain in his own home. He cried out, screamed and groaned loudly. The worlds of light heard his voice and beheld the shape of the stupid dēv. The perishable army rallied: they reviewed and examined one another like a body in which a limb suddenly begins to shake, and they resounded like a copper vessel.

Then a voice went forth from the sublime King of Light, he spoke to the worlds of light (and) the škinas and uthras: "Be calm, (you) uthras, and remain where you are in your škinas. do not be alarmed at the fury of the stupid, evil dēv who is worked up into a rage.

In his own container (*kanna*) he shall be imprisoned, he shall be imprisoned in his own container (*kanna*).

> All his plans shall be spoilt,
> spoilt shall be all his plans,
> and his (evil) works will come to nothing."

> When I stood in the House of Life,
> I beheld the rebellious.
> I beheld the gates of darkness,
> I beheld the depths full of darkness.
> I beheld the destructive
> and the lords of the gloomy abode.
> I beheld the warriors,
> who are buried in darkness.
> I beheld the gates of fire,

how they burn and glow.
The wicked burn and glow
and deliberate on imperfection and deficiency.
I beheld Hewath the female,
how she speaks in (the) darkness and malice.
She speaks in malice,
in witchcraft, and sorcery, which she practises.
She speaks with illusory wisdom
and sits enthroned in falsehood.
I beheld the gate of darkness
and the arteries of the earth Siniawis, just as they are (there).
I beheld the black water in it,
which rose up, boiled, and bubbled.
Whoever enters there dies,
and whoever beholds it is scorched.
I beheld the dragons,
who were hurled there and writhe about.
I beheld dragons
of every type and every kind.
I beheld the chariots of (the sons of) darkness,
which do not resemble one another.
I beheld the wicked rebels,
as they are seated in their chariots.
I beheld the wicked rebels,
how they are arrayed with weapons of evil.
They are arrayed in weapons of evil
and plot evil against the Place of Light.

Whence is the darkness,
Whence are its inhabitants, who sit in it?
Whence are their works, which are so hideous
and frightful?
Whence is their deficiency,
which is so far-reaching,
whose appearance is hideous and fearful
and is crammed with flaws?
It is crammed with flaws
[. . .]
Whence are the mighty, evil monsters
who live in the fire?

Whence are the black waters
which seethe and boil?
Whoever enters there, dies,
and whoever sees it, is consumed.
Whence are the dragons
which are cast therein and contort themselves?
Whence are their chariots,
whence are the wicked who are in them?
Whence is Hewath, the female
[. . .]
"Since you, Life, were there,
how did darkness come into being (there)?
How did darkness come into being (there),
how did imperfection and deficiency come into being?"

There is no boundary for the light
and it was not known when it came into being.
Nothing was when light was not,
nothing was when radiance was not.
Nothing was when the Mighty (Life) was not;
there never was a boundary for the light.
Nothing was when the water was not;
the water is prior to the darkness.
Prior to the darkness is the water:
there is nothing without an end.
There is no number of which we could say,
how (great) it was before the uthras came into being.
The uthras are prior to the darkness,
prior to the darkness are the uthras and more ancient than
    its inhabitants.
Goodness is prior
to the malice of the Place of Darkness.
Gentleness is prior
to the bitterness of the Place of Darkness.
The living fire is prior
to the bitterness of the Place of Darkness.
The living fire is prior
to the consuming fire of the Place of Darkness.
Praise is prior
to sorcery and witchcraft, which the wicked practise.

The third jordan is prior
to the flowing water of the Place of Darkness.
Perception (or: instruction in the faith) is prior
to this or that, which the wicked of the Place of Darkness
    practise.
The call of the uthras is prior
to that of the powerful wicked ones of the Palace of Darkness.
The throne of rest is prior
to the throne of rebellion.
Hymns and recitations (or: books) are prior
to the sorcery of Hewath, the terrible woman.
The kanna of ether is prior
to the talk which Ruha produces.

*   *   *   *   *

B'haq-Ziwa is prior
to Ruha, as she was (or: came into being).
The design of all the uthras
is prior to the rebellious call.
The boundary of the good is prior
to the master of the whole place of darkness.
The elect righteous are prior
to all the creations of darkness, as they (also) are.

Water mixes not with pitch,
and darkness cannot be reckoned with light.
Darkness cannot be reckoned with light,
the gloomy abode is not illuminated.
The gloomy abode is not illuminated
and the turbid water does not sparkle.
Darkness increased,
and its inhabitants were formed.
Darkness was formed,
and its inhabitants were formed.
Darkness was formed,
and when it was formed, immediately it tested its strength.
Because of the malice which it harboured in its mind,
it is imprisoned in its own kanna.
It is imprisoned in its own kanna,
and all its works come to nothing.

The sons of darkness come to nothing,
but the sons of the Mighty (Life) remain steadfast.
The house of the wicked comes to nothing,
and the consuming fire goes out.
Its sorcery dies and ceases to be,
since it does not exist from eternity.
Its works come to an end,
but the generations of the Life remain steadfast for ever and ever.
The living instruction rises up
and illuminates the perishable dwelling.

The attack of Darkness

What caused the Darkness to mount up and fight against the Light? In terms of external occasion: the perception of the Light, which heretofore had been unknown to it. To get to such a perception, the Darkness had first to reach its own outer limits, and to these it was pushed at some time in the course of the internal warfare in which the destructive passion of its members was ceaselessly engaged. For the nature of Darkness is hate and strife, and it must fulfill this nature against itself until the encounter with the Light presents an external and better object. We render this piece of doctrine in the following compilation from Severus, Theodoret, and Titus:[1]

The Darkness was divided against itself – the tree against its fruits and the fruits against the tree. Strife and bitterness belong to the nature of its parts; the gentle stillness is alien to them who are filled with every malignity, and each destroys what is close to him.

Yet it was their very tumult which gave them the occasion to rise up to the worlds of Light. For truly, these members of the tree of death did not even know one another to begin with. Each one had but his own mind, each knew nothing but his own voice and saw but what was before his eyes. Only when one of them screamed did they hear him and turned impetuously towards the sound.

Thus aroused and mutually incited they fought and devoured one another, and they did not cease to press each other hard, until at last they caught sight of the Light. For in the course of the war they came, some pursued and some pursuing, to the boundaries of the Light, and when they beheld the Light – a sight wondrous and glorious, by far superior to their own – it pleased them and they marvelled at it; and they assembled – all the Matter of Darkness – and conferred how they could mingle with the Light. But because of the disorder of their minds they failed to perceive that the strong and mighty God dwelt there. And they strove to rise upward to the height, because never a knowledge of the Good and the Godhead had come to them. Thus without understanding, they cast a mad glance upon it from lust for the spectacle of these blessed worlds, and they thought it could become theirs. And carried away by the passion within them, they now wished with all their might to fight against it in order to bring it into their power and to mix with the Light their own Darkness. They united the whole dark pernicious Hyle and with their innumerable forces rose all together, and in desire for the better opened the attack. They attacked in one body, as it were without knowing their adversary, for they had never heard of the Deity.

Note

1   The beginning of this section is taken from Hans Jonas (ed.) *The Gnostic Religion* (Boston: Beacon Press, 1958). The remainder comes from Severus of Antioch, *123 Homily*; Theodoret, Haereticorum Fabularum Compendium (I. 26) (Migne PP.Gr.83); Titus of Bostra, *Adversus Manichaeos* (Migne PP.Gr.18).

The wisdom of the Zohar[1]

Regarding the matter of the Tree of Knowledge, of which Adam was commanded not to eat: Fix your mind on this matter and as to why God kept him away from this tree more than from the others. Notice that, according to the wording in Scripture, He did not enjoin him against gathering [the fruit], but only against eating it. For Adam did not pluck and take the fruit, but the woman gave it to him, as is written, "And she gave also unto her husband" (Gen. 3:6). The Scriptural verse also only has Him saying: "Hast thou eaten of the tree, whereof I commanded thee that thou shouldest not eat?" Likewise, Scripture says about the Tree of Life: "lest he put forth his hand, and take also of the tree of life, and eat, and live for ever." From here we may infer that it is the act of eating that causes sin, and indeed, this is so. Know that the eating of the fruits of the Garden [of Eden] provided nourishment for the soul; therefore, he was punished for eating, which involves both body and soul. But the soul has no share or benefit in gathering the fruit: even though [he thereby brought about] a separation in the lower realms, it does not cause separation in the upper realms, but the soul only partakes in the act of eating the fruit, and is nourished by its fruits. But damage is caused [to the soul] if the fruit contains damaging things, and [things that] stimulate the Evil Urge and diminish it [the soul] in its rank and its health, and reduces its strength in the upper realm – and this was [Adam's] sin.

You already know that the Tree of Life and the Tree of Knowledge are one [tree] below but two [trees] above: the Tree of Knowledge is from the northern side, but the Tree of Life is from the eastern side, from whence light emanates into the entire world, and the potency of Satan is there. And it is written in the "Jerusalem Talmud":"What is Satan? This teaches that the Holy One blessed be He has a quality whose name is Evil, and it lies to the north of God, as is written, 'Out of the north the evil shall break forth' (Jer. 1:14), and from the north it comes. And what is it? It is the form of the [left] hand, and it has many emissaries, and every single one of them is called Evil, Evil; however, there are among them lesser and greater ones, and they make the world culpable," as it is written there. And it is also written in the above-quoted "Jerusalem Talmud": "What is meant by, 'And the Lord showed him a tree, and he cast it into the waters' (Exod. 15:25)? This refers to the Tree of Life that Satan threw down, etc.," as it is written there.

Now this is the meaning: So long as the Tree of Life, which comes from the side of the east and is the Good Urge and the quality of peace [harmony], is connected with the Tree of Knowledge, which comes from the side of the north, from the side of Satan and evil, then Satan can do nothing, for the Tree of Life, which is the quality of peace [i.e., harmony], shall overwhelm him. But the moment it [the Tree of Knowledge] is separated [from the Tree of Life], its strength is freed and Satan is able to act. Therefore, when Satan wished to lead Israel astray [at Marah], he cast [the Tree of Life] away and separated it from them and tested Israel, and was therefore able to seduce Israel into sinning. And this is the matter known as "chopping down of the plantings" (*kitsuts baneti'oth*), for had he been connected [with the Tree of Life], he would have been unable to do this thing. Moreover, had Adam not first separated the fruit, Satan would have been unable to separate him from the Tree of Life.

And let the matter that he [Adam?] was not involved in the eating [that is, that he did not participate in the eating with Eve] not seem difficult to you; for he performed separation in his thought, which is more a part of the soul. For you already know that a human being is composed of all things, and his soul is connected to the supernal soul, for which reason the Torah states, "Ye shall be holy, for I am Holy" (Lev. 19:2), as well as, "Sanctify yourselves therefore, and be ye holy" (Lev. 20:7). Therefore, the righteous man, who raises his pure and immaculate soul to the supernal holy soul, unites with it and knows the future; and that is the meaning of the prophet and his path, for the Evil Urge has no power over him to separate him from the upper soul. That is why the prophet's soul unites completely with the upper soul, and with his intellect fulfills the Torah, for they [the commandments] are incorporated within him [in his intellect]. That is why our sages said that the Patriarchs fulfilled the Torah in their intellect, and they said that the Patriarchs are themselves the *Merkavah*, and the same is also true of their children after them, and of every righteous man. About this, Scripture says, "And I will dwell among the children of Israel" (Exod. 29:45), for the Holy Spirit rests upon them and joins itself to them. But if a man walks in the path of evil, which is Satan, then he chops and separates his soul from the supernal soul; and concerning this it is written in the Torah, "and My soul shall abhor you" (Lev. 26:30) – that is, the soul is separated and distanced from the supernal soul, and this is like a chopping away. And that is why in the words "that ye should be defiled thereby" (Lev. 11:43), the Hebrew word [for "defiled"] *ve-nitmeitem* is written without an *'alef* – signifying that they are not worthy to have the crown of God's reign that animates everything [symbolized in the *'alef*] be on their heads, but they are culpable of death [because of their separation from the supernal soul and because they destroyed the divine unity].

It is written in the Prophets, "But your iniquities have separated between you and your God" (Isa. 59:2), and similar verses. And the Talmud says: "It is not the Serpent that kills, but sin that kills." Hence, when Adam ate of the fruit of the Tree of Knowledge, which is of the side of evil, and separated it [through his awareness or his contemplation] from the Tree of Life, the Evil Urge dominated him in his eating and in his soul, for his soul took part in the eating of the fruits of the Garden, as we said above. Thus, impurity and death and removal of the soul from the [supernal] soul took place [within Adam]. This explains that by his eating he caused destruction above and below in the plantings and separated the forces of the Tree of Knowledge by themselves, and separated them from the forces of the Tree of Life – and this is the great offense against both body and soul, above and below, and that is why it is said of Adam that he chopped away at the plantings. For after he separated the fruit of the Tree of Knowledge, which is of the side of evil, from the Tree of Life, and increased the strength of the Evil Urge and sated his soul with it, he separated the [lower] from the [upper] soul, and gave the emissaries of the Tree of Knowledge the strength to do evil, and he thereby separated the Tree of Knowledge from the Tree of Life, and also separated his soul from all the good qualities of the supernal soul, and united himself with the Evil Urge . . .

And the Sages expressly said: "He is Satan, he is the Evil Urge, he is the Angel of Death." For prior to his eating, Adam was completely spiritual and had the nature of the angels, like Enoch and Elijah, hence, he was worthy to eat of the fruits of Paradise, which are the fruits of the soul. And let not the expression "eating of the fruit" be difficult to you, for "eating" signifies enjoyment or benefit, as in [their saying], "'Its flesh shall not be eaten' (Exod. 21:28): this implies both the prohibition of eating and the prohibition of deriving benefit therefrom" – and this refers to the benefit or enjoyment obtained by the soul. After that, it states – "Behold, the man is become as one of us" (Gen. 3:22). And the Sages said, "like the One of the world," that is, he was composed of all [intellectual–spiritual] things and potencies. And the words "Behold, the man . . .," etc. refer to the time before he sinned; but now, in his sin, he has become mortal. Before sinning, he was worthy of eating of the fruits of the Garden, which were the fruits of the soul; therefore it was necessary to send him away from there. There was also another reason to drive him away from there: "lest he put forth his hand, and take also of the Tree of Life" – the Tree of Life which causes life, for it stems from the force of the "Bundle of Life" – "and eat, and live for ever" – for that is whence the strength of life comes from. And he was deprived of two things: the eating of the fruit of the Garden, which are life for the soul, just as the eating of [ordinary] fruit is life for the body; and the eating of the Tree of Life, which refers to eternal life. And it is to this that the two expressions refer: "He sent him forth," and "He drove out the man."

35

Note

1 Quoted from *On the Mystical Shape of the Godhead: Basic Concepts of the Kabbalah*, ed. Gershom Scholem (New York: Shocken Books, 1995).

Part 2

FROM
SIN TO VICE

Chartres Cathedral, "The Devil and Greed."

The concept of evil enters a new phase with Christianity. The primary focus of attention is directed to a metaphysical extension of the question raised by Job: how can an omnipotent benevolent deity create a world in which men knowingly and voluntarily disobey divine commands? Why do the just and the innocent suffer? The second set of issues centers around analyzing the primary locus and sources of disobedience and sin. Are acts in and of themselves sinful, or must the agent intend harm? Is the intention to sin sufficient for the imputation of guilt? Is the tendency to sin inherited? If it is innate, how can man be held guilty? Are there sins of omission as well as commission?

Although Augustine (354–430) at one time held the Manichaean view that the forces of good and evil are opposed in metaphysical and psychological combat, he repudiated those beliefs, and developed a Christian synthesis of neo-Platonism and Stoicism. The problem of evil came to be centered on explaining human wayward-ness and malevolence. How could a benevolent and omnipotent deity have created a wayward being capable of transgressing divine commands, violating his innate knowledge of the difference between good and evil? Augustine's answer was complex: the world was created, and is wholly directed by divine love and benev-olence. Man is endowed with innate knowledge of the difference between right and wrong. But because he has also been endowed with the dignity of a free will, capable of genuine and not merely programmed choice, his knowledge of good and evil is not always immediately accessible or effective. Although man is informed by divinity, he is nevertheless finite, frail and vulnerable. His desires are deformed by his self-centered partiality. Since the world contains nothing which is intrinsi-cally bad, human desires are directed to things – food, sex, power – that are in themselves genuine goods. But a self-oriented will perceives and desires these things in the wrong way, for the wrong reason. Benevolent divine grace – following its counsels of eternal order – can reorient the will, return the soul to its proper harmony. The neo-Platonic strand in Augustine's thought emphasized the redemp-tive power of love – divine love and love of the divine – as a guiding force towards the good.

Augustine set the frame – formulated the questions, supplied the terminology and premises – for a great deal of later discussions of evil. Influenced by earlier Sufi writers, al-Ghazali's (1058–1111) exhortations develop the Koranic emphasis on the unity and benevolence of the divine. As one of Ghazali's defenders put it, "his purpose is to incite man to the utmost . . . trust . . . and reliance on God . . . so that he may not despair over evils [that may] befall him or good[s that may] which elude him."[1] The world is not only ordered reasonably well enough: it is so ordered that not an iota, not a gnat's wing or speck of dust, can be changed for the better.

Abelard (1079–1142) poses a set of penetrating questions, pressing for greater precision in locating the scene of sin. Does it consist in faulty – unGodly –

action? Is it a response to the lure of bodily desires? Is the will itself infected? Does sin emerge from malformed character traits? Strongly influenced by Augustine, anxious to preserve the freedom of choice – the absolutely voluntary character of sin – Abelard locates sin in the *consent* to what is willed, desired, or done. He argues that a person can sin by consenting to a wrong without himself having had a defective intention; he can also rightly, morally consent to an action that is normally culpable. To preserve absolute moral responsibility, sinfulness has moved to the core self, the self who has the freedom and the power to affirm or deny his own psychology as well as his actions.

Maimonides (1135–1204) catalogues the sources of human frailty. Most men mistake their place in the universe. Instead of recognizing that what befalls them is incidental to the larger working of the cosmos, they think that the world is – or should be – constructed around them, their needs and benefits. "It is because of our own deficiencies that we lament." The evils that befall men have three sources, all of them due to his own nature. He is a temporal, material being, capable of decay and mortality; he is given to tyrannical domination over others; and he harms himself through his own defective character, his lack of foresight and moderation. Attempting to use Aristotelian insights to flesh out the commands of the Torah, Maimonides analyzes the virtues that conduce to obeying the Law.

Pope Innocent III (Lothari dei Segni, 1161–1216) catalogues the varieties of human wickedness, the sources of the shameful desires for riches, pleasures and honors. It is these desires that issue in the sins of envy, avarice, gluttony, lechery, and pride. The wrath that is an expression of Divine justice decrees the punishment, the tortures, the eternal damnation of the wicked. Having loved their transgressions, sinners will continue to live in sin, even through the fires of hell that burn within their hearts.

Aquinas (1225–1274) treated virtually every traditional problem surrounding the existence of evil: Is evil ontologically real? Is it compatible with a perfectly ordered world? Are there sins of omission? What is the difference between sin and vice? Does sin consists in a defective will or in defective action or both taken together? How can a good man fall into sin? What are the major sources of vice and sin? Many of the legion of distinctions Aquinas offered to reconcile opposing views on the answers to these questions were derived from Aristotelian ethics and philosophical psychology. He distinguishes between evil means and evil ends, between actual and potential evil, between vice and characterological weakness, between the viciousness of excess and that of deficiency.

In describing the architecture of the Inferno, Dante (1265–1321) provides a taxonomic map of the vices, in their order of dependence and heinousness. Violence and fraud are species of malice, "the sin most hated by God." Each of these sins has distinctive varieties, ranged in degree of viciousness. Violence can be directed to goods or to persons; violence to persons can be directed to one's fellows, to oneself or to God. Flattery, theft, usury, suicide, treachery have distinctive punishments, crafted to suit its nature. At the very pit of hell is treachery to God.

"The Parson's Tale" in Chaucer's (1340–1400) *Canterbury Tales* gives a succinct stereotypic description of popular views of the seven deadly sins. Inherited from Adam's original disobedience, sin is transmitted through the body, "vile and corrupt matter." Venial sins involve loving Christ less than one should. Without repentance, they can gradually become the mortal sin of loving something worldly more than God. The principal mortal sin – the "trunk from which [the others] branch" – is the dominance of self-love in pride, which in turn generates varieties of anger, envy, melancholia, avarice, gluttony, lechery.

Note

1   Murtada al-Zabidi (d. 1205) *Ithaf*, IX, 450, quoted by Eric Ormsby, *Theodicy in Islamic Thought* (Princeton, NJ: Princeton University Press, 1984), p. 38.

7

ST AUGUSTINE

The discoveries of guilt and
divine benevolence

The Confessions

Nothing is utterly condemnable save vice: yet I grew in vice through desire of praise; and when I lacked opportunity to equal others in vice, I invented things I had not done, lest I might be held cowardly for being innocent, or contemptible for being chaste. With the basest companions I walked the streets of Babylon [the city of this World as opposed to the city of God] and wallowed in its filth as if it had been a bed of spices and precious ointments. To make me cleave closer to that city's very center, the invisible Enemy trod me down and seduced me, for I was easy to seduce. My mother had by now fled out of the center of Babylon, but she still lingered in its outskirts. She had urged me to chastity but she did not follow up what my father had told her of me: and though she saw my sexual passions as most evil now and full of peril for the future, she did not consider that if they could not be pared down to the quick, they had better be brought under control within the bounds of married love. She did not want me married because she feared that a wife might be a hindrance to my prospects – not those hopes of the world to come which my mother had in You, O God, but my prospects as a student. Both my parents were unduly set upon the success of my studies, my father because he had practically no thought of You and only vain ambition for me, my mother because she thought that the usual course of studies would be not only no hindrance to my coming to You but an actual help. Recalling the past as well as I can, that is how I read my parents' characters. Anyhow, I was left to do pretty well as I liked, and go after pleasure not only beyond the limit of reasonable discipline but to sheer dissoluteness in many kinds of evil. And in all this, O God, a mist hung between my eyes and the brightness of Your truth: *and mine iniquity had come forth as it were from fatness.*

Confessions (source: *The Confessions of Saint Augustine*, trans. F. J. Sheed, New York: Sheed & Ward, 1943); *The City of God* (source: *The City of God*, trans. Marens Dod, New York: The Modern Library, 1950); *The Problem of Free Choice* (source: *The Problem of Free Choice*, trans. Mon Mark Pontifex, Westminster, MD: Newman Press, 1955)

Your law, O Lord, punishes theft; and this law is so written in the hearts of men that not even the breaking of it blots it out: for no thief bears calmly being stolen from – not even if he is rich and the other steals through want. Yet I chose to steal, and not because want drove me to it – unless a want of justice and contempt for it and an excess for iniquity. For I stole things which I already had in plenty and of better quality. Nor had I any desire to enjoy the things I stole, but only the stealing of them and the sin. There was a pear tree near our vineyard, heavy with fruit, but fruit that was not particularly tempting either to look at or to taste. A group of young blackguards, and I among them, went out to knock down the pears and carry them off late one night, for it was our bad habit to carry on our games in the streets till very late. We carried off an immense load of pears, not to eat – for we barely tasted them before throwing them to the hogs. Our only pleasure in doing it was that it was forbidden. Such was my heart, O God, such was my heart: yet in the depth of the abyss You had pity on it. Let that heart now tell You what it sought when I was thus evil for no object, having no cause for wrongdoing save my wrongness. The malice of the act was base and I loved it – that is to say I loved my own undoing, I loved the evil in me – not the thing for which I did the evil, simply the evil: my soul was depraved, and hurled itself down from security in You into utter destruction, seeking no profit from wickedness but only to be wicked.

There is an appeal to the eye in beautiful things, in gold and silver and all such; the sense of touch has its own powerful pleasures; and the other senses find qualities in things suited to them. Worldly success has its glory, and the power to command and to overcome: and from this springs the thirst for revenge. But in our quest of all these things, we must not depart from You, Lord, or deviate from Your Law. This life we live here below has its own attractiveness, grounded in the measure of beauty it has and its harmony with the beauty of all lesser things. The bond of human friendship is admirable, holding many souls as one. Yet in the enjoyment of all such things we commit sin if through immoderate inclination to them – for though they are good, they are the lowest order of good – things higher and better are forgotten, even You, O Lord our God, and Your Truth and Your Law. These lower things have their delights but not such as my God has, for He made them all: *and in Him doth the righteous delight, and He is the joy of the upright of heart.*

Now when we ask why this or that particular evil act was done, it is normal to assume that it could not have been done save through the desire of gaining or the fear of losing some one of these lower goods. For they have their own charm and their own beauty, though compared with the higher values of heaven they are poor and mean enough. Such a man has committed a murder. Why? He wanted the other man's wife or his property; or he had chosen robbery as a means of livelihood; or he feared to lose this or that through his victim's act; or he had been wronged and was aflame for vengeance. Would any man commit a murder for no cause, for the sheer delight of murdering? The thing would be incredible. There is of course the case of the man [Catiline] who was said to be so stupidly and savagely cruel that he practiced cruelty and evil even when he had nothing to gain by them. But even there a cause was stated – he did it, he said, lest through idleness his hand or his resolution should grow slack. And why did he want to prevent that? So that one day by the multiplication of his crimes the city should be his, and he would have gained honors and authority and riches, and would no longer be in fear of the law or in the difficulties that want of money and the awareness of his crimes had brought him. So that not even Catiline loved his crimes as crimes: he loved some other thing which was his reason for committing them.

What was it then that in my wretched folly I loved in you, O theft of mine, deed wrought in that dark night when I was sixteen? For you were not lovely: you were a theft. Or are you anything at all, that I should talk with you? The pears that we stole were beautiful for they were created by Thee, Thou most Beautiful of all, Creator of all, Thou good God, my Sovereign and true Good. The pears were beautiful but it was not pears that my empty soul desired. For I had any number of better pears of my own, and plucked those only that I might steal. For once I had gathered them I threw them away, tasting only my own sin and savouring that with delight; for if I took so much as a bite of any one of those pears, it was the sin that sweetened it. And now, Lord my God, I ask what was it that attracted me in that theft, for there was no beauty in it to attract. I do not mean merely that it lacked the beauty that there is in injustice and prudence, or in the mind of man or his senses and vegetative life: or even so much as the beauty and glory of the stars in the heavens, or of earth and sea with their oncoming of new life to replace the generations that pass. It had not even that false show or shadow of beauty by which sin tempts us.

For there *is* a certain show of beauty in sin . . . . Thus pride wears the mask of loftiness of spirit, although You alone, O God, are high over all. Ambition seeks honor and glory, although You alone are to be honored before all and glorious forever. By cruelty the great seek to be feared, yet who is to be feared but God alone: from His power what can be wrested away, or when or where or how or by whom? The caresses by which the lustful seduce are a seeking for love: but nothing is more caressing than Your charity, nor is anything more healthfully loved than Your supremely lovely, supremely luminous, Truth. Curiosity may be regarded as a desire for knowledge, whereas You supremely know all things. Ignorance and sheer stupidity hide under the names of simplicity and innocence: yet no being has simplicity like to Yours: and none is more innocent than You, for it is their own deeds that harm the wicked. Sloth pretends that it wants quietude: but what sure rest is there save the Lord? Luxuriousness would be called abundance and completeness; but You are the fullness and inexhaustible abundance of incorruptible delight. Wastefulness is a parody of generosity: but You are the infinitely generous giver of all good. Avarice wants to possess overmuch: but You possess all. Enviousness claims that it strives to excel: but what can excel before You? Anger clamors for just vengeance: but whose vengeance is so just as Yours? Fear is the recoil from a new and sudden threat to something one holds dear, and a cautious regard for one's own safety: but nothing new or sudden can happen to You, nothing can threaten Your hold upon things loved, and where is safety secure save in You? Grief pines at the loss of things in which desire delighted: for it wills to be like to You from whom nothing can be taken away.

Thus the soul is guilty of fornication when she turns from You and seeks from any other source what she will nowhere find pure and without taint unless she returns to You. Thus even those who go from You and stand up against You are still perversely imitating You. But by the mere fact of their imitation, they declare that You are the creator of all that is, and that there is nowhere for them to go where You are not.

So once again what did I enjoy in that theft of mine? Of what excellence of my Lord was I making perverse and vicious imitation? Perhaps it was the thrill of acting against Your law — at least in appearance, since I had no power to do so in fact, the delight a prisoner might have in making some small gesture of liberty — getting a deceptive sense of omnipotence from doing something forbidden without immediate punishment. I was that slave, who fled from his Lord and pursued his Lord's shadow. O rottenness, O monstrousness of life and abyss of death! Could you find pleasure only in what was forbidden, and only because it was forbidden?

What shall I render unto the Lord, that I can recall these things and yet not be afraid! *I shall love Thee, Lord, and shall give thanks to Thee and confess Thy name*, because Thou has forgiven me such great sins and evil deeds. I know that it is only by Thy grace and mercy that Thou hast melted away the ice of my sins. And the evil I have not done, that also I know is by Thy grace: for what might I not have done, seeing that I loved evil solely because it was evil? I confess that Thou hast forgiven all alike — the sins I committed of my own motion, the sins I would have committed but for Thy grace.

Would any man, considering his own weakness, dare to attribute his chastity or his innocence to his own powers and so love Thee less — as if he did not need the same mercy as those who return to Thee after sin. If any man has heard Thy voice and followed it and done none of the things he finds me here recording and confessing, still he must not scorn me: for I am healed by the same doctor who preserved him from falling into sickness, or at least into such grievous sickness. But let him love Thee even more: seeing me rescued out of such sickness of sin, and himself saved from falling into such sickness of sin, by one same Saviour.

What fruit therefore had I (in my vileness) *in those things of which I am now ashamed?* Especially in that piece of thieving, in which I loved nothing except the thievery — though that in itself was no *thing* and I only the more wretched for it. Now — as I think back on the state of my mind then — I am altogether certain that I would not have done it alone. Perhaps then what I really loved was the companionship of those with whom I did it. If so, can I still say that I loved nothing over and above the thievery? Surely I can; that companionship was nothing over and above, because it was nothing. What is the truth of it? Who shall show me, unless He that illuminates my heart and brings light into its dark places? What is the thing that I am trying to get at in all this discussion? If I had liked the pears that I stole and wanted to enjoy eating them, I might have committed the offence alone, if that had been sufficient, to get me the pleasure I wanted; I should not have needed to inflame the itch of my desires by rubbing against accomplices. But since the pleasure I got was not in the pears, it must have been in the crime itself, and put there by the companionship of others sinning with me.

What was my feeling in all this? Depraved, undoubtedly, and woe is me that I had it. But what exactly was it? *Who can understand sins?* We laughed together as if our hearts were tickled to be playing a trick upon the owners, who had no notion of what we were doing and would very strongly have objected. But what delight did I find in that, which I would not equally have found if I had done it alone? Because we are not much given to laughing when we are alone? Not much given, perhaps, but laughter does sometimes overcome a man when no one else is about, if something especially ridiculous is seen or heard or floats into the mind. Yet I would not have done this by myself: quite definitely I would not have done it myself.

Here, then, O God, is the memory still livid in my mind. I would not have committed that theft alone: my pleasure in it was not what I stole but that I stole: yet I would not have enjoyed doing it, I would not have done it, alone. O friendship unfriendly, unanalysable attraction for the mind, greediness to do damage for the mere sport and jest of it, desire for another's loss with no gain to oneself or vengeance to be satisfied! Someone cries "Come on, let's do it" – and we would be ashamed to be ashamed?

Who can unravel that complex twisted knottedness? It is unclean, I hate to think of it or look at it. I long for Thee, O Justice and Innocence, Joy and Beauty of the clear of sight, I long for Thee with unquenchable longing. There is sure repose in Thee and life untroubled. He that enters into Thee, enters into the joy of his Lord and shall not fear and shall be well in Him who is the Best. I went away from Thee, my God, in my youth I strayed too far from Thy sustaining power, and I became to myself a barren land.

The City of God

It is with reference to the nature, then, and not to the wickedness of the devil, that we are to understand these words, "This is the beginning of God's handiwork"; for, without doubt, wickedness can be a flaw or vice only where the nature previously was not vitiated. Vice, too, is so contrary to nature, that it cannot but damage it. And therefore departure from God would be no vice, unless in a nature whose property it was to abide with God. So that even the wicked will is a strong proof of the goodness of the nature. But God, as He is the supremely good Creator of good natures, so is He of evil wills the most just Ruler; so that, while they make an ill use of good natures, He makes a good use even of evil wills. Accordingly, He caused the devil (good by God's creation, wicked by his own will) to be cast down from his high position, and to become the mockery of His angels – that is, He caused his temptations to benefit those whom he wishes to injure by them. And because God, when He created him, was certainly not ignorant of his future malignity, and foresaw the good which He Himself would bring out of his evil, therefore says the psalm, "This leviathan whom Thou hast made to be a sport therein," that we may see that, even while God in His goodness created him good, He yet had already foreseen and arranged how He would make use of him when he became wicked . . .

This may be enough to prevent any one from supposing, when we speak of the apostate angels, that they could have another nature, derived, as it were, from some different origin, and not from God. From the great impiety of this error we shall disentangle ourselves the more readily and easily, the more distinctly we understand that which God spoke by the angel when He sent Moses to the children of Israel: "I am that I am." For since God is the supreme existence, that is to say, supreme is, and is therefore unchangeable, the things that He made He empowered to be, but not to be supremely like Himself. To some He communicated a more ample, to others a more limited existence, and thus arranged the natures of beings in ranks. For as from *sapere* comes *sapientia*, so from *esse* comes *essentia* – a new word indeed, which the old Latin writers did not use, but which is naturalized in our day, that our language may not want an equivalent for the Greek οἰσία. For this is expressed word for word by *essentia*. Consequently, to that nature which supremely is, and which created all else that exists, no nature is contrary save that which does not exist. For nonentity is the contrary of that which is. And thus there is no being contrary to God, the Supreme Being, and Author of all beings whatsoever . . .

In Scripture they are called God's enemies who oppose His rule, not by nature, but by vice; having no power to hurt Him, but only themselves. For they are His enemies, not through their power to hurt, but by their will to oppose Him. For God is unchangeable, and wholly proof against injury. Therefore the vice which makes those who are called His enemies resist Him, is an evil not to God, but to themselves. And to them it is an evil, solely because it corrupts the good of their nature. It is not nature, therefore, but vice, which is contrary to God. For that which is evil is contrary to the good. And who will deny that God is the supreme good? Vice, therefore, is contrary to God, as evil to good. Further, the nature it vitiates is a good, and therefore to this good also it is contrary. But while it is contrary to God only as evil to good, it is contrary to the nature it vitiates, both as evil and as hurtful. For to God no evils are hurtful; but only to natures mutable and corruptible, though, by the testimony of the vices themselves, originally good. For were they not good, vices could not hurt them. For how do they hurt them but by depriving them of integrity, beauty, welfare, virtue, and, in short, whatever natural good vice is wont to diminish or destroy? But if there be no good to take away, then no injury can be done, and consequently there can be no vice. For it is impossible that there should be a harmless vice. Whence we gather, that though vice cannot injure the unchangeable good, it can injure nothing but good; because it does not exist where it does not injure. This, then, may be thus formulated: Vice cannot be in the highest good, and cannot be but in some good. Things solely good, therefore, can in some circumstances exist; things solely evil, never, for even those natures which are vitiated by an evil will, so far indeed as they are vitiated, are evil, but in so far as they are natures they are good. And when a vitiated nature is punished, besides the good it has in being a nature, it has this also, that it is not unpunished. For this is just, and certainly everything just is a good. For no one is punished for natural, but for voluntary vices. For even the vice which by the force of habit and long continuance has become a second nature, had its origin in the will. For at present we are speaking of the vices of the nature, which has a mental capacity for that enlightenment which discriminates between what is just and what is unjust . . .

Let no one look for an efficient cause of the evil will; for it is not efficient, but deficient, as the will itself is not an effecting of something, but a defect. For defection from that which supremely is, to that which has less of being – this is to begin to have an evil will. Now, to seek to discover the causes of these defections – causes, as I have said, not efficient, but deficient – is as if some one sought to see darkness, or hear silence. Yet both of these are known by us, and the former by means only of the eye, the latter only by the ear; but not by their positive actuality, but by their want of it. Let no one, then, seek to know from me what I know that I do not know; unless he perhaps wishes to learn to be ignorant of that of which all we know is, that it cannot be known. For those things which are known not by their actuality, but by their want of it, are known, if our expression may be allowed and understood, by not knowing them, that by knowing them they may be not known. For when the eyesight surveys objects that strike the sense, it nowhere sees darkness but where it begins not to see. And so no other sense but the ear can perceive silence, and yet it is only perceived by not hearing. Thus, too, our mind perceives intelligible forms by understanding them; but when they are deficient, it knows them by not knowing them; for "who can understand defects?"[1]

This I do know, that the nature of God can never, nowhere, nowise be defective, and that natures made of nothing can. These latter, however, the more being they have, and the more good they do (for then they do something positive), the more they have efficient causes; but in so far as they are defective in being, and consequently do evil (for then what is their work but vanity?), they have deficient causes. And I know likewise, that the will could not become evil, were it unwilling to become so; and therefore its failings are justly punished, being not necessary, but voluntary. For its defections are not to evil things, but are themselves evil; that is to say, are not towards things that are naturally and in themselves evil, but the defection of the will is evil, because it is contrary to the order of nature, and an abandonment of that which has supreme being for that which has less. For avarice is not a fault inherent in gold, but in the man who inordinately loves gold, to the detriment of justice, which ought to be held in incomparably higher regard than gold. Neither is luxury the fault of lovely and charming objects, but of the heart that inordinately loves sensual pleasures, to the neglect of temperance, which attaches us to objects more lovely in their spirituality, and more delectable by their incorruptibility. Nor yet is boasting the fault of human praise, but of the soul that is inordinately fond of the applause of men, and that makes light of the voice of conscience. Pride, too, is not the fault of him who delegates power, nor of power itself, but of the soul that is inordinately enamoured of its own power, and despises the more just dominion of a higher authority. Consequently he who inordinately loves the good which any nature possesses, even though he obtain it, himself becomes evil in the good, and wretched because deprived of a greater good . . .

[W]ho does not see that idolatries, witchcrafts, hatreds, variance, emulations, wrath, strife, heresies, envyings, are vices rather of the soul than of the flesh? For it is quite possible for a man to abstain from fleshly pleasures for the sake of idolatry or some heretical error; and yet, even when he does so, he is proved by this apostolic authority to be living after the flesh; and in abstaining from fleshly pleasure, he is proved to be practising damnable works of the flesh. Who that has enmity has it not in his soul? or who would say to his enemy, or to the man he thinks his enemy, You have a bad flesh towards me, and not rather, You have a bad spirit towards me? In fine, if any one heard of what I may call "carnalities," he would not fail to attribute them to the carnal part of man; so no one doubts that "animosities" belong to the soul of man. Why then does the doctor of the Gentiles in faith and verity call all these and similar things works of the flesh, unless because, by that mode of speech whereby the part is used for the whole, he means us to understand by the word flesh and man himself? . . .

But if any one says that the flesh is the cause of all vices and ill conduct, inasmuch as the soul lives wickedly only because it is moved by the flesh, it is certain he has not carefully considered the whole nature of man. For "the corruptible body, indeed, weigheth down the soul."[2] Whence, too, the apostle, speaking of this corruptible body, of which he had shortly before said, "though our outward man perish,"[3] says, "We know that if our earthly house of this tabernacle were dissolved, we have a building of God, an house not made with hands, eternal in the heavens. For in this we groan, earnestly desiring to be clothed upon with our house which is from heaven: if so be that being clothed we shall not be found naked. For we that are in this tabernacle do groan, being burdened: not for that we would be unclothed, but clothed upon, that mortality might be swallowed up in life."[4] We are then burdened with this corruptible body; but knowing that the cause of this burdensomeness is not the nature and substance of the body, but its corruption, we do not desire to be deprived of the body, but to be clothed with its immortality. For then, also, there will be a body, but it shall no longer be a burden, being no longer corruptible. At present, then, "the corruptible body presseth down the soul, and the earthly tabernacle weigheth down the mind that museth upon many things," nevertheless they are in error who suppose that all the evils of the soul proceed from the body.

Virgil [in the *Aeneid*], indeed, seems to express the sentiments of Plato in the beautiful lines, where he says:

"A fiery strength inspires their lives,
An essence that from heaven derives,
Though clogged in part by limbs of clay,
And the dull 'vesture of decay'";

but though he goes on to mention the four most common mental emotions – desire, fear, joy, sorrow – with the intention of showing that the body is the origin of all sins and vices, saying:

"Hence wild desires and groveling fears,
And human laughter, human tears,
Immured in dungeon-seeming night,
They look abroad, yet see no light."

yet we believe quite otherwise. For the corruption of the body, which weighs down the soul, is not the cause but the punishment of the first sin; and it was not the corruptible flesh that made the soul sinful, but the sinful soul that made the flesh corruptible. And though from this corruption of the flesh there arise certain incitements to vice, and indeed vicious desires, yet we must not attribute to the flesh all the vices of a wicked life, in case we thereby clear the devil of all these, for he has no flesh. For though we cannot call the devil a fornicator or drunkard, or ascribe to him any sensual indulgence (though he is the secret instigator and prompter of those who sin in these ways), yet he is exceedingly proud and envious. And this viciousness has so possessed him, that on account of it he is reserved in chains of darkness to everlasting punishment. Now these vices, which have dominion over the devil, the apostle attributes to the flesh, which certainly the devil has not. For he says "hatred, variance, emulations, strife, envying" are the works of the flesh; and of all these evils pride is the origin and head, and it rules in the devil though he has no flesh. For who shows more hatred to the saints? who is more at variance with them? who more envious, bitter, and jealous? And since he exhibits all these works, though he has no flesh, how are they works of the flesh, unless because they are the works of man, who is, as I said, spoken of under the name of flesh? For it is not by having flesh, which the devil has not, but by living according to himself – that is, according to man – that man became like the devil. For the devil too, wished to live according to himself when he did not abide in the truth; so that when he lied, this was not of God, but of himself, who is not only a liar, but the father of lies, he being the first who lied, and the originator of lying as of sin . . .

No sin is committed save by that desire or will by which we desire that it be well with us, and shrink from it being ill with us. That, therefore, is a lie which we do in order that it may be well with us, but which makes us more miserable than we were. And why is this, but because the source of man's happiness lies only in God, whom he abandons when he sins, and not in himself, by living according to whom he sins? . . .

Notes

1   Ps. xix:12.
2   Wisd. ix:15.
3   2 Cor. iv:16.
4   2 Cor. v:1–4.

The Problem of Free Choice

The mind becomes the slave of passion only through its own will. It cannot be forced to a shameful act by anything above it, nor by anything equal, for this would be unjust, nor by anything below it, for this would be impossible. The movement, therefore, must be due to itself, by which it turns its will to enjoyment of the creature from enjoyment of the Creator. If this movement is called culpable – and to doubt this is . . . absurd – it is certainly not natural, but voluntary. In one respect it is like the movement by which a stone comes down to the ground again, because, as the one belongs to the stone, so the other belongs to the soul; but in another respect it is unlike, because the stone is not able to check the movement by which it comes down, whereas the soul does not move against its will to leave the higher and choose the lower. Hence the movement is natural to the stone, but voluntary to the soul.

Consequently if anyone says the stone sins because it falls down through its own weight, he is not perhaps more stupid than the stone but he is certainly considered mad. But we convict the soul of sin, when we prove that it abandons what is higher and prefers the enjoyment of what is lower.

So what need is there to ask the source of that movement by which the will turns from the unchangeable good to the changeable good? We agree that it belongs only to the soul, and is voluntary and therefore culpable; and the whole value of teaching in this matter consists in its power to make us censure and check this movement, and turn our wills away from temporal things below us to enjoyment of the everlasting good . . .

The will is the cause of sin; [if there were] a cause of the will . . . [w]hat could precede the will and be its cause? Either it is the will itself, and nothing else than the will is the root, or it is not the will which is not sinful. Either the will itself is the original cause of sin, or no sin is the original cause of sin. Sin cannot be attributed to anything except to the sinner. It cannot rightly be attributed to anything except to him who wills it: I do not know why you should wish to look for anything further.

Again, whatever is the cause of the will, is either just or unjust. If just, we shall not sin by submitting to it; if unjust, let us not submit to it, and we shall not sin. But perhaps it uses compulsion and forces a man against his will? Need we repeat ourselves over and over again? Remember all that we said before about sin and free will. If it is difficult to keep it all in mind, do remember this summary. Whatever is the cause of the will, if we can resist, we must not yield and we shall not sin. Perhaps it tricks us when off our guard? We must be careful not to be tricked. Or is the trickery such that we cannot possibly be on our guard against it? If so, there is no sin, for no one sins when he cannot guard against it. Yet sin is committed, and therefore we can guard against it.

8

ABU HAMID AL-GHAZALI

There Is No evil in Allah's Perfect World

Everything which God apportions to man, such as
sustenance, life-span, pleasure and pain, capacity
and incapacity, belief and disbelief, obedience
and sin, is all of it sheer justice, with no injustice
in it; and pure right, with no wrong in it.   (40)
Indeed, it is according to the necessarily right
order, in accord with what must be and as it must
be and in the measure in which it must be; and
there is not in possibility anything whatever more
excellent, more perfect, and more complete than it.   (45)
For if there were and He had withheld it, having
power to create it but not deigning to do so, this
would be miserliness contrary to the divine generosity
and injustice contrary to the divine justice.
But if He were not able, it would be incapability   (50)
contrary to divinity.
Indeed, all poverty and loss in this world is a
diminution in this world but an increase in the
next. Every lack in the next world in relation to
one individual is a boon in relation to someone   (55)
else. For were it not for night, the value of day
would be unknown. Were it not for illness, the
healthy would not enjoy health. Were it not for
hell, the blessed in paradise would not know the
extent of their blessedness. In the same way, the   (60)

Source: *There Is No Evil in Allah's Perfect World*, from Iḥyā.

lives of animals serve as ransom for human souls,
and the power to kill them which is given to humans
is no injustice.
Indeed, giving precedence to the perfect over
the imperfect is justice itself. So too is   (65)
heaping favors on the inhabitants of paradise
by increasing the punishment of the inhabitants
of hell. The ransom of the faithful by means of
the unfaithful is justice itself.
As long as the imperfect is not created, the   (70)
perfect will remain unknown. If beasts had not
been created, the dignity of man would not be
manifest. The perfect and the imperfect are
correlated. Divine generosity and wisdom require
the simultaneous creation of the perfect and   (75)
the imperfect.
Just as the amputation of a gangrenous hand in
order to preserve life is justice, since it involves
ransoming the perfect through the imperfect, so
too the matter of the discrepancy which exists   (80)
among people in their portion in this world and
the next. That is all justice, without any wrong;
and right in which there is no caprice.
Now this is a vast and deep sea with wide shores
and tossed by billows. In extent it is comparable   (85)
to the sea of God's unity. Whole groups of the
inept drown in it without realizing that it is an
arcane matter which only the knowing comprehend.
Behind this sea is the mystery of predestination
where the many wander in perplexity and which   (90)
those who have been illuminated are forbidden
to divulge.
The gist is that good and evil are foreordained.
What is foreordained comes necessarily to be after
a prior act of divine volition. No one can rebel   (95)
against God's judgement; no one can appeal His
decree and command. Rather, everything small and
large is written and comes to be in a known and
expected measure. "What strikes you was not there to
miss you; what misses you was not there to strike you."

9
PETER ABELARD
Sin moves inward

"Know Yourself"

We call "morals" the mind's vices or virtues that make us disposed to bad or good deeds.

Not only are there the mind's vices or goods, but also the body's. For example, weakness of the body or the strength we call vigor, sluggardness or nimbleness, lameness or walking erect, blindness or sight. That is why when we said "vices" we prefixed the words "the mind's," in order to exclude such bodily vices. Now these vices (that is, the mind's) are contrary to virtues. For example, injustice to justice, laziness to perseverance, immoderateness to moderation.

On mental vice relevant to morals

But there are also some vices or goods of the mind that are unconnected to morals and don't make a human life deserving of censure or praise. For example, mental obtuseness or a quick wit, being forgetful or having a good memory, ignorance or knowledge. Since all these things turn up among reprobates and good people alike, they are irrelevant to the make-up of morals and don't make a life shameful or respectable. Thus when we said "the mind's vices," we were right to add, in order to exclude such morally irrelevant vices, the words "that make us disposed to bad deeds" – that is, they incline the will to something that isn't properly to be done or renounced at all.

What difference is there between a sin and a vice inclining one to evil?

This kind of mental vice isn't the same as a sin. And a sin isn't the same as a bad action. For instance, being hot-tempered – that is, disposed or easily given to the turmoil that

Source: *Ethical Writings: His Ethics or "Know Yourself" and His Dialogue between a Philosopher, a Jew and a Christian*, trans. Paul Vincent Spade, Indianapolis, Ind.: Hackett Publishing Company Inc., 1995.

is anger – is a vice. It inclines the mind to doing something impulsively and irrationally that isn't fit to be done at all. Now this vice is in the soul in such a way that the soul is easily given to getting angry even when it isn't being moved to anger, just as the lameness whereby a person is called "lame" is in him even when he isn't limping around. For the vice is present even when the action is absent.

So also the body's very nature or structure makes many people prone to wantonness, just as it does to anger. But they don't sin by the fact that they are like this. Rather they get from it material for a fight, so that victorious over themselves through the virtue of moderation they might obtain a crown. Thus Solomon says, "The long-suffering man is better than the mighty man, and the one who rules his mind than the capturer of cities." For religion doesn't think it shameful to be defeated by a human being, but by a vice. The former surely happens to good people too, but in the latter we depart from goods.

In recommending this victory to us, the Apostle says, "No one will be crowned unless he struggles according to the Law." Struggles, I say, in resisting not people so much as vices, lest they drag us away to improper consent. They don't stop assaulting us, even if people do stop, so that the vices' attack against us is more dangerous the more it is repeated, and victory is more glorious the more difficult it is. But no matter how much people influence us, they force nothing shameful on our life unless, having so to speak been *turned* into vices for us, they subject us to shameful consent the way vices do. There is no risk to true liberty while others rule the body; we don't run into any abominable slavery as long as the mind is free. For it isn't shameful to serve a human being but to serve a vice, and it isn't bodily slavery that disfigures the soul but submission to vices. For whatever is common to good and bad people equally is irrelevant to virtue or vice.

What is mental vice, and what is properly called "sin"?

So it is vice that makes us disposed to sin – that is, we are inclined to consent to what is inappropriate, so that we do it or renounce it. This consent is what we properly call "sin," the fault of the soul whereby it merits damnation or is held guilty before God. For what is this consent but scorn for God and an affront against him? God cannot be offended by injury but he can by scorn. For he is the ultimate power, not diminished by any injury but wreaking vengeance on scorn for him.

Thus our sin is scorn for the creator, and to sin is to scorn the creator – not to do for his sake what we believe we ought to do for his sake, or not to renounce for his sake what we believe ought to be renounced. And so when we define sin negatively, saying it is *not* doing or *not* renouncing what is appropriate, we show clearly that there is no substance to a sin; it consists of non-being rather than of being. It is as if we define shadows by saying they are the absence of light where light did have being.

But perhaps you will say that *willing* a bad deed is also a sin; it renders us guilty before God, just as willing a good deed makes us just. As a result, in the same way as there is virtue in a good will so there is sin in a bad will, and there is sin not only in non-being but also in being, just as with virtue. For just as by willing to do what we believe pleases God we do please him, so by willing to do what we believe displeases God we do displease him, and appear to affront or scorn him.

But I say that if we look more closely, we have to view this matter quite otherwise than it appears. For sometimes we sin *without* any bad will. And when a bad will is curbed without being extinguished, it wins the palm-branch of victory for those resisting it, and provides the material for a fight and a crown of glory. It shouldn't itself be called a "sin" but a kind of illness that is now necessary.

Look, here is some innocent person. His cruel master is so enraged with fury at him that with bared blade he hunts him down to kill him. The innocent man flees him for a long time, and avoids his own murder as long as he can. Finally, under duress and against his will, he kills his master in order not to be killed by him.

Whoever you are, tell me what bad will he had in doing this deed! If he wanted to flee death, he also wanted to save his own life. But was this willing a bad one?

You will say: It isn't *this* will, I·think, that is bad, but the will he had for killing the master who was hunting him down.

I reply: You speak well and astutely, if you can point to a will in what you are saying. . . . [I]t was against his will and under duress that he did what kept his life intact as long as possible. Also, he knew danger would threaten his own life as a result of this slaying. How then did he *willingly* do what he did with this danger even to his own life?

If you reply that this too was done because of a willing, since obviously he was brought to this point by willing to escape death, not by willing to kill his master, we aren't contesting that. But as was already said, this willing isn't to be condemned as bad. As you say, through it he wanted to escape death, not to kill his master. Yet he did wrong in consenting (even though he was under duress from the fear of death) to an unjust slaying he should have borne rather than inflicted. He certainly took up the sword on his own; he didn't have it entrusted to him by some power.

Hence Truth says, "Everyone who takes up the sword will perish by the sword." "Who," he says, "takes up the sword" out of presumptuousness, not someone to whom it was entrusted for the sake of administering punishment. "Will perish by the sword" – that is, brings upon himself damnation and the slaying of his own soul by this foolhardiness. And so, as was said, he wanted to escape death, not to kill his master. But because he consented to a killing he shouldn't have consented to, his unjust consent that preceded the killing was a sin . . .

Surely a so called "willing" like this, one that consists of great mental sorrow, isn't to be called a "willing" but instead a "suffering." To say he "wants" one thing because of another is like saying he tolerates what he doesn't want because of something else he does desire. So too a sick person is said to "want" to be cauterized or to be operated on in order to be cured. And the martyrs "wanted" to suffer in order to reach Christ, or Christ himself "wanted" to suffer that we might be saved by his suffering. But we aren't thereby forced to grant without qualification that they wanted this. For there cannot be a "suffering" at all except where something happens against one's will; no one "suffers" when he accomplishes his will and when what happens delights him. Surely the Apostle who says, "I long to be dissolved and to be with Christ" – that is, to die in order to reach him – elsewhere comments, "We do not want to be disrobed but to be clothed over, so that what is mortal be absorbed by life."

Blessed Augustine also mentions this view, stated by the Lord where he says to Peter, "You will hold out your hands, and someone else will gird you and lead you where you do not want to go." In accordance with human nature's assumed infirmity, the Lord also says to the Father: "If it is possible, let this chalice pass from me. Yet not as I will, but as you do." Surely his soul was naturally terrified at the great suffering of his death, and what he knew would be a penalty couldn't be a matter of "willing" for him. Even though elsewhere it is written about him, "He was offered up because he himself willed it," either this has to be taken in accordance with the nature of divinity, the will of which included the assumed man's suffering, or else "willed it" is here used in the sense of "arranged it," in accordance with the Psalmist's statement, "He has done whatever he willed."

Hence it is plain that sin is sometimes committed without any bad will at all, so that it is clear from this that willing isn't said to be what sin is.

Of course, you will say, this holds where we sin under duress, but it doesn't hold where we sin willingly. For example, if we want to commit some deed we know shouldn't be committed by us. In that case, surely, the bad willing and the sin appear to be the same. For example, someone sees a woman and falls into lust. His mind is stirred by the pleasure of the flesh, with the result that he is set on fire for the shamefulness of sex. So, you say, what else is this willing and shameful desire but sin?

I reply: What if this willing is curbed by the virtue of moderation but not extinguished, stays for the fight, holds out for the struggle, and doesn't give up even when defeated? For where is the fight if the material for the fight is absent? Where does the great reward come from if there is nothing serious we put up with? When the struggle has passed, there is no fighting left but only the receiving of the reward. We struggle by fighting here in order that, triumphant in the struggle, we might receive a crown elsewhere. But to have a fight it's proper to have an enemy who resists, not one who gives up altogether. Now this enemy is our bad will, the one we triumph over when we subject it to the divine will. But we don't entirely extinguish it, so that we always have a will we might strive against.

For what great deed do we do for God's sake if we don't put up with anything opposed to our willing but instead accomplish what we will? Indeed who thanks us if, in what we say we are doing for his sake, we are accomplishing our own will?

Rather, you will say, what do we merit before God from what we do, either willingly or unwillingly?

I reply: Nothing, of course, since in giving out rewards he takes account of the mind rather than the action. The action doesn't add anything to the merit, whether it springs from good or bad willing . . .

But when we prefer his will to ours, so that we follow his rather than ours, we do obtain great merit before him, according to the perfection of Truth, "I did not come to do my will but his who sent me." In encouraging us to do this, he says "If anyone comes to me and does not hate his father and mother, indeed even his own soul, he is not worthy of me." That is, unless he refuses their suggestions or his own will and submits himself entirely to my commands. Therefore, if we are ordered to hate our father but not kill him, so too for our will; the order is that we not follow it, not that we destroy it entirely.

For he who says, "Do not pursue your lusts, and turn away from your will," commanded us not to *satisfy* our lusts, but not to do without them altogether. For satisfying them is wicked, but going without them is impossible in our feeble state. And so it isn't the lusting after a woman but the consenting to the lust that is the sin. It isn't the will to have sex with her that is damnable but the will's consent . . .

Adding on the performance of the deed doesn't add anything to increase the sin. Instead, for God, someone who tries as hard as he can to go through with it is just as guilty as one who does go through with it insofar as he is able. It is just as if he too had been apprehended in the very deed . . .

But although the willing isn't the sin and sometimes we even commit sins *against* our will, nevertheless some people say every sin is "voluntary." In so doing they find a kind of difference between the sin and the willing. For one thing is called the "will," and another thing is called "voluntary"; that is, the will is other than what is committed *by* the will. But if we call a sin what we have said above is properly called a sin — namely scorn for God, consenting to what we believe should be renounced for his sake — then how do we say the sin is "voluntary"? That is, how do we say we *want* to scorn God (which is what sinning is), or to grow worse or to be made deserving of damnation? For although we might want to do what we know ought to be punished, or that whereby we might be deserving of punishment, nevertheless we don't want to be punished. In this respect we are plainly being unfair, because we want to do what is unfair but don't want to yield to the fairness of a penalty that is just. The penalty, which is just, displeases; the action, which is unjust, pleases . . .

There are also people who entirely regret being drawn into consenting to lust or into an evil will, and are compelled by the flesh's weakness to want what they don't *want* to want at all.

Therefore, I really don't see how this consent that we don't want is going to be called "voluntary" so that . . . we call *every* sin "voluntary" — unless we understand the "voluntary" as merely excluding the necessary (since no sin is inevitable), or call the "voluntary" whatever arises from some will (for although he who killed his master under duress didn't have a will for killing, nevertheless he committed it from *some* will, since he wanted to escape or put off death).

Some people may be more than a little upset because they hear us say that doing the sin doesn't add anything to the guilt or to the damnation before God. For they object that in acting out a sin there follows a kind of pleasure that increases the sin, as in sex or in the eating we talked about.

It wouldn't be absurd of them to say this, if they proved that this kind of bodily pleasure is a sin and that no one can commit anything like that without sinning. If they actually accept that, then surely it is illicit for *anyone* to have this bodily pleasure. Hence not even married couples are exempt from sin when they are brought together by this bodily pleasure that is permitted to them, and neither is one who enjoys a delicious meal of his own fruit. All sick people too would be at fault who favor sweeter foods for refreshment, in order to recuperate from their illness. They surely don't take these foods *without* pleasure; otherwise if they took them they wouldn't help . . .

But again, they say sex in marriage and the eating of delicious food are only permitted in such a way that the pleasure itself is *not* permitted. Rather, they should be done entirely *without* pleasure. But surely if this is so, then they were permitted to be done in a way such that they cannot be done at all. And authorization that permitted their being done in a way that they certainly *cannot* be done is unreasonable . . .

No natural bodily pleasure is to be counted as a sin. It isn't to be regarded as a fault that we take pleasure in what is such that, when it has occurred, pleasure is necessarily felt. For example, if someone forces someone in religious orders, bound by chains, to lie among women, and he is led into pleasure – but *not* into consent – by the bed's softness and the touch of the women around him, who can venture to call this pleasure nature has made necessary a "sin"? . . .

Surely one who doesn't yet perceive by reason what he ought to do doesn't have any fault because of scorn the God. yet he isn't immune to the stain of his earlier parents' sin, from which he already incurs punishment even if not fault; he preserves in his punishment what they committed in their fault. Thus when David says he was conceived in iniquities or sins, he perceived that he was subject to the general pronouncement of damnation from the fault of his parents. And he referred these offenses not so much to his immediate parents as to earlier ones . . .

We have brought up these matters so that no one, perhaps wanting every pleasure of the flesh to be a sin, would say that sin itself is increased by the action when one extends the mind's consent to the point of performing the deed, so that one is defiled not only by consent to shamefulness but also by the stains of the act. As if what occurred outside in the body could defile the soul!

Therefore, any kind of carrying out of deeds is irrelevant to increasing a sin. Nothing taints the soul but what belongs to it, namely the consent that we've said is alone the sin, not the will preceding it or the subsequent doing of the deed. For even if we want or do what is improper, we don't *thereby* sin, since these things frequently occur without sin, just as, conversely, consent occurs without these things. We have already shown this in part: the point about the will without consent, in the example of the man who fell into lust for a woman he saw, or for someone else's fruit, yet wasn't enticed to consent, the point about bad consent without a bad will, in the example of the person who killed his master unwillingly.

Now as for things that ought not to be done, I don't think it escapes anyone how often they *are* done without sin, for example when they are committed through force or ignorance. For instance, if a women subjected to force has sex with someone else's husband, or if a man somehow deceived sleeps with a woman he thought was his wife, or if by mistake he kills someone he believed *should* be killed by him in his role as a judge. So it isn't a sin to lust after someone else's wife, or to have sex with her; the sin is rather to *consent* to this lust or to this action.

Indeed the Law calls this *consent* to lust "lust" when it says, "Thou shalt not lust." For it isn't the *lusting* that had to be prohibited (which we cannot avoid and wherein we do not sin), but rather the *assent* to it. The Lord's words too, "He who shall look at a woman in order to lust after her," have to be understood in this way: he who shall look at her in order to fall into *consent* to lust "has already committed adultery in his heart," even if he hasn't committed adultery in deed. That is, he already has the guilt for the sin, even if he is still lacking the performance of it.

If we look carefully, wherever deeds appear to be included under a command or prohibition, they are to be referred more to the will or the consent to the deeds than to the deeds themselves. Otherwise, nothing relevant to merit would come under the scope of a command. For things less in our power are less worth commanding. There are surely many things we are prevented from doing, but we always have will and consent within our power of choosing.

Why the doing of sin is punished more than the sin itself

There are people too who get more than a little upset when they hear us say the *doing* of a sin isn't properly said to be the sin, or doesn't add anything to enlarge the sin. Why, they ask, is a harder atonement exacted of penitents for performing the deed than for being guilty of the fault?

I give them this reply first: Why aren't you especially surprised at the fact that sometimes a great penalty is imposed as atonement where *no* fault occurred, and that sometimes we ought to punish those we know are innocent?

For look, some poverty-stricken woman has a little baby at the breast and doesn't have enough clothes to be able to meet the needs both of the little one in the crib and of herself. So, moved by pity for the little baby, she puts him by her side to warm him with her own rags. In the end, overwhelmed in her own feebleness by the force of nature, she is driven to smother the one she embraces with the greatest love.

Augustine says, "Have charity and do whatever you want." Yet when she comes to the bishop for atonement, a heavy penalty is exacted from her, not for a fault she committed but to make her or other women more careful about anticipating such dangers.

Sometimes too it happens that someone is accused by his enemies before a judge. They attribute to him something such that the judge thereby knows he is innocent. Yet because they pursue the matter and demand a hearing in court, they begin the proceedings on the assigned day. They bring forward witnesses, although false ones, to convict the one they are accusing. Yet since the judge cannot in any way refute the witnesses by clear reasons, he is forced by the law to accept them. Admitting their proof, he punishes the innocent. Therefore, he should punish one who shouldn't be punished. He should do it anyway, because it is in accordance with the law that the judge does justly here what the person didn't deserve.

So it is clear from these cases that sometimes a penalty is reasonably exacted from one in whom no fault has occurred. What then is there to wonder at, if where a fault *has* occurred, the ensuing deed increases the penalty before human beings in *this* life, but not before God in the future one? For human beings don't judge about what is hidden but about what is plain. They don't think so much of the guilt belonging to the fault as of the performance of the deed. Rather God alone, who pays attention not so much to the deeds that are done as to the mind with which they are done, is truly thinking about the guilt in our intention and tries the fault in a true court.

Thus he is called the tester of the heart and reins, and is said to see in darkness. For where no one sees, there he sees most of all, because in punishing sin he doesn't pay attention to the deed but to the mind, just as conversely we don't pay attention to the mind that we don't see but to the deed we know. Thus often we punish the innocent or free culprits, either by mistake or through being forced by the law, as we said. God is called the tester and knower of the heart and [flesh] — that is, of any intentions coming from an emotion of the soul or from bodily weakness or pleasure . . .

Why God is called the examiner of the heart and [flesh]

Therefore, God has been called the "tester o the heart and [flesh]" — that is, the examiner of the intentions of consents stemming from there — with respect to the two things we've just mentioned: lust of the flesh and lust of the soul. But we, who aren't in a position to discriminate or decide this, turn our judgment mostly to the deeds . . .

So when the Lord distinguished deeds according to whether their intention is right or not right, he was careful to call the mind's eye (that is, its intention) "simple" and so to speak pure of dirt so it can see clearly, or conversely "cloudy." He said, "If your eye is simple, your whole body will be shining." That is, if the intention is right, the whole mass of deeds arising from it – which, like corporeal things, can be seen – will be worthy of light, that is, will be good. So too the other way around.

Thus an intention isn't to be called good because it *appears* good, but more than that, because it *is* such as it is considered to be – that is, when if one believes that what he is aiming at is pleasing to God, he is in addition not deceived in his evaluation. Otherwise the infidels themselves would also have good deeds, just as we do, since they too believe no less than we do that through their deeds they are saved or are pleasing to God . . .

How many ways is something called a "sin"?

But to reply more fully to objections, one needs to know that the name "sin" is taken in different ways. Properly, sin is said to be scorn for God or consent to evil. Children and those who are naturally fools are exempt from this. Since they lack reason so to speak, they don't have any merits, nothing is charged against them as a sin, and they are saved only through the sacraments.

10

MOSES MAIMONIDES

Divine rationality and moral character

Imagining evil

Often it occurs to the imagination of the multitude that there are more evils in the world than there are good things. As a consequence, this thought is contained in many sermons and poems of all the religious communities, which say that it is surprising if good exists in the temporal, whereas the evils of the temporal are numerous and constant. This error is not found only among the multitude, but also among those who deem that they know something.

[Some have said] that there is more evil than good in what exists; if you compare man's well-being and his pleasures in the time span of his well-being with the pains, the heavy sufferings, the infirmities, the paralytic afflictions, the wretchedness, the sorrows, and the calamities that befall him, you find that his existence – that is the existence of man – is a punishment and a great evil inflicted upon him. He began to establish this opinion by inductively examining these misfortunes, so as to oppose all that is thought by the adherents of the truth regarding the beneficence and manifest munificence of the deity and regarding His being, may He be exalted, the absolute good and regarding all that proceeds from Him being indubitably an absolute good. The reason for this whole mistake lies in the fact that this ignoramus and those like him among the multitude consider that which exists only with reference to a human individual. Every ignoramus imagines that all that exists exists with a view to his individual sake; it is as if there were nothing that exists except him. And if something happens to him that is contrary to what he wishes, he makes the trenchant judgment that all that exists is an evil. However, if man considered and represented to himself that which exists and knew the smallness of his part in it, the truth would become clear and manifest to him. For this

Source: *The Guide to the Perplexed*, trans. Shlomo Pines, Chicago, Ill.: University of Chicago Press, 1963; "Laws Concerning Character Traits" (source: *The Ethical Writings of Maimonides*, eds R. L. Weis and C. E. Butterworth, New York: Dover, 1975).

extensive raving entertained by men with regard to the multitude of evils in the world is not said by them to hold good with regard to the angels or with regard to the spheres and the stars or with regard to the elements and the minerals and the plants composed of them or with regard to the various species of animals, but their whole thought only goes out to some individuals belonging to the human species. If someone has eaten bad food and consequently was stricken with leprosy, they are astonished how this great ill has befallen him and how this great evil exists. They are also astonished when one who frequently copulates is stricken blind, and they think it a marvelous thing the calamity of blindness that has befallen such a man and other such calamities.

Now the true way of considering this is that all the existent individuals of the human species and, all the more, those of the other species of the animals are things of no value at all in comparison with the whole that exists and endures: *Man is like unto vanity, and so on.*[1] *Man, that is a worm; and the son of man, that is a maggot.*[2] *How much less in them that dwell in houses of clay, and so on.*[3] *Behold, the nations are as a drop of a bucket, and so on.*[4] . . . [M]an [should know his] true value, so that he should not make the mistake of thinking that what exists is in existence only for the sake of him as an individual. According to us, on the other hand, what exists is in existence because of the will of its Creator; and among the things that are in existence, the species of man is the least in comparison to the superior existents – I refer to the spheres and the stars. As far as comparison with the angels is concerned, there is in true reality no relation between man and them. Man is merely the most noble among the things that are subject to genera-tion, namely, in this our nether world; I mean to say that he is the noblest thing that is composed of the elements. Withal his existence is for him a great good and a benefit on the part of God because of the properties with which He has singled him out and perfected him. The greater part of the evils that befall its individuals are due to the latter, I mean the deficient individuals of the human species. It is because of our own deficiencies that we lament and we call for aid. We suffer because of evils that we have produced ourselves of our free will; but we attribute them to God, may He be exalted above this; just as He explains in His book, saying: *Is corruption His? No; His children's is the blemish, and so on.*[5] *Solomon* too has explained this, saying: *The foolishness of man perverteth his way; and his heart fretteth against the Lord.*[6] The explanation of this lies in the fact that all the evils that befall man fall under one of three species.

The first species of evil is that which befalls man because of the nature of coming-to-be and passing-away, I mean to say because of his being endowed with matter. Because of this, infirmities and paralytic afflictions befall some individuals either in consequence of their original natural disposition, or they supervene because of changes occurring in the elements, such as corruption of the air or a fire from heaven and a landslide. We have already explained that divine wisdom has made it obligatory that there should be no coming-to-be except through passing-away. Were it not for the passing-away of the individuals, the coming-to-be relating to the species would not continue. Thus that pure beneficence, that munificence, that activity causing good to overflow, are made clear. He who wishes to be endowed with flesh and bones and at the same time not be subject to impressions and not to be attained by any of the concomitants of matter merely wishes, without being aware of it, to combine two contraries, namely, to be subject to impressions and not to be subject to them. For if he were not liable to receive impressions, he would not have been generated, and what exists of him would have been one single individual and not a multitude of individuals belonging to one species. . . . Everything that is capable of being generated from any matter whatever, is generated in the most perfect way in which it is possible to be generated out of that specific matter; the deficiency attaining the individuals of the species corresponds to the deficiency of the particular matter of the individual. Now the ultimate term and the most perfect thing that may be generated out of blood and sperm is the human species with its well-known nature consisting in man's being a living, rational, and mortal being. Thus this species of evils must necessarily exist. Withal you will find that the evils of this kind that befall men are very few and occur only seldom. For you will find cities, existing for thousands of years, that have never been flooded or burned. Also thousands of people are born in perfect health whereas the birth of an infirm human being is an anomaly, or at least – if someone objects to the word anomaly and does not use it – such an individual is very rare; for they do not form a hundredth or even a thousandth part of those born in good health.

The evils of the second kind are those that men inflict upon one another, such as tyrannical domination of some of them over others. These evils are more numerous than those belonging to the first kind, and the reasons for that are numerous and well known. The evils in question also come from us. However, the wronged man has no device against them. At the same time, there is no city existing anywhere in the whole world in which evil of this kind is in any way widespread and predominant among the inhabitants of that city; but its existence is also rare – in the cases, for instance, when one individual surprises another individual and kills him or robs him by night. This kind of evil becomes common, reaching many people, only in the course of great wars; and such events too do not form the majority of occurrences upon the earth taken as a whole.

The evils of the third kind are those that are inflicted upon any individual among us by his own action; this is what happens in the majority of cases, and these evils are much more numerous than those of the second kind. All men lament over evils of this kind; and it is only seldom that you find one who is not guilty of having brought them upon himself. He who is reached by them deserves truly to be blamed. To him one may say what has been said: *This hath been to you of your own doing.* It has also been said: *He doeth it that would destroy his own soul*[7]. *Solomon* has said about evils of this kind: *The foolishness of man perverteth his way, and so on.*[8] He also has explained with reference to evils of this kind that they are done by man to himself; his dictum being: *Behold, this only have I found, that God made man upright; but they have sought out many thoughts;*[9] these thoughts are those that have been vanquished by these evils. About this kind it has also been said: *For affliction cometh not forth from the dust, neither doth trouble spring out of the ground.*[10] Immediately afterwards it is explained that this sort of evil is brought into existence by man, for it is said: *For man is born unto trouble, and so on.*[11] This kind is consequent upon all vices, I mean concupiscence for eating, drinking, and copulation, and doing these things with excess in regard to quantity or irregularly or when the quality of the food-stuffs is bad. For this is the cause of all corporeal and psychical diseases and ailments. With regard to the diseases of the body, this is manifest. With regard to the diseases of the soul due to this evil regimen, they arise in two ways: In the first place, through the alteration necessarily affecting the soul in consequence of the alteration of the body, the soul being a corporeal faculty – it having already been said that the moral qualities of the soul are consequent upon the temperament of the body. And in the second place, because of the fact that the soul becomes familiarized with, and accustomed to, unnec-essary things and consequently acquires the habit of desiring things that are unnecessary either for the preservation of the individual or for the preservation of the species; and this desire is something infinite. For whereas all necessary things are restricted and limited, that which is superfluous is unlimited. If, for instance, your desire is directed to having silver plate, it would be better if it were of gold; some have crystal plate; and perhaps plate is procured that is made out of emeralds and rubies, whenever these stones are to be found. Thus every ignoramus who thinks worthless thoughts is always sad and despon-dent because he is not able to achieve the luxury attained by someone else. In most cases such a man exposes himself to great dangers, such as arise in sea voyages and the services of kings; his aim therein being to obtain these unnecessary luxuries. When, however, he is stricken by misfortunes in these courses he has pursued, he complains about God's decree and predestination and begins to put the blame on the temporal and to be aston-ished at the latter's injustice in not helping him to obtain great wealth, which would permit him to procure a great deal of wine so as always to be drunk and a number of concubines adorned with gold and precious stones of various kinds so as to move him to copulate more than he is able so as to experience pleasure – as if the end of existence consisted merely in the pleasure of such an ignoble man. The error of the multitude has arrived at the point where they impute to the Creator deficiency of power because of His having produced that which exists and endowed it with a nature entailing, according to their imagination, these great evils; inasmuch as this nature does not help every vicious man to achieve the satisfaction of his vice so that his corrupt soul should reach the term of its demand, which, according to what we have explained, has no limit. On the other hand, men of excellence and knowledge have grasped and understood the wisdom mani-fested in that which exists, as *David* has set forth, saying: *All the paths of the Lord are mercy and truth unto such as keep His covenant and His testimonies.*[12] By this he says that those who keep to the nature of that which exists, keep the commandments of the Law, and know the ends of both, apprehend clearly the excellency and the true reality of the whole. For this reason they take as their end that for which they were intended as men, namely, apprehension. And because of the necessity of the body, they seek what is necessary for it, *bread to eat, and raiment to put on,*[13] without any luxury. If one restricts oneself to what is necessary, this is the easiest of things and may be obtained with a very small effort . . .

All natural, psychic, and animal faculties and all the parts that are found in one particular individual are also found, as far as essence is concerned, in another – even though there be accidentally a deficiency because of something that has supervened and that is not according to nature. But this is rare, as we have made clear. There in no way exists a relation of superiority and inferiority between individuals conforming to the course of nature except that which follows necessarily from the differences in the disposition of the various kinds of matter; this being necessary on account of the nature of the matter of the particular species and not specially intended for one individual rather than another.

Laws concerning character traits

They include altogether eleven commandments, five positive commandments and six negative commandments. These are: 1) to imitate His ways, 2) to cleave to those who know Him, 3) to love neighbors, 4) to love the converts, 5) not to hate brothers, 6) to rebuke, 7) not to put [anyone] to shame, 8) not to afflict the distressed, 9) not to go about as a talebearer, 10) not to take revenge, 11) not to bear a grudge. The explanation of all these commandments [follows].

Every single human being has many character traits. [As for character traits in general,] one differs from another and they are exceedingly far apart from each other. One man is irascible, perpetually angry, and another man has a tranquil mind and does not become angry at all; if he does become angry, his anger is mild and only rarely aroused during a period of several years. One man has an exceedingly haughty heart, and another has an extremely lowly spirit. One is so full of desire that his soul is never satisfied by pursuing its desire; another has a body so exceedingly pure that he does not even desire the few things the body needs. One has a desire so great that his soul would not be satisfied with all the wealth in the world. As it is said: "He that loves silver shall not be satisfied with silver." Another is so constrained that he would be satisfied with some small thing not adequate for him, and he does not press to acquire whatever he needs.

One torments himself with hunger and is so tightfisted that he does not eat the worth of a small coin except when in great pain; another intentionally squanders all his wealth. All the rest of the character traits follow these patterns, which are [also] exemplified by the gay and the mournful, the miserly and the prodigal, the cruel and the merciful, the soft-hearted and the hard-hearted, and so on.

Between two character traits at opposite extremes, there is a character trait in the middle, equidistant from the extremes. Some character traits a man has from the beginning of his creation, depending upon the nature of his body; some character traits a certain man's nature is disposed to receive in the future more quickly than other character traits; and some a man does not have from the beginning of his creation but learns from others, or he himself turns to them due to a thought that arose in his heart, or he hears that a certain character trait is good for him and that it is proper to acquire it and he trains himself in it until it is firmly established within him.

For any character trait, the two opposite extremes are not the good way, and it is not proper for a man to follow them nor to teach them to himself. If he finds his nature inclined toward one extreme or if he is disposed to receive one of them or if he has already learned one of them and has become accustomed to it, he shall make himself return to the good way and follow the way of good men, which is the right way.

The right way is the mean in every single one of a man's character traits. It is the character trait that is equally distant from the two extremes, not close to one or the other. Therefore the wise men of old commanded that a man continuously appraise his character traits and evaluate them and direct them in the middle way so that he becomes perfect.

How so? A man shall not be irascible and easily angered, nor like a corpse which feels nothing, but in between; he shall only become angry about a large matter that deserves anger so that something like it not be done again.

So too, he shall only desire the things which the body needs and without which it is impossible to live. As it is said: *A just man eats to satisfy his desire.* Likewise, he shall only labor at his work to acquire what he needs for the present. As it is said: *Good is a little for the just man.* He shall not be exceedingly tightfisted, nor squander all his wealth, but he shall give charity according to his means and lend a fitting amount to the needy. He shall not be gay and buffoonish nor sad and mournful, but rejoice all his days, calmly, with a cheerful demeanor. And thus shall he order the rest of his character traits. This way is the way of the wise men.

Every man whose character traits all lie in the mean is called a wise man. Whoever is exceedingly scrupulous with himself and moves a little toward one side or the other, away from the character trait in the mean, is called a pious man.

How so? Whoever moves away from a haughty heart to the opposite extreme so that he exceedingly lowly in spirit is called a pious man; this is the measure of piety. If he moves only to the mean and is humble, he is called a wise man; this is the measure of wisdom. The same applies to all the rest of the character traits. The pious men of old used to direct their character traits from the middle way toward [one of] the two extremes; some character traits toward the last extreme, and some toward the first extreme. This is the meaning of "inside the line of the law."

We are commanded to walk in these middle ways, which are the good and right ways. As it is said: *And you shall walk in His ways.* Thus they taught in explaining this commandment: Just as He is called gracious, you too be gracious; just as He is called merciful, you too be merciful; just as He is called holy, you too be holy.

In like manner, the prophets applied all these terms to God: slow to anger and abundant in loving-kindness, just and righteous, perfect, powerful, strong, and the like. They did so to proclaim that these ways are good and right, and a man is obliged to train himself to follow them and to imitate according to his strength.

How so? A man shall habituate himself in these character traits until they are firmly established in him. Time after time, he shall perform actions in accordance with the character traits that are in the mean. He shall repeat them continually until performing them is easy for him and they are not burdensome and these character traits are firmly established in his soul.

Since these terms applied to the Creator refer to the middle way that we are obliged to follow, this way is called the way of the Lord. That is what Abraham taught to his sons. As it is said: *For I have known him so that he will command his sons and his household after him to keep the way of the Lord, to do justice and righteousness.* Whoever walks in this way brings good and blessing upon himself. As it is said: "In order that the Lord render unto Abraham that which He said concerning him."

Those whose bodies are sick taste the bitter as sweet and the sweet as bitter. Some of the sick desire and long for foods that are not fit to eat, such as soil and charcoal, and they hate good foods, such as bread and meat. It all depends upon the extent of the illness. Likewise, people with sick souls crave and love the bad character traits and hate the good way. They are careless about following it, and it is very difficult for them, depending upon the extent of their illness. Thus says Isaiah about these men: *Woe unto them who call evil good, and good evil; who turn darkness into light, and light into darkness; who turn the bitter into the sweet, and the sweet into the bitter.* Of them it is said: *They forsake the paths of righteousness to walk in the ways of darkness.*

What is the remedy for those whose souls are sick? Let them go to the wise men — who are physicians of the soul — and they will cure their disease by means of the character traits that they shall teach them, until they make them return to the middle way. Solomon said about those who recognize their bad character traits and do not go to the wise men to be cured: Fools despise admonition.

How are they to be cured? Whoever is irascible is told to train himself so that if he is beaten and cursed, he will not feel anything. He shall follow this way for a long time until the rage is uprooted from his heart. If his heart is haughty, he shall train himself to endure much degradation. He shall sit lower than anyone else and wear worn-out, shabby garments, which make the wearer despised, and do similar things, until his haughty heart is uprooted. Then he shall return to the middle way, which is the good way, and when he returns to the middle way he shall follow it all his days.

He shall do the same with all the other character traits. If he is at one extreme, he shall move to the other extreme and accustom himself to it for a long time until he returns to the good way, which is the mean in every single character trait.

In the case of some character traits, a man is forbidden to accustom himself to the mean. Rather, he shall move to the other [i.e., far] extreme. One such [character trait] is a haughty heart, for the good way is not that a man be merely humble, but that he have a lowly spirit, that his spirit be very submissive. Therefore it was said of Moses our master that he was "very humble," and not merely humble. And therefore the wise men commanded: *Have a very, very lowly spirit.* Moreover they said that everyone who makes his heart haughty denies the existence of God. As it is said: *And your heart shall swell, and you shall forget the Lord your God.* In addition they said: *Whoever has an arrogant spirit – even a little – deserves excommunication.* Likewise, anger is an extremely bad character trait, and it is proper for a man to move away from it to the other extreme and to teach himself not to become angry, even over something it is proper to be angry about. Now, he might wish to arouse fear in his children and the members of his household or in the community (if he is a leader) and to become angry at them in order that they return to what is good. Then he shall pretend to be angry in their presence in order to admonish them, but his mind shall be tranquil within himself, like a man who feigns anger but is not angry. The wise men of old said: *Anyone who is angry – it is as if he worships idols.* They said about anyone who is angry: If he is a wise man, his wisdom departs from him, and if he is a prophet, his prophecy departs from him. And [they said] the life of irascible men is no life. Therefore they commanded a man to refrain from becoming angry, until he trains himself not to feel anything even in response to things that provoke anger; this is the good way. The way of the just men is to be insulted but not to insult; they hear themselves reviled and do not reply; they act out of love and rejoice in afflictions. Scripture says about them: *And those who love Him are like the sun rising in its power.*

There shall always be much silence in a man's conduct. He shall speak only about a matter concerned with wisdom or matters that are necessary to keep his body alive. They said about Rav, a student of our holy master, that during his entire life he did not engage in idle conversation. The latter is characteristic of most men. A man shall not use many words, even in connection with the needs of the body. Concerning this, the wise men commanded, saying: *Anyone who multiplies words brings about sin.* They also said: *I have found nothing better for the body than silence.* Likewise, concerning words of Torah and words of wisdom, the words of the wise man shall be few, but full of content. This is what the wise men commanded, saying: *A man shall always teach his students by the shortest path.* But if the words are many and the content slight, that is indeed foolishness. Concerning this it is said: *For a dream comes with much content, but a fool's voice with many words.*

Silence is a fence around wisdom. Therefore he shall not hasten to reply, nor speak much; he shall teach his students quietly and calmly, without shouting or prolixity. That is in keeping with the saying of Solomon: *Words of wise men, spoken calmly, are listened to.*

A man is forbidden to make a habit of using smooth and deceptive language. There shall not be one thing in his mouth and another in his heart, but what is within shall be like what is without. The matter in his heart shall be the same as what is in his mouth. It is forbidden to delude one's fellow creatures, even a Gentile.

How so? He shall not sell to a Gentile meat not ritually slaughtered as though it were ritually slaughtered, nor a shoe made from an animal that died by itself in place of one ritually slaughtered. He shall not urge his friend to eat with him when he knows he will not eat, nor press refreshment upon him when he knows it will not be accepted, nor open casks of wine (which he needs to open to sell anyway) to deceive him into thinking they were opened to honor him. Likewise with everything like that — even one word of deception and fraud is forbidden. Rather, he shall have lips of truth, a steadfast spirit, and a heart pure of all mischief and intrigue.

A man shall not be full of laughter and mockery, nor sad and mournful, but joyful. Thus the wise men said: *Laughter and levity bring about illicit sexual conduct.* They commanded that a man not be unrestrained in laughter, nor sad and mournful, but that he receive every man with a cheerful demeanor. Likewise his desire shall not be so great that he rushes for wealth, nor shall he be lazy and refrain from working. But he shall live in contentment, have a modest occupation, and be occupied [mainly] with the Torah. No matter how small his portion, let him rejoice in it. He shall not be full of contention, envy, or desire, nor shall he seek honor. Thus the wise men said: *Envy, desire, and honor remove a man from the world.* The general rule is that he follow the mean for every single character trait, until all his character traits are ordered according to the mean. That is in keeping with what Solomon says: *And all your ways will be upright.*

Perhaps a man will say: *Since desire, honor, and the like constitute a bad way and remove a man from the world, I shall completely separate myself from them and go to the other extreme.* So he does not eat meat, nor drink wine, nor take a wife, nor live in a decent dwelling, nor wear decent clothing, but sackcloth, coarse wool, and so on, like the priests of Edom. This, too, is a bad way and it is forbidden to follow it . . .

Therefore the wise men commanded that a man only abstain from things forbidden by the Torah alone. He shall not prohibit for himself, by vows and oaths, things that are permitted. Thus the wise men said: *Is what the Torah has prohibited not enough for you, that you prohibit other things for yourself?*

Those who fast continuously are in this class; they do not follow the good way. The wise men prohibited a man from tormenting himself by fasting. Concerning all these things and others like them, Solomon commanded, saying: *Do not be overly righteous and do not be excessively wise; why should you destroy yourself?*

Man needs to direct every single one of his deeds solely toward attaining knowledge of the Name, blessed be He. His sitting down, his standing up, and his speech, everything shall be directed toward this goal. How so? When he conducts business or works to receive a wage, his heart shall not only be set upon taking in money, but he shall do these things in order to acquire what the body needs, such as food, drink, shelter, and a wife.

Likewise when he eats, drinks, and has sexual intercourse, his purpose shall not be to do these things only for pleasure, eating and drinking only what is sweet to the palate and having sexual intercourse only for pleasure. Rather, his only purpose in eating and drinking shall be to keep his body and limbs healthy. Therefore he shall not eat everything that the palate desires, like a dog or an ass, but he shall eat things that are useful for him, whether bitter or sweet, and he shall not eat things bad for the body, even if they are sweet to the palate.

How so? Whoever has warm flesh shall not eat meat or honey, nor drink wine. As Solomon, for example, said: *It is not good to eat much honey, etc.* He shall drink chicory water, even though it is bitter. Since it is impossible for a man to live except by eating and drinking, he shall eat and drink only in accordance with the directive of medicine, in order that he become healthy and remain perfect. Likewise when he has sexual intercourse, he shall do so only to keep his body healthy and to have offspring Therefore he shall not have sexual intercourse every time he has the desire, but whenever he knows that he needs to discharge sperm in accordance with the directive of medicine, or to have offspring.

If one conducts himself in accordance with the [art of] medicine and sets his heart only upon making his body and limbs perfect and strong, and upon having sons who will do his work and labor for his needs, this is not a good way. Rather, he shall set his heart upon making his body perfect and strong so that his soul will be upright to know the Lord. For it is impossible for him to understand and reflect upon wisdom when he is sick or when one of his limbs is in pain. He shall set his heart upon having a son who perhaps will be a wise and great man in Israel. Whoever follows this way all his days serves the Lord continuously, even when he engages in business and even when he has sexual intercourse, because his thought in everything is to fulfill his needs so that his body will be perfect to serve the Lord.

Even when he sleeps, if he sleeps with the intention of resting his mind and his body so that he does not become sick — for he is unable to serve the Lord when he is sick — his sleep shall become a service of the Lord, blessed be He. Concerning this subject, the wise men commanded, saying: *Let all your deeds be for the sake of Heaven.* That is what Solomon said in his wisdom: *In all your ways know Him, and He will make your paths straight.*

Man is created in such a way that his character traits and actions are influenced by his neighbours and friends, and he follows the custom of the people in his country. Therefore a man needs to associate with the just and be with the wise continually in order to learn [from] their actions, and to keep away from the wicked, who walk in darkness, so that he avoids learning from their actions. That is what Solomon said: *He who walks with wise men will become wise, but he who associates with fools will become evil.* And it says: *Blessed is the man who does not walk in the counsel of the wicked, etc.* Likewise, if he is in a country with evil customs where men do not follow the right way, he shall go to a place where men are just and they follow the way of good men. If all the countries he knows or hears about follow a way that is not good, as in our time, or if because of military campaigns or illness, he is unable to go to a city with good customs, he shall dwell alone in solitude. As it is said: *Let him dwell alone and be silent.* If there are evil men and sinners who do not let him live in the country unless he mingles with them and follows their evil customs, he shall go off to the caves, the briers, or the desert, and not accustom himself to the way of sinners. As it is said: *O that I were in the desert, in a lodging place of wayfaring men.*

It is a positive commandment to cleave to the wise men in order to learn from their actions. As it is said: And to Him shall you cleave. It is possible for a man to cleave to the *Shekhinah* [Presence]? But thus said the wise men in explaining this commandment: cleave to the wise men and their disciples . . .

It is a commandment for every man to love every single individual of Israel like his own body. As it is said: *And you shall love your neighbor and yourself.* Therefore he needs to speak in praise of him and to have concern for his possessions, just as he has concern for his own possessions and wants to be honored himself. Whoever glorifies himself through the humiliation of his fellow man has no portion in the world-to-come.

There are two positive commandments to love the convert who comes under the wings of the *Shekhinah*; one, because he is in the class of neighbors, and the other, because he is a convert and the Torah said: *And you shall love the stranger.* He [God] commanded the love of the convert, just as He commanded the love of His Name. As it is said: *And you shall love the Lord your God.* The Holy One Himself, blessed be He, loves the converts. As it is said: *And He loves the stranger.*

Anyone who hates one Israelite in his heart transgresses a prohibition. As it is said: *You shall not hate your brother in your heart.* They do not give lashes in connection with this prohibition, since it does not refer to an action. The Torah warned [here] only about hatred in the heart, but whoever strikes his fellow man and reviles him, even though it is not permitted, does not transgress what is prohibited by the verse, "You shall not hate . . ."

When a man sins against another man, he [the latter] shall not hate him and remain silent. As it is said about the wicked: *And Absalom spoke to Amnon neither good nor evil, although Absalom hated Amnon.* Rather, he is commanded to speak to him, and to say to him: *Why did you do such-and-such to me? Why did you sin against me in such-and-such a matter?* As it is said: *You shall surely rebuke your neighbor.* If he repents and requests forgiveness from him, he needs to forgive and shall not be cruel. As it is said: *And Abraham prayed to God, etc.*

If someone sees his fellow man who has sinned or who follows a way that is not good, it is a commandment to make him return to the good and to make known to him that he sins against himself by his evil actions. As it is said: *You shall surely rebuke your neighbor.*

Whoever rebukes his fellow man, whether concerning matters between the two of them or between him [the fellow man] and God, needs to rebuke him in private. He shall speak to him calmly and gently, and make known to him that he talks to him only for his own good, to bring him to the life of the world-to-come. If he accepts it from him, good; if not, he shall rebuke him a second and a third time. Thus he is always obliged to rebuke him until the sinner strikes him and says to him, *I will not listen.* If he does not prevent everything he can possibly prevent, he is ensnared in the sin of all those he could have prevented from sinning.

Whoever rebukes his fellow man shall not at first speak harshly so as to put him to shame. As it is said: *You shall not bear sin on his account.* Thus said the wise men: *Are we to assume he should rebuke him until his face changes* [its expression or color]? *The text therefore says: "You shall not bear sin on his account."* From this we learn it is forbidden to humiliate an Israelite; all the more [is it forbidden] in public.

Even though the one who humiliates his fellow man is not given lashes, it is a great sin. Thus said the wise men: *Whoever puts his fellow man to shame in public has no portion in the world-to-come.*

Therefore a man needs to be careful that he not shame his fellow man — be he young or old — in public, nor call him by a name he is ashamed of, nor speak about something in front of him that would make him ashamed.

To what matters does the above refer? To matters between a man and his fellow man, but in matters of Heaven if he does not repent in private, he is to be humiliated in public, his sin is proclaimed, and he is reviled to his face and degraded and cursed until he returns to the good. That is what all the prophets did with Israel.

If someone is sinned against by his fellow man and does not wish to rebuke him or to say anything to him — because the sinner is exceedingly simple or his mind is distraught — and if he forgives him in his heart and bears no animosity toward him and does not rebuke him, this is indeed the measure of piety. The Torah was particularly concerned only about animosity . . .

Notes

1 Ps. 144:4.
2 Job 25:6.
3 Job 4:19.
4 Isa. 40:15.
5 Deut. 32:5.
6 Prov. 19:3.
7 Prov. 6:32.

 8 Prov. 19:3.
 9 Eccles. 7:29.
10 Job 5:6.
11 Job 5:7.
12 Ps. 25:10.
13 Gen. 28:20.

11

POPE
INNOCENT III

On the Misery of the Human Condition

Of the vile matter from which man is made

"God made the planets and stars from fire, the breeze and winds from air, the fishes and birds from water; but He made men and beasts from earth. Thus a man, looking upon sea life, will find himself low; looking upon creatures of the air he will know he is lower; and looking upon the creatures of fire he will see he is lowest of all. Nor can he equal heavenly things, nor dare put himself above the earthly; for he finds himself on a level with the beasts and knows he is like them.

"Therefore the death of man and the beast is the same, and the condition of them both is equal, and man has nothing more than the beast. Of earth they were made, and into earth they return together."[1] These are not just the words of any man, but of wisest Solomon. What then is a man but slime and ashes? Man addresses God: "Remember, I beseech thee, that thou hast made me as the clay, and thou wilt bring me into dust again."[2] And God addresses man: "Dust thou art, and unto dust thou shalt return."[3] "I am compared to mud and am likened to embers and ashes."[4] Now, mud is made of water and dirt, both remaining what they are; but ashes are made of fire and wood, both being consumed. In this a mystery is revealed, but it will be expounded elsewhere. Therefore, mud, why art thou proud? dust, what hast thou to boast about? ashes, why art thou so insolent?

But perhaps you will reply that although Adam himself was formed of the earth's slime *you* were conceived of human seed. On the contrary, Adam was formed of earth, but of virgin earth; you were made of seed, and that unclean. "For who can make clean what was conceived from unclean seed?"[5] "What is man that he should be without spot, and he that is born of a woman that he should appear just?"[6] "Behold, I was conceived in iniquities and in sins did my mother conceive me."[7] Not in one sin alone, not in one

Source: *On the Misery of the Human Condition*, translated by Margaret Mary Dietz, Indianapolis, Ind.: Hackett Publishing Company Inc., 1969.

transgression alone, but in many sins and many transgressions: in her own sins and transgressions, and the sins and transgressions of others. . . .

Of the misery of the good and the evil

It is not for the wicked to rejoice, says the Lord, "For by what things a man sins, by the same also he is tormented."[8] For the worm of conscience never dies, and reason's light is never put out. "I have seen those who work iniquity and sow sorrows and reap them perishing by the blast of God and consumed by the spirit of His wrath."[9] Pride inflates, envy gnaws, avarice goads, wrath inflames, gluttony chokes, lechery destroys, lying ensnares, murder defiles. So, too, other vices have their portents, for the sinful delights which entice men are the very instruments of God's punishment. "The envious man loses weight when he sees someone else getting fat."[10] But,

The tyrants of Sicily never discovered a worse form of torment than envy.[11]

For vice corrupts nature as the Apostle witnesses: "Because they have become vain in their thoughts, and their foolish hearts have been darkened, therefore God gave them up to the desires of their hearts unto uncleanness, to dishonor their own bodies, and as they liked not to have God in their knowledge, God delivered them up to a reprobate sense, to do those things which are not convenient."[12]

But even those "who will to live godly in Christ Jesus will suffer persecution."[13] "The saints had the experience of mockery and stripes, yes, even of chains and prisons. They were stoned, they were cut asunder, they were tempted, they were put to death by the sword for the Lord. They went about in sheepskins and goatskins, being in want, distressed, and afflicted, of whom the world was not worthy, wandering in deserts in mountains, and in dens and in caves of the earth."[14] In peril from floods, in peril from robbers, in peril from the gentiles, in peril from the city, in peril from false brethren. In labor and hardship, in many watchings, in hunger and thirst, in fastings often, in cold and nakedness,"[15] in many hardships.

For the just man "denies himself,"[16] crucifying his body on the cross of its own vices and concupiscences, so that the world is crucified to him and he to the world. He does not have in this life a lasting city of this world, but seeks the future city of God. He endures the world as an exile, shut up in the body as in a prison. "I am a sojourner on the earth"[17] "and a pilgrim like all my fathers. Turn thy eyes from me, that I may recover, before I go and am no more."[18] "Who is me that my sojourning is prolonged; I have dwelt with the inhabitants of Cedar, my soul has long been a sojourner."[19] "Who is weak and I am not weak? Who is scandalized and I am not on fire?"[20] For the sins of those about us are a torment to the righteous. And this teaching is the flowing water which Caleb gave for dowry to his daughter Axa.

On the enemies of man

"The life of man on the earth is warfare."[21] Is it not truly warfare when a manifold enemy – the devil and man, the world and the flesh – always and everywhere lie in wait to seize us, follow us about to slay us? – the world through the four elements, the flesh through the senses, man through the beasts, and the devil through vices. "For the flesh lusts against the spirit and the spirit against the flesh."[22] For "our wrestling is not against flesh and blood, but against principalities and powers, against the rulers of the world of darkness."[23] For your adversary the devil, as a roaring lion, goes about seeking whom he may devour."[24] . . .

Of the guilty progress of the human condition

Men strive especially for three things: riches, pleasures, and honors. Riches lead to immorality, pleasures to shame, and honors to vanity. Hence the Apostle John says, "Do not love the world or the things that are in the world; because all that is in the world is the concupiscence of the flesh and the concupiscence of the eyes and the pride of life." The concupiscence of the flesh pertains to pleasures, the concupiscence of the eyes to riches, and the pride of life to honors. Riches beget covetousness and avarice, pleasures give birth to gluttony and lechery, and honors nourish pride and boasting.

Of covetousness

"Nothing is more wicked than a covetous man and there is not a more wicked thing than to love money."[25] That is the statement of the wise man, and the Apostle confirms it by saying, "They that will become rich fall into temptations and into the snare of the devil and into many unprofitable and hurtful desires, which drown men into destruction and perdition. For the desire of money is the root of all evils."[26] It causes sacrilege and theft, incites robbery and plunder, starts wars and prompts murders; it buys and sells in simony, seeks and takes without fairness, trades and lends without justice, presses with guile and threatens with fraud; it violates agreements and breaks oaths, corrupts witnesses, and perverts judges . . .

On respect of persons

Woe to you who have been corrupted by pressure of bribery, influenced by love or hate to "call evil good and good evil, who put darkness for light and light for darkness,"[27] killing souls which do not die and giving life to souls which do not live. [Judges] pay no attention to the value of a case, but to the value of a person; not to laws but to bribes; not to justice but to money; not to reason's dictate but to your will's desire: not to the law's decree but to your mind's urging. You do not bend your mind to justice, but bend justice to your mind; not in order that you desire what is lawful but that it may be made lawful to do what you desire. For your eye is never so pure as to keep the brightness of the whole body: you add always some yeast that corrupts the whole . . .

On the despair of the damned

"They are laid in hell like sheep; death will feed on them."[28] This text is based upon the similarity of damned souls to beasts of burden, who do not tear up the grass by the roots but only chew the top, so that the grass grows again for pasture. Thus the wicked, as if eaten by death, spring to life again to die once more, and so are eternally dying.

> The liver of Tityus, unconsumed and ever growing,
> Wastes not – whence it can be devoured many times.[29]

Then death will never die, and those who are dead to life will live for death alone. They will seek death and never find it, having had life and lost it. Hear what John says in the Apocalypse: "In those days men will seek death and they will not find it, and they will desire to die and death will flee from them."[30] O death, how sweet you would be to these souls who when alive thought you so bitter; they will long for you and you alone – they who had despised you so in life.

Why the wicked will never be released from punishment

Therefore let no man flatter himself, saying "The Lord will not always be angry, nor will He threaten forever,"[31] and "His mercy is over all His works."[32] For "when He was angry He did not forget to be merciful,"[33] nor does He hate anything which He has made. They take up this erroneous argument because of what our Lord said through the prophet, "And they shall be gathered together as in the gathering of one bundle into the pit. And they shall be shut up there in prison, and after many days they shall be visited."[34] And therefore – so they argue – because man sinned in time, he will not be punished in eternity.

O vain hope, O false presumption! "He shall not believe, being vainly deceived by error, that he may be redeemed with any price,"[35] "for there is no redemption in hell."[36] Therefore sinners shall be gathered in a pit and shut in a prison, which is Hell; and there they will be tortured without their bodies until Doomsday, and then after many days they shall be visited, that is, after they rise with their bodies on the last day; but they will be visited with vengeance, not salvation, for they will be punished still more grievously after the day of judgment. Thus it is said in another place, "I will visit their iniquities with a rod and their sins with stripes."[37]

Therefore God will be angry with those who are saved only for a time, for "He scourges every son whom he receives."[38] From this it is understood that "He will not always be angry."[39] But with the wicked He will be angry forever, for it is just and right that those who go astray in *their* portion of eternity shall have God's wrath throughout *His* eternity. For although the sinner in Hell has lost the opportunity of sinning, still he does not lose his will to sin. It is written: "The pride of those who hate thee ascends continually."[40]

The wicked will not be humbled, having already despaired of mercy. Malignant hate will grow in them, so much that they will wish God, through whom they know they exist so unhappily, could altogether cease to exist. They will curse the Almighty and blaspheme the Everlasting, complaining that He is evil who created them for punishment and never inclines to mercy. Hear what John says in the Apocalypse: "And great hail came down from heaven upon men, and men blasphemed God for the plague of the hail because it was exceeding great."[41]

Therefore the will of the damned, although it lose the effect of its power, will always retain the love of evil; it will of itself be a punishment in hell, which had been a sin in the world, though perhaps even in hell it will still be a sin, but not worth punishment. Thus the sinner, having always had within himself the accusation of guilt, will always feel within himself the anguish of punishment: what he did not wipe away through penitence, God will not remit through indulgence. "There it pertains to the great justice of the judge that they never lack punishment in hell who never wished to lack sin in life. They would have certainly wished, if they could, to live forever so that they might sin forever."[42] For they show that they want always to live in sin who never cease to sin while they are alive.

Notes

1 Eccles. 3:19–20.
2 Job 10:9.
3 Gen. 3:19.
4 Job 30:19.
5 Job 14:4.
6 Job 15:14.
7 Ps. 50:7.
8 Wisd. 11:17.
9 Job 4:8–9.
10 Horace, *Epistles* I. ii. 56.
11 *Ibid.*, 57–59.
12 Rom. 1:21, 24, 28.
13 II Tim. 3:12.
14 Heb. 11:36–38.
15 II Cor. 11:26–27.
16 Luke 9:23.
17 Ps. 118:19.
18 Ps. 38:13–14.
19 Ps. 119:5.

20 II Cor. 11:29.
21 Job 7:1.
22 Gal. 5:17.
23 Eph. 6:12.
24 I Pet. 5:8.
25 Ecclus. 10:9, 10.
26 I Tim. 6:9–10.
27 Isa. 5:20.
28 Ps. 48:15.
29 Ovid, *Epistulae ex Ponto* I. ii. 42.
30 Apoc. 9:6.
31 Ps. 102:9.
32 Ps. 144:9.
33 Cf. Ps. 76:10.
34 Isa. 24:22.
35 Job 15:31.
36 Resp. III Noct. *Officium Defunctorum.*
37 Ps. 88:33.
38 Heb. 12:6.
39 Ps. 102:9.
40 Ps. 73:23.
41 Apoc. 16:21.
42 St. Gregory, *Dialogues* IV. 44.

12

ST THOMAS AQUINAS

On Evil

Q. 1, Art. 1   Whether evil is something?

Something is said to be evil in two ways; in one way simply, in another way in some particular respect. And that is called evil simply, which is in itself evil; and this is inasmuch as a thing is deprived of some particular good that pertains to its due or proper perfection, as sickness in an animal is an evil because it deprives it of the equilibrium of humors which is required for the well-being of the animal. But that is said to be evil in some respect, which is not evil in itself but to something else because, namely, it is not deprived of some good that belongs to its own due perfection but that belongs to the due perfection of another, as in fire there is a privation of water's form which does not belong to the due perfection of fire but to the due perfection of water; hence fire is not of itself evil but is evil to water. And likewise the order of justice has an adjunct the privation of water's form which does not belong to the due perfection of fire but to the due perfection of water; hence fire is not of itself evil but is evil to water. And likewise the order of justice has as an adjunct the privation of a particular good of a transgressor, inasmuch as the order of justice requires that a transgressor be deprived of a good he desires. So accordingly, the punishment itself is good simply, but an evil to this person. And God is said to create this evil and to make peace because the desire of the transgressor does not cooperate with the punishment, but the desire of the recipient of peace does cooperate with peace; but to create is to make something with nothing presupposed. And therefore it is clear that evil is said to be created not inasmuch as it is evil but inasmuch as it is good simply and evil only in a certain respect.

Good and evil are properly opposed as privation and possession of a quality because . . . those things are properly called contraries, each of which is something in keeping with nature, for example hot and cold, white and black; but those of which one is in conformity

Source: *On Evil*, trans. Jean Oesterle, Notre Dame, Ill.: University of Notre Dame Press, 1995.

with nature and the other a departure from nature are not properly opposed as contraries but as privation and possession of a quality. But privation is twofold: one of which consists of an actual loss of being, like death or blindness; the other which consists of a gradual loss of being, like sickness which is a process leading to death or ophthalmia, which is a process leading to blindness. And privations of this latter kind are sometimes called contraries, inasmuch as they still retain something of that which is being lost; and in this way evil is called a contrary, since it does not deprive of all good, but something of the good remains.

The reason why evil is more properly called contrary to good in moral matters than in natural things is that moral acts depend on the will, and the object of the will is good and evil. But every act is denominated and receives its species from its object. So accordingly, the act of the will, inasmuch as it turns to evil, receives the nature and name of evil; and this evil is properly contrary to good. And this contrariety passes on from acts to habits, inasmuch as acts and habits are akin to one another.

Evil taken abstractly, i.e., evil itself, is said to corrupt, not indeed actively but formally, namely, inasmuch as it is the corruption itself of [something] good, as also blindness is said to corrupt sight, inasmuch as blindness is the corruption or privation itself of sight. But that which is evil, if it is evil simply, i.e., in itself, so corrupts or actively and effectively makes the thing corrupt not by acting but by dis-acting, i.e., by failing to act, by reason of a deficiency of active power, as for example defective seed generates defectively and produces a monstrosity, which is a corruption of the natural order. But that which is not simply and in itself evil, by its active power brings about complete corruption [or destruction, as e.g. water extinguishes fire].

Corruption that comes about from that which is simply and in itself evil cannot be natural, but is rather a lapse from nature. But corruption that comes about from that which is evil with reference to something else can be [in accordance with nature].

Q. I, Art. 2   Whether evil exists in good?

Evil cannot exist except in good. To prove this we must consider that we may speak of good in two ways: in one way of good absolutely, in another way of "a good this," for instance a good man or a good eye. Speaking then of good absolutely, good has the greatest extension, even greater than being . . . For since good is that which is desirable, what is in itself desirable is in itself good; and this is the end, the object or goal of the appetite. But from this, that we desire the end, it follows that we desire those things that are ordered to the end. Consequently those things that are ordered to the end, from the very fact that they are ordered to the end or good, have the nature of good; hence useful things are contained under the division of good . . .

But although any being whatsoever, whether actual or potential, can be called good simply, i.e., in itself, nevertheless it does not follow from this alone that anything without distinction is "a good this": for example if a man is good simply, it does not follow that he is a good flute player but only when he has attained skill in the art of flute playing. So accordingly, although man precisely as he is a man is a certain good, nevertheless it does not follow from this alone that he is a good man, rather that which makes each thing good is its proper virtue. . . . [S]omething is called "a good this" when it has the perfection proper to it, for example "a good man" when he has the perfection proper to man, "a good eye" when it has the perfection proper to the eye.

Good and evil are differences only in moral matters, in which evil is something affirmed in a positive way, inasmuch a the very act of the will is denominated evil from what is willed, although the evil itself cannot be willed except under the aspect of good.

From the foregoing analysis then it is evident that good is taken in three ways. For in one way the very perfection of the thing is called its good, as sharpness of vision is called the good of the eye and virtue is called the good of man. Secondly, the thing that has its proper perfection is called good, for instance a virtuous man and a sharp eye. In the third way the subject itself is called good inasmuch as it is in potentiality to perfection, for example the soul to virtue, and the substance of the eye to acuteness of sight. But since evil, as we have said above (in article 1), is nothing else but the privation of a due perfection, and privation exists only in a being in potentiality because we say a thing is deprived which is designed by nature to have something and does not have it, it follows that evil exists in good inasmuch as being in potentiality is called good.

Now the good which is perfection is free from [evil] i.e., is without evil; consequently in such a good, evil cannot exist. But the good which is a composite of subject and perfection is seriously damaged by evil, inasmuch as the perfection is removed and the subject remains, for instance blindness deprives of vision and leaves the eye without sight, and exists in the substance of the eye or even in the animal itself as in a subject.

Hence if there is a good which is pure act having no admixture of potency, such as God is, in such a good evil in no way can exist.

Q. 2, Art. 1 Whether every sin involves an act?

[S]ome have asserted that in any sin, even a sin of omission, there is an act: either an interior act of the will, as when someone sins in not giving an alms he wills not to give the alms, or even a connected exterior act by which a person is kept from doing an act he ought to do; whether that act be done simultaneously with the omission, as when someone desiring to play forgoes going to church, or it be a preceding act, as when a person is prevented from getting up for morning prayer because he stayed up too late the night before engrossed in something . . .

Others, however, asserted that the sin of omission does not involve an act but that the sin of omission is the very desistance from an act, and they explain Augustine's statement that sin is a word or deed or desire as implying that desiring and not desiring, saying and not saying, doing and not doing are taken as the same so far as the nature of sin is concerned . . .

And in fact each opinion is true in a certain respect. . . . For a sin of omission an act is not required; and indeed (*per se*) absolutely speaking the sin of omission consists in the very cessation or desistance from an act, i.e., not-doing an act. And this is obvious if we consider the nature of sin: for fault occurs both in those things which are according to nature and in those according to art when nature or art does not attain the end for which it acts. And that an agent operating by art or by nature does not attain the end occurs from this that it deviates from the measure or rule of proper operation . . . . [I]n natural things [this] is the natural inclination itself that follows on the form, [while] in works of art it is the rule of [each] art. So accordingly, in fault two things can be considered: departure from the rule or measure, and departure from the end.

But sometimes a departure from the end occurs and not a departure from the rule or measure by which an agent operates for an end both in nature and in art. In nature, for example, if something indigestible like a piece of metal or a stone is ingested, a failure of digestion occurs without any fault of nature; likewise if a doctor in conformity with his art prescribes some medicine and the patient is not cured, either because he has an incurable disease or because he does something contrary to his health, clearly the doctor is not at fault although the end is not attained; but if, conversely, he attained the end but nevertheless deviated from the rule of art, nonetheless he would be said to be at fault. From which it is evident that it pertains more to the nature of fault to disregard the rule of action than to fail to attain the end of the action. It is therefore intrinsically (*per se*) of the nature of fault, whether in nature or in art or in morals, that it is opposed to a rule of action.

But since a rule of action establishes a mean between too much and too little, it is necessary that one rule forbid and another prescribe. Hence certain negative and certain affirmative precepts are contained both in natural reason and in divine law, according to which our actions ought to be regulated. . . . [J]ust as doing [something is] a sin [when] it is opposed to a negative precept of the law, so too not-doing [something] is a sin [when] it is opposed to an affirmative precept. So then there can be [sins of omission].

But [in another sense] an act is required for any sin, even [for] a sin of omission. . . . [I]f someone does not do what he ought to do, there must be a cause of this. But if the cause is wholly extrinsic, an omission of this kind does not have the nature of sin, for example if someone injured by a falling rock is prevented from going to church, or being robbed by someone is prevented from giving an alms. Therefore only at that time is the omission imputed as a sin when it has an intrinsic cause not just of any kind whatsoever but a voluntary one; because if a person were impeded by an intrinsic cause which was not voluntary, say a fever, the same reasoning would hold as in the case of an extrinsic cause. Therefore for an omission to be a sin the omission must be caused by a voluntary act.

But the will is the cause of a thing sometimes directly (*per se*) and sometimes indirectly (*per accidens*); directly, as when it acts intentionally to attain such an effect, for example if someone seeking to find a treasure, finds it while digging; but indirectly, as when it is apart from his intention, for example if someone intending to dig a grave while digging uncovers a treasure. So then the voluntary act sometimes is the direct cause of an omission, not however in such a way that the will directly intends the omission, since non-being and evil are contrary to the intention and the will, and the object of the will is being and good; but indirectly the will is moved to something positive with foresight of the consequent omission, as when a person wills to play knowing that this is concomitant with not going to church; just as likewise in transgression we say that a thief wills (to have) the gold in not shunning the deformity of injustice. On the other hand sometimes the voluntary act is required as a cause . . .

[It] is on account of the will that an act is praiseworthy, i.e., meritorious and virtuous, or is blameworthy and demeritorious or vicious. And therefore any virtue and vice is said to be a habit of the mind and will, not that the exterior acts do not likewise pertain to the acts of virtue and vice, but because the exterior acts are acts of virtue and vice only according as they are commanded by the mind's will.

Only the will is said to be rewarded or condemned because nothing is condemned or rewarded except insofar as it is from the will . . .

The act of that person whose hand someone used to kill would indeed be a disordered act but would not have the nature of fault except in relation to him who uses the other person's hand. And similarly the exterior act of the member [of the body] has deformity, but it does not have the nature of fault unless it is from the will. Hence if the will and the hand belong to two persons, the hand would not sin but the will would sin not only by its own act which is to will but also by the act of the hand that it uses; and in the cases presented here there is one man to whom both acts belong and he is punished for both . . .

But it must be noted that these three — evil, sin, and fault — are related to each other as more general and less general. For evil is more general: indeed any privation whatever of form or of order or of due measure either in the subject or in the act, has the nature of evil. But any act lacking due order or form or measure is called a sin (or defect). Hence it can be said that a crooked leg is an evil or bad leg, but it cannot be said that it is a sin except perhaps in that manner of speaking in which the effect of sin is called a sin; but the limping itself is called a sin or defect: indeed any disordered act either in nature or in art or in morals can be called a sin. But sin has the nature of fault only from the fact that as it is voluntary: for no disordered act is imputed to anyone as a fault except in consequence of the fact that it is within his power. And so it is clear that sin is more general than fault, although according to the common usage among theologians, sin and fault are taken for the same thing.

Consequently those who considered in sin only the nature of evil said that the substance of the act is not a sin but the deformity of the act is; but those who considered in sin only that from which it has the nature of fault said that sin consists in the will alone. But in sin it is necessary to consider not only the deformity itself but also the act underlying the deformity, since sin is not the deformity but a deformed act. Now the deformity of the act is owing to this that it is discordant with the due rule of reason or of the law of God, which deformity is found not only in the interior act, but also in the exterior act: but nevertheless the very fact that the exterior deformed act is imputed to man as a fault is on account of the will. And so clearly if we wish to consider all that is in sin, sin consists not only in the privation (of the due rule of reason or the divine law) nor only in the interior act, but also in the exterior act . . .

What is not really good appears good for two reasons: sometimes because of a defect of the intellect, as when a person has an erroneous opinion about doing an act, as is obvious in him who thinks fornication is not a sin, or in a person who lacks the use of reason; and such a defect on the part of the intellect lessens the fault or excuses it entirely. But sometimes the defect is not on the part of the intellect but rather on the part of the will, for according to the character of a man so does the end appear to him . . . [W]e know by experience that in respect to those things that we love or those we hate, so does something seem good or bad to us. And therefore when a person is inordinately disposed toward something, the judgment of his intellect in regard to a particular eligible object is impeded owing to inordinate affection. And thus the fault is not principally in the cognition but in the affection. And therefore he who sins in this way is not said to sin on account of ignorance, but in ignorance . . .

Q. 3, Art. 1 Whether God is the cause of sin?

Someone is the cause of sin in two ways: in one way because he himself sins, in another way because he causes another to sin. Neither of which can belong to God.

That God cannot sin is evident both from the general nature of sin and from the particular nature of moral sin which is called fault. For sin commonly so called as it is found in the things of nature and of art arises from this that someone in acting does not attain the end for which he acts. Which occurs from a defect of the active principle; for example, if a grammarian writes incorrectly, it happens from a deficiency of the art, at least if he intended to write correctly; and that nature sins, i.e., fails in the formation of an animal, as occurs in the birth of monstrosities, happens from a defect in the active power of the seed. But sin as it is properly so called in moral matters and has the nature of fault arises from this that the will fails to attain its proper end owing to the fact that it is aim[ed] at an improper end. But in God the active principle cannot be deficient because His power is infinite, nor can His will fail to attain its proper end because His very will, which is identical with His nature, is the supreme goodness which is the ultimate end and first rule of all wills; hence His will naturally adheres to the supreme good and cannot depart from it, just as the natural appetite of a thing cannot fail to desire its own natural good. So accordingly He cannot be the cause of sin in that He Himself sins.

Likewise He cannot be the cause of sin in that He causes others to sin. For sin as we are now speaking of it consists in a turning away of the created will from the ultimate end. But it is impossible that God should cause the will of anyone to be turned away from the ultimate end, since He Himself is the ultimate end. For whatever is commonly found in all created agents is necessarily had after the manner of an imitation of the first agent, Who bestows His likeness on all things according to their capacity to partake thereof. Now every created agent as a result of its own action is found to draw other things to itself in a certain manner by making them similar to itself, either by a likeness of form, as when heat makes something warm, or by conversion of others to its own end, as man moves others by his command to the end he intends. This then is proper to God that He turns all things to Himself and consequently that He turns nothing away from Himself. But He Himself is the greatest good. Hence He cannot be the cause of turning the will away from the greatest, i.e., the ultimate good, in which the nature of fault consists, according as we are now speaking of fault.

It is therefore impossible for God to be the cause of sin.

Q. 3, Art. 9   Whether someone who knows the difference between good and evil can tell sin from weakness?

[J]ust as there is a certain regulative power of the body, so reason is the regulative power of all the internal affections: hence when some affection is not regulated according to the rule of reason, but is excessive or deficient, it is said to be a weakness of the soul. And this occurs especially in regard to the affections of the sense appetite, which are called passions, for instance fear, anger, concupiscence, and the like; hence the ancient authors called such passions of the soul sicknesses of the soul . . . Therefore a person is said to do that from weakness, which he does from some passion, for instance from anger or fear or concupiscence or some such passion.

But Socrates . . . held that knowledge cannot be overcome by passion. . . . [N]o one by reason of passion can do anything contrary to his knowledge; hence he called all virtues kinds of . . . knowledge and he called all vices or sins kinds of ignorance. From which it follows that no one having knowledge sins from weakness; which clearly is contrary to our daily experience. And therefore we must consider that one may have knowledge in many ways: in one way in general, in another way in particular, and in one way habitually, in another way actually. In the first place it can happen by reason of passion that what is known habitually is not actually considered. For it is obvious that . . . when a person concentrates on hearing someone, he does not notice a man passing by. And the reason for this is that . . . when a person is resolutely intent on the act of one power, his attention to the act of another power is reduced. In this way, then, when [desire] or anger or something of this kind is intense, man is impeded from the consideration of knowledge.

Secondly ... the passions of the soul ... are concerned with particulars: a person desires *this* pleasure, as for instance he tastes this sweet thing. But knowledge (*scientia*) concerns the universal; and nevertheless ... acts are about particulars. When, then, passion is vehement concerning some particular, it repulses the contrary movement of knowledge about the same particular, not only by distracting from a consideration of knowledge ... but by perverting it ... And so he who is in a vehement passion, even if in some way he should consider the universal, nevertheless his deliberation about the particular is impeded.

Thirdly we must consider that by reason of some bodily change the use of reason may be fettered, so that either it considers nothing at all or cannot freely consider, as is apparent in those asleep and those delirious. And indeed by reason of the passions, a change takes place in the body in such a way that sometimes people have fallen into madness on account of anger or concupiscence or some such passion. And therefore, when such passions are intense, by reason of the bodily change itself, such passions so to speak fetter the reason so that it does not exercise free judgment about particular acts to be done. And so nothing prevents someone who has knowledge according to habit and of general applicability from sinning out of weakness.

Q. 3, Art. 10   Whether sins committed from weakness are imputed to man as a mortal fault?

[When] reason is fettered by passion ... [it is still] within the power of the will to repulse this fettering of reason. For ... reason is fettered [when] attention ... is vehemently applied to [some] appetite ... it is diverted from considering in particular what it knows universally and habitually. But the will has the power to apply or not to apply its attention to something; hence it is within the power of the will to exclude the fettering of reason. Therefore the act committed, which proceeds from this fettering, is voluntary; hence it is not excused even from mortal fault. But if the fettering of reason by passion advanced to such a point that it would not be within the power of the will to exclude this fettering, for example, if from some passion of the soul someone were to become insane, whatever he committed would not be imputed to him nor to another insane person as a sin, except perhaps so far as concerns the beginning of such a passion, that it was voluntary; for the will was able in the beginning to prevent passion from advancing so far, just as homicide committed by reason of drunkenness is imputed to a man as a sin because the beginning of drunkenness was voluntary.

Q. 8, Art. 1   How many capital [mortal] vices are there?[1]

The good of man is three-fold: the good of the soul, the good of the man and the good of external things. The sin of pride pertains to the imaginatively grasped good of the soul, which should be directed to the excellence of honor. Gluttony is the sin that pertains to the good of the body in preserving the individual through food. Lust is the sin that pertains to the preservation of the species in sexual intercourse. The sin of avarice pertains to the good of exterior things. Appetite moves in two directions: pursuit or avoidance. There are three vices concerning avoidance and pursuit. Acedia [melancholia] is sadness or antipathy towards a spiritual good; it is avoidance of proper pleasure. Envy is sorrow over another's good; anger involves recrimination; it implies pursuit of revenge.

Note

1   I have substituted my translation for that of Jean Oesterle. Ed.

13

DANTE ALIGHIERI

The suffering of the damned

Midway in our life's journey, I went astray
　　from the straight road and woke to find myself
　　alone in a dark wood. How shall I say

what wood that was! I never saw so drear,
　　so rank, so arduous a wilderness!
　　Its very memory gives a shape to fear.

Death could scarce be more bitter than that place!
　　But since it came to good, I will recount
　　all that I found revealed there by God's grace.

How I came to it I cannot rightly say,
　　so drugged and loose with sleep had I become
　　when I first wandered there from the True Way.

But at the far end of that valley of evil
　　whose maze had sapped my very heart with fear!
　　I found myself before a little hill

and lifted up my eyes. Its shoulders glowed
　　already with the sweet rays of that planet
　　whose virtue leads men straight on every road,

Source: *The Inferno*, cantos 1, 3, 11–14, translated by John Ciardi, New York: New American Library, 1954.

and the shining strengthened me against the fright
   whose agony had wracked the lake of my heart
   through all the terrors of that piteous night.

[. . .]

I AM THE WAY INTO THE CITY OF WOE.
I AM THE WAY TO A FORSAKEN PEOPLE.
I AM THE WAY INTO ETERNAL SORROW.

SACRED JUSTICE MOVED MY ARCHITECT.
I WAS RAISED HERE BY DIVINE OMNIPOTENCE,
PRIMORDIAL LOVE AND ULTIMATE INTELLECT.

ONLY THOSE ELEMENTS TIME CANNOT WEAR
WERE MADE BEFORE ME, AND BEYOND TIME I STAND.
ABANDON ALL HOPE YE WHO ENTER HERE.

These mysteries I read cut into stone
   above a gate. And turning I said: "Master,
   what is the meaning of this harsh inscription?"

And he then as initiate to novice:
   "Here must you put by all division of spirit
   and gather your soul against all cowardice.

This is the place I told you to expect.
   Here you shall pass among the fallen people,
   souls who have lost the good of intellect."

So saying, he put forth his hand to me,
   and with a gentle and encouraging smile
   he led me through the gate of mystery.

Here sighs and cries and wails coiled and recoiled
   on the starless air, spilling my soul to tears.
   A confusion of tongues and monstruous accents toiled

in pain and anger. Voices hoarse and shrill
    and sounds of blows, all intermingled, raised
    tumult and pandemonium that still

whirls on the air forever dirty with it
    as if a whirlwind sucked at sand. And I,
    holding my head in horror, cried: "Sweet Spirit,

what souls are these who run through this black haze?"
    And he to me: "These are the nearly soulless
    whose lives concluded neither blame nor praise.

They are mixed here with that despicable corps
    of angels who were neither for God nor Satan,
    but only for themselves. The High Creator

scourged them from Heaven for its perfect beauty,
    and Hell will not receive them since the wicked
    might feel some glory over them." And I:

"Master, what gnaws at them so hideously
    their lamentation stuns the very air?"
    "They have no hope of death," he answered me,

"and in their blind and unattaining state
    their miserable lives have sunk so low
    that they must envy every other fate.

No word of them survives their living season.
    Mercy and Justice deny them even a name.
    Let us not speak of them: look, and pass on."

I saw a banner there upon the mist.
    Circling and circling, it seemed to scorn all pause.
    So it ran on, and still behind it pressed

a never-ending rout of souls in pain.
    I had not thought death had undone so many
    as passed before me in that mournful train.

And some I knew among them; last of all
    I recognized the shadow of that soul
     who, in his cowardice, made the Great Denial.

At once I understood for certain: these
    were of that retrograde and faithless crew
     hateful to God and to His enemies.

These wretches never born and never dead
    ran naked in a swarm of wasps and hornets
     that goaded them the more the more they fled,

and made their faces stream with bloody gouts
    of pus and tears that dribbled to their feet
     to be swallowed there by loathsome worms and maggots.

[. . .]

"My son," [Virgil] began, "there are below this wall
    three smaller circles, each in its degree
     like those you are about to leave, and all

are crammed with God's accurst. Accordingly,
    that you may understand their sins at sight,
     I will explain how each is prisoned, and why.

Malice is the sin most hated by God.
    And the aim of malice is to injure others
     whether by fraud or violence. But since fraud

is the vice of which man alone is capable,
    God loathes it most. Therefore, the fraudulent
     are placed below, and their torment is more painful.

The first below are the violent. But as violence
    sins in three persons, so is that circle formed
     of three descending rounds of crueler torments.

Against God, self, and neighbor is violence shown.
    Against their persons and their goods, I say,
      as you shall hear set forth with open reason.

Murder and mayhem are the violation
    of the person of one's neighbor: and of his goods;
      harassment, plunder, arson, and extortion.

Therefore, homicides, and those who strike
    in malice – destroyers and plunderers – all lie
      in that first round, and like suffers with like.

A man may lay violent hands upon his own
    person and substance; so in that second round
      eternally in vain repentance moan

the suicides and all who gamble away
    and waste the good and substance of their lives
      and weep in that sweet time when they should be gay.

Violence may be offered the deity
    in the heart that blasphemes and refuses Him
      and scorns the gifts of Nature, her beauty and bounty.

Therefore, the smallest round brands with its mark
    both Sodom and Cahors, and all who rail
      at God and His commands in their hearts' dark.

Fraud, which is a canker to every conscience,
    may be practiced by a man on those who trust him,
      and on those who have reposed no confidence.

The latter mode seems only to deny
    the bond of love which all men have from Nature;
      therefore within the second circle lie

simoniacs, sycophants, and hypocrites,
    falsifiers, thieves, and sorcerers,
      grafters, pimps, and all such filthy cheats.

The former mode of fraud not only denies
    the bond of Nature, but the special trust
    added by bonds of friendship or blood-ties.

Hence, at the center point of all creation,
    in the smallest circle, on which Dis is founded,
    the traitors lie in endless expiation."

"Master," I said, "the clarity of your mind
    impresses all you touch; I see quite clearly
    the orders of this dark pit of the blind.

But tell me: those who lie in the swamp's bowels,
    those the wind blows about, those the rain beats,
    and those who meet and clash with such mad howls —

why are *they* not punished in the rust-red city
    if God's wrath be upon them? and if it is not,
    why must they grieve through all eternity?"

And he: "Why does your understanding stray
    so far from its own habit? or can it be
    your thoughts are turned along some other way?

Have you forgotten that your *Ethics* states
    the three main dispositions of the soul
    that lead to those offenses Heaven hates —

incontinence, malice, and bestiality?
    and how incontinence offends God least
    and earns least blame from Justice and Charity?

Now if you weight this doctrine and recall
    exactly who they are whose punishment
    lies in that upper Hell outside the wall,

you will understand at once why they are confined
    apart from these fierce wraiths, and why less anger
    beats down on them from the Eternal Mind."

"O sun which clears all mists from troubled sight,
    such joy attends your rising that I feel
    as grateful to the dark as to the light.

Go back a little further," I said, "to where
    you spoke of usury as an offence
    against God's goodness. How is that made clear?"

"Philosophy makes plain by many reasons,"
    he answered me, "to those who heed her teachings,
    how all of Nature, – her laws, her fruits, her seasons, –

springs from the Ultimate Intellect and Its art:
    and if you read your *Physics* with due care,
    you will note, not many pages from the start,

that Art strives after her by imitation,
    as the disciple imitates the master;
    Art, as it were, is the Grandchild of Creation.

By this, recalling the Old Testament
    near the beginning of Genesis, you will see
    that in the will of Providence, man was meant

to labor and to prosper. But userers,
    by seeking their increase in other ways,
    scorn Nature in herself and her followers.

But come, for it is my wish now to go on:
    the wheel turns and the Wain lies over Caurus,
    the Fish are quivering low on the horizon

and there beyond us runs the road we go
down the dark scarp into the depths below."

14

GEOFFREY CHAUCER

The seven deadly sins

The Parson's Tale

Of the birth of sins, Saint Paul says thus: that "as by one man sin entered into the world, and death by sin; . . . so death passed upon all men, for that all have sinned." And this man was Adam, by whom sin entered into the world when he broke the commandment of God. And therefore, he that at first was so mighty that he should never have died became such a one as must needs die, whether he would or no; and all his progeny in this world, since they, in that man, sinned . . .

From that same Adam caught we all that original sin; for we are all descended from him in the flesh, engendered of vile and corrupt matter. And when the soul is put into a body, immediately is contracted original sin; and that which was at first merely the penalty of concupiscence becomes afterwards both penalty and sin. And therefore are we all born the sons of wrath and of everlasting damnation, were it not for the baptism we receive, which washes away the culpability; but, forsooth, the penalty remains within us, as temptation, and that penalty is called concupiscence. When it is wrongly disposed or established in man, it makes him desire, by the lust of the flesh, fleshly sin; desire, by the sight of his eyes, earthly things; and desire high place, what of the pride of his heart . . .

[T]hey are deceived who say that they are never tempted in the flesh. Witness Saint James the apostle, who says that everyone is tempted in his own concupiscence. That is to say, each of us has cause and occasion to be tempted by the sin that is nourished in the body. And thereupon says Saint John the Evangelist: "If we say that we have no sin, we deceive ourselves, and the truth is not in us." . . .

[S]in is of two kinds; it is either venial or mortal sin. Verily, when man loves any creature more than he loves Jesus Christ our Creator, then is it mortal sin. And venial

Source: *The Canterbury Tales*, "The Parson's Tale".

sin it is if a man love Jesus Christ less than he ought. Forsooth the effect of this venial sin is very dangerous; for it diminishes more and more the love that man should have for God. And therefore, if a man charge himself with many such venial sins, then certainly, unless he discharge them occasionally by shriving, they may easily lessen in him all the love that he has for Jesus Christ; and in this wise venial sin passes over into mortal sin . . .

[T]he love for everything that is not fixed or rooted in God, or done principally for God's sake, though a man love it less than he love God, yet is it venial sin; and it is mortal sin when the love for anything weighs in the heart of man as much as the love for God, or more. "Mortal sin," as Saint Augustine says, "is when a man turns his heart from God, Who is the truly sovereign goodness and may not change, and gives his heart unto things that may change and pas away." And true it is that if a man give his love, the which he owes all to God, with all his heart, unto a creature, then certainly so much of his love as he gives unto the said creature he takes away form God; and thereby does he sin. For he, who is debtor to God, yields not unto God all of his debt, which is to say, all the love of his heart.

Now since man understands generally what venial sin is, it is fitting to tell especially of sins which many a man perhaps holds not to be sins at all, and for which he shrives not himself; yet, nevertheless, they are sins. Truly, as clerics write, every time a man eats or drinks more than suffices for the sustenance of his body, it is certain that he thereby sins. And, too, when he speaks more than it is necessary it is sin. Also, when he hears not benignly the complaint of the poor. Also, when he is in health of body and will not fast when other folk fast, and that without a reasonable excuse. Also, when he sleeps more than he needs, or when he comes, for that reason, too late to church, or to other places where works of charity are done. Also, when he enjoys his wife without a sovereign desire to procreate children to the honour of God, or when he does it without intention to yield to his wife the duty of his body. Also, when he will not visit the sick and the imprisoned, if he may do so. Also, if he love wife or child or any other worldly thing more than reason requires. Also, if he flatter or blandish more than, of necessity, he ought. Also, if he diminish or withdraw his alms to the poor. Also, if he prepare his food more delicately than is needful, or eat it too hastily or too greedily. Also, if he talk about vain and trifling matters in a church or at God's service, or if he be a user of idle words of folly or of obscenity; for he shall yield up an accounting of it at the day of doom. Also, when he promises or assures one that he will do what he cannot perform. Also, when he, through thoughtlessness or folly, slanders or scorns his neighbour. Also, when he suspects a thing to be evil when he has no certain knowledge of it. These things, and more without number, are sins . . .

Now it is a needful thing to tell which are the mortal sins, that is to say, the principal sins; they are all leashed together, but are different in their ways. Now they are called principal sins because they are the chief sins and the trunk from which branch all others. And the root of these seven sins is pride, which is the general root of all evils; for from this root spring certain branches, as anger, envy, acedia [melancholia] or sloth, avarice (or covetousness, for vulgar understanding), gluttony, and lechery. And each of these principal sins has its branches and its twigs.

Pride

And though it be true that no man can absolutely tell the number of the twigs and of the evil branches that spring from pride, yet will I show forth a number of them, as you shall understand. There are disobedience, boasting, hypocrisy, scorn, arrogance, impudence, swelling of the heart, insolence, elation, impatience, strife, contumacy, presumption, irreverence, obstinacy, vainglory; and many another twig that I cannot declare. Disobedient is he that disobeys for spite the commandments of God, of his rulers, and of his spiritual father. Braggart is he that boasts of the evil or the good that he has done. Hypocrite is he that hides his true self and shows himself such as he is not. Scorner is he who has disdain for his neighbour, that is to say for his fellow Christian, or who scorns to do that which he ought to do. Arrogant is he who thinks he has within himself those virtues which he has not, or who holds that he should so have them as his desert; or else he deems that he is that which he is not. Impudent is he who, for his pride's sake, has no shame for his sins. Swelling of heart is what a man has when he rejoices in evil that he has done. Insolent is he that despises in his judgments all other folk in comparing theirs with his worth, and with his understanding, and with his conversation, and with his bearing. Elated is he who will suffer neither a master nor a peer. Impatient is he who will not be taught nor reproved for his vice, and who, by strife, knowingly wars on truth and defends his folly. *Contumax* is he who, because of his indignation, is against all authority or power of those that are his rulers. Presumption is when a man undertakes an enterprise that he ought not to attempt, or one which he cannot accomplish; and that is called over-confidence. Irreverence is when men do not show honour where they ought, and themselves wait to be reverenced. Obstinacy is when man defends his folly and trusts too much in his own judgment. Vainglory is delight in pomp and temporal rank, and glorification in this worldly estate. Chattering is when men speak too much before folk, clattering like a mill and taking no care of what they say.

Envy

After pride I will speak of the foul sin of envy, which is, according to the word of the philosopher, sorrow for other men's prosperity; and according to the word of Saint Augustine, it is sorrow for other men's weal and joy for other men's harm. . . . Now malice has two species, that is to say, a heart hardened in wickedness, or else the flesh of man is so blind that he does not consider himself to be in sin, or he cares not that he is in sin, which is the hardihood of the Devil. The other kind of malice is, when a man wars against the truth, knowing that it is truth. Also, when he wars against the grace that God has given to his neighbour; and all this is envy. Certainly, then, envy is the worst sin there is. For truly, all other sins are sometime against only one special virtue; but truly, envy is against all virtues and against all goodnesses; for it is sorry for all the virtues of its neighbour; and in this way it differs from all other sins. For hardly is there any sin that has not some delight in itself, save only envy, which ever has of itself but anguish and sorrow. The kinds of envy are these: there is, first, sorrow for other men's goodness and prosperity; and prosperity being naturally a thing for joy, then envy is a sin against nature. The second kind of envy is joy in other men's harm; and this is naturally like the Devil, who always rejoices in man's harm . . .

Anger

After envy will I describe the sin of anger. For truly, whoso has envy of his neighbour will generally find himself showing anger, in word or in deed, against him whom he envies. And anger comes as well from pride as from envy; for certainly, he that is proud or envious is easily angered.

This sin of anger, according to Saint Augustine, is a wicked determination to be avenged by word or by deed. Anger, according to the philosopher, is the hot blood of man quickened in his heart, because of which he wishes to harm him whom he hates. For truly, the heart of man, by the heating and stirring of his blood, grows so disturbed that he is put out of all ability to judge reasonably. But you shall understand that anger manifests itself in two manners; one of them is good, the other bad. The good anger is caused by zeal for goodness, whereof a man is enraged by wickedness and against wickedness; and thereupon a wise man says that "Anger is better than play." This anger is gentle and without bitterness; not felt against the man, but against the misdeed of the man, as the Prophet David says: *Irascimini et nolite peccare.* Now understand, that wicked anger is manifested in two manners, that is to say, sudden or hasty anger, without the advice and counsel of reason. The meaning and the sense of this is, that the reason of man consents not to this sudden anger, and so it is venial. Another anger is full wicked, which comes of sullenness of heart, with malice aforethought and with wicked determination to take vengeance, and to which reason assents; and this, truly, is mortal sin. This form of anger is so displeasing to God that it troubles His house and drives the Holy Ghost out of man's soul, and wastes and destroys the likeness of God, that is to say, the virtue that is in man's soul; and it puts within him the likeness of the Devil, and takes the man away from God, his rightful Lord. This form of anger is a great joy to the Devil; for it is the Devil's furnace, heated with the fire of Hell . . .

From anger come these stinking engenderings: first hate, which is old wrath; discord, by which a man forsakes his old friend whom he has long loved. And then come strife and every kind of wrong that man does to his neighbour, in body or in goods. Of this cursed sin of anger comes manslaughter also. And understand well that homicide, manslaughter, that is, is of different kinds. Some kinds of homicide are spiritual, and some are bodily. Spiritual manslaughter lies in six things. First, hate; and as Saint John says: "He that hateth his brother committeth homicide." Homicide is also accomplished by backbiting; and of backbiters Solomon says that "They have two swords wherewith they slay their neighbours." For truly, it is as wicked to take away a man's good name as his life. Homicide consists also in the giving of wicked counsel deceitfully, as in counselling one to levy wrongful duties and taxes . . .

Melancholia

After the sins of envy and of anger, now will I speak of the sin of acedia, or sloth. For envy blinds the heart of a man and anger troubles a man; and acedia makes him heavy, thoughtful, and peevish. Envy and anger cause bitterness of heart; which bitterness is the mother of acedia, and takes from a man the love of all goodness. Then is acedia the anguish of a troubled heart; and Saint Augustine says: "It is the sadness of goodness and the joy of evil." Certainly this is a damnable sin; for it wrongs Jesus Christ in as much as it lessens the service that men ought to give to Christ with due diligence, as says Solomon. But sloth has no such diligence; it does everything sadly and with peevishness, slackness, and false excusing, and with slovenliness and unwillingness . . .

[F]rom the sin of acedia it happens that a man is too sad and hindered to be able to do anything good . . .

Now enters despair, which is despair of the mercy of God, and comes sometimes of too extravagant sorrows and sometimes of too great fear: for the victim imagines that he has done so much sin that it will avail him not to repent and forgo sin . . .

Avarice

After acedia I will speak of avarice and of covetousness, of which sin Saint Paul says that "The love of money is the root of all evil:" *ad Timotheum, sexto capitulo.* For verily, when the heart of a man is confounded within itself, and troubled, and when the soul has lost the comforting of God, then seeks a man a vain solace in worldly things.

Avarice, according to the description of Saint Augustine, is the eagerness of the heart to have earthly things. Others say that avarice is the desire to acquire earthly goods and give nothing to those that need. And understand that avarice consists not only of greed for land and chattels, but sometimes for learning and for glory, and for every kind of immoderate thing. And the difference between avarice and covetousness is this. Covetousness is to covet such things as one has not; and avarice is to keep and withhold such things as one has when there is no need to do so . . .

Gluttony

After avarice comes gluttony, which also is entirely against the commandment of God. Gluttony is immoderate appetite to eat or to drink, or else to yield to the immoderate desire to eat or to drink. This sin corrupted all this world, as is well shown by the sin of Adam and Eve. Read, also, what Saint Paul says of gluttony: "For many walk, of whom I have told you often, and now tell you even weeping, that they are the enemies of the cross of Christ: whose end is destruction, whose God is their belly, and whose glory is in their shame, who mind earthly things." He that is addicted to this sin of gluttony may withstand no other sin. He may even be in the service of all the vices, for it is in the Devil's treasure house that he hides himself and rests . . .

Lechery

After gluttony, then comes lechery; for these two sins are such close cousins that oftentimes they will not be separated. God knows, this sin is unpleasing to God; for He said Himself, "Do no lechery." . . .

Let us speak, then, of that stinking sin of lechery that men call adultery of wedded folk, which is to say, if one of them be wedded, or both. Saint John says that adulterers shall be in Hell "in the lake which burneth with fire and brimstone" – in the fire for the lechery, in brimstone for the stink of their filthiness. Certainly, the breaking of this sacrament is a horrible thing; it was ordained by God Himself in Paradise, and confirmed by Jesus Christ . . .

And not only did God forbid adultery in deed, but also he commanded that "thou shalt not covet thy neighbour's wife." This behest, says Saint Augustine, contains the forbidding of all desire to do lechery. Behold what Saint Matthew says in the gospel: "Whatsoever looketh on a woman to lust after her, hath committed adultery with her already in his heart." Here you may see that not only the doing of this sin is forbidden, but also the desire to do that sin. This accursed sin grievously troubles those whom it haunts. And first, it does harm to the soul; for it constrains it to sin and to the pain of everlasting death. Unto the body it is a tribulation also, for it drains it, and wastes and ruins it, and makes of its blood a sacrifice to the Field of Hell; also it wastes wealth and substance.

Part 3

EVIL AS
WILLFULNESS

George Grosz: "The Wilful Possessors."

Augustine and Abelard had, each in his own way, brought the locus of evil inward to the conditions of ultimate choice – Augustine to the disposition of the will, Abelard to the moment of consent. As they saw it, the soul has the power, as well as the authority, to resist whatever the world offers as temptation to the self's natural, but debased inclinations. They held that both sin and the possibility of avoiding it arise from the power and the freedom of the will to deny divine commands . . . and to deny the inclination to iniquity.

Luther (1483–1546) carried that tradition forward. He pressed the question: from where, in what form, does temptation present itself? His answer is simple, direct and unequivocal: it is from the flesh, from the desires of the flesh. Luther understands the lure of the flesh broadly: moved by his finitude and mortality, his vulnerability and fear, man is inclined to wrath, envy, impatience, pride as well as gluttony and lust. But men are composed of spirit as well as flesh: they have the power to overcome the temptations of the flesh. Luther's message is one of comfort as well as despair: the battle between the flesh and the spirit is a condition of life. Not even the faithful, not even monks and saints escape it. Indeed "the more godly a man is, the more does he feel that battle." But even the worst sinner can overcome his flesh by his faith. That faith – his belief in his salvation through the redemption of Christ – brings his forgiveness. Sin he must, but "to him that believeth, it is forgiven and not imputed."

Calvin (1509–1564) returns to Genesis to locate the origin of sin. The outward form of Adam's Fall was his disobedience; the inward motion was faithlessness and pride, along with the ingratitude and ambition that follow it. Once the human soul estranged itself from God, its original nature became depraved. No longer "in the image of God," it suffers the death of the spirit. By contrast to Luther, Calvin holds that post-Adamic depravity is "diffused into all parts of the soul. . . . By this corruption, we stand justly condemned by God." Although human nature was corrupted by a natural process, it was man's own disobedience rather than God's will or an evil force that brought his fall.

Milton (1608–1674) sets himself to "justify the ways of God to man." If God is righteous, damnation is the just punishment of sin. Satan is the external projection of man's disobedience, the pride of his willful spirit. Once among the most powerful of the angels, the Arch-Angel's overweening ambition exemplifies as well as causes his fall. Divine Providence seeks to "bring forth good . . . out of our evil"; Satan sets himself to reverse divine Providence: "out of good to find means of evil." That desire *is* the fall. And fall to the domain of absolute willfulness he does, "from dawn to dewy eve." Once fallen, he exercises his power by bringing mankind into sin with him. We are to see ourselves in Satan, in his power and his pride; and we are to see ourselves in Satan's hell. "The mind is its own place, and in itself can make a Heav'n of Hell, a Hell of Heav'n." The Satan within continues to corrupt the Eve and then the Adam within.

109

Jonathan Edwards (1703–1758) justifies God's severity more directly: "the heart of man is naturally of a corrupt and evil disposition." Human depravity and corruption are not the outcome of a single event, nor does it consist in occasional lapses of the soul. They pervade every act, every motion of the soul. Man's fate cannot be redeemed by the balance of good over evil in his soul, nor by the victory of obedient love over self-aggrandizing pride. Because man's evil disposition is rightly odious to God, because his sins are "too heinous to be atoned for," he deserves God's wrath, his eternal condemnation.

15

MARTIN LUTHER

Flesh against spirit

For the flesh lusteth against the spirit,
and the spirit against the flesh

When Paul saith that the flesh lusteth against the spirit, and the spirit against the flesh, he admonisheth us that we shall feel the concupiscence of the flesh, that is to say, not only carnal lust, but also pride, wrath, heaviness, impatience, incredulity, and such-like. Notwithstanding he would have us so to feel them, that we consent not unto them, nor accomplish them: that is, that we neither think, speak, nor do those things which the flesh provoketh us unto. As, if it move us to anger, yet we should be angry in such wise as we are taught in the fourth Psalm, that we sin not. As if Paul would thus say: I know that the flesh will provoke you unto wrath, envy, doubting, incredulity, and such-like: but resist it by the Spirit, that ye sin not. But if ye forsake the guiding of the Spirit, and follow the flesh, ye shall fulfil the lust of the flesh, and ye shall die, as Paul saith in the eighth to the Romans. So this saying of the Apostle is to be understood, not of fleshly lusts only, but of the whole kingdom of sin.

And these are contrary one to the other, so that ye cannot do
the things that ye would

These two captains or leaders, saith he, the flesh and the spirit, are one against another in your body, so that ye cannot do what ye would. And this place witnesseth plainly that Paul writeth these things to the saints, that is, to the Church believing in Christ, baptized, justified, renewed, and having full forgiveness of sins. Yet notwithstanding he saith that she hath flesh rebelling against the spirit. After the same manner he speaketh of himself in the seventh to the Romans: "I (saith he) am carnal and sold under sin"; and again:"I see another law in my members rebelling against the law of my mind," &c.; also: "O wretched man that I am," &c.

Source: *Selections From His Writings*, "A Commentry on St. Paul's Epistle to the Galatians," Garden City, N.Y.: Doubleday, 1961.

Here, not only the schoolmen, but also some of the old fathers are much troubled, seeking how they may excuse Paul. For it seemeth unto them absurd and unseemly to say, that that elect vessel of Christ should have sin. But we credit Paul's own words, wherein he plainly confesseth that he is sold under sin, that he is led captive of sin, that he hath a law in his members rebelling against him, and that in the flesh he serveth the law of sin. Here again they answer, that the Apostle speaketh in the person of the ungodly. But the ungodly do not complain of the rebellion of their flesh, of any battle or conflict, or of the captivity and bondage of sin: for sin mightily reigneth in them. This is therefore the very complaint of Paul and of all the saints. Wherefore they have done very wickedly which have excused Paul and other saints to have no sin. For by this persuasion (which proceedeth of ignorance of the doctrine of faith) they have robbed the Church of a singular consolation: they have abolished the forgiveness of sins, and made Christ of none effect.

Wherefore when Paul saith: "I see another law in my members," &c., he denieth not that he hath flesh, and the vices of the flesh in him. It is likely therefore that he felt sometimes the motions of carnal lust. But yet (I have no doubt) these motions were well suppressed in him by the great and grievous [afflictions and] temptations both of mind and body, wherewith he was in a manner continually exercised and vexed, as his epistles do declare; or if he at any time being merry and strong, felt the lust of the flesh, wrath, impatiency, and such-like, yet he resisted them by the Spirit, and suffered not those motions to bear rule in him. Therefore let us in no wise suffer such comfortable places (whereby Paul describeth the battle of the flesh against the spirit in his own body) to be corrupted with such foolish glosses. The schoolmen, the monks, and such other, never felt any spiritual temptations, and therefore they fought only for the repressing and overcoming of fleshly lust and lechery, and being proud of that victory which they never yet obtained, they thought themselves far better and more holy than married men. I will not say, that under this holy pretence they nourished and maintained all kinds of horrible sins, as dissension, pride, hatred, disdain, and despising of their neighbours, trust in their own righteousness, presumption, contempt of godliness and of the Word of God, infidelity, blasphemy, and such-like. Against these sins they never fought, nay rather they took them to be no sins at all: they put righteousness in the keeping of their foolish and wicked vows, and unrighteousness in the neglecting and contemning of the same . . .

Let no man therefore despair if he feel the flesh oftentimes to stir up new battles against the spirit, or if he cannot by and by subdue the flesh, and make it obedient unto the spirit. I also do wish myself to have a more valiant and constant heart, which might be able, not only boldly to contemn the threatenings of tyrants, the heresies, offences and tumults which the fantastical spirits stir up; but also might by and by shake off the vexations and anguish of spirit, and briefly, might not fear the sharpness of death, but receive and embrace it as a most friendly guest. But I find another law in my members, rebelling against the law of my mind, &c. Some other do wrestle with inferior temptations, as poverty, reproach, impatiency and such-like.

Let no man marvel therefore or be dismayed, when he feeleth in his body this battle of the flesh against the spirit: but let him pluck up his heart and comfort himself with these words of Paul:

"The flesh lusteth against the spirit," &c., and: "These are contrary one to another, so that ye do not those things that ye would." For by these sentences he comforteth them that be tempted. As if he should say: It is impossible for you to follow the guiding of the Spirit in all things without any feeling or hindrance of the flesh; nay, the flesh will resist: and so resist and hinder you that ye cannot do those things that gladly ye would. Here, it shall be enough if ye resist the flesh and fulfil not the lust thereof: that is to say, if ye follow the spirit and not the flesh, which easily is overthrown by impatiency, coveteth to revenge, biteth, grudgeth, hateth God, is angry with him, despaireth &c. Therefore when a man feeleth this battle of the flesh, let him not be discouraged therewith, but let him resist in the Spirit, and say: I am a sinner, and I feel sin in me, for I have not yet put off the flesh, in which sin dwelleth so long as it liveth; but I will obey the spirit and not the flesh: that is, I will by faith and hope lay hold upon Christ, and by his word I will raise up myself, and being so raised up, I will not fulfil the lust of the flesh.

It is very profitable for the godly to know this, and to bear it well in mind; for it wonderfully comforteth them when they are tempted. When I was a monk I thought by and by that I was utterly cast away, if at any time I felt the concupiscence of the flesh: that is to say, if I felt any evil motion, fleshly lust, wrath, hatred, or envy against any brother. I assayed many ways, I went to confession daily, &c., but it profited me not; for the concupiscence of my flesh did always return, so that I could not rest, but was continually vexed with these thoughts: This or that sin thou hast committed; thou art infected with envy, with impatiency, and such other sins; therefore thou art entered into this holy order in vain, and all thy good works are unprofitable. If then I had rightly understood these sentences of Paul: "The flesh lusteth contrary to the spirit, and the spirit contrary to the flesh," &c. and "these two are one against another, so that ye cannot do the things that ye would do," I should not have so miserably tormented myself, but should have thought and said to myself, as now commonly I do: Martin, thou shalt not utterly be without sin, for thou hast yet flesh; thou shalt therefore feel the battle thereof, according to that saying of Paul: "The flesh resisteth the spirit." Despair not therefore, but resist it strongly, and fulfil not the lust thereof. Thus doing thou art not under the law . . .

The faithful therefore receive great consolation by this doctrine of Paul, in that they know themselves to have partly the flesh, and partly the spirit, but yet so notwithstanding that the spirit ruleth and the flesh is subdued, that righteousness reigneth and sin serveth. He that knoweth not this doctrine, and thinketh that the faithful ought to be without all fault, and yet seeth the contrary in himself, must needs at the length be swallowed up by the spirit of heaviness, and fall into desperation. But whoso knoweth this doctrine well and useth it rightly, to him the things that are evil turn unto good. For when the flesh provoketh him to sin, by occasion thereof he is stirred up and forced to seek forgiveness of sins by Christ, and to embrace the righteousness of faith, which else he would not so greatly esteem, nor seek for the same with so great desire. Therefore it profiteth us very much to feel sometimes the wickedness of our nature and corruption of our flesh, that even by this means we may be waked and stirred up to faith and to call upon Christ. And by this occasion a Christian becometh a mighty workman and a wonderful creator, which of heaviness can make joy, of terror comfort, of sin righteousness, and of death life, when he by this means repressing and bridling the flesh, maketh it subject to the Spirit.

Wherefore let not them which feel the concupiscence of the flesh, despair of their salvation. Let them feel it and all the force thereof, so that they consent not to it. Let the passions of lust, wrath and such other vices shake them, so that they do not overthrow them. Let sin assail them, so that they do not accomplish it. Yea the more godly a man is, the more doth he feel that battle. And hereof come those lamentable complaints of the saints in the Psalms and in all the holy Scripture. Of this battle the hermits, the monks, and the schoolmen, and all that seek righteousness and salvation by works, know nothing at all.

But here may some man say, that it is a dangerous matter to teach that a man is not condemned, if by and by he overcome not the motions and passions of the flesh which he feeleth. For when this doctrine is taught amongst the common people, it maketh them careless, negligent and slothful. This is it which I said a little before, that if we teach faith, then carnal men neglect and reject works: if works be required, then is faith and consolation of conscience lost. Here no man can be compelled, neither can there be any certain rule prescribed. But let every man diligently try himself to what passion of the flesh he is most subject, and when he findeth that, let him not be careless, nor flatter himself: but let him watch and wrestle in Spirit against it, that if he cannot altogether bridle it, yet at the least he do not fulfil the lust thereof.

This battle of the flesh against the spirit, all the saints have had and felt: and the selfsame do we also feel and prove. He that searcheth his own conscience, if he be not an hypocrite, shall well perceive that to be true in himself which Paul here saith: that the flesh lusteth against the spirit. All the faithful therefore do feel and confess that their flesh resisteth against the spirit, and that these two are so contrary the one to the other in themselves, that, do what they can, they are not able to perform that which they would do. Therefore the flesh hindereth us that we cannot keep the commandments of God, that we cannot love our neighbours as ourselves, much less can we love God with all our heart, &c. Therefore it is impossible for us to become righteous by the works of the law. Indeed there is a good will in us, and so must there be (for it is the Spirit itself which resisteth the flesh), which would gladly do good, fulfil the law, love God and his neighbour, and such-like, but the flesh obeyeth not this good will, but resisteth it: and yet God imputeth not unto us this sin, for he is merciful to those that believe, for Christ's sake.

But it followeth not therefore that thou shouldest make a light matter of sin, because God doth not impute it. True it is that he doth not impute it: but to whom, and for what cause? Not to them that are hard-hearted and secure, but to such as repent and lay hold by faith upon Christ the mercy-seat, for whose sake, as all their sins are forgiven them, even so the remnants of sin which are in them, be not imputed unto them. They make not their sin less than it is, but amplify it and set it out as it is indeed; for they know that it cannot be put away by satisfactions, works, or righteousness, but only by the death of Christ. And yet notwithstanding, the greatness and enormity of their sin doth not cause them to despair, but they assure themselves that the same shall not be imputed unto them [or laid unto their charge], for Christ's sake.

This I say, lest any man should think that after faith is received, there is little account to be made of sin. Sin is truly sin, whether a man commit it before he hath received the knowledge of Christ or after. And God always hateth sin: yea all sin is damnable as touching the fact itself. But in that it is not damnable to him that believeth, it cometh of Christ the reconciler, who by his death hath expiated sin. But to him that believeth not in Christ, not only all his sins are damnable, but even his good works also are sin; according to that saying: "Whatsoever is not of faith is sin" [Rom. 14:23]. Therefore the error of the schoolmen is most pernicious, which do distinguish sins according to the fact, and not according to the person. He that believeth hath as great sin as the believer. But to him that believeth, it is forgiven and not imputed: to the unbeliever it is not pardoned but imputed. To the believer it is venial: to the unbeliever it is mortal [and damnable]: not for any difference of sins, or because the sin of the believer is less, and the sin of the unbeliever greater: but for the difference of the persons. For the believer assureth himself by faith that his sin is forgiven him, forasmuch as Christ hath given himself for it. Therefore although he have sin in him and daily sinneth, yet he continueth godly: but contrariwise, the unbeliever continueth wicked. And this is the true wisdom and consolation of the godly, that although they have and commit sins, yet they know that for Christ's sake they are not imputed unto them . . .

Every age, even in the faithful hath his peculiar temptations: as fleshly lusts assail a man most of all in his youth, in his middle-age ambition and vain-glory, and in his old-age covetousness. There was never yet (as I have said already) any of the saints whom the flesh hath not often in his lifetime provoked to impatiency, anger . . .

Notwithstanding sometimes it happeneth that the saints also do fall and perform the desires of the flesh: as David fell horribly into adultery. Also he was the cause of the slaughter of many men, when he caused Uriah to be slain in the forefront of the battle. . . . Peter also fell most grievously and horribly when he denied Christ. But although these sins were great and heinous, yet were they not committed upon any contempt of God or of a wilful and obstinate mind, but through infirmity and weakness. Again, when they were admonished, they did not obstinately continue in their sins, but repented.... To those therefore which sin and fall through infirmity, pardon is not denied, so that they rise again and continue not in their sin: for of all things continuance in sin is the worst. But if they repent not, but still obstinately continue in their wickedness and perform the desires of the flesh, it is a certain token that there is deceit in their spirit.

No man therefore shall be without [lusts and] desires so long as he liveth in the flesh, and therefore no man shall be free from temptations. Notwithstanding some are tempted one way and some another, according to the difference of the persons. One man is assailed with more vehement and grievous motions, as with bitterness and anguish of spirit, blasphemy, distrust, and desperation: another with more gross temptations, as with fleshly lusts, wrath, envy, hatred and such-like. But in this case Paul requireth us that we walk in the Spirit, and resist the flesh. But whoso obeyeth the flesh, and continueth without fear or remorse in accomplishing the desires and lusts thereof, let him know that he pertaineth not unto Christ; and although he brag of the name of a Christian never so much, yet doth he but deceive himself. For they which are of Christ, do crucify their flesh with the affections and lusts thereof...

[Ye should] endeavour with diligence, that ye may discern and rightly judge between true righteousness and holiness, and that which is hypocritical: then shall ye behold the kingdom of Christ with other eyes that [carnal] reason doth, that is, with spiritual eyes, and certainly judge those to be true saints indeed which are baptized and believe in Christ, and afterwards in the same faith whereby they are justified, and their sins both past and present are forgiven, do abstain from the desires of the flesh. But from these desires they are not thoroughly cleansed; for the flesh lusteth against the spirit. Notwithstanding these uncleannesses do still remain in them to this end, that they may be humbled, and being so humbled, they may feel the sweetness of the grace and benefit of Christ. So these unclean remnants of sin do nothing at all hinder, but greatly further the godly; for the more they feel their infirmities and sins, so much the more they fly unto Christ the throne of grace, and more heartily crave his aid and succour: to wit, that he will adorn them with his righteousness, that he will increase their faith, that he will endue them with his Spirit, by whose [gracious leading and] guiding they may overcome the lusts of the flesh, that they may not rule and reign over them, but may be subject unto them. Thus true Christians do continually wrestle with sin, and yet notwithstanding in wrestling they are not overcome, but obtain the victory.

This have I said, that ye may understand, not by men's dreams, but by the Word of God, who be true saints indeed. We see then how greatly Christian doctrine helpeth to the raising up and comforting of [weak] consciences; which treateth not of cowls, shavings, rosaries, and such-like toys, but of high and weighty matters, as how we may overcome the flesh, sin, death, and the devil. This doctrine, as it is unknown to the justiciaries [and such as trust in their own works,] so is it impossible for them to instruct or bring into the right way one [poor] conscience wandering and going astray; or to pacify and comfort the same when it is in heaviness, terror, or desperation.

16

JOHN CALVIN

Human corruption

The history of the Fall shows us that sin is unfaithfulness
[Gen. 3]

Because what God so severely punished must have been no light sin but a detestable crime, we must consider what kind of sin there was in Adam's desertion that enkindled God's fearful vengeance against the whole of mankind. To regard Adam's sin as gluttonous intemperance (a common notion) is childish. As if the sum and head of all virtues lay in abstaining solely from one fruit, when all sorts of desirable delights abounded everywhere; and not only abundance but also magnificent variety was at hand in that blessed fruitfulness of earth!

We ought therefore to look more deeply. Adam was denied the tree of the knowledge of good and evil to test his obedience and prove that he was willingly under God's command. The very name of the tree shows the sole purpose of the precept was to keep him content with his lot and to prevent him from becoming puffed up with wicked lust. But the promise by which he was bidden to hope for eternal life so long as he ate from the tree of life, and, conversely, the terrible threat of death once he tasted of the tree of the knowledge of good and evil, served to prove and exercise his faith. Hence it is not hard to deduce by what means Adam provoked God's wrath upon himself. Indeed, Augustine speaks rightly when he declares that pride was the beginning of all evils. For if ambition had not raised man higher than was meet and right, he could have remained in his original state.

But we must take a fuller definition from the nature of the temptation which Moses describes. Since the woman through unfaithfulness was led away from God's Word by the serpent's deceit, it is already clear that disobedience was the beginning of the Fall. This Paul also confirms, teaching that all were lost through the disobedience of one man [Rom. 5:19]. Yet it is at the same time to be noted that the first man revolted from God's authority, not only because he was seized by Satan's blandishments, but also because,

Source: *Calvin: Institutes of the Christian Religion*, trans. Ford Lewis Battles, Philadelphia, PA: Westminster Press, 1960.

contemptuous of truth, he turned aside to falsehood. And surely, once we hold God's Word in contempt, we shake off all reverence for him. For, unless we listen attentively to him, his majesty will not dwell among us, nor his worship remain perfect. Unfaithfulness, then, was the root of the Fall. But thereafter ambition and pride, together with ungratefulness, arose, because Adam by seeking more than was granted him shamefully spurned God's great bounty, which had been lavished upon him. To have been made in the likeness of God seemed a small matter to a son of earth unless he also attained equality with God – a monstrous wickedness! If apostasy, by which man withdraws from the authority of his Maker – indeed insolently shakes off his yoke – is a foul and detestable offense, it is vain to extenuate Adam's sin. Yet it was not simple apostasy, but was joined with vile reproaches against God. These assented to Satan's slanders, which accused God of falsehood and envy and ill will. Lastly, faithlessness opened the door to ambition, and ambition was indeed the mother of obstinate disobedience; as a result, men, having cast off the fear of God, threw themselves wherever lust carried them. Hence Bernard rightly teaches that the door of salvation is opened to us when we receive the gospel today with our ears, even as death was then admitted by those same windows when they were opened to Satan [cf. Jer. 9:21]. For Adam would never have dared oppose God's authority unless he had disbelieved in God's Word. Here, indeed, was the best bridle to control all passions: the thought that nothing is better than to practice righteousness by obeying God's commandments; then, that the ultimate goal of the happy life is to be loved by him. Therefore Adam, carried away by the devil's blasphemies, as far as he was able, extinguished the whole glory of God.

The first sin as original sin

As it was the spiritual life of Adam to remain united and bound to his Maker, so estrangement from him was the death of his soul. Nor is it any wonder that he consigned his race to ruin by his rebellion when he perverted the whole order of nature in heaven and on earth. "All creatures," says Paul, "are groaning" [Rom. 8:22], "subject to corruption, not of their own will" [Rom. 8:20]. If the cause is sought, there is no doubt that they are bearing part of the punishment deserved by man, for whose use they were created. Since, therefore, the curse, which goes about through all the regions of the world, flowed hither and yon from Adam's guilt, it is not unreasonable if it is spread to all his offspring. Therefore, after the heavenly image was obliterated in him, he was not the only one to suffer this punishment – that, in place of wisdom, virtue, holiness, truth, and justice, with which adornments he had been clad, there came forth the most filthy plagues, blindness, impotence, impurity, vanity, and injustice – but he also entangled and immersed his offspring in the same miseries.

This is the inherited corruption, which the church fathers termed "original sin," meaning by the word "sin" the depravation of a nature previously good and pure . . .

Original sin does not rest upon imitation

We hear that the uncleanness of the parents is so transmitted to the children that all without any exception are defiled at their begetting. But we will not find the beginning of this pollution unless we go back to the first parent of all, as its source. We must surely hold that Adam was not only the progenitor but, as it were, the root of human nature; and that therefore in his corruption mankind deserved to be vitiated. This the apostle makes clear from a comparison of Adam with Christ. "As through one man sin came into the world and through sin death, which spread among all men when all sinned" [Rom. 5:12], thus through Christ's grace righteousness and life are restored to us [Rom. 5:17] . . .

Adam, by sinning, not only took upon himself misfortune and ruin but also plunged our nature into like destruction. This was not due to the guilt of himself alone, which would not pertain to us at all, but was because he infected all his posterity with that corruption into which he had fallen . . .

Adam so corrupted himself that infection spread from him to all his descendants. Christ himself, our heavenly judge, clearly enough proclaims that all men are born wicked and depraved when he says that "whatever is born of flesh is flesh" [John 3:6], and therefore the door of life is closed to all until they have been reborn [John 3:5].

The nature of original sin

Original sin seems to be a hereditary depravity and corruption of our nature, diffused into all parts of the soul, which first makes us liable to God's wrath, then also brings forth in us those works which Scripture calls "works of the flesh" [Gal. 5:19]. And that is properly what Paul often calls sin. The works that come forth from it – such as adulteries, fornications, thefts, hatreds, murders, carousings – he accordingly calls "fruits of sin" [Gal. 5:19–21], although they are also commonly called "sins" in Scripture, and even by Paul himself.

We must, therefore, distinctly note these two things. First, we are so vitiated and perverted in every part of our nature that by this great corruption we stand justly condemned and convicted before God, to whom nothing is acceptable but righteousness, innocence, and purity. And this is not liability for another's transgression. For, since it is said that we became subject to God's judgment through Adam's sin, we are to understand it not as if we, guiltless and undeserving, bore the guilt of his offense but in the sense that, since we through his transgression have become entangled in the curse, he is said to have made us guilty. Yet not only has punishment fallen upon us from Adam, but a contagion imparted by him resides in us, which justly deserves punishment. For this reason, Augustine, though he often calls sin "another's" to show more clearly that it is distributed among us through propagation, nevertheless declares at the same time that it is peculiar to each. And the apostle himself most eloquently testifies that "death has spread to all because all have sinned" [Rom. 5:12]. That is, they have been enveloped in original sin and defiled by its stains. For that reason, even infants themselves, while they carry their condemnation along with them from the mother's womb, are guilty not of another's fault but of their own. For, even though the fruits of their iniquity have not yet come forth, they have the seed enclosed within them. Indeed, their whole nature is a seed of sin; hence it can be only hateful and abhorrent to God. From this it follows that it is rightly considered sin in God's sight, for without guilt there would be no accusation.

Then comes the second consideration: that this perversity never ceases in us, but continually bears new fruits — the works of the flesh that we have already described — just as a burning furnace gives forth flame and sparks, or water ceaselessly bubbles up from a spring. Thus those who have defined original sin as "the lack of the original righteousness, which ought to reside in us," although they comprehend in this definition the whole meaning of the term, have still not expressed effectively enough its power and energy. For our nature is not only destitute and empty of good, but so fertile and fruitful of every evil that it cannot be idle. Those who have said that original sin is "concupiscence" have used an appropriate word, if only it be added — something that most will by no means concede — that whatever is in man, from the understanding to the will, from the soul even to the flesh, has been defiled and crammed with this concupiscence. Or, to put it more briefly, the whole man is of himself nothing but concupiscence.

Sin overturns the whole man

For this reason, I have said that all parts of the soul were possessed by sin after Adam deserted the fountain of righteousness. For not only did a lower appetite seduce him, but unspeakable impiety occupied the very citadel of his mind, and pride penetrated to the depths of his heart. Thus it is pointless and foolish to restrict the corruption that arises thence only to what are called the impulses of the senses; or to call it the "kindling wood" that attracts, arouses, and drags into sin only that part which they term "sensuality.". . . . [The] part in which the excellence and nobility of the soul especially shine has not only been wounded, but so corrupted that it needs to be healed and to put on a new nature as well. . . . [T]he whole man is overwhelmed — as by a deluge — from head to foot, so that no part is immune from sin and all that proceeds from him is to be imputed to sin. As Paul says, all turnings of the thoughts to the flesh are enmities against God [Rom. 8:7], and are therefore death [Rom. 8:6].

Sin is not our nature, but its derangement

Now away with those persons who dare write God's name upon their faults, because we declare that men are vicious by nature! They perversely search out God's handiwork in

121

their own pollution, when they ought rather to have sought it in that unimpaired and uncorrupted nature of Adam. Our destruction, therefore, comes from the guilt of our flesh, not from God, inasmuch as we have perished solely because we have degenerated from our original condition.

Let no one grumble here that God could have provided better for our salvation if he had forestalled Adam's fall. Pious minds ought to loathe this objection, because it manifests inordinate curiosity. Furthermore, the matter has to do with the secret of predestination, which will be discussed later in its proper place. Let us accordingly remember to impute our ruin to depravity of nature, in order that we may not accuse God himself, the Author of nature. True, this deadly wound clings to nature, but it is a very important question whether the wound has been inflicted from outside or has been present from the beginning. Yet it is evident that the wound was inflicted through sin. We have, therefore, no reason to complain except against ourselves. Scripture has diligently noted this fact. For Ecclesiastes says: "This I know, that God made man upright, but they have sought out many devices" [Ch. 7:29]. Obviously, man's ruin is to be ascribed to man alone; for he, having acquired righteousness by God's kindness, has by his own folly sunk into vanity.

"Natural" corruption of the "nature" created by God

Therefore we declare that man is corrupted through natural vitiation, but a vitiation that did not flow from nature. We deny that it has flowed from nature in order to indicate that it is an adventitious quality which comes upon man rather than a substantial property which has been implanted from the beginning. Yet we call it "natural" in order that no man may think that anyone obtains it through bad conduct, since it holds all men fast by hereditary right. Our usage of the term is not without authority. The apostle states: "We are all by nature children of wrath" [Eph. 2:3]. How could God, who is pleased by the least of his works, have been hostile to the noblest of all his creatures? But he is hostile toward the corruption of his work rather than toward the work itself. Therefore if it is right to declare that man, because of his vitiated nature, is naturally abominable to God, it is also proper to say that man is naturally depraved and faulty. Hence Augustine, in view of man's corrupted nature, is not afraid to call "natural" those sins which necessarily reign in our flesh wherever God's grace is absent. Thus vanishes the foolish trifling of the Manichees, who, when they imagined wickedness of substance in man, dared fashion another creator for him in order that they might not seem to assign the cause and beginning of evil to the righteous God.

17

JOHN MILTON

The voice of Satan

Paradise Lost

This first Book proposes, first in brief, the whole Subject, *Man's disobedience, and the loss thereupon of Paradise wherein he was plac't:* Then touches *the prime cause of his fall, the Serpent, or rather* Satan *in the Serpent; who revolting from God, and drawing to his side many Legions of Angels, was by the command of God driven out of Heaven with all his Crew into the great Deep.* Which action past over, the Poem hastes into the midst of things, presenting *Satan with his Angels now fallen into Hell,* describ'd here, *not in the Centre* (for Heaven and Earth may be suppos'd as yet not made, certainly not yet accurst) *but in a place of utter darkness, fitliest call'd* Chaos: Here Satan *with his Angels lying on the burning Lake, thunder-struck and astonisht, after a certain space recovers, as from confusion, calls up him who next in Order and Dignity lay by him; they confer of thir miserable fall.* Satan *awakens all his Legions, who lay till then in the same manner confounded; They rise, thir Numbers, array of Battle, thir chief Leaders nam'd, according to the Idols known afterwards in* Canaan *and the Countries adjoining. To these* Satan *directs his Speech, comforts them with hope yet of regaining Heaven, but tells them lastly of a new World and new kind of Creature to be created, according to an ancient Prophecy or report in Heaven;* for that Angels were long before this visible Creation, was the opinion of many ancient Fathers. *To find out the truth of this Prophecy, and what to determine thereon he refers to a full Council. What his Associates thence attempt.* Pandemonium *the Palace of* Satan *rises, suddenly built out of the Deep: The infernal Peers there sit in Council.*

Of Man's First Disobedience, and the Fruit
Of that Forbidden Tree, whose mortal taste
Brought Death into the World, and all our woe,
With loss of *Eden*, till one greater Man
Restore us, and regain the blissful Seat,
Sing Heav'nly Muse, that on the secret top

Source: *Complete Poems and Major Prose: Book 1*, Indianapolis, Ind.: Bobbs–Merrill Company Inc., 1975.

Of *Oreb*, or of *Sinai*, didst inspire
That Shepherd, who first taught the chosen Seed,
In the Beginning how the Heav'ns and Earth
Rose out of *Chaos*: Or if *Sion* Hill
Delight thee more, and *Siloa's* Brook that flow'd
Fast by the Oracle of God; I thence
Invoke thy aid to my advent'rous Song,
[W]ith speedy works th' Arch-fiend [thus] repli'd.
. . . [T]o be weak is miserable
Doing or Suffering: but of this be sure,
To do aught good never will be our task,
But ever to do ill our sole delight,
As being the contrary to his high will
Whom we resist. If then his Providence
Out of our evil seek to bring forth good,
Our labor must be to pervert that end,
And out of good still to find means of evil;
Which oft-times may succeed, so as perhaps
Shall grieve him, if I fail not, and disturb
His inmost counsels from thir destin'd aim.
But see the angry Victor hath recall'd
His Ministers of vengeance and pursuit
Back to the Gates of Heav'n: the Sulphurous Hail
Shot after us in storm, o'erblown hath laid
The fiery Surge, that from the Precipice
Of Heav'n receiv'd us falling, and the Thunder,
Wing'd with red Lightning and impetuous rage,
Perhaps hath spent his shafts, and ceases now
To bellow through the vast and boundless Deep.
Let us not slip th' occasion, whether scorn,
Or satiate fury yield it from our Foe.
Seest thou yon dreary Plain, forlorn and wild,
The seat of desolation, void of light,
Save what the glimmering of these livid flames
Casts pale and dreadful? Thither let us tend
From off the tossing of these fiery waves,
There rest, if any rest can harbor there,
And reassembling our afflicted Powers,
Consult how we may henceforth most offend
Our Enemy, our own loss how repair,

How overcome this dire Calamity,
What reinforcement we may gain from Hope,
If not what resolution from despair.
　　Is this the Region, this the Soil, the Clime,
Said then the lost Arch-Angel, this the seat
That we must change for Heav'n, this mournful gloom
For that celestial light? Be it so, since he
Who now is Sovran can dispose and bid
What shall be right: fardest from him is best
Whom reason hath equall'd, force hath made supreme
Above his equals. Farewell happy fields
Where Joy for ever dwells: Hail horrors, hail
Infernal world, and thou profoundest Hell
Receive thy new Possessor: One who brings
A mind not to be chang'd by Place or Time.
The mind is its own place, and in itself
Can make a Heav'n of Hell, a Hell of Heav'n.
What matter where, if I be still the same,
And what I should be, all but less than hee
Whom Thunder hath made greater? Here at least
We shall be free; th' Almighty hath not built
Here for his envy, will not drive us hence:
Here we may reign secure, and in my choice
To reign is worth ambition though in Hell:
Better to reign in Hell, than serve in Heav'n.
But wherefore let we then our faithful friends,
Th' associates and copartners of our loss
Lie thus astonisht on th' oblivious Pool,
And call them not to share with us their part
In this unhappy Mansion: or once more
With rallied Arms to try what may be yet
Regain'd in Heav'n, or what more lost in Hell?

18

JONATHAN
EDWARDS

Sinners in the hand of an angry God

The evidence of original sin from what appears in fact of the sinfulness of mankind

All mankind do constantly in all ages, without fail in any one instance, run into that moral evil, which is in effect their own utter and eternal perdition, in a total privation of God's favor and suffering of his vengeance and wrath

By original sin, as the phrase has been most commonly used by divines, is meant the *innate sinful depravity of the heart*. But yet when the doctrine of original sin is spoken of, it is vulgarly understood in that latitude, as to include not only the depravity of nature, but the *imputation* of Adam's first sin; or in other words, the liableness or exposedness of Adam's posterity, in the divine judgment, to partake of the punishment of that sin. So far as I know, most of those who have held one of these, have maintained the other; and most of those who have opposed one, have opposed the other. Both are opposed by the author chiefly attended to in the following discourse, in his book against original sin. And it may perhaps appear in our future consideration of the subject, that they are closely connected, and that the arguments which prove the one establish the other, and that there are no more difficulties attending the allowing of one than the other.

I shall in the first place consider this doctrine more especially with regard to the corruption of nature; and as we treat of this, the other will naturally come into consideration in the prosecution of the discourse, as connected with it.

As all moral qualities, all principles, either of virtue of vice, lie in the disposition of the heart, I shall consider whether we have any evidence, that the heart of man is naturally of a corrupt and evil disposition. This is strenuously denied by many late writers, who are enemies to the doctrine of original sin . . .

Source: *Original Sin*, New Haven, Conn.: Yale University Press, 1970.

126

The way we come by the idea of any such thing as disposition or tendency, is by observing what is constant or general in event; especially under a great variety of circumstances; and above all, when the effect or event continues the same through great and various opposition, much and manifold force and means used to the contrary not prevailing to hinder the effect. I don't know that such a prevalence of effects is denied to be an evidence of prevailing tendency in causes and agents; or that it is expressly denied by the opposers of the doctrine of original sin, that if, in the course of events, it universally or generally proves that mankind are actually corrupt, this would be an evidence of a prior corrupt propensity in the world of mankind; whatever may be said by some, which, if taken with its plain consequences, may seem to imply a denial of this; which may be considered afterwards . . .

That is to be looked upon as the true tendency of the natural or innate disposition of man's heart, which appears to be its tendency when we consider things as they are in themselves, or in their own nature, without the *interposition of divine grace*. Thus, the state of man's nature, that disposition of the mind, is to be looked upon as evil and pernicious, which, as it is in itself, tends to extremely pernicious consequences, and would certainly end therein, were it not that the free mercy and kindness of God interposes to prevent that issue. It would be very strange, if any should argue that there is no evil tendency in the case, because the mere favor and compassion of the Most High may step in and oppose the tendency, and prevent the sad effect tended to. Particularly, if there by anything in the nature of man, whereby he has an universal, unfailing tendency to that moral evil, which according to the real nature and true demerit of things, as they are in themselves, implies his utter ruin, that must be looked upon as an evil tendency or propensity; however divine grace may interpose, to save him from deserved ruin, and to overrule things to an issue contrary to that which they tend to of themselves. Grace is a sovereign thing, exercised according to the good pleasure of God, bringing good out of evil; the effect of it belongs not to the nature of things themselves, that otherwise have an ill tendency, any more than the remedy belongs to the disease; but is something altogether independent on it, introduced to oppose the natural tendency, and reverse the course of things. . . . Nothing is more precisely according to the truth of things, than divine justice; it weighs things in an even balance; it views and estimates things no otherwise than they are truly in their own nature. Therefore undoubtedly that which implies a tendency to ruin according to the estimate of divine justice, does indeed imply such a tendency in its own nature.

And then it must be remembered, that it is a *moral depravity* we are speaking of; and therefore when we are considering whether such depravity don't appear by a tendency to a bad effect or issue, 'tis a *moral tendency* to such an issue, that is what is to be taken into the account. A moral tendency or influence is by desert. Then it may be said, man's nature or state is attended with a pernicious or destructive tendency, in a moral sense, when it tends to that which deserves misery and destruction. And therefore it equally shews the moral depravity of the nature of mankind in their present state, whether that nature be universally attended with an effectual tendency to destructive vengeance actually executed, or to their deserving misery and ruin, or their just exposedness to destruction, however that fatal consequence may be prevented by grace, or whatever the actual event be.

One thing more is to be observed here, viz. that the topic mainly insisted on by the opposers of the doctrine of original sin, is the justice of God; both in their objections against the imputation of Adam's sin, and also against its being so ordered that men should come into the world with a corrupt and ruined nature, without having merited the displeasure of their Creator by any personal fault. But the latter is not repugnant to God's justice, if men can be, and actually are, born into the world with a tendency to sin, and to misery and ruin for their sin, which actually will be the consequence, unless *mere grace* steps in and prevents it. If this be allowed, the argument from *justice* is given up; for it is to suppose that their liableness to misery and ruin comes in a way of justice; otherwise there would be no need of the interposition of divine grace to save 'em. Justice alone would be sufficient security, if exercised, without grace. 'Tis all one in this dispute about what is just and righteous, whether men are born in a miserable state, by a tendency to ruin, which actually follows, and that justly; or whether they are born in such a state as tends to a desert of ruin, which might justly follow, and would actually follow, did not grace prevent. For the controversy is not, what grace will do, but what justice might do . . .

[D]ivine grace [does] not [alter] the nature of things, as they are in themselves; and accordingly, when I speak of such and such an evil tendency of things, belonging to the present nature and state of mankind, understand me to mean their tendency *as they are in themselves*, abstracted from any consideration of that remedy the sovereign and infinite grace of God has provided.

Having premised these things, I now proceed to say, that mankind are all naturally in such a state, as is attended, without fail, with this consequence or issue; that they universally run themselves into that which is, in effect, their own utter eternal perdition, as being finally accursed of God, and the subjects of his remedy-less wrath, through sin.

From which I infer, that the natural state of the mind of man is attended with a propensity of nature, which is prevalent and effectual, to such in issue; and that therefore their nature is corrupt and depraved with a moral depravity, that amounts to and implies their utter undoing . . .

That propensity which has been proved to be in the nature of all mankind, must be a very evil, depraved and pernicious propensity; making it manifest that the soul of man, as it is by nature, is in a corrupt, fallen and ruined state: which is the other part of the consequence, drawn from the proposition {already} laid down

The question to be considered, in order to determine whether man's nature is not depraved and ruined, is not whether he is not inclined to perform as many *good deeds* as *bad ones*, but, which of these two he preponderates to, in the frame of his heart, and state of his nature, a state of innocence and righteousness, and favor with God; or a state of sin, guiltiness and abhorrence in the sight of God. Persevering sinless righteousness, or else the guilt of sin, is the alternative, on the decision of which depends (as is confessed) according to the nature and truth of things, as they are in themselves, and according to the rule of right and perfect justice, man's being approved and accepted of his Maker, and eternally blessed as good; or his being rejected, thrown away and cursed as bad. And therefore the determination of the tendency of man's heart and nature with respect to these terms, is that which is to be looked at, in order to determine whether his nature is good or evil, pure or corrupt, sound or ruined. If such be man's nature, and state of his heart, that he has an infallibly effectual propensity to the latter of those terms; then it is wholly impertinent, to talk of the innocent and kind actions, even of criminals themselves, surpassing their crimes in numbers; and of the prevailing innocence, good nature, industry, felicity and cheerfulness of the greater part of mankind. Let never so many thousands, of millions of acts of honesty, good nature, etc. be supposed; yet, by the supposition, there is an unfailing propensity to such moral evil, as in its dreadful consequences infinitely outweighs all effects or consequences of any supposed good. Surely that tendency, which, in effect, is an infallible tendency to eternal destruction, is an infinitely dreadful and pernicious tendency: and that nature and frame of mind, which implies such a tendency, must be an infinitely dreadful and pernicious frame of mind. It would be much more absurd, to suppose that such a state of nature is good, or not bad, under a notion of men's doing more honest and kind things, than evil ones; than to say, the state of that ship is good, to cross the Atlantick Ocean in, that is such as cannot hold together through the voyage, but will infallibly founder and sink by the way; under a notion that it may probably go great part of the way before it sinks, or that it will proceed and sail above water more hours than it will be sinking: or to pronounce that road a good road to go to such a place, the greater part of which is plain and safe, though some parts of it are dangerous, and certainly fatal to them that travel in it; or to call that a good propensity, which is an inflexible inclination to travel in such a way.

A propensity to that sin which brings God's eternal wrath and curse (which has been proved to belong to the nature of man) is not evil, only as it is calamitous and sorrowful, ending in great *natural evil*; but it is *odious* too, and *detestable*; as, by the supposition, it tends to that *moral evil*, by which the subject becomes odious in the sight of God, and liable, as such, to be condemned, and utterly rejected and cursed by him. This also makes it evident, that the state which it has been proved mankind are in, is a corrupt state in a moral sense, that it is inconsistent with the fulfillment of the law of God, which is the rule of moral rectitude and goodness. That tendency, which is opposite to that which the moral law requires and insists upon, and prone to that which the moral law utterly forbids, and eternally condemns the subject for, is doubtless a corrupt tendency, in a moral sense.

So that this depravity is both odious, and also pernicious, fatal and destructive, in the highest sense, as inevitably tending to that which implies man's eternal ruin; it shews, that man, as he is by nature, is in a deplorable and undone state, in the highest sense. And this proves that men don't come into the world perfectly innocent in the sight of God, and without any just exposedness to his displeasure. For the being by nature in a lost and ruined state, in the highest sense, is not consistent with being by nature in a state of favor with God.

But if any should still insist on a notion of men's good deeds exceeding their bad ones, and that seeing the good that is in men more than countervails the evil, they can't be properly denominated evil; all persons and things being most properly denominated from that which prevails, and has the ascendent in them: I would say further, that I presume it will be allowed, that if there is in man's nature a tendency to guilt and ill-desert, in a vast over-balance to virtue and merit; or a propensity to that sin, the evil and demerit of which is so great, that the value and merit that is in him, or in all the virtuous acts that ever he performs, are as nothing to it; then truly the nature of man may be said to be corrupt and evil.

That this is the true case, may be demonstrated by what is evident of the infinite heinousness of sin against God, from the nature of things. The heinousness of this must rise in some proportion to the obligation we are under to regard the Divine Being; and that must be in some proportion to his worthiness of regard; which doubtless is infinitely beyond the worthiness of any of our fellow creatures. But the merit of our respect or obedience to God is not infinite. The merit of respect to any being don't increase, but is rather diminished in proportion to the obligations we are under in strict justice to pay him that respect. There is no great merit in paying a debt we owe, and by the highest possible obligations in strict justice are obliged to pay; but there is great demerit in refusing to pay it. That on such accounts as these there is an infinite demerit in all sin against God, which must therefore immensely outweigh all the merit which can be supposed to be in our virtue, I think, is capable of full demonstration; and that the futility of the objections, which some have made against the argument, might most plainly be demonstrated. But I shall omit a particular consideration of the evidence of this matter from the nature of things, as I study brevity, and lest any should cry out, "Metaphysicks!" as the manner of some is, when any argument is handled, against any tenet they are fond of, with a close and exact consideration of the nature of things. And this is not so necessary in the present case, inasmuch as the point asserted, namely, that he who commits any one sin, has guilt and ill-desert which is so great, that the value and merit of all the good which it is possible he should do in his whole life, is as nothing to it; I say, this point is not only evident by metaphysics, but is plainly demonstrated by what has been shewn to be *fact*, with respect to God's own constitutions and dispensations towards mankind: as particularly by this, that whatever acts of virtue and obedience a man performs, yet if he trespasses in one point, is guilty of any the least sin, he, according to the law of God, and so according to the exact truth of things and the proper demerit of sin, is exposed to be wholly cast out of favor with God, and subjected to his curse, to be utterly and eternally destroyed. . . . [H]ow can it be agreeable to the nature of things, and exactly consonant to everlasting truth and righteousness, thus to deal with a creature for the least sinful act, though he should perform ever so many thousands of honest and virtuous acts, to countervail the evil of that sin? Or how can it be agreeable to the exact truth and real demerit of things, thus wholly to cast off the deficient creature, without any regard to the merit of all his good deeds, unless that be in truth the case, that the value and merit of all those good actions bear no proportion to the heinousness of the least sin? If it were not so, one would think, that however the offending person might have some proper punishment, yet seeing there is so much virtue to lay in the balance against the guilt, it would be agreeable to the nature of things, that he should find some favor, and not be altogether rejected, and made the subject of perfect and eternal destruction; and thus no account at all be made of all his virtue, so much as to procure him the least relief or hope. How can such a constitution represent sin in its proper colors and according to its true nature and desert . . . unless this be its true nature, that it is so bad, that even in the least instance it perfectly swallows up all the value of the sinner's supposed good deeds, let 'em be ever so many? So that this matter is not left to our metaphysics or philosophy; the great Lawgiver and infallible Judge of the universe has clearly decided it, in the revelation he has made of what is agreeable to exact truth, justice and the nature of things, in his revealed law or rule of righteousness.

He that in any respect or degree is a transgressor of God's law, is a wicked man, yea, wholly wicked in the eye of the law; all his goodness being esteemed nothing, having no account made of it, when taken together with his wickedness. And therefore, without any regard to his righteousness, he is, by the sentence of the law, and so by the voice of truth and justice to be treated as worthy to be rejected, abhorred and cursed forever; and must be so, unless grace interposes, to cover his transgression. But men are really, in themselves, what they are in the eye of the law, and by the voice of strict equity and justice; however they may be looked upon, and treated by infinite and unmerited mercy.

So that, on the whole, it appears, all mankind have an infallibly effectual propensity to that moral evil, which infinitely outweighs the value of all the good that can be in them; and have such a disposition of heart, that the certain consequence of it is, their being, in the eye of perfect truth and righteousness, wicked men. And I leave all to judge, whether such a disposition be not in the eye of truth a depraved disposition.

Agreeable to these things, the Scripture represents all mankind, not only as having guilt, but immense guilt, which they can have no merit or worthiness to countervail. Such is the representation we have in Matt. 18:21, to the end. There, on Peter's inquiring how often his brother should trespass against him and he forgive him, whether until seven times? Christ replies, "I say not unto thee, until seven times, but until seventy times seven'; apparently meaning, that he should esteem no number of offenses too many, and no degree of injury it is possible our neighbor should be guilty of towards us, too great to be forgiven. For which this reason is given in the parable there following, that if ever we obtain forgiveness and favor with God, he must pardon that guilt and injury towards his majesty, which is immensely greater than the greatest injuries that ever men are guilty of, one towards another, yea, than the sum of all their injuries put together; let 'em be ever so many, and ever so great: so that the latter would be put as an hundred pence to ten thousand talents: which immense debt we owe to God, and have nothing to pay; which implies that we have no merit, to countervail any part of our guilt. And this must be because, if all that may be called virtue in us, be compared with our ill-desert, it is in the sight of God as nothing to it. The parable is not to represent *Peter's* case in particular, but that of all who then were, or ever should be Christ's disciples. It appears by the conclusion of the discourse; "*So likewise shall my heavenly Father do . . .* if ye, from your hearts, forgive not every one his brother their trespasses."

Therefore how absurd must it be for Christians to object, against the depravity of man's nature, a greater number of innocent and kind actions, than of crimes; and to talk of a prevailing innocency, good nature, industry, and cheerfulness of the greater part of mankind? Infinitely more absurd, than it would be to insist, that the domestic of a prince was not a bad servant, because though sometimes he contemned and affronted his master to a great degree, yet he did not spit in his master's face so often as he performed acts of service; or, than it would be to affirm, that his spouse was a good wife to him, because, although she committed adultery, and that with the slaves and scoundrels sometimes, yet she did not do this so often as she did the duties of a wife. These notions would be absurd, because the crimes are too heinous to be atoned for, by many honest actions of the servant or spouse of the prince; there being a vast disproportion between the merit of the one, and the ill-desert of the other: but in no measure so great, nay infinitely less than that between the demerit of our offenses against God and the value of our acts of obedience . . .

Part 4

THE CRUEL FACE OF JUSTICE

JUSTICE

King Zaleucus had made a very severe law. His son having broken it,
he commanded that one of his own eyes and one of his son's be gouged out.
This is to be attributed to his love of justice.

JUSTICE

Zaleucus lets no lawless act go by;
He and his erring son each lose an eye.

Cesare Ripa: "Justicia."

Although theologians and philosophers continued to debate the problem of evil in the fifteenth and sixteenth centuries, the problem also took new, secular, forms. Might a prince sometimes have a civic obligation to perform actions that he himself also regards as vicious? Are men by nature either just or unjust, virtuous or vicious, or do these terms only have meaning and force within a legal or social contextual frame?

Machiavelli (1469–1527) replaces a focus on salvation with one on statecraft, and replaces the language of redemption and sin with that of virtue and vice. Moralist that he is, he retains the distinction between virtue and vice; realist as he proclaims himself to be, he argues that the successful prince – the prince who brings security and glory to his city – must be able to have what the world calls *vices*. He must be animal and man, a fox and a lion, able to gauge exactly when and how to be cruel without risking being hated, to be thought generous without wasting resources, to break promises without being thought unjust, to be devious while being thought straightforward. A sense of timing, the ability to control appearances are essential to secure and to maintain authority. Certainly a vicious despot must also have these traits to be successful in his tyranny, but Machiavelli is describing the directed and controlled use of selected vices as necessary but certainly not sufficient for a prince worthy of respect and admiration.

Hobbes (1588–1679) conducts a thought experiment to gauge human nature in its natural, pre-social, condition. As he sees it, man is endowed with certain capacities and powers, with strength, imagination, cunning and foresight; but he is neither naturally virtuous nor vicious, neither sociable nor destructive. Because the goods that sustain life are scarce and because men are roughly equal in ability, they suffer an insatiable need for "power after power." Insecurity places men in a war of each against all in competition for a marginal advantage. It is, finally, rationality (foresight, the capacity to calculate benefits and risks, the ability to use signs and language) and the passions (the fear of death and the desire for security) that prompt men to move towards safety and security. Recognizing that only an absolute Power can secure peace and keep them from mutual destruction, men willingly resign their natural right to violent self-protection to "a common Power to keep them all in awe . . . Where there is no common power, there is no law; where no law, no justice and injustice." The distinctions between right and wrong, justice and injustice, obedience and disobedience come into being with the existence of the Sovereign state.

Even when they were directed against other men, the seven deadly sins described by medieval Christians were treated as offenses against God. With Samuel Butler (1612–1680), they become forms of social depravity, detestable, somewhat laughable. A corrupt judge is an avaricious thief, a debauched man is a glutton and a lecher, the malicious knave man is hateful and false. Social corruption is the subject of satire rather than eternal damnation; it brings its own retribution: illness, contempt, ostracism.

19

NICCOLÒ MACHIAVELLI

A prince's virtue: timely ruthlessness

About those factors that cause men, and especially rulers, to be praised or censured

Our next task is to consider the policies and principles a ruler ought to follow in dealing with his subjects or with his friends. Since I know many people have written on this subject, I am concerned it may be thought presumptuous for me to write on it as well, especially since what I have to say, as regards this question in particular, will differ greatly from the recommendations of others. But my hope is to write a book that will be useful, at least to those who read it intelligently, and so I thought it sensible to go straight to a discussion of how things are in real life and not waste time with a discussion of an imaginary world. For many authors have constructed imaginary republics and principalities that have never existed in practice and never could; for the gap between how people actually behave and how they ought to behave is so great that anyone who ignores everyday reality in order to live up to an ideal will soon discover he has been taught how to destroy himself, not how to preserve himself. For anyone who wants to act the part of a good man in all circumstances will bring about his own ruin, for those he has to deal with will not all be good. So it is necessary for a ruler, if he wants to hold on to power, to learn how not to be good, and to know when it is and when it is not necessary to use this knowledge.

Let us leave to one side, then, all discussion of imaginary rulers and talk about practical realities. I maintain that all men, when people talk about them, and especially rulers, because they hold positions of authority, are described in terms of qualities that are inextricably linked to censure or to praise. So one man is described as generous, another as a miser [*misero*] (to use the Tuscan term; for "avaricious," in our language, is used of someone who has a rapacious desire to acquire wealth, while we call someone a "miser"

Source: *The Prince*, ch. 15–18, translated by David Wootton, Indianapolis, Ind.: Hackett Publishing Company Inc., 1995.

when he is unduly reluctant to spend the money he has); one is called open-handed, another tight-fisted; one man is cruel, another gentle; one untrustworthy, another reliable; one effeminate and cowardly, another bold and violent; one sympathetic, another self-important; one promiscuous, another monogamous; one straightforward, another duplicitous; one tough, another easy-going; one serious, another cheerful; one religious, another atheistical; and so on. Now I know everyone will agree that if a ruler could have all the good qualities I have listed and none of the bad ones, then this would be an excellent state of affairs. But one cannot have all the good qualities, nor always act in a praiseworthy fashion, for we do not live in an ideal world. You have to be astute enough to avoid being thought to have those evil qualities that would make it impossible for you to retain power; as for those that are compatible with holding on to power, you should avoid them if you can; but if you cannot, then you should not worry too much if people say you have them. Above all, do not be upset if you are supposed to have those vices a ruler needs if he is going to stay securely in power, for, if you think about it, you will realize there are some ways of behaving that are supposed to be virtuous [*che parrà virtù*], but would lead to your downfall, and others that are supposed to be wicked, but will lead to your welfare and peace of mind.

On generosity and parsimony

Let me begin, then, with the qualities I mentioned first. I argue it would be good to be thought generous; nevertheless, if you act in the way that will get you a reputation for generosity, you will do yourself damage. For generosity used skillfully [*virtuosamente*] and practiced as it ought to be, is hidden from sight, and being truly generous will not protect you from acquiring a reputation for parsimony. So, if you want to have a reputation for generosity, you must throw yourself into lavish and ostentatious expenditure. Consequently, a ruler who pursues a reputation for generosity will always end up wasting all his resources; and he will be obliged in the end, if he wants to preserve his reputation, to impose crushing taxes upon the people, to pursue every possible source of income, and to be preoccupied with maximizing his revenues. This will begin to make him hateful to his subjects, and will ensure no one thinks well of him, for no one admires poverty. The result is his supposed generosity will have caused him to offend the vast majority and to have won favor with few. Anything that goes wrong will destabilize him, and the slightest danger will imperil him. Recognizing the problem, and trying to economize, he will quickly find he has acquired a reputation as a miser.

So we see a ruler cannot seek to benefit from a reputation as generous [*questa virtù del liberale*] without harming himself. Recognizing this, he ought, if he is wise, not to mind being called miserly. For, as time goes by, he will be thought of as growing ever more generous, for people will recognize that as a result of his parsomony he is able to live on his income, maintain an adequate army, and undertake new initiatives without imposing new taxes. The result is he will be thought to be generous towards all those whose income he does not tax, which is almost everybody, and stingy towards those who miss out on handouts, who are only a few. In modern times nobody has succeeded on a large scale except those who have been thought miserly; the others came to nothing. Pope Julius II took advantage of a reputation for generosity in order to win election, but once elected he made no effort to keep his reputation, for he wanted to go to war. The present King of France has fought many wars without having to impose additional taxes on his people, because his occasional additional expenditures are offset by his long-term parsimony. The present King of Spain could not have aspired to, or achieved, so many conquests if he had had a reputation for generosity.

So a ruler should not care about being thought miserly, for it means he will be able to avoid robbing his subjects; he will be able to defend himself; he will not become poor and despicable, and he will not be forced to become rapacious. This is one of those vices that make successful government possible. And if you say: But Caesar rose to power thanks to his generosity, and many others have made their way to the highest positions of authority because they have both been and have been thought to be generous. I reply, either you are already a ruler, or you are on your way to becoming one. If you are already a ruler, generosity is a mistake; if you are trying to become one then you do, indeed, need to be thought of as generous. Caesar was one of those competing to become the ruler of Rome; but if, having acquired power, he had lived longer and had not learned to reduce his expenditures, he would have destroyed his own position. You may be tempted to reply: Many established rulers who have been thought to be immensely generous have been successful in war. But my answer is: Rulers either spend their own wealth and that of their subjects, or that of other people. Those who spend their own and their subjects' wealth should be abstemious; those who spend the wealth of others should seize every opportunity to be generous. Rulers who march with their armies, living off plunder, pillage, and confiscations are spending other people's money, and it is essential they should seem generous, for otherwise their soldiers will not follow them. With goods that belong neither to you nor to your subjects, you can afford to be generous, as Cyrus, Caesar, and Alexander were. Squandering other people's money does not do your reputation any harm, quite the reverse. The problem is with squandering your own. There is nothing so self-defeating as generosity, for the more generous you are, the less you are able to be generous. Generosity leads to poverty and disgrace, or, if you try to escape that, to rapacity and hostility. Among all the things a ruler should try to avoid, he must avoid above all being hated and despised. Generosity leads to your being both. So it is wiser to accept a reputation as miserly, which people despise but do not hate, than to aspire to a reputation as generous, and as a consequence, be obliged to face criticism for rapacity, which people both despise and hate.

About cruelty and compassion; and about whether it is better to be loved than feared, or the reverse

Going further down our list of qualities, I recognize every ruler should want to be thought of as compassionate and not cruel. Nevertheless, I have to warn you to be careful about being compassionate. . . . [A] ruler ought not to mind the disgrace of being called cruel, if he keeps his subjects peaceful and law-abiding, for it is more compassionate to impose harsh punishments on a few than, out of excessive compassion, to allow disorder to spread, which leads to murders or looting. The whole community suffers if there are riots, while to maintain order the ruler only has to execute one or two individuals. Of all rulers, he who is new to power cannot escape a reputation for cruelty, for he is surrounded by dangers. Virgil [*Aeneid* I, 563–4] has Dido say:

Harsh necessity, and the fact my kingdom is new, oblige me to do
  these things,
And to mass my armies on the frontiers.

Nevertheless, you should be careful how you assess the situation and should think twice before you act. Do not be afraid of your own shadow. Employ policies that are moderated by prudence and sympathy. Avoid excessive self-confidence, which leads to carelessness, and avoid excessive timidity, which will make you insupportable.

This leads us to a question that is in dispute: Is it better to be loved than feared, or vice versa? My reply is one ought to be both loved and feared; but, since it is difficult to accomplish both at the same time, I maintain it is much safer to be feared than loved, if you have to do without one of the two. For of men one can, in general, say this: They are ungrateful, fickle, deceptive and deceiving, avoiders of danger, eager to gain. As long as you serve their interests, they are devoted to you. They promise you their blood, so long as you seem to have no need of them. But as soon as you need help, they turn against you. Any ruler who relies simply on their promises and makes no other preparations, will be destroyed. For you will find that those whose support you buy, who do not rally to you because they admire your strength of character and nobility of soul, these are people you pay for, but they are never yours, and in the end you cannot get the benefit of your investment. Men are less nervous of offending someone who makes himself lovable, than someone who makes himself frightening. For love attaches men by ties of obligation, which, since men are wicked, they break whenever their interests are at stake. But fear restrains men because they are afraid of punishment, and this fear never leaves them. Still, a ruler should make himself feared in such a way that, if he does not inspire love, at least he does not provoke hatred. For it is perfectly possible to be feared and not hated. You will only be hated if you seize the property or the women of your subjects and citizens. Whenever you have to kill someone, make sure you have a suitable excuse and an obvious reason; but, above all else, keep your hands off other people's property;

for men are quicker to forget the death of their father than the loss of their inheritance. Moreover, there are always reasons why you might want to seize people's property; and he who begins to live by plundering others will always find an excuse for seizing other people's possessions; but there are fewer reasons for killing people, and one killing need not lead to another.

When a ruler is at the head of his army and has a vast number of soldiers under his command, then it is absolutely essential to be prepared to be thought cruel; for it is absolutely impossible to keep an army united and ready for action without acquiring a reputation for cruelty. Among the extraordinary accomplishments of Hannibal, we may note one in particular: He commanded a vast army, made up of men of many different nations, who were fighting far from home, yet they never mutinied and they never fell out with one another, either when things were going badly, or when things were going well. The only possible explanation for this is that he was known to be harsh and cruel. This, together with his numerous virtues [*virtù*], meant his soldiers always regarded him with admiration and fear. Without cruelty, his other virtues [*virtù*] would not have done the job . . .

I conclude, then, that, as far as being feared and loved is concerned, since men decide for themselves whom they love, and rulers decide whom they fear, a wise ruler should rely on the emotion he can control, not on the one he cannot. But he must take care to avoid being hated, as I have said.

How far rulers are to keep their word

Everybody recognizes how praiseworthy it is for a ruler to keep his word and to live a life of integrity, without relying on craftiness. Nevertheless, we see that in practice, in these days, those rulers who have not thought it important to keep their word have achieved great things, and have known how to employ cunning to confuse and disorientate other men. In the end, they have been able to overcome those who have placed store in integrity.

You should therefore know there are two ways to fight: one while respecting the rules, the other with no holds barred. Men alone fight in the first fashion, and animals fight in the second. But because you cannot always win if you respect the rules, you must be prepared to break them. A ruler, in particular, needs to know how to be both an animal and a man. The classical writers, without saying it explicitly, taught rulers to behave like this. They described how Achilles, and many other rulers in ancient times, were given to Chiron the centaur to be raised, so he could bring them up as he thought best. What they intended to convey, with this story of rulers being educated by someone who was half beast and half man, was that it is necessary for a ruler to know when to act like an animal and when like a man; and if he relies on just one or the other mode of behavior he cannot hope to survive.

Since a ruler, then, needs to know how to make good use of beastly qualities, he should take as his models among the animals both the fox and the lion, for the lion does not know how to avoid traps, and the fox is easily empowered by wolves. So you must be a fox when it comes to suspecting a trap, and a lion when it comes to making the wolves turn tail. Those who simply act like a lion all the time do not understand their business. So you see a wise ruler cannot, and should not, keep his word when doing so is to his disadvantage, and when the reasons that led him to promise to do so no longer apply. Of course, if all men were good, this advice would be bad; but since men are wicked and will not keep faith with you, you need not keep faith with them. Nor is a ruler ever short of legitimate reasons to justify breaking his word. I could give an infinite number of contemporary examples to support my argument and to show how treaties and promises have been rendered null and void by the dishonesty of rulers; and he who has known best how to act the fox has come out of it the best. But it is essential to know how to conceal how crafty one is, to know how to be a clever counterfeit and hypocrite. You will find people are so simple-minded and so preoccupied with their immediate concerns, that if you set out to deceive them, you will always find plenty of them who will let themselves be deceived . . .

So a ruler need not have all the positive qualities I listed earlier, but he must seem to have them. Indeed, I would go so far as to say that if you have them and never make any exceptions, then you will suffer for it; while if you merely appear to have them, they will benefit you. So you should seem to be compassionate, trustworthy, sympathetic, honest, religious, and, indeed, be all these things; but at the same time you should be constantly prepared, so that, if these become liabilities, you are trained and ready to become their opposites. You need to understand this: a ruler, and particularly a ruler who is new to power, cannot conform to all those rules that men who are thought good are expected to respect, for he is often obliged, in order to hold on to power, to break his word, to be uncharitable, inhumane, and irreligious. So he must be mentally prepared to act as circumstances and changes in fortune require. As I have said, he should do what is right if he can; but he must be prepared to do wrong if necessary.

A ruler must, therefore, take great care that he never carelessly says anything that is not imbued with the five qualities I listed above. He must seem, to those who listen to him and watch him, entirely pious, truthful, reliable, sympathetic, and religious. There is no quality that it is more important he should seem to have than this last one. In general, men judge more by sight than by touch. Everyone sees what is happening, but not everyone feels the consequences. Everyone sees what you seem to be; few have direct experience of who you really are. Those few will not dare speak out in the face of public opinion when that opinion is reinforced by the authority of the state. In the behavior of all men, and particularly of rulers, against whom there is no recourse at law, people judge by the outcome. So if a ruler wins wars and holds on to power, the means he has employed will always be judged honorable, and everyone will praise them. The common man accepts external appearances and judges by the outcome; and when it comes down to it only the masses count; for the elite are powerless if the masses have someone to provide them with leadership . . .

How one should avoid hatred and contempt

Because I have spoken of the more important of the qualities I mentioned earlier, I want now to discuss the rest of them briefly under this general heading, that a ruler must take care (I have already referred to this in passing) to avoid those things that will make him an object of hatred or contempt. As long as he avoids these he will have done what is required of him, and he will find having a reputation for any of the other vices will do him no harm at all. You become hateful, above all, as I have said, if you prey on the possessions and the women of your subjects. You should leave both alone. The vast majority of men, so long as their goods and their honor are not taken from them, will live contentedly, so you will only have to contend with the small minority who are ambitious, and there are lots of straightforward ways of keeping them under control. You become contemptible if you are thought to be erratic, capricious, effeminate, pusillanimous, irresolute. You should avoid acquiring such a reputation as a pilot steers clear of the rocks. Make every effort to ensure your actions suggest greatness and endurance, strength of character and of purpose. When it comes to the private business of your subjects, you should aim to ensure you never have to change your decisions once they have been taken, and that you acquire a reputation that will discourage people from even considering tricking or deceiving you.

A ruler who is thought of in these terms has the sort of reputation he needs; and it is difficult to conspire against someone who is respected in this way, difficult to attack him, because people realize he is on top of his job and has the loyalty of his employees. For rulers ought to be afraid of two things: Within the state, they should fear their subjects; abroad, they should fear other rulers. Against foreign powers, a good army and reliable allies are the only defense; and, if you have a good army, you will always find your allies reliable. And you will find it easy to maintain order at home if you are secure from external threats, provided, that is, conspiracies against you have not undermined your authority. Even if foreign powers do attack, if you have followed my advice and lived according to the principles I have outlined, then, as long as you keep a grip on yourself, you will be able to resist any attack. . . . But where your subjects are concerned, when you are not being attacked by foreign powers, you have to be wary of secret conspiracies. The best protection against these is to ensure you are not hated or despised, and the people are satisfied with your rule. It is essential to accomplish this, as I have already explained at length.

Indeed, one of the most effective defenses a ruler has against conspiracies is to make sure he is not generally hated. For conspirators always believe the assassination of the ruler will be approved by the people. If they believe the people will be angered, then they cannot screw up the courage to embark on such an enterprise, for conspirators have to overcome endless difficulties to achieve success. Experience shows the vast majority of conspiracies fail. For a conspirator cannot act alone, and he can only find associates among those whom he believes are discontented. As soon as you tell someone who is discontented what you are planning, you give him the means to satisfy his ambitions, because it is obvious he can expect to be richly rewarded if he betrays you. If he betrays you, his reward is certain; if he keeps faith with you, he faces danger, with little prospect of reward. So, you see, he needs either to be an exceptionally loyal friend or to be a completely intransigent enemy of the ruler, if he is to keep faith with you. So we can sum up as follows: The conspirators face nothing but fear, mutual distrust, and the prospect of punishment, so they lose heart; while the ruler is supported by the authority of his office and by the laws, and protected both by his supporters and by the forces of government. So, if you add to this inbuilt advantage the goodwill of the populace, then it is impossible to find anyone who is so foolhardy as to conspire against you. For in most situations a conspirator has to fear capture before he does the deed; but if the ruler has the goodwill of the people, he has to fear it afterwards as well, for the people will turn on him when the deed is done, and he will have nowhere to hide . . .

I conclude, then, that a ruler need not worry much about conspiracies as long as the people wish him well; but if the people are hostile to him and hate him, then he should fear everything and everyone. States that are well-governed and rulers who are wise make every effort to ensure the elite are not driven to despair, and to satisfy the masses and keep them content; for this is one of the most important tasks a ruler must set himself.

20

THOMAS HOBBES

The natural condition of mankind: every man is enemy to every man

Of the difference of manners

I put for a generall inclination of all mankind, a perpetuall and restlesse desire of Power after power, that ceaseth onely in Death. And the cause of this, is not alwayes that a man hopes for a more intensive delight, than he has already attained to; or that he cannot be content with a moderate power: but because he cannot assure the power and means to live well, which he hath present, without the acquisition of more. And from hence it is, that Kings, whose power is greatest, turn their endeavours to the assuring it at home by Lawes, or abroad by Wars: and when that is done, there succeedeth a new desire; in some, of Fame from new Conquest; in others, of ease and sensuall pleasure; in others, of admiration, or being flattered for excellence in some art, or other ability of the mind.

Competition of Riches, Honour, Command, or other power, enclineth to Contention, Enmity, and War: Because the way of one Competitor, to the attaining of his desire, is to kill, subdue, supplant, or repell the other. Particularly, competition of praise, enclineth to a reverence of Antiquity. For men contend with the living, not with the dead; to these ascribing more than due, that they may obscure the glory of the other.

Desire of Ease, and sensuall Delight, disposeth men to obey a common Power: Because by such Desires, a man doth abandon the protection might be hoped for from his own Industry, and labour. Fear of Death, and Wounds, disposeth to the same; and for the same reason. On the contrary, needy men, and hardy, not contented with their present condition; as also, all men that are ambitious of Military command, are enclined to continue the causes of warre; and to stirre up trouble and sedition: for there is no honour Military but by warre; nor any such hope to mend an ill game, as by causing a new shuffle.

Desire of knowledge, and Arts of Peace, enclineth men to obey a common Power: For such Desire, containeth a desire of leasure; and consequently protection from some other Power than their own.

Source: *Leviathan*, I, ch. 11, 13, Baltimore, MD: Penguin Books, 1968.

Desire of Praise, disposeth to laudable actions, such as please them whose judgement they value; for of those men whom we contemn, we contemn also the Praises. Desire of Fame after death does the same. And though after death, there be no sense of the praise given us on Earth, as being joyes, that are either swallowed up in the unspeakable joyes of Heaven, or extinguished in the extreme torments of Hell: yet is not such Fame vain; because men have a present delight therein, from the foresight of it, and of the benefit that may rebound thereby to their posterity: which though they now see not, yet they imagine; and any thing that is pleasure in the sense, the same also is pleasure in the imagination.

To have received from one, to whom we think our selves equall, greater benefits than there is hope to Requite, disposeth to counterfeit love; but really secret hatred; and puts a man into the estate of a desperate debtor, that in declining the sight of his creditor, tacitely wishes him there, where he might never see him more. For benefits oblige; and obligation is thraldome; and unrequitable obligation, perpetuall thraldome; which is to ones equall, hatefull. But to have received benefits from one, whom we acknowledge for superiour, enclines to love; because the obligation is no new depression: and cheerfull acceptation, (which men call *Gratitude*,) is such an honour done to the obliger, as is taken generally for retribution. Also to receive benefits, though from an equall, or inferiour, as long as there is hope of requitall, disposeth to love: for in the intention of the receiver, the obligation is of ayd, and service mutuall; from whence proceedeth an Emulation of who shall exceed in benefiting; the most noble and profitable contention possible; wherein the victor is pleased with his victory, and the other revenged by confessing it.

To have done more hurt to a man, than he can, or is willing to expiate, enclineth the doer to hate the sufferer. For he must expect revenge, or forgivenesse; both which are hatefull.

Feare of oppression, disposeth a man to anticipate, or to seek ayd by society: for there is no other way by which a man can secure his life and liberty.

Men that distrust their own subtilty, are in tumult, and sedition, better disposed for victory, than they that suppose themselves wise, or crafty. For these love to consult, the other (fearing to be circumvented,) to strike first. And in sedition, men being alwayes in the procincts of battell, to hold together, and use all advantages of force, is a better strategem, than any that can proceed from subtility of Wit.

Vain-glorious men, such as without being conscious to themselves of great sufficiency, delight in supposing themselves gallant men, are enclined onely to ostentation; but not to attempt: Because when danger or difficulty appears, they look for nothing but to have their insufficiency discovered.

Vain-glorious men, such as estimate their sufficiency by the flattery of other men, or the fortune of some precedent action, without assured ground of hope from the true knowledge of themselves, are enclined to rash engaging; and in the approach of danger, or difficulty, to retire if they can: because not seeing the way of safety, they will rather hazard their honour, which may be salved with an excuse; than their lives, for which no salve is sufficient.

Men that have a strong opinion of their own wisdome in matter of government, are disposed to Ambition. Because without publique Employment in counsell or magistracy, the honour of their wisdome is lost. And therefore Eloquent speakers are enclined to Ambition; for Eloquence seemeth wisedome, both to themselves and others.

Pusillanimity disposeth men to Irresolution, and consequently to lose the occasions, and fittest opportunities of action. For after men have been in deliberation till the time of action approach, if it be not then manifest what is best to be done, 'tis a signe, the difference of Motives, the one way and the other, are not great: Therefore not to resolve then, is to lose the occasion by weighing of trifles; which is pusillanimity.

Frugality, (though in poor men a Vertue,) maketh a man unapt to atchieve such actions, as require the strength of many men at once: For it weakeneth their Endeavour, which is to be nourished and kept in vigor by Reward.

Eloquence, with flattery, disposeth men to confide in them that have it; because the former is seeming Wisdome, the later seeming Kindnesse. Adde to them Military reputation, and it disposeth men to adhære, and subject themselves to those men that have them. The two former, having given them caution against danger from him; the later gives them caution against danger from others.

Want of Science, that is, Ignorance of causes, disposeth, or rather constraineth a man to rely on the advise, and authority of others. For all men whom the truth concernes, if they rely not on the opinion of some other, whom they think wiser than themselves, and see not why he should deceive them.

Ignorance of the signification of words; which is, want of understanding, disposeth men to take on trust, not onely the truth they know not; but also the errors; and which is more, the non-sense of them they trust: For neither Error, nor non-sense, can without a perfect understanding of words, be detected.

From the same it proceedeth, that men give different names, to one and the same thing, from the difference of their own passions: As they that approve a private opinion, call it Opinion; but they that mislike it, Hæresie: and yet hæresie signifies no more than private opinion; but has onely a greater tincture of choler . . .

Of the naturall condition of mankind, as concerning their felicity, and misery

Nature hath made men so equall, in the faculties of body, and mind; as that though there bee found one man sometimes manifestly stronger in body, or of quicker mind than another; yet when all is reckoned together, the difference between man, and man, is not so considerable, as that one man can thereupon claim to himselfe any benefit, to which another may not pretend, as well as he. For as to the strength of body, the weakest has strength enough to kill the strongest, either by secret machination, or by confederacy with others, that are in the same danger with himselfe.

And as to the faculties of the mind, (setting aside the arts grounded upon words, and especially that skill of proceeding upon generall, and infallible rules, called Science; which very few have, and but in few things; as being not a native faculty, born with us; nor attained, (as Prudence,) while we look after somewhat els,) I find yet a greater equality amongst men, than that of strength. For Prudence, is but Experience; which equall time, equally bestowes on all men, in those things they equally apply themselves unto. That which may perhaps make such equality incredible, is but a vain conceipt of ones owne wisdome, which almost all men think they have in a greater degree, than the Vulgar; that is, than all men but themselves, and a few others, whom by Fame, or for concurring with themselves, they approve. For such is the nature of men, that howsoever they may acknowledge many others to be more witty, or more eloquent, or more learned; Yet they will hardly believe there be many so wise as themselves: For they see their own wit at hand, and other men's at a distance. But this proveth rather that men are in that point equall, than unequall. For there is not ordinarily a greater signe of the equall distribution of any thing, than that every man is contented with his share.

From this equality of ability, ariseth equality of hope in the attaining of our Ends. And therefore if any two men desire the same thing, which nevertheless they cannot both enjoy, they become enemies; and in the way to their End, (which is principally their owne conservation, and sometimes their delectation only,) endeavour to destroy, or subdue one an other. And from hence it comes to passe, that where an Invader hath no more to feare, than an other mans single power; if one plant, sow, build, or possesse a convenient Seat, others may probably be expected to come prepared with forces united, to dispossesse, and deprive him, not only of the fruit of his labour, but also of his life, or liberty. And the Invader again is in the like danger of another.

And from this diffidence of one another, there is no way for any man to secure himselfe, so reasonable, as Anticipation; that is, by force, or wiles, to master the persons of all men he can, so long, till he see no other power great enough to endanger him: And this is no more than his own conservation requireth, and is generally allowed. Also because there be some, that taking pleasure in contemplating their own power in the acts of conquest, which they pursue farther than their security requires; if others, that otherwise would be glad to be at ease within modest bounds, should not by invasion increase their power, they would not be able, long time, by standing only on their defence, to subsist. And by consequence, such augmentation of dominion over men, being necessary to a mans conservation, it ought to be allowed him.

Againe, men have no pleasure, (but on the contrary a great deale of griefe) in keeping company, where there is no power able to over-awe them all. For every man looketh that his companion should value him, at the same rate he sets upon himselfe: And upon all signes of contempt, or undervaluing, naturally endeavours, as far as he dares (which amongst them that have no common power, to keep them in quiet, is far enough to make them destroy each other,) to extort a greater value from his contemners, by dommage; and from others, by the example.

So that in the nature of man, we find three principall causes of quarrell. First, Competition; Secondly, Diffidence; Thirdly, Glory.

The first, maketh men invade for Gain; the second, for Safety; and the third, for Reputation. The first use Violence, to make themselves Masters of other mens persons, wives, children, and cattell; the second, to defend them; the third, for trifles, as a word, a smile, a different opinion, and any other signe of undervalue, either direct in their Persons, or by reflexion in their Kindred, their Friends, their Nation, their Profession, or their Name.

Hereby it is manifest, that during the time men live without a common Power to keep them all in awe, they are in that condition which is called Warre; and such a warre, as is of every man, against every man. For Warre, consisteth not in Battell onely, or the act of fighting; but in a tract of time, wherein the Will to contend by Battell is sufficiently known: and therefore the notion of *Time*, is to be considered in the nature of Warre; as it is in the nature of Weather. For as the nature of Foule weather, lyeth not in a showre or two of rain; but in an inclination thereto of many dayes together: So the nature of War, consisteth not in actuall fighting; but in the known disposition thereto, during all the time there is no assurance to the contrary. All other time is Peace.

Whatsoever therefore is consequent to a time of Warre, where every man is Enemy to every man; the same is consequent to the time, wherein men live without other security, than what their own strength, and their own invention shall furnish them withall. In such condition, there is no place for Industry; because the fruit thereof is uncertain: and consequently no Culture of the Earth; no Navigation, nor use of the commodities that may be imported by Sea; no commodious Building; no Instruments of moving, and removing such things as require much force; no Knowledge of the face of the Earth; no account of Time; no Arts; no Letters; no Society; and which is worst of all, continuall feare, and danger of violent death; And the life of man, solitary, poore, nasty, brutish, and short.

It may seem strange to some man, that has not well weighted these things; that nature should thus dissociate, and render men apt to invade, and destroy one another: and he may therefore, not trusting to this Inference, made from the Passions, desire perhaps to have the same confirmed by Experience. Let him therefore consider with himselfe, when taking a journey, he armes himselfe, and seeks to go well accompanied; when going to sleep, he locks his dores; when even in his house he locks his chests; and this when he knows there bee Lawes, and publike Officers, armed, to revenge all injuries shall bee done him; what opinion he has of his fellow subjects, when he rides armed; of his fellow Citizens, when he locks his dores; and of his children, and servants, when he locks his chests. Does he not there as much accuse mankind by his actions, as I do by my words?

But neither of us accuse mans nature in it. The Desires, and other Passions of man, are in themselves no Sin. No more are the Actions, that proceed from those Passions, till they know a Law that forbids them: which till Lawes be made they cannot know: nor can any Law be made, till they have agreed upon the person that shall make it.

It may peradventure be thought, there was never such a time, nor condition of warre as this; and I believe it was never generally so, over all the world: but there are many places, where they live so now. For the savage people in many places of *America*, except the government of small Families, the concord whereof dependeth on naturall lust, have no government at all; and live at this day in that brutish manner, as I said before. Howsoever, it may be perceived what manner of life there would be, where there were no common Power to feare; by the manner of life, which men that have formerly lived under a peacefull government, use to degenerate into, in a civill Warre.

But though there had never been any time, wherein particular men were in a condition of warre one against another; yet in all times, Kings, and Persons of Soveraigne authority, because of their Independency, are in continuall jealousies, and in the state and posture of Gladiators; having their weapons pointing, and their eyes fixed on one another; that is, their Forts, Garrisons, and Guns upon the Frontiers of their Kingdomes; and continuall Spyes upon their neighbours; which is a posture of War. But because they uphold thereby, the Industry of their Subjects; there does not follow from it, that misery, which accompanies the Liberty of particular men.

To this warre of every man against every man, this also is consequent; that nothing can be Unjust. The notions of Right and Wrong, Justice and Injustice have there no place. Where there is no common Power, there is no Law: where no Law, no Injustice. Force, and Fraud, are in warre the two Cardinall vertues. Justice, and Injustice are none of the Faculties neither of the Body, nor Mind. If they were, they might be in a man that were alone in the world, as well as his Senses, and Passions. They are Qualities, that relate to men in Society, not in Solitude. It is consequent also to the same condition, that there be no Propriety, no Dominion, no *Mine* and *Thine* distinct; but onely that to be every mans that he can get; and for so long, as he can keep it. And thus much for the ill condition, which man by meer Nature is actually placed in; though with a possibility to come out of it, consisting partly in the Passions, partly in his Reason.

The Passions that encline men to Peace, are Feare of Death; Desire of such things as are necessary to commodious living; and a Hope by their Industry to obtain them. And Reason suggesteth convenient Articles of Peace, upon which men may be drawn to agreement. These Articles, are they, which otherwise are called the Lawes of Nature[.]

21

SAMUEL BUTLER

Varieties of malice and corruption

A corrupt judge

Passes Judgment as a Gamester does false Dice. The first Thing he takes is his Oath and his Commission, and afterwards the strongest Side and Bribes. He gives Judgment, as the Council at the Bar are said to give Advice, when they are paid for it. He wraps himself warm in Furs, that the cold Air may not strike his Conscience inward. He is never an upright Judge, but when he is weary of sitting and stands for his Ease. . . . [H]e takes his Liberty to do what he pleases; this he maintains with Canting, of which himself being the only Judge, he can give it what arbitrary Interpretation he pleases; yet is a great Enemy to arbitrary Power, because he would have no Body use it but himself. If he have Hopes of Preferment he makes all the Law run on the King's Side; if not, it always takes part against him; for as he was bred to make any Thing right or wrong between Man and Man, so he can do between the King and his Subjects. He calls himself *Capitalis*, *&c.* which Word he never uses but to Crimes of the highest Nature. He usurps unsufferable Tyranny over Words; for when he has enslaved and debased them from their original Sense, he makes them serve against themselves to support him, and their own Abuse. He is as stiff to Delinquents, and makes as harsh a Noise as a new Cart-wheel, until he is greased, and then he turns about as easily. He calls all necessary and unavoidable Proceedings of State, without the punctual Formality of Law, arbitrary and illegal, but never considers, that his own Interpretations of Law are more arbitrary, and, when he pleases, illegal. He cannot be denied to be a very impartial Judge; for right or wrong are all one to him. He takes Bribes, as pious Men give Alms, with so much Caution, that his right Hand never knows what his left receives.

A debauched man

Saves the Devil a Labour, and leads himself into Temptation, being loath to lose his good Favour in giving him any Trouble, where he can do the Business himself without

Source: *Samuel Butler 1612–1680: Characters*, Cleveland, O.: The Press of Case Western Reserve University, 1970.

his Assistance, which he very prudently reserves for matters of greater Concernment. He governs himself in an arbitrary Way, and is absolute, without being confined to any Thing but his own Will and Pleasure, which he makes his Law. His Life is all Recreation, and his Diversions nothing but turning from one Vice, that he is weary of, to entertain himself with another that is fresh. He lives above the State of his Body as well as his Fortune, and runs out of his Health and Money, as if he had made a Match and betted on the Race, or bid the Devil take the Hindmost. He is an amphibious Animal, that lives in two Elements wet and dry; and never comes out of the first, but, like a Sea-Calf, to sleep on the Shore. His Language is very suitable to his Conversation, and he talks as loosely as he lives. Ribaldry and Profanation are his Doctrine and Use; and what he professes publicly he practices very carefully in his Life and Conversation, not like those Clergymen, that to save the Souls of other Men condemn themselves out of their own Mouths. His whole Life is nothing but a perpetual Lordship of Misrule, and a constant Ramble Day and Night as long as it lasts, which is not according to the Course of Nature, but its own Course; for he cuts off the latter End of it, like a pruned Vine, that it may bear the more Wine, although it be the shorter. As for that which is left, he is as lavish of it as he is of every Thing else; for he sleeps all Day, and sits up all Night, that he may not see how it passes, until, like one that travels in a Litter and sleeps, he is at his Journey's End before he is aware; for he is spirited away by his Vices, and clapped under Hatches, where he never knows whither he is going, until he is at the End of his Voyage.

A malicious man

Has a strange natural Inclination to all ill Intents and Purposes. He bears nothing so resolutely as Ill-will, which he takes naturally to, as some do to Gaming, and will rather hate for nothing than sit out. He believes the *Devil* is not so bad as he should be, and therefore endeavours to make him worse by drawing him into his own Party offensive and defensive; and if he would but be ruled by him does not doubt but to make him understand his Business much better than he does. He lays nothing to Heart but Malice, which is so far from doing him hurt, that it is the only Cordial that preserves him. Let him use a Man never so civilly to his Face, he is sure to hate him behind his Back. He has no Memory for any good that is done him; but Evil, whether it be done him or not, never leaves him, as Things of the same Kind always keep together. Love and Hatred, though contrary Passions, meet in him as a third, and unite; for he loves nothing but to hate, and hates nothing but to love. All the Truths in the World are not able to produce so much Hatred, as he is able to supply. He is a common Enemy to the World; for being born to the Hatred of it, Nature that provides for every Thing she brings forth, has furnished him with a Competence suitable to his Occasions; for all Men together cannot hate him so much, as he does them one by one. He loses no Occasion of Offence, but very thriftily lays it up, and endeavours to improve it to the best Advantage. He makes Issues in his Skin, to vent his ill Humours, and is sensible of no Pleasure so much as the Itching of his Sores. He hates Death for nothing so much, as because he fears it will take him away, before he has paid all the Ill-will he owes, and deprive him of all those precious Feuds, he has been scraping together all his Life-time. He is troubled to think what a Disparagement it will be to him to die before those, that will be glad to hear he is gone; and desires very charitably, they might come to an Agreement like good Friends, and go Hand in Hand out of the World together. He loves his Neighbour as well as he does himself, and is willing to endure any Misery, so they may but take Part with him, and undergo any Mischief rather than they should want it. He is ready to spend his Blood, and lay down his Life for theirs, that would not do half so much for him; and rather than fail would give the *Devil* suck, and his Soul into the Bargain, if he would but make him his Plenipotentiary, to determine all Differences between himself and others. He contracts Enmities as others do Friendships, out of Likenesses, Sympathies, and Instincts; and when he lights upon one of his own Temper, as Contraries produce the same Effects, they perform all the Offices of Friendship, have the same thoughts, Affections, and Desires of one another's Destruction, and please themselves as heartily, and perhaps as securely, in hating one another, as others do in loving. He seeks out Enemies to avoid falling out with himself; for his Temper is like that of a flourishing Kingdom, if it have not a foreign Enemy it will fall into a civil War, and turn its Arms upon it self, and so does but hate in his own Defence. His Malice is all Sorts of Gain to him; for as Men take Pleasure in pursuing, entrapping, and destroying all Sorts of Beasts and Fowl, and call it Sports, so would he do Men, and if he had equal Power would never be at a Loss, nor give over his Game without his Prey, and in this he does nothing but Justice; for as Men take Delight to destroy Beasts, he being a Beast does but do as he is done by in endeavouring to destroy Men. The Philosopher said – *Man to Man is a God and a Wolf*; but he being incapable of the first does his Endeavour to make as much of the last as he can, and shews himself as excellent in his Kind, as it is in his Power to do.

A knave

Is like a Tooth-drawer, that maintains his own Teeth in constant eating by pulling out those of other Men. He is an ill moral Philosopher, of villainous Principles, and as bad Practice. His Tenets are to hold what he can get, right or wrong. His Tongue and his Heart are always at Variance, and fall out, like Rogues in the Street, to pick somebody's Pocket. They never agree but, like *Herod* and *Pilate*, to do Mischief. His Conscience never stands in his Light, when the *Devil* holds a Candle to him; for he has stretched it so thin, that it is transparent. He is an Engineer of Treachery, Fraud, and Perfidiousness, and knows how to manage Matters of great Weight with very little Force, by the

Advantage of his trepanning Screws. He is very skilful in all the Mechanics of Cheat, the mathematical Magic of Imposture; and will outdo the Expectation of the most Credulous, to their own Admiration and Undoing. He is an excellent Founder, and will melt down a leaden Fool, and cast him into what Form he pleases. He is like a Pike in a Pond, that lives by Rapine, and will sometimes venture on one of his own Kind, and devour a Knave as big as himself – He will swallow a Fool a great deal bigger than himself; and if he can but get his Head within his Jaws, will carry the rest of him hanging out at his Mouth, until by Degrees he has digested him all. He has a hundred Tricks, to slip his Neck out of the Pillory, without leaving his Ears behind. As for the Gallows, he never ventures to show his Tricks upon the high-Rope, for fear of breaking his Neck. He seldom commits any Villany, but in a legal Way, and makes the Law bear him out in that, for which it hangs others. He always robs under the Vizard of Law, and picks Pockets with Tricks in Equity. By his Means the Law makes more Knaves than it hangs, and, like the *Inns-of-Court* protects Offenders against itself. He gets within the Law, and disarms it. His hardest Labour is to wriggle himself into Trust, which if he can but compass, his Business is done; for Fraud and Treachery follow as easily, as a Thread does a Needle. He grows rich by the Ruin of his Neighbours, like Grass in the Streets in a great Sickness. He shelters himself under the Covert of the Law, like a Thief in a Hemp-Plot, and makes that secure him, which was intended for his Destruction.

An oppressor

Is said to grind the faces of the poor, because he holds their noses to the grindstone. He is like the Spaniards of Potosi, that make their sheep bear burdens, as well as fleeces, on their backs, and supply him by extraordinary ways more heavy than those they were design'd for. He lays the heaviest weights upon those that yield easiest to them; like the foundation of London bridge upon woolsacks, that rests upon a soft cushion for its case; and, therefore, the poorer and weaker men are, the fitter and easier he always finds them for his purpose. Where Fortune has begun to oppress a man he presently strikes in and seconds her, and like a right bloodhound hunts none but a wounded deer. He is as barbarous as those inhuman people that dwell upon the coasts of rugged seas, and live by robbing all those, whom the less cruel sea has spared and cast upon them; for he makes other mens wrecks his returns, and ships that are cast away bring him a prosperous voyage. He is a Hun, that when he is thirsty opens a vein and sucks the blood of the poor beast that bears him. He loves his neighbour's goods better than his own, and rejoices more over one pound that he comes sinfully by, than ninety nine that are righteously gotten, and need no repentance. He believes a man gains nothing by that which is his due, and therefore is not at all the better for it; but that which comes, where nothing could be expected or demanded, is like a present that he makes himself, and how mean soever ought to receive a value from the good will of the giver. He is so kind and goodnatur'd, that he loves to have something of every mans to remember him by; but does not care to put any man to the trouble of preserving any thing that is his. Tis natural for gamesters to love other mens money better than their own, else they would never venture to lose that which they are certain of to win that which is uncertain; and as the philosopher said, of all wines another mans wines are ever the best, he is confident it is much more true of another man's money.

Part 5

THE IRRATIONALITY OF WAYWARDNESS

Francisco Goya: "The Sleep of Reason Produces Monsters."

Gnostics and Neo-Platonists placed human psychology within a metaphysical frame: the state of the soul is a reflection – an expression – of the hierarchical order of the universe. Christian Neo-Platonists had to find a way to reconcile divine order with the freedom necessary for man's ultimate moral accountability. A double solution was forged: (1) God permits, but does not cause human wickedness; (2) a world in which free choice between good and evil is possible is more perfect than one in which there is no freedom.

Leibniz (1646–1716) continues the metaphysical tradition while refusing its dilemmas. Distinguishing metaphysical evil (which consists in comparative inferiority), physical evil (which consists in suffering or destruction), and moral evil (which consists in viciousness), he argues that none of these evils indicates that the world is imperfect. All evils, including what is called *sin*, conform to the divine plan. "God wills order and good; but it sometimes happens that what is disorder in the part is order in the whole.... The permission of evils [which is not the *cause* of their being evil] comes from a kind of moral necessity: God is constrained to this by his wisdom and by his goodness.... Supreme reason ... permits [local] evil. If God chose what would not be best absolutely and in all, that would be a greater evil than all the individual evils which he could prevent by this means."

Mandeville (1670–1733) develops a social, secular version of Leibniz's theodicy. Like Leibniz, he does not deny the existence of suffering and (what is ordinarily called) vice; but like Machiavelli, he argues that the vices promote harmony, as well as conduce to it, and flourish when they are exercised in a well-regulated system. Indeed he claims that prosperity, progress and civilization itself depend on greed, hypocrisy, vanity. Private vices are offensive: they often do local, short-range harm. They are nevertheless more effective in promoting the long-range public good than sweetness and light could possibly be.

Voltaire (1694–1778) will have none of it. If viciousness is vile, it cannot be excused or justified by some notional benign effects; the suffering caused by wars, cruelty, natural disasters remains inconsolable. A promissory note of metaphysical harmony is worse than superstitious nonsense: it is offensive. What theologians call conscience, what they argue to be the divine gift of innate knowledge of right and wrong is nothing more than social convention, variable with circumstance, hypocritically trumped up to make men obedient.

Like Hobbes, Rousseau (1712–1778) thinks that men are not naturally either good or wicked, sociable nor anti-social. Unlike Hobbes, he does not envision the conditions of nature to be so harsh that men must compete for their basic survival. Rather, he thinks that circumstances bring them together so that they discover the benefits of cooperation and the charms of society. Originally beneficial, the division of labor, the discoveries of natural regularities, the diversions of music and song become debilitating, crippling and eventually corrupting. The division of labor naturally leads to specialization and dependency: men who had originally been self-sufficient become passive and enfeebled. The discoveries of natural regularities that overcame fearful superstition and that promoted fore-sighted self-protection become the jealous competitive obsessions of science and philosophy. When the development of the arts moved from naive songs and dances to elaborate theatrical displays, imagination began to rule good sense. When everything seems possible, simple contentment disappears. In short, society becomes the source of the vices that it pretends to cure. Attacking Mandeville's contention that the vices promote public progress, Rousseau argued that the very idea of public progress engenders the vices.

Intent on accounting for responsible agency of rational beings, Kant (1724–1804) argues that they are capable of freely choosing to act either against or in accord with the moral law. Although men are, as a species, neither good nor bad, individuals can willingly act from immoral maxims. By nature, men have three basic dispositions or tendencies that typically serve the species well, but that can be debased by malformed inclinations. As living organisms, they are predisposed to individual physical self-preservation, which can sometimes lead them to weigh their own inclinations more than their moral obligations. As specifically human beings, they endeavor "to acquire worth in the opinion of others." From this disposition, originally expressed in a desire for equality, comes a host of the dangerous social vices that Rousseau anatomized: rivalry, envy, spite. As rational beings, men are predisposed to be held, and to hold themselves, accountable for their choices. But if their choices are free, they are capable of deviating from the moral law. As freedom of the will holds open the possibility of immorality as well as morality, so rationality holds open the possibility of irra-tionality. Kant acknowledges that "the perversion of the will . . . [and] the propensity to evil [remain] inscrutable."

160

22

G.W. VON LEIBNIZ

The justice of God and the problem of evil

Freedom of man and the origin of evil

Evil may be taken metaphysically, physically and morally. *Metaphysical evil* consists in mere imperfection; *physical evil* in suffering, and *moral evil* in sin.

Concerning sin or moral evil, although it happens very often that it may serve as a means of obtaining good or of preventing another evil, it is not this that renders it a sufficient object of the divine will or a legitimate object of a created will. It must only be admitted or *permitted* in so far as it is considered to be a certain consequence of an indispensable duty: as for instance if a man who was determined not to permit another's sin were to fail of his own duty, or as if an officer on guard at an important post were to leave it, especially in time of danger, in order to prevent a quarrel in the town between two soldiers of the garrison who wanted to kill each other . . .

It is again well to consider that moral evil is an evil so great only because it is a source of physical evils, a source existing in one of the most powerful of creatures, who is also most capable of causing those evils . . .

It is indeed beyond question that we must refrain from preventing the sin of others when we cannot prevent their sin without sinning ourselves. But someone will perhaps bring up the objection that it is God himself who acts and who effects all that is real in the sin of the creature. This objection leads us to consider the *physical co-operation* of God with the creature, after we have examined the *moral co-operation*, which was the more perplexing . . .

The objection will be made that God . . . creates man a sinner, he that in the beginning created him innocent. But here it must be said, with regard to the moral aspect, that God being supremely wise cannot fail to observe certain laws, and to act according

Source: *Theodicy: Essays on the Goodness of God, the Freedom of Man and the Origin of Evil*, translated by E.M. Huggard, La Salle, Ill.: Open Court, 1985.

to the rules, as well physical as moral, that wisdom has made him choose. And the same reason that has made him create man innocent, but liable to fall, makes him re-create man when he falls; for God's knowledge causes the future to be for him as the present, and prevents him from rescinding the resolutions made.

[In the best of all possible worlds that God could have created, there must] be choice; [and if choice, then the possibility of bad choice.] But I do not think one must seek the reason altogether in the good or bad nature of men. For if with some people one assume[s] that God, choosing the plan which produces the most good, but which involves sin and damnation, has been prompted by his wisdom to choose the best natures in order to make them objects of his grace, this grace would not sufficiently appear to be a free gift. Accordingly man will be distinguishable by a kind of inborn merit, and this assumption seems remote from the principles of St Paul, and even from those of Supreme Reason.

It is true that there are reasons for God's choice, and the consideration of the object, that is, the nature of man, must needs enter therein; but it does not seem that this choice can be subjected to a rule such as we are capable of conceiving, and such as may flatter the pride of men. Some famous theologians believe that God offers more grace, and in a more favourable way, to those whose resistance he foresees will be less, and that he abandons the rest to their self-will. We may readily suppose that this is often the case, and this expedient, among those which make man distinguishable by anything favourable in his nature, is the farthest removed from Pelagianism. But I would not venture, notwithstanding, to make of it a universal rule. Moreover, that we may not have cause to vaunt ourselves, it is necessary that we be ignorant of the reasons for God's choice. Those reasons are too diverse to become known to us; and it may be that God at times shows the power of his grace by overcoming the most obstinate resistance, to the end that none may have cause either to despair or to be puffed up. St Paul, as it would seem, had this in mind when he offered himself as an example. God, he said, has had mercy upon me, to give a great example of his patience.

It may be that fundamentally all men are equally bad, and consequently incapable of being distinguished the one from the other through their good or less bad natural qualities; but they are not bad all in the same way: for there is an inherent individual difference between souls. . . . Some are more or less inclined towards a particular good or a particular evil, or towards their opposites, all in accordance with their natural dispositions. But since the general plan of the universe, chosen by God for superior reasons, causes men to be in different circumstances, those who meet with such as are more favourable to their nature will become more readily the least wicked, the most virtuous, the most happy; yet it will be always by aid of the influence of that inward grace which God unites with the circumstances. Sometimes it even comes to pass, in the progress of human life, that a more excellent nature succeeds less, for lack of cultivation or opportunities. One may say that men are chosen and ranged not so much according to their excellence as according to their conformity with God's plan. Even so it may occur that a stone of lesser quality is made use of in a building or in a group because it proves to be the particular one for filling a certain gap.

But, in fine, all these attempts to find reasons, where there is no need to adhere altogether to certain hypotheses, serve only to make clear to us that there are a thousand ways of justifying the conduct of God. All the disadvantages we see, all the obstacles we meet with, all the difficulties one may raise for oneself, are no hindrance to a belief founded on reason, even when it cannot stand on conclusive proof . . . that there is nothing so exalted as the wisdom of God, nothing so just as his judgements, nothing so pure as his holiness, and nothing more vast than his goodness . . .

To make men better, God does all that is due, and even all that can be done on his side without detriment to what is due. The most usual aim of punishment is amendment; but it is not the sole aim, nor that which God always intends. . . . Original sin, which disposes men towards evil, is not merely a penalty for the first sin; it is a natural consequence thereof. . . . It is like drunkenness, which is a penalty for excess in drinking and is at the same time a natural consequence that easily leads to new sins.

[Some may object:] "To permit the evil that one could prevent is not to care whether it be committed or not, or is even to wish that it be committed."

By no means. How many times do men permit evils which they could prevent if they turned all their efforts in that direction? But other more important cares prevent them from doing so. One will rarely resolve upon adjusting irregularities in the coinage while one is involved in a great war. . . . Can one conclude from this that the State has no anxiety about this irregularity, or even that it desires it? God has a far stronger reason, and one far more worthy of him, for tolerating evils. Not only does he derive from them greater goods, but he finds them connected with the greatest goods of all those that are possible: so that it would be a fault not to permit them.

[Others may object:] "It is a very great fault in those who govern, if they do not care whether there be disorder in their States or not. The fault is still greater if they wish and even desire disorder there. If by hidden and indirect, but infallible, ways they stirred up a sedition in their States to bring them to the brink of ruin, in order to gain for themselves the glory of showing that they have the courage and the prudence necessary for saving a great kingdom on the point of perishing, they would be most deserving of condemnation. But if they stirred up this sedition because there were no other means than that, of averting the total ruin of their subjects and of strengthening on new foundations, and for several centuries, the happiness of nations, one must needs lament the unfortunate necessity . . . to which they were reduced, and praise them for the use that they made thereof."

This maxim, with divers others set forth here, is not applicable to the government of God. Not to mention the fact that it is only the disorders of a very small part of his kingdom which are brought up in objection, it is untrue that he has no anxiety about evils, that he desires them, that he brings them into being, to have the glory of allaying them. God wills order and good; but it happens sometimes that what is disorder in the part is order in the whole. . . . The permission of evils comes from a kind of moral necessity: God is constrained to this by his wisdom and by his goodness; *this necessity is happy*, whereas that of the prince spoken of in the maxim is *unhappy*. His State is one of the most corrupt; and the government of God is the best State possible.

[Some may say:] "The permission of a certain evil is only excusable when one cannot remedy it without introducing a greater evil; but it cannot be excusable in those who have in hand a remedy more efficacious against this evil, and against all the other evils that could spring from the suppression of this one."

The maxim is true, but it cannot be brought forward against the government of God. Supreme reason constrains him to permit the evil. If God chose what would not be the best absolutely and in all, that would be a greater evil than all the individual evils which he could prevent by this means. This wrong choice would destroy his wisdom and his goodness.

[Others may say:] "The Being infinitely powerful, Creator of matter and of spirits, makes whatever he wills of this matter and these spirits. There is no situation or shape that he cannot communicate to spirits. If he then permitted a physical or a moral evil, this would not be for the reason that otherwise some other still greater physical or moral evil would be altogether inevitable. None of those reasons for the mixture of good and evil which are founded on the limitation of the forces of benefactors can apply to him."

It is true that God makes of matter and of spirits whatever he wills; but he is like a good sculptor, who will make from his block of marble only that which he judges to be the best, and who judges well. God makes of matter the most excellent of all possible machines; he makes of spirits the most excellent of all governments conceivable; and over and above all that, he establishes for their union the most perfect of all harmonies, according to the system I have proposed. Now since physical evil and moral evil occur in this perfect work, one must conclude . . . that *otherwise a still greater evil would have been altogether inevitable*. This great evil would be that God would have chosen ill if he had chosen otherwise than he has chosen. It is true that God is infinitely powerful; but his power is indeterminate, goodness and wisdom combined determine him to produce the best.

23

BERNARD MANDEVILLE

Private Vices, Public Benefits

Laws and Government are to the Political Bodies of Civil Societies, what the Vital Spirits and life it self are to the Natural Bodies of Animated Creatures; and as those that study the Anatomy of Dead Carcases may see, that the chief Organs and nicest Springs more immediately required to continue the Motion of our Machine, are not hard Bones, strong Muscles and Nerves, nor the smooth white Skin that so beautifully covers them, but small trifling Films and little Pipes that are either over-look'd, or else seem inconsiderable to Vulgar Eyes; so they that examine into the Nature of Man, abstract from Art and Education, may observe, that what renders him a Sociable Animal, consists not in his desire of Company, Good-nature, Pity, Affability, and other Graces of a fair Outside; but that his vilest and most hateful Qualities are the most necessary Accomplishments to fit him for the largest, and, according to the World, the happiest and most flourishing Societies.

[My design is] to shew the Impossibility of enjoying all the most elegant Comforts of Life that are to be met with in an industrious, wealthy and powerful nation, and at the same time be bless'd with all the Virtue and Innocence that can be wish'd for in a Golden Age; from thence to expose the Unreasonableness and Folly of those, that desirous of being an opulent and flourishing People, and wonderfully greedy after all the Benefits they can receive as such, are yet always murmuring at and exclaiming against those Vices and Inconveniences, that from the Beginning of the World to this present Day, have been inseparable from all Kingdoms and States that ever were fam'd for Strength, Riches, and Politeness, at the same time.

To do this, I first slightly touch upon some of the Faults and Corruptions the several Professions and Callings are generally charged with. After that I shew that those very Vices of every particular Person by skilful Management, were made subservient to the Grandeur and worldly Happiness of the whole. Lastly, by setting forth what of necessity

Source: *The Fable of the Bees: or, Private Vices, Public Benefits.*

must be the consequence of general Honesty and Virtue, and National Temperance, Innocence and Content, I demonstrate that if Mankind could be cured of the Failings they are Naturally guilty of, they would cease to be capable of being rais'd into such vast, potent and polite Societies, as they have been under the several great Commonwealths and Monarchies that have flourish'd since the Creation.

[E]very Part was full of Vice,
Yet the whole Mass a Paradise;
Flatter'd in Peace, and fear'd in Wars,
They were th' Esteem of Foreigners,
And lavish of their Wealth and Lives,
The Balance of all other Hives.
Such were the Blessings of that State;
Their Crimes conspir'd to make them Great:
And Virtue, who from Politicks
Had learn'd a Thousand Cunning Tricks,
Was, by their happy Influence,
Made Friends with Vice: And ever since,
The worst of all the Multitude
Did something for the Common Good.

This was the State's Craft, that maintain'd
The Whole of which each Part complain'd:
This, as in Musick harmony,
Made Jarrings in the main agree;
Parties directly opposite,
Assist each other, as 'twere for spite;
And Temp'rance with Sobriety,
Serve Drunkenness and Gluttony.

The Root of Evil, Avarice,
That damn'd ill-natur'd Baneful Vice,
Was Slave to Prodigality,
That noble Sin; whilst Luxury
Employ'd a Million of the Poor,
And odious Pride a Million more:
Envy it self, and Vanity,
Were Ministers of Industry;
Their darling Folly, Fickleness,
In Diet, Furniture and Dress,

That strange ridic'lous Vice, was made
The very Wheel that turn'd the Trade.
Their Laws and Clothes were equally
Objects of Mutability;
For, what was well done for a time,
In half a Year became a Crime;
Yet while they alter'd thus their Laws,
Still finding and correcting Flaws,
They mended by Inconstancy
Faults, which no Prudence could foresee.

Thus Vice nurs'd Ingenuity,
Which join'd with Time and Industry,
Had carry'd Life's Conveniencies,
Its real Pleasures, Comforts, Ease,
To such a Height, the very Poor
Liv'd better than the Rich before,
And nothing could be added more.

24

VOLTAIRE

Conscience and original sin

Conscience

We have no other conscience than what is created in us by the spirit of the age, by example, and by our own dispositions and reflections.

Man is born without principles, but with the faculty of receiving them. His natural disposition will incline him either to cruelty or kindness; his understanding will in time inform him that the square of twelve is a hundred and forty-four, and that he ought not to do to others what he would not that others should do to him; but he will not, of himself, acquire these truths in early childhood. He will not understand the first, and he will not feel the second.

A young savage who, when hungry, has received from his father a piece of another savage to eat, will, on the morrow, ask for the like meal, without thinking about any obligation not to treat a neighbor otherwise than he would be treated himself. He acts, mechanically and irresistibly, directly contrary to the eternal principle.

Nature has made a provision against such horrors. She has given to man a disposition to pity, and the power of comprehending truth. These two gifts of God constitute the foundation of civil society. This is the reason there have ever been but few cannibals; and which renders life, among civilized nations, a little tolerable. Fathers and mothers bestow on their children an education which soon renders them social, and this education confers on them a conscience.

Pure religion and morality, early inculcated, so strongly impress the human heart that, from the age of sixteen or seventeen, a single bad action will not be performed without the upbraidings of conscience. Then rush on those headlong passions which war against conscience, and sometimes destroy it. During the conflict, men, hurried on by the tempest of their feelings, on various occasions consult the advice of others; as, in physical diseases, they ask it of those who appear to enjoy good health.

Source: *A Philosophical Dictionary*, New York: Coventry House, 1932.

Whether a judge should decide according to his conscience, or according to the evidence

Thomas Aquinas, you are a great saint, and a great divine, and no Dominican has a greater veneration for you than I have; but you have decided, in your "Summary," that a judge ought to give sentence according to the evidence produced against the person accused, although he knows that person to be perfectly innocent. You maintain that the deposition of witnesses, which must inevitably be false, and the pretended proofs resulting from the process, which are impertinent, ought to weigh down the testimony of his own senses. He saw the crime committed by another; and yet, according to you, he ought in conscience to condemn the accused, although his conscience tells him the accused is innocent. According to your doctrine, therefore, if the judge had himself committed the crime in question, his conscience ought to oblige him to condemn the man falsely accused of it.

In my conscience, great saint, I conceive that you are most absurdly and most dreadfully deceived. It is a pity that, while possessing such a knowledge of canon law, you should be so little acquainted with natural law. The duty of a magistrate to be just, precedes that of being a formalist. If, in virtue of evidence which can never exceed probability, I were to condemn a man whose innocence I was otherwise convinced of, I should consider myself a fool and an assassin.

Original sin

This is the alleged triumph of [those who call original sin the] foundation of the Christian religion[.] It is to offend god, they say, it is to accuse him of the most absurd barbarity, to dare to say that he made all the generations of men in order to torment them by eternal sufferings on the pretext that their first father ate some fruit in a garden. This sacrilegious imputation is all the more inexcusable in Christians because there is not a single word about this invention of original sin in the Pentateuch or the prophets or the gospels whether apocryphal or canonical, or in any of the writers who are called the first fathers of the church.

It is not even said in Genesis that god condemned Adam to death because he swallowed an apple. He did tell him: "in the day that thou eatest thereof thou shalt surely die"; but this same Genesis makes Adam live 930 years after this criminal meal. The animals and plants which did not eat this fruit died in the time prescribed by nature. Man is born to die, like all the rest.

Besides the punishment of Adam formed no part of the Jewish law. Adam was no more a Jew than a Persian or a Chaldean. The first chapters of Genesis (whatever the period of their composition) were regarded by all Jewish scholars as an allegory, and even as a very dangerous fable, since the reading of it was forbidden before the age of twenty-five.

In a word, the Jews knew original sin no better than Chinese ceremonies, and although theologians find whatever they want in the scriptures, *totidem verbis* or *totidem litteris*, it can be asserted that no reasonable theologian will ever find this surprising mystery in it.

Let us admit that saint Augustine was the first to authorize this strange idea, worthy of the fiery and romantic head of a debauched and repentant African, Manichean and Christian, indulgent and persecuted, who spent his life contradicting himself.

"How horrible," exclaim the strict Unitarians, "to calumniate the author of nature to the point of imputing to him continual miracles in order to damn for ever men whom he has given life for so little time! Either he created souls from all eternity, and by this system, being infinitely older than Adam's sin, they have no connection with him. Or these souls are formed every time a man lies with a woman, and in that case god is continually on the watch for all the assignations in the universe in order to create the spirits whom he will make eternally unhappy. Or god is himself the soul of all men, and in that case he damns himself. Which of these three suppositions is the most horrible and most senseless? There is not a fourth, for the view that god waits for six weeks to create a damned soul in a foetus is equivalent to that which holds it to be created at the moment of copulation: what matter six weeks more or less?"

I have reported the view of the Unitarians, and men have attained to such profound superstition that I shuddered in reporting it.

Explication of original sin

The difficulty is the same with respect to this substituted limbo as with respect to hell. Why should these poor little wretches be placed in this limbo? what had they done? how could their souls which they had not in their possession a single day, be guilty of a gormandizing that merited a punishment of six thousand years?

St Augustine, who damns them, assigns as a reason, that the souls of all men being comprised in that of Adam, it is probable that they were all accomplices. But, as the Church subsequently decided that souls are not made before the bodies which they are to inhabit are originated, that system falls to the ground, notwithstanding the celebrity of its author.

Others said that original sin was transmitted from soul to soul, in the way of emanation, and that one soul, derived from another, came into the world with all the corruption of the mother-soul. This opinion was condemned.

After the divines had done with the question, the philosophers tried at it. Leibniz, while sporting with his monads, amused himself with collecting together in Adam all the human monads with their little bodies of monads. This was going further than St Augustine. But this idea, which was worthy of Cyrano de Bergerac, met with very few to adopt and defend it. Malebranche explains the matter by the influence of the imagination on mothers. Eve's brain was so strongly inflamed with the desire of eating the fruit that her children had the same desire; just like the irresistibly authenticated case of the woman who, after having seen a man racked, was brought to bed of a dislocated infant.

25

J.-J. ROUSSEAU
Social corruption

So many reflections on the weakness of our nature often do no more than divert us from generous enterprises. The more we think about the miseries of mankind, the more our imagination oppresses us with their weight, and too much forethought robs us of courage by robbing us of confidence. It is in vain that we strive to provide against unforeseen accidents "if science, trying to arm us with new defenses against natural inconveniences, has impressed our imagination more deeply with their magnitude and weight than with its own reasons and the vain subtleties that lead us to seek cover behind it."

A taste for philosophy loosens all the bonds of esteem and benevolence that tie men to society, and this is perhaps the most dangerous of the evils it engenders. The charm of study soon dulls all other attachments. What is more, continued reflection on mankind, continued observation of men, teach the Philosopher to judge them at their worth, and it is difficult to have much affection for what one holds in contempt. Before long he comes to focus on himself alone all the interest which virtuous men share with their fellows; his contempt for others heightens his pride: his *amour propre* grows in direct proportion to his indifference to the rest of the universe. Family, fatherland, become for him words devoid of meaning: he is neither parent, nor citizen, nor man; he is a philosopher.

While the pursuit of the sciences draws the philosopher's heart away from the crowd, as it were, in another sense it draws in the heart of the man of letters, and in both cases it does so with equal prejudice to virtue. Anyone who cultivates the agreeable talents wants to please, to be admired, and indeed wants to be admired more than anyone else is. Public applause is to be his alone: I would say that he does everything to obtain it, if he did not do even more to deprive his competitors of it. Hence arise, on the one hand, the refinements of taste and politeness; vile and obsequious flattery, seductive, insidious, childish attentions which in time diminish the soul and corrupt the heart; and, on the other hand, the jealousies, the rivalries, the well-known hatred of artists for one another, sly slander, deceit, treachery, and all the most cowardly and odious aspects of

Source: *The Discourses and Other Early Political Writings, First Discourse*: "Replies," Preface to Narcissus and *Second Discourse*, translated by Victor Gourevitch, Cambridge: Cambridge University Press, 1993.

vice. If the philosopher holds men in contempt, the artist soon causes them to hold him in contempt, and in the end both conspire to render them contemptible.

There is more; and of all the truths I submitted to the judgment of the wise, this is the most arresting and the most cruel. All our Writers regard the crowning achievement of our century's politics to be the sciences, the arts, luxury, commerce, laws, and all the other bonds which, by tightening the social ties[1] among men through self-interest, place them all in a position of mutual dependence, impose on them mutual needs and common interests, and oblige everyone to contribute to everyone else's happiness in order to secure his own. These are certainly fine ideas, and they are presented in an attractive light. But when they are examined carefully and impartially, the advantages which they seem at first to hold out prove to be subject to a good many reservations.

What a wonderful thing, then, to have put men in a position where they can only live together by obstructing, supplanting, deceiving, betraying, destroying one another! From now on we must take care never to let ourselves be seen as we are: because for every two men whose interests coincide, perhaps a hundred thousand oppose them, and the only way to succeed is either to deceive or to ruin all those people. This is the fatal source of the violence, the betrayals, the treacheries and all the horrors necessarily required by a state of affairs in which everyone pretends to be working for the profit or reputation of the rest, while only seeking to raise his own above theirs and at their expense.

What have we gained from all this? Much chatter, rich men and argumentative ones, that is to say enemies of virtue and common sense. In return we have lost innocence and morals. The multitude grovels in poverty; all are the slaves of vice. Uncommitted crimes dwell deep inside men's hearts, and all that keeps them from being carried out is the assurance of impunity.

What a strange and ruinous constitution, where having wealth invariably makes it easier to get more, and it is impossible for the man who has nothing to acquire anything; where a good man has no escape from his misery; where the basest are the most honored, and where one has to renounce virtue in order to become an honest man! I know that sermonizers have said all this a hundred times; but they were delivering sermons, whereas I give reasons; they perceived the evil, and I lay bare its causes, and above all I point out something highly consoling and useful by showing that all these vices belong not so much to man, as to man badly governed.[2] . . .

Science is not suited to man in general. He forever goes astray in his quest for it; and if he sometimes attains it, he almost always does so to his detriment. He is born to act and to think, not to reflect. Reflection only makes him unhappy without making him better or wiser: it causes him to regret past benefits and keeps him from enjoying the present: it shows him a happy future that his imagination might seduce and his desires torment him, and an unhappy future that he might experience it in anticipation. Study corrupts his morals, affects his health, ruins his temperament, and often spoils his reason: even if it did teach him something, it would seem to me to be a poor compensation.

I acknowledge that there are a few sublime geniuses capable of piercing the veils in which the truth wraps itself, a few privileged souls able to resist the folly of vanity, base jealousy, and the other passions aroused by a taste for letters. The small number who have the good fortune of combining these qualities are the beacon and the honor of mankind; only they may properly engage in study for the good of all, and this very exception confirms the rule; for if all men were Socrates, science would do them no harm, but neither would they need it.

Any people with morals, and hence with respect for its laws and without desire to improve on its traditional ways, must carefully guard against the sciences, and above all against men of science and learning whose sententious and dogmatic maxims would soon teach it to despise both its ways and its laws; which is something a nation can never do without being corrupted. The slightest change in customs, even if it is in some respects for the better, invariably proves prejudicial to morals. For customs are the morality of the people; and as soon as the people ceases to respect them, it is left with no rule but its passions, and no curb but the laws, which can sometimes keep the wicked in check, but can never make them good. Besides, once philosophy has taught the people to despise its customs, it soon learns the secret of eluding its laws. I therefore say that a people's morals are like a man's honor; they are a treasure to be preserved, but which cannot be recovered once lost.

But once a people is to a certain extent corrupted, should the sciences – regardless of whether they did or did not contribute to the corruption – be banished, or the people be shielded from them, either in order to be improved, or to be kept from becoming worse? This is another question about which I positively declared for the negative. For, in the first place, since a vicious people never returns to virtue, the problem is not how to make good those who are no longer so, but how to keep good those who are fortunate enough to be so. In the second place, the same causes that have corrupted peoples sometimes help prevent a greater corruption; thus, a man who has ruined his temperament by an injudicious use of medicines is forced to continue to rely on doctors in order to stay alive; and that is how the arts and sciences, having fostered the vices, become necessary to keep them from turning into crimes; at least they coat with a varnish that prevents the poison from being exuded quite so freely. They destroy virtue, but preserve its public semblance,[3] and this at least is a fine thing to do. They introduce politeness and propriety in its stead, and for the fear of appearing wicked they substitute the fear of appearing ridiculous . . .

It would at first seem that men in that state having neither moral relations of any sort between them, nor known duties, could be neither good nor wicked, and had neither vices nor virtues, unless these words are taken in a physical sense and the qualities that can harm an individual's self-preservation are called vices, and those that can contribute to it, virtues; in which case he who least resists the simple impulsions of Nature would have to be called the most virtuous: But without straying from the ordinary sense, we should suspend the judgment we might pass on such a situation and be wary of our Prejudices until it has been established, Scale in hand, whether there are more virtues than vices among civilized men, or whether their virtues are more advantageous than their vices are detrimental, or whether the progress of their knowledge is sufficient compensation for the harms they do one another in proportion as they learn of the good they should do, or whether their situation would not, on the whole, be happier if they had neither harm to fear nor good to hope for from anyone, than they are by having subjected themselves to universal dependence and obligated themselves to receive everything from those who do not obligate themselves to give them anything.

Above all, let us not conclude with Hobbes that because he has no idea of goodness man is naturally wicked, that he is vicious because he does not know virtue, that he always refuses to those of his kind services which he does not believe he owes them, or that by virtue of the right which he reasonably claims to the things he needs, he insanely imagines himself to be the sole owner of the entire Universe. Hobbes very clearly saw the defect of all modern definitions of Natural right: but the conclusions he draws from his own definition show that he understands it in a sense that is no less false. By reasoning on the basis of the principles he establishes, this Author should have said that, since the state of Nature is the state in which the care for our own preservation is least prejudicial to the self-preservation of others, it follows that this state was the most conducive to Peace and the best suited to Mankind. He says precisely the contrary because he improperly included in Savage man's care for his preservation the need to satisfy a multitude of passions that are the product of Society and have made Laws necessary. A wicked man is, he says, a sturdy Child; it remains to be seen whether Savage Man is a sturdy Child; Even if it were granted him that he is, what would he conclude? That if this man, when sturdy, were as dependent on others as when he is weak, he would not stop at any kind of excess, that he would strike his Mother if she were slow to give him the breast, that he would strangle one of his young brothers if he discommoded him, that he would bite the other's leg if he hurt or bothered him; but being sturdy and being dependent are two contradictory assumptions in the state of Nature; Man is weak when he is dependent, and he is emancipated before he is sturdy. Hobbes did not see that the same cause that keeps Savages from using their reason, as our Jurists claim they do, at the same time keeps them from abusing their faculties, as he himself claims they do; so that one might say that Savages are not wicked precisely because they do not know what it is to be good; for it is neither the growth of enlightenment nor the curb of the Law, but the calm of the passions and the ignorance of vice that keep them from evil-doing; *so much more does the ignorance of vice profit these than the knowledge of virtue profits those.* There is, besides, another Principle which Hobbes did not notice and which, having been given to man in order under certain circumstances to soften the ferociousness of his *amour propre* or of the desire for self-preservation prior to the birth of *amour propre*, tempers his ardor for well-being with an innate repugnance to see his kind suffer. I do not believe I need fear any contradiction in granting to man the only Natural virtue which the most extreme Detractor of human virtues was forced to acknowledge. I speak of Pity, a disposition suited to beings as weak and as subject to so many ills as we are; a virtue all the more universal and useful to man as it precedes the exercise of all reflection in him, and so Natural that even the Beasts sometimes show evident signs of it. To say nothing of the tenderness Mothers feel for their young and of the dangers they brave in order to protect them, one daily sees the repugnance of Horses to trample a living Body underfoot; An animal never goes past a dead animal of his own Species without some restlessness: Some even give them a kind of burial; and the mournful lowing of Cattle entering a Slaughter-House conveys their impression of the horrible sight that strikes them. It is a pleasure to see the author of the *Fable of the Bees* forced to recognize man as a compassionate and sensitive Being, and abandon, in the example he gives of it, his cold and subtle style, to offer us the pathetic picture of a man locked up, who outside sees a ferocious Beast tearing a Child from his Mother's breast, breaking his weak limbs with its murderous fangs, and tearing the Child's throbbing entrails with its claws. What a dreadful agitation must not this witness to an event in which he takes no personal interest whatsoever experience? What anguish must he not suffer at this sight, for not being able to give any help to the fainted Mother or the dying Child?

Such is the pure movement of Nature prior to all reflection: such is the force of natural pity, which the most depraved morals still have difficulty destroying, since in our theaters one daily sees being moved and weeping at the miseries of some unfortunate person people who, if they were in the Tyrant's place, would only increase their enemy's torments; like bloodthirsty Sulla, so sensitive to ills which he had not caused, or that Alexander of Pherae who dared not attend the performance of a single tragedy for fear that he might be seen to moan with Andromache and Priam, but who listened without emotion to the cries of so many citizens daily being murdered on his orders.

> *When nature gave man tears,*
> *She proclaimed that he was tender-hearted.*

Mandeville clearly sensed that, for all their morality, men would never have been anything but monsters if Nature had not given them pity in support of reason: but he did not see that from this single attribute flow all the social virtues he wants to deny men. Indeed, what are generosity, Clemency, Humanity, if not Pity applied to the weak, the guilty, or the species in general? Even Benevolence and friendship, properly understood, are the products of a steady pity focused on a particular object; for what else is it to wish that someone not suffer, than to wish that he be happy? Even if it were true that commiseration is nothing but a sentiment that puts us in the place of him who suffers, a sentiment that is obscure and lively in Savage man, developed but weak in Civil man, what difference could this idea make to the truth of what I say, except to give it additional force? Indeed commiseration will be all the more energetic in proportion as the Onlooking animal identifies more intimately with the suffering animal: Now this identification must, clearly, have been infinitely closer in the state of Nature than in the state of reasoning. It is reason that engenders *amour propre*, and reflection that reinforces it; reason that turns man back upon himself; reason that separates him from everything that troubles and afflicts him: It is Philosophy that isolates him; by means of Philosophy he secretly says, at the sight of a suffering man, perish if you wish, I am safe. Only dangers that threaten the entire society still disturb the Philosopher's tranquil slumber, and rouse him from his bed. One of his kind can with impunity be murdered beneath his window; he only has to put his hands over his ears and to argue with himself a little in order to prevent Nature, which rebels within him, from letting him identify with the man being assassinated. Savage man has not this admirable talent; and for want of wisdom and of reason he is always seen to yield impetuously to the first sentiment of Humanity. In Riots, in Street-brawls, the Populace gathers, the prudent man withdraws; it is the rabble, it is the Marketwomen who separate the combatants, and keeps honest folk from murdering one another.

It is therefore quite certain that pity is a natural sentiment which, by moderating in every individual the activity of self-love, contributes to the mutual preservation of the entire species. It is pity that carries us without reflection to the assistance of those we see suffer; pity that, in the state of Nature, takes the place of Laws, morals, and virtue, with the advantage that no one is tempted to disobey its gentle voice; pity that will keep any sturdy Savage from robbing a weak child or an infirm old man of his hard-won subsistence if he can hope to find his own elsewhere: pity that, in place of that sublime maxim of reasoned justice *Do unto others as you would have them do unto you*, inspires in all Men this other maxim of natural goodness, much less perfect but perhaps more useful than the first: *Do your good with the least possible harm to others*. It is, in a word, in this Natural sentiment rather than in subtle arguments that one has to seek the cause of the repugnance to evil-doing which every human being would feel even independently of the maxims of education. While Socrates and minds of his stamp may be able to acquire virtue through reason, mankind would long ago have ceased to be if its preservation had depended solely on the reasonings of those who make it up.

Notes

1   I complain that Philosophy loosens the bonds of society formed by mutual esteem and benevolence, and I complain that the sciences, the arts and all the other objects of commerce tighten the bonds of society through self-interest. And it is indeed impossible to tighten one of these bonds without the other relaxing by as much. There is therefore no contradiction here.

2   I have noticed that at present a great many petty maxims hold sway in the world which seduce simple minds with a false semblance of philosophy and are, besides, very handy for cutting off discussions in an authoritative and peremptory tone without having to consider the issue. One of them is: "Men are everywhere subject to the same passions; everywhere *amour propre* and self-interest guide them; hence they are everywhere the same." When Geometers make an assumption which, argument by argument, leads them to an absurd conclusion, they retrace their steps, and so show the assumption false. The same method, applied to the maxim in question, would readily show its absurdity: But let us argue differently. A Savage is a man, and a European is a man. The half philosopher immediately concludes that the one is no better than the other; but the philosopher says: In Europe the government, the laws, the customs, self-interest, everything places individuals under the necessity of deceiving one another, and of doing so incessantly; everything conspires to make vice a duty for them; they must be wicked if they are to be wise, since there is no greater folly than to provide for the happiness of scoundrels at the expense of one's own. Among Savages self-interest speaks as insistently as it does among us, but it does not say the same things: love of society and care for their common defense are the only bonds that unite them: the word *property*, which causes so many crimes among our honest folk, is, for them, almost devoid of meaning; discussions about interests that divide them simply do not arise among them; nothing leads them to deceive one another; public esteem is the only good to which everyone aspires and which they all deserve. It is perfectly possible that a Savage might commit a bad action, but it is not possible that he will acquire the habit of doing evil, because it would profit him nothing. I believe that men's morals can be very accurately gauged by how much business they have with one another: the more dealings they have, the more they admire their talents and their industry, the more decorously and cunningly are they villains, and the more contemptible they are. I say it reluctantly: the good man is he who has no need to deceive anyone, and the Savage is that man.

> *He is not moved by the people's fasces, nor by the King's purple,*
> *Nor by the discord that pits faithless brothers against one another:*
> *Nor by Rome's affairs, nor by kingdoms doomed to fall. Neither does he*
> *In his misery pity the poor, or envy the rich.*

3   This semblance consists in a certain mildness of morals which sometimes compensates for their lack of purity, a certain appearance of order which averts terrible confusion, a certain admiration for what is fine which keeps what is good from being entirely forgotten. Vice here dons the mask of virtue not as hypocrisy does, in order to deceive and betray, but rather in order to escape, behind this pleasing and sacred effigy, its horror at itself when it sees itself uncovered.

26

IMMANUEL KANT

The rational will overcomes base inclinations

Concerning the indwelling of the evil principle with the good, or, on the radical evil in human nature

That "the world lieth in evil" is a plaint as old as history, old even as the older art, poetry; indeed, as old as that oldest of all fictions, the religion of priest-craft. All agree that the world began in a good estate, whether in a Golden Age, a life in Eden, or a yet more happy community with celestial beings. But they represent that this happiness vanished like a dream and that a Fall into evil (moral evil, with which physical evil ever went hand in hand) presently hurried mankind from bad to worse with accelerated descent; so that now (this "now" is also as old as history) we live in the final age, with the Last Day and the destruction of the world at hand . . .

More modern, though far less prevalent, is the contrasted optimistic belief, which indeed has gained a following solely among philosophers and, of late, especially among those interested in education – the belief that the world steadily (though almost imperceptibly) forges in the other direction, to wit, from bad to better; at least that the predisposition to such a movement is discoverable in human nature. If this belief, however, is meant to apply to *moral* goodness and badness (not simply to the process of civilization), it has certainly not been deduced from experience; the history of all times cries too loudly against it. The belief, we may presume, is a well-intentioned assumption of the moralists, from Seneca to Rousseau, designed to encourage the sedulous cultivation of that seed of goodness which perhaps lies in us – if, indeed, we can count on any such natural basis of goodness in man. We may note that since we take for granted that man is by nature sound of body (as at birth he usually is), no reason appears why, by nature,

Source: *Religion Within the Limits of Reason Alone*, translated by Theodore H. Greene and Hoyt H. Hudson, New York: Harper & Row, 1960.

his soul should not be deemed similarly healthy and free from evil. Is not nature herself, then, inclined to lend her aid to developing in us this moral predisposition to goodness? In the words of Seneca: *Sanabilibus ægrotamus malis*, nosque in rectum genitos *natura, si sanari velimus, adiuvat*.[1]

But since it well may be that both sides have erred in their reading of experience, the question arises whether a middle ground may not at least be possible, namely, that man as a species is neither good nor bad, or at all events that he is as much the one as the other, partly good, partly bad. We call a man evil, however, not because he performs actions that are evil (contrary to law) but because he performs actions that are of such a nature that we may infer from them the presence in him of evil maxims. In and through experience we can observe actions contrary to law, and we can observe (at least in ourselves) that they are performed in the consciousness that they are unlawful; but a man's maxims, sometimes even his own, are not thus observable; consequently the judgment that the agent is an evil man cannot be made with certainty if grounded on experience. In order, then, to call a man evil, it would have to be possible *a priori* to infer from several evil acts done with consciousness of their evil, or from one such act, an underlying evil maxim; and further, from this maxim to infer the presence in the agent of an underlying common ground, itself a maxim, of all particular morally-evil maxims.

Lest difficulty at once be encountered in the expression *nature*, which, if it meant (as it usually does) the opposite of *freedom* as a basis of action, would flatly contradict the predicates *morally* good or evil, let it be noted that by "nature of man" we here intend only the subjective ground of the exercise (under objective moral laws) of man's freedom in general; this ground – whatever is its character – is the necessary antecedent of every act apparent to the senses. But this subjective ground, again, must itself always be an expression of freedom (for otherwise the use or abuse of man's power of choice in respect of the moral law could not be imputed to him nor could the good or bad in him be called moral). Hence the source of evil cannot lie in an object *determining* the will through inclination, nor yet in a natural impulse; it can lie only in a rule made by the will for the use of its freedom, that is, in a maxim. But now it must not be considered permissible to inquire into the subjective ground in man of the adoption of this maxim rather than of its opposite. If this ground itself were not ultimately a maxim, but a mere natural impulse, it would be possible to trace the use of our freedom wholly to determination by natural causes; this, however, is contradictory to the very notion of freedom. When we say, then, Man is by nature good, or, Man is by nature evil, this means only that there is in him an ultimate ground (inscrutable to us) of the adoption of good maxims or of evil maxims (i.e., those contrary to law), and this he has, being a man; and hence he thereby expresses the character of his species.

We shall say, therefore, of the character (good or evil) distinguishing man from other possible rational beings, that it is *innate* in him. Yet in doing so we shall ever take the position that nature is not to bear the blame (if it is evil) or take the credit (if it is good), but that man himself is its author. But since the ultimate ground of the adoption of our maxims, which must itself lie in free choice, cannot be a fact revealed in experience, it follows that the good or evil in man (as the ultimate subjective ground of the adoption of this or that maxim with reference to the moral law) is termed innate only in *this* sense, that it is posited as the ground antecedent to every use of freedom in experience (in earliest youth as far back as birth) and is thus conceived of as present in man at birth – though birth need not be the cause of it.

Observation

The conflict between the two hypotheses presented above is based on a disjunctive proposition: *Man is* (by nature) *either morally good or morally evil.* It might easily occur to any one, however, to ask whether this disjunction is valid, and whether some might not assert that man is by nature either of the two, others, that man is at once both, in some respects good, in other respects evil. Experience actually seems to substantiate the middle ground between the two extremes.

It is, however, of great consequence to ethics in general to avoid admitting, so long as it is possible, of anything morally intermediate, whether in actions (*adiophora*) or in human characters; for with such ambiguity all maxims are in danger of forfeiting their precision and stability. Those who are partial to this strict mode of thinking are usually called *rigorists* (a name which is intended to carry reproach, but which actually praises); their opposites may be called *latitudinarians*. These latter, again, are either latitudinarians of neutrality, whom we may call *indifferentists*, or else latitudinarians of coalition, whom we may call *syncretists*.

According to the rigoristic diagnosis, the answer to the question at issue rests upon the observation, of great importance to morality, that freedom of the will is of a wholly unique nature in that an incentive can determine the will to an action *only so far as the individual has incorporated it into his maxim* (has made it the general rule in accordance with which he will conduct himself); only thus can an incentive, whatever it may be, co-exist with the absolute spontaneity of the will (i.e., freedom). But the moral law, in the judgment of reason, is in itself an incentive, and whoever makes it his maxim is *morally* good. If, now, this law does not determine a person's will in the case of an action which has reference to the law, an incentive contrary to it must influence his choice; and since, by hypothesis, this can only happen when a man adopts this incentive (and thereby the deviation from the moral law) into his maxim (in which case he is an evil man) it follows that his disposition in respect to the moral law is never indifferent, never neither good nor evil.

Neither can a man be morally good in some ways and at the same time morally evil in others. His being good in one way means that he has incorporated the moral law into his maxim; were he, therefore, at the same time evil in another way, while his maxim would be universal as based on the moral law of obedience to duty, which is essentially single and universal, it would at the same time be only particular; but this is a contradiction.[2]

To have a good or an evil disposition as an inborn natural constitution does not here mean that it has not been acquired by the man who harbors it, that he is not author of it, but rather, that it has not been acquired in time (that he has *always* been good, or evil, *from his youth up*). . . . Yet this disposition itself must have been adopted by free choice, for otherwise it could not be imputed. . . . [T]he man of whom we say, "He is by nature good or evil," is to be understood not as the single individual (for then one man could be considered as good, by nature, another as evil), but as the entire race; that we are entitled so to do can only be proved when anthropological research shows that the evidence, which justifies us in attributing to a man one of these characters as innate, is such as to give no ground for excepting anyone, and that the attribution therefore holds for the race.

Concerning the original predisposition to good in human nature

We may conveniently divide this predisposition, with respect to function, into three divisions, to be considered as elements in the fixed character and destiny of man:

1   The predisposition to *animality* in man, taken as a *living* being;
2   The predisposition to *humanity* in man, taken as a living and at the same time a *rational* being;
3   The predisposition to *personality* in man, taken as a rational and at the same time an *accountable* being.

The predisposition to *animality* in mankind may be brought under the general title of physical and purely *mechanical* self-love, wherein no reason is demanded. It is threefold: first, for self-preservation; second, for the propagation of the species, through the sexual impulse, and for the care of offspring so begotten; and third, for community with other men, i.e., the social impulse. On these three stems can be grafted all kinds of vices (which, however, do not spring from this predisposition itself as a root). They may be termed vices of the coarseness of nature, and in their greatest deviation from natural purposes are called the *beastly* vices of *gluttony* and *drunkenness*, *lasciviousness*, and *wild lawlessness* (in relation to other men).

The predisposition to humanity can be brought under the general title of a self-love which is physical and yet *compares* (for which reason is required); that is to say, we judge ourselves happy or unhappy only by making comparison with others. Out of this self-love springs the inclination *to acquire worth in the opinion of others*. This is originally a desire merely for *equality*, to allow no one superiority above oneself, bound up with a constant care lest others strive to attain such superiority; but from this arises gradually the unjustifiable craving to win it for oneself over others. Upon this twin stem of *jealousy* and *rivalry* may be grafted the very great vices of secret and open animosity against all whom we look upon as not belonging to us – vices, however, which really do not sprout of themselves from nature as their root; rather are they inclinations, aroused in us by the anxious endeavors of others to attain a hated superiority over us, to attain for ourselves as a measure of precaution and for the sake of safety such a position over others. For nature, indeed, wanted to use the idea of such rivalry (which in itself does not exclude mutual love) only as a spur to culture. Hence the vices which are grafted upon this inclination might be their termed vices of *culture*; in highest degree of malignancy, as, for example, in *envy, ingratitude, spitefulness*, etc. (where they are simply the idea of a maximum of evil going beyond what is human), they can be called the *diabolical vices*.

Man is evil by nature

Viliis nemo sine nascitur. – Horace

In view of what has been said above, the proposition, Man is *evil*, can mean only, He is conscious of the moral law but has nevertheless adopted into his maxim the (occasional) deviation therefrom. He is evil *by nature*, means but this, that evil can be predicated of man as a species; not that such a quality can be inferred from the concept of his species (that is, of man in general) – for then it would be necessary; but rather that from what we know of man through experience we cannot judge otherwise of him, or, that we may presuppose evil to be subjectively necessary to every man, even to the best. Now this propensity must itself be considered as morally evil, yet not as a natural predisposition but rather as something that can be imputed to man, and consequently it must consist in maxims of the will which are contrary to the law. Further, for the sake of freedom, these maxims must in themselves be considered contingent, a circumstance which, on the other hand, will not tally with the universality of this evil *unless* the ultimate subjective ground of all maxims somehow or other is entwined with and, as it were, rooted in humanity itself. Hence we can call this a natural propensity to evil, and as we must, after all, ever hold man himself responsible for it, we can further call it a *radical* innate *evil* in human nature (yet none the less brought upon us by ourselves).

Concerning the origin of evil in human nature

An origin (a first origin) is the derivation of an effect from its first cause, that is, from that cause which is not in turn the effect of another cause of the same kind. It can be considered either as an *origin in reason* or as an *origin in time*. In the former sense, regard is had only to the *existence* of the effect; in the latter, to its *occurrence*, and hence it is related as an event to its *first cause in time*. If an effect is referred to a cause to which it is bound under the laws of freedom, as is true in the case of moral evil, then the determination of the will to the production of this effect is conceived of as bound up with its determining ground not in time but merely in rational representation; such an effect cannot be derived from any *preceding* state whatsoever. Yet derivation of this sort is always necessary when an evil action, as an *event* in the world, is referred to its natural cause. To seek the temporal origin of free acts as such (as though they were natural effects) is thus a contradiction. Hence it is also a contradiction to seek the temporal origin of man's moral character, so far as it is considered as contingent, since this character signifies the ground of the *exercise* of freedom; this ground (like the determining ground of the free will generally) must be sought in purely rational representations.

However the origin of moral evil in man is constituted, surely of all the explanations of the spread and propagation of this evil through all members and generations of our race, the most inept is that which describes it as descending to us as an *inheritance* from our first parents; for one can say of moral evil precisely what the poet said of good: *genus et proavos, et* quae non fecimus ipsi, *vix ea nostra puto*. Yet we should note that, in our search for the origin of this evil, we do not deal first of all with the propensity thereto (as *peccatum in potentia*); rather do we direct our attention to the actual evil of given actions with respect to its inner possibility – to what must take place within the will if evil is to be performed.

In the search for the rational origin of evil actions, every such action must be regarded as though the individual had fallen into it directly from a state of innocence. For whatever his previous deportment may have been, whatever natural causes may have been influencing him, and whether these causes were to be found within him or outside him, his action is yet free and determined by none of these causes; hence it can and must always be judged as an *original* use of his will. He should have refrained from that action, whatever his temporal circumstances and entanglements; for through no cause in the world can he cease to be a freely acting being. Rightly is it said that to a man's account are set down the *consequences* arising from his former free acts which were contrary to the law; but this merely amounts to saying that man need not involve himself in the evasion of seeking to establish whether or not these consequences are free, since there exists in the admittedly free action, which was their cause, ground sufficient for holding him accountable. However evil a man has been up to the very moment of an impending free act (so that evil has actually become custom or second nature) it was not only his duty to have been better [in the past], it is *now* still his duty to better himself. To do so must be within his power, and if he does not do so, he is susceptible of, and subjected to, imputability in the very moment of that action, just as much as though, endowed with a predisposition to good (which is inseparable from freedom), he had stepped out of a state of innocence into evil. Hence we cannot inquire into the temporal origin of this deed, but solely into its rational origin, if we are thereby to determine and, wherever possible, to elucidate the propensity, if it exists, i.e., the general subjective ground of the adoption of transgression into our maxim.

The foregoing agrees well with that manner of presentation which the Scriptures use, whereby the origin of evil in the human race is depicted as having a [temporal] *beginning*, this beginning being presented in a narrative, wherein what in its essence must be considered as primary (without regard to the element of time) appears as coming first in time. According to this account, evil does not start from a propensity thereto as its underlying basis, for otherwise the beginning of evil would not have its source in freedom; rather does it start from *sin* (by which is meant the transgressing of the moral law as a *divine command*). The state of man prior to all propensity to evil is called the state of *innocence*. The moral law became known to mankind, as it must to any being not pure but tempted by desires, in the form of a *prohibition* (Genesis II, 16–17). Now instead of straightway following this law as an adequate incentive (the only incentive which is unconditionally good and regarding which there is no further doubt), man looked about for other incentives (Genesis III, 6) such as can be good only conditionally (namely, so far as they involve no infringement of the law). He then made it his maxim — if one thinks of his action as consciously springing from freedom — to follow the law of duty, not as duty, but, if need be, with regard to other aims. Thereupon he began to call in question the severity of the commandment which excludes the influence of all other incentives; then by sophistry he reduced obedience to the law to the merely conditional character of a means (subject to the principle of self-love); and finally he adopted into his maxim of conduct the ascendancy of the sensuous impulse over the incentive which springs from the law — and thus occurred sin (Genesis III, 6). *Mutato nomine de te fabula narratur.* From all this it is clear that we daily act in the same way, and that therefore "in Adam all have sinned" and still sin; except that in us there is presupposed an innate propensity to transgression, whereas in the first man, from the point of view of time, there is presupposed no such propensity but rather innocence; hence transgression on his part is called a *fall into sin*; but with us sin is represented as resulting from an already innate wickedness in our nature. This propensity, however, signifies no more than this, that if we wish to address ourselves to the explanation of evil in terms of its *beginning in time*, we must search for the causes of each deliberate transgression in a previous period of our lives, far back to that period wherein the use of reason had not yet developed, and thus back to a propensity to evil (as a natural ground) which is therefore called innate — the source of evil. But to trace the causes of evil in the instance of the first man, who is depicted as already in full command of the use of his reason, is neither necessary nor feasible, since otherwise this basis (the evil propensity) would have had to be created in him; therefore his sin is set forth as engendered directly from innocence. We must not, however, look for an origin in time of a moral character for which we are to be held responsible; though to do so is inevitable if we wish to *explain* the contingent existence of this character (and perhaps it is for this reason that Scripture, in conformity with this weakness of ours, has thus pictured the temporal origin of evil).

But the rational origin of this perversion of our will whereby it makes lower incentives supreme among its maxims, that is, of the propensity to evil, remains inscrutable to us, because this propensity itself must be set down to our account and because, as a result, that ultimate ground of all maxims would in turn involve the adoption of an evil maxim [as its basis]. Evil could have sprung only from the morally-evil (not from mere limitations in our nature); and yet the original predisposition (which no one other than man himself could have corrupted, if he is to be held responsible for this corruption) is a predisposition to good; there is then for us no conceivable ground from which the moral evil in us could originally have come. This inconceivability, together with a more accurate specification of the wickedness of our race, the Bible expresses in the historical narrative as follows. It finds a place for evil at the creation of the world, yet not in man, but in a *spirit* of an originally loftier destiny. Thus is the *first* beginning of all evil represented as inconceivable by us (for whence came evil to that spirit?); but man is represented as having fallen into evil only *through seduction*, and hence as being *not basically* corrupt (even as regards his original predisposition to good) but rather as still capable of an improvement, in contrast to a seducing *spirit*, that is, a being for whom temptation of the flesh cannot be accounted as an alleviation of guilt. For man, therefore, who despite a corrupted heart yet possesses a good will, there remains hope of a return to the good from which he has strayed.

Natural inclinations, *considered in themselves*, are *good*, that is, not a matter of reproach, and it is not only futile to want to extirpate them but to do so would also be harmful and blameworthy. Rather, let them be tamed and instead of clashing with one another they can be brought into harmony in a wholeness which is called happiness. Now the reason which accomplishes this is termed *prudence*. But only what is opposed to the moral law is evil in itself, absolutely reprehensible, and must be completely eradicated; and that reason which teaches this truth, and more especially that which puts it into actual practice, alone deserves the name of *wisdom*. The vice corresponding to this may indeed be termed *folly*, but again only when reason feels itself strong enough not merely to *hate* vice as something to be feared, and to arm itself against it, but to *scorn* vice (with all its temptations) . . .

Now a change of heart is a departure from evil and an entrance into goodness, the laying off of the old man and the putting on of the new, since the man becomes dead unto sin (and therefore to all inclinations so far as they lead thereto) in order to become alive unto righteousness. But in this charge, regarded as an intellectual determination, there are not two moral acts separated by an interval of time but only a single act, for the departure from evil is possible only through the agency of the good disposition which effects the individual's entrance into goodness, and vice versa. So the good principle is present quite as much in the desertion of the evil as in the adoption of the good disposition, and the pain, which by rights accompanies the former disposition, ensues wholly from the latter. The coming forth from the corrupted into the good disposition is, in itself (as "the death of the old man," "the crucifying of the flesh"), a sacrifice and an entrance upon a long train of life's ills. These the new man undertakes in the disposition of the Son of God, that is, merely for the sake of the good, though really they are due as *punishments* to another, namely to the old man (for the old man is indeed morally another).

Although the man (regarded from the point of view of his empirical nature as a sentient being) is *physically* the self-same guilty person as before and must be judged as such before a moral tribunal and hence by himself; yet, because of his new disposition, he is (regarded as an intelligible being) *morally* another in the eyes of a divine judge for whom this disposition takes the place of action. And this moral disposition which in all its purity (like unto the purity of the Son of God) the man has made his own – or, (if we personify this idea) this Son of God, Himself – bears as *vicarious substitute* the guilt of sin for him, and indeed for all who believe (practically) in Him; as *savior* He renders satisfaction to supreme justice by His sufferings and death; and as *advocate* He makes it possible for men to hope to appear before their judge as justified. Only it must be remembered that (in this mode of representation) the suffering which the new man, in becoming dead to the *old*, must accept throughout life is pictured as a death endured once for all by the representative of mankind.

Notes

1   *De ira*, II, 13, 1: "We are sick with curable diseases, and if we wish to be cured, nature comes to our aid, *for we were born to health.*"
2   The ancient moral philosophers, who pretty well exhausted all that can be said upon virtue, have not left untouched the two questions mentioned above. The first they expressed thus: Must virtue be learned? (Is man by nature indifferent as regards virtue and vice?) The second they put thus: Is there more than one virtue (so that man might be virtuous in some respects, in others vicious)? Both questions were answered by them, with rigoristic precision, in the negative, and rightly so; for they were considering virtue *as such*, as it is in the idea of reason (that which man ought to be). If, however, we wish to pass moral judgment on this moral being, man *as he appears*, i.e., as experience reveals him to us, we can answer both questions in the affirmative; for in this case we judge him not according to the standard of pure reason (at a divine tribunal) but by an empirical standard (before a human judge).

Part 6

THE ROMANTICISM OF EVIL

Aubrey Beardsley: "Salome."

When divinity is primarily seen in its form as Creator, evil becomes associated with the will-to-self-creation rather than with lawless disobedience. As creativity rather than obedience, calculation or sociability becomes the distinguishing mark of humankind, its boundless presumption – a transformation of the sin of pride – becomes the source of evil.

The Marquis de Sade (1740–1814) described himself as a *libertine*: he linked his defense of political liberty to his defiant exposure of the pieties of religion and of conventional morality. While he acknowledged that "murder is . . . the cruelest . . . irreparable . . . offense that man commits against his fellows," de Sade argued that the impulse to murder is, along with incest, rape and other forms of cruelty, a natural impulse. Indeed, Nature is, as he sees it, itself engaged in destructive, murderous activity as a form of self-creation.

Goethe (1749–1832) has Faust characterize "the endless Power" as "creative, living and benign." Like Milton's Satan, Goethe's Mephistopheles is searingly truthful. Claiming the part of Mother Night, he says "I am the Darkness which gave birth to Light . . . the Spirit that constantly denies." Able to transmute himself as well as the elements, Satan denies the natural order. Ironies abound, the Spirit of denial finds itself to be the force "which would do evil [but which] forever works the good." In offering Faust the power of living fantasy, Mephistopheles intends to claim Faust's soul for hell. But Faust is, in the end, redeemed by creative love.

Blake (1757–1827) completes the creative reversal of good and evil. The true evils of mankind are the opposition between spirit and body exemplified in the chains of the Law, in the charge of pious obedience and in the lure of material progress. Creativity, energy, sheer delight – these are the forces of the true God. Blake's vision of Hell is a vision of a world confined by the Bible, by Aristotle's *Analytics*, by the works of Locke and Newton. His vision of Heaven is a vision of delight in the vitality of the senses, in ever renewing gratified desire, in the exuberant imagination.

Hawthorne's (1804–1864) stories and novels reverse Blake's paean to the imagination. They evoke its corrupting lure. Young Goodman Brown was captured by the evils evoked by his own imagination. They affected his perceptions, subjected him to terror and dread. Neither his goodly neighbors nor his true wife Faith were able to free him from the fearful enchantments of evil conjured by a night in a dark encompassing forest. While references to Gnostic works like "The Pearl," to Dante, to Jonathan Edwards and Puritan sermons abound, it is difficult to locate Hawthorne's own attitudes. Does he share the Puritan vision, the Puritan fears of Darkness? Or is he portraying these so darkly that we shudder at a world so filled with horror?

In "Flowers of Evil," Baudelaire (1821–1881) envelops the reader with sensory images of evil, the fetid corruption of flesh, the scent of decaying flowers, the names of vices, the instruments of destruction. But he declares that all these are as nothing to the BOREDOM from which the lust to evil springs. Baudelaire evokes the seductive enchantment of over-ripe corruption.

Schopenhauer (1788–1860) abandons all attempts to rationalize and reinterpret metaphysical, physical and moral evil. The will that has been the glory of man's freedom – his claim to morality or to creativity – is now revealed as raw, mindless energy. Growth is a form of strife and suffering; the creativity of the imagination issues in illusion; desires are doomed to defeat; pain is far more salient than pleasure; men are unjust and cruel to one another. In all this, there is no hope for redemption by a hidden hand, designing an underlying or an emergent order.

Nietzsche (1844–1900) locates the origins of morality in admiration and disgust. Initially the opposition of "good and bad" connoted the difference between excellent and defective examples of the species. (Analogy: good and bad apples.) He projects the archaic Greek heroes as free and independent, joyous and creative, bent on celebrating and achieving excellence. By contrast, the weak, the debilitated, the passive and submissive are inferior examples of the species, further scarred by animus and resentment. As all men, strong and weak alike, are moved by the will to power, the resentful weak move to their debased forms of power: to self-righteousness, condemning exuberance while affirming humility. Nietzsche's genealogical history of the transformations of the will to power conjectures that the weak unite to form a rancorous herd, insidiously bent on acquiring their own forms of domination. Themselves swayed by the poetic magic of prophets and priests, the weak lure the strong and free to the mysteries of religion; in their turn, sovereigns and judges subject them to the restrictions of Law; the sanctimonious bind them to the obligations of Morality and, finally, scholars subdue them to the awe of Knowledge. The notion of conscience, with its imputation of punishment and guilt (*geld*) as payment or reparation, has its origins in a mercantile society, where the infraction of law incurs debt (*schuld*) to society. "Bad conscience" is an illness: the weak turn their corrosive rancor against themselves.

27

THE MARQUIS
DE SADE

Murdering nature

Philosophy in the Bedroom

Man follows Nature's impulses when he indulges in homicide; it is Nature who advises him, and the man who destroys his fellow is to Nature what are the plague and famine, like them sent by her hand which employs every possible means more speedily to obtain of destruction this primary matter, itself absolutely essential to her works . . .

[W]hat other than Nature's voice suggests to us personal hatreds, revenges, wars, in a word, all those causes of perpetual murder? Now, if she incites us to murderous acts, she has need of them; that once grasped, how may we suppose ourselves guilty in her regard when we do nothing more than obey her intentions?

But that is more than what is needed to convince any enlightened reader, that for murder ever to be an outrage to nature is impossible.

Is it a political crime? We must avow, on the contrary, that it is, unhappily, merely one of policy's and politics' greatest instruments. It is not by dint of murders that France is free today? Needless to say, here we are referring to the murders occasioned by war, not to the atrocities committed by plotters and rebels; the latter, destined to the public's execration, have only to be recollected to arouse forever general horror and indignation. What study, what science, has greater need of murder's support than that which tends only to deceive, whose sole end is the expansion of one nation at another's expense? Are wars, the unique fruit of this political barbarism, anything but the means whereby a nation is nourished, whereby it is strengthened, whereby it is buttressed? And what is war if not the science of destruction?

Is murder then a crime against society? But how could that reasonably be imagined? What difference does it make to this murderous society, whether it have one member more, or less? Will its laws, its manners, its customs be vitiated? Has an individual's

Source: *The Marquis de Sade: Justine, Philosophy in the Bedroom, and Other Writings*, compiled and translated by Richard Seaver and Austryn Wainhouse, New York: Grove Weidenfeld, 1965.

death ever had any influence upon the general mass? And after the loss of the greatest battle, what am I saying? after the obliteration of half the world – or, if one wishes, of the entire world – would the little number of survivors, should there by any, notice even the faintest difference in things? No, alas. Nor would Nature notice any either, and the stupid pride of man, who believes everything created for him, would be dashed indeed, after the total extinction of the human species, were it to be seen that nothing in Nature had changed, and that the stars' flight had not for that been retarded . . .

Destruction being one of the chief laws of Nature, nothing that destroys can be criminal; how might an action which so well serves Nature ever be outrageous to her? This destruction of which man is wont to boast is, moreover, nothing but an illusion; murder is no destruction; he who commits it does but alter forms, he gives back to Nature the elements whereof the hand of this skilled artisan instantly re-creates other beings: now, as creations cannot but afford delight to him by whom they are wrought, the murderer thus prepares for Nature a pleasure most agreeable, he furnishes her materials, she employs them without delay, and the act fools have had the madness to blame is nothing but meritorious in the universal agent's eye. 'Tis our pride prompts us to elevate murder into crime. Esteeming ourselves the foremost of the universe's creatures, we have stupidly imagined that every hurt this sublime creature endures must perforce be an enormity; we have believed Nature would perish should our marvelous species chance to be blotted out of existence, while the whole extirpation of the breed would, by returning to Nature the creative faculty she has entrusted to us, reinvigorate her, she would have again that energy we deprive her of by propagating our own selves . . . . [A]n ambitious sovereign can destroy, at his ease and without the least scruple, the enemies prejudicial to his grandiose designs. . . . Cruel laws, arbitrary, imperious laws can likewise every century assassinate millions of individuals and we, feeble and wretched creatures, we are not allowed to sacrifice a single being to our vengeance or our caprice!

28

J.W. VON GOETHE

Mephistopheles speaks

(As the mist falls away, MEPHISTOPHELES steps forth from behind the stove, dressed as a traveling scholar.)

MEPHISTOPHELES. What is the gentleman's pleasure? . . .

[. . .]

    I salute you, learned Sir.

FAUST. What is your name?

MEPHISTOPHELES.   For one so disesteeming

    The word, the question seems so small to me,

    And for a man disdainful of all seeming,

    Who searches only for reality.

FAUST. With gentlemen like you, their nature is deduced

    Quite often from the name that's used,

    As all too patently applies

    When you are named Corrupter, Liar, God of Flies.

    All right, who are you then?

MEPHISTOPHELES.   Part of that Force which would

    Do evil ever yet forever works the good.

FAUST. What sense is there beneath that riddling guise?

MEPHISTOPHELES. I am the Spirit that constantly denies!

    And rightly so; for everything that's ever brought

    To life deserves to come to naught.

    Better if nothing ever came to be.

    Thus all that you call sin, you see,

    And havoc – evil, in short – is meant

    To be my proper element.

FAUST. You call yourself a part, yet stand quite whole before me there?

Source: *Faust*, translated by Charles E. Passage, Indianapolis, Ind.: Bobbs–Merrill Company, Inc., 1965.

MEPHISTOPHELES. It is the modest truth that I declare.
  Now folly's little microcosm, man,
  Boasts *him*self whole as often as he can. . . .
  I am part of the part which once was absolute,
  Part of the Darkness which gave birth to Light,
  The haughty Light, which now seeks to dispute
  The ancient rank and range of Mother Night,
  But unsuccessfully, because, try as it will,
  It is stuck fast to bodies still.
  It streams from bodies, bodies it makes fair,
  A body hinders its progression; thus I hope
  It won't be long before its scope
  Will in the bodies' ruination share.
FAUST. I see your fine objectives now!
  Wholesale annihilation fails somehow,
  So you go at it one by one.
MEPHISTOPHELES. I don't get far, when all is said and done.
  The thing opposed to Nothingness,
  This stupid earth, this Somethingness,
  For all that I have undertaken
  Against it, still remains unshaken;
  In spite of tempest, earthquake, flood, and flame
  The earth and ocean calmly stay the same.
  And as for that damned stuff, the brood of beasts and man,
  With them there's nothing I can do.
  To think how many I have buried too!
  Fresh blood runs in their veins just as it always ran.
  And so it goes. Sometimes I could despair!
  In earth, in water, and in air
  A thousand growing things unfold,
  In dryness, wetness, warmth, and cold!
  Had I not specially reserved the flame,
  I wouldn't have a thing in my own name.
FAUST. So you shake your cold devil's fist
  Clenched in futile rage malign,
  So you the endless Power resist,
  The creative, living, and benign!
  Some other goal had best be sought,
  Chaos' own fantastic son!
[. . .]

FAUST.   So hell has its own law?
  I find that good, because a pact could then
  Perhaps be worked out with you gentlemen?

29
WILLIAM BLAKE
Shame is pride's cloak

The Marriage of Heaven and Hell

The argument

Rintrah roars & shakes his fires in the burden'd air;
Hungry clouds swag on the deep.

Once meek, and in a perilous path,
The just man kept his course along
The vale of death . . .

Then the perilous path was planted:
And a river and a spring
On every cliff and tomb:
And on the bleached bones
Red clay brought forth.

Till the villain left the paths of ease,
To walk in perilous paths, and drive
The just man into barren climes.

Now the sneaking serpent walks
In mild humility,
And the just man rages in the wilds
Where lions roam.

Source: *The Marriage of Heaven and Hell*, London: Oxford University Press, 1975.

Rintrah roars & shakes his fires in the burden'd air;
Hungry clouds swag on the deep.

Without Contraries is no progression. Attraction and Repulsion, Reason and Energy, Love and Hate, are necessary to Human existence.

From these contraries spring what the religious call Good & Evil. Good is the passive that obeys Reason. Evil is the active springing from Energy.

Good is Heaven. Evil is Hell.

The voice of the Devil

All Bibles or sacred codes have been the causes of the following Errors:

1 That Man has two real existing principles: Viz: a Body & a Soul.
2 That Energy, call'd Evil, is alone from the Body, & that Reason, call'd Good, is alone from the Soul.
3 That God will torment Man in Eternity for following his Energies.

But the following Contraries to these are True:

1 Man has no Body distinct from his Soul; for that call'd Body is a portion of Soul discern'd by the five Senses, the chief inlets of Soul in this age.
2 Energy is the only life and is from the Body and Reason is the bound or outward circumference of Energy.
3 Energy is Eternal Delight.

Those who restrain desire, do so because theirs is weak enough to be restrained; and the restrainer or Reason usurps its place & governs the unwilling.

And being restrain'd, it by degrees becomes passive, till it is only the shadow of desire.

The history of this is written in Paradise Lost, & the Governor or Reason is call'd Messiah.

And the original Archangel, or possessor of the command of the heavenly host, is call'd the Devil or Satan, and his children are call'd Sin & Death.

But in the Book of Job, Milton's Messiah is call'd Satan.

For this history has been adopted by both parties.

It indeed appear'd to Reason as if Desire was cast out, but the Devil's account is, that the Messiah fell, & formed a heaven of what he stole from the Abyss.

This is shewn in the Gospel, where he prays to the Father to send the comforter, or Desire, that Reason may have Ideas to build on, the Jehovah of the Bible being no other than [the Devil] he who dwells in flaming fire.

Know that after Christ's death, he became Jehovah.

But in Milton, the Father is Destiny, the Son, a Ratio of the five senses, & the Holy-ghost, Vacuum!

Note: The reason Milton wrote in fetters when he wrote of Angels & God, and at liberty when of Devils & Hell, is because he was a true Poet and of the Devil's party without knowing it.

A memorable fancy

As I was walking among the fires of hell, delighted with the enjoyments of Genius, which to Angels look like torment and insanity, I collected some of their Proverbs; thinking that as the sayings used in a nation mark its character, so the Proverbs of Hell shew the nature of Infernal wisdom better than any description of buildings or garments.

When I came home: on the abyss of the five senses, where a flat sided steep frowns over the present world, I saw a mighty Devil folded in black clouds, hovering on the sides of the rock, with corroding fires he wrote the following sentence now perceived by the minds of men, & read by them on earth:

> How do you know but ev'ry Bird that cuts the airy way,
> Is an immense world of delight, clos'd by your senses five?

Proverbs of hell

In seed time learn, in harvest teach, in winter enjoy.

Drive your cart and your plow over the bones of the dead.

The road of excess leads to the palace of wisdom.

Prudence is a rich ugly old maid courted by Incapacity.

He who desires but acts not, breeds pestilence.

The cut worm forgives the plow.

Dip him in the river who loves water.

A fool sees not the same tree that a wise man sees.

He whose face gives no light, shall never become a star.

Eternity is in love with the productions of time.

The busy bee has no time for sorrow.

The hours of folly are measur'd by the clock; but of wisdom, no
    clock can measure.

All wholsom food is caught without a net or a trap.

Bring out number, weight & measure in a year of dearth.

No bird soars too high, if he soars with his own wings.

A dead body revenges not injuries.

The most sublime act is to set another before you.

If the fool would persist in his folly he would become wise.

Folly is the cloke of knavery.

Shame is Pride's cloke.

Prisons are built with stones of Law, Brothels with bricks of
   Religion.

The pride of the peacock is the glory of God.

The lust of the goat is the bounty of God.

The wrath of the lion is the wisdom of God.

The nakedness of woman is the work of God.

Excess of sorrow laughs. Excess of joy weeps.

The roaring of lions, the howling of wolves, the raging of the
   stormy sea, and the destructive sword, are portions of eternity
   too great for the eye of man.

The fox condemns the trap, not himself.

Joys impregnate. Sorrows bring forth.

Let man wear the fell of the lion, woman the fleece of the sheep.

The bird a nest, the spider a web, man friendship.

The selfish smiling fool, & the sullen, frowning fool shall be both
   thought wise, that they may be a rod.

What is now proved was once only imagin'd.

The rat, the mouse, the fox, the rabbet watch the roots; the lion,
   the tyger, the horse, the elephant, watch the fruits.

The cistern contains: the fountain overflows.

One thought fills immensity.

Always be ready to speak your mind, and a base man will avoid
   you.

Every thing possible to be believ'd is an image of truth.

The eagle never lost so much time, as when he submitted to learn
   of the crow.

The fox provides for himself, but God provides for the lion.

Think in the morning. Act in the noon. Eat in the evening. Sleep
   in the night.

He who has suffer'd you to impose on him knows you.

As the plow follows words, so God rewards prayers.

The tygers of wrath are wiser than the horses of instruction.

Expect poison from the standing water.

You never know what is enough unless you know what is more
   than enough.

Listen to the fool's reproach! it is a kingly title!

The eyes of fire, the nostrils of air, the mouth of water, the beard of earth.

The weak in courage is strong in cunning.

The apple tree never asks the beech how he shall grow; nor the lion, the horse, how he shall take his prey.

The thankful receiver bears a plentiful harvest.

If others had not been foolish, we should be so.

The soul of sweet delight can never be defil'd.

When thou seest an Eagle, thou seest a portion of Genius; lift up thy head!

As the catterpiller chooses the fairest leaves to lay her eggs on, so the priest lays his curse on the fairest joys.

To create a little flower is the labour of ages.

Damn braces: Bless relaxes.

The best wine is the oldest, the best water the newest.

Prayers plow not! Praises reap not!

Joys laugh not! Sorrows weep not!

The head Sublime, the heart Pathos, the genitals Beauty, the hands & feet Proportion.

As the air to a bird or the sea to a fish, so is contempt to the contemptible.

The crow wish'd every thing was black, the owl that every thing was white.

Exuberance is Beauty.

If the lion was advised by the fox, he would be cunning.

Improve[me]nt makes strait roads; but the crooked roads without Improvement are roads of Genius.

Sooner murder an infant in its cradle than nurse unacted desires.

Where man is not, nature is barren.

Truth can never be told so as to be understood, and not be believ'd.

Enough! or Too much . . .

. . . The ancient tradition that the world will be consumed in fire at the end of six thousand years is true, as I have heard from Hell.

For the cherub with his flaming sword is hereby commanded to leave his guard at tree of life; and when he does, the whole creation will be consumed and appear infinite and holy, whereas it now appears finite & corrupt.

This will come to pass by an improvement of sensual enjoyment.

But first the notion that man has a body distinct from his soul is to be expunged; this I shall do by printing in the infernal method, by corrosives, which in Hell are salutary and medicinal, melting apparent surfaces away, and displaying the infinite which was hid.

If the doors of perception were cleansed every thing would appear to man as it is, Infinite.

For man has closed himself up, till he sees all things thro' narrow chinks of his cavern.

A *memorable fancy*

I was in a Printing house in Hell & saw the method in which knowledge is transmitted from generation to generation.

In the first chamber was a Dragon-Man, clearing away the rubbish from a cave's mouth; within, a number of Dragons were hollowing the cave.

In the second chamber was a Viper folding round the rock & the cave, and others adorning it with gold, silver and precious stones.

In the third chamber was an Eagle with wings and feathers of air: he caused the inside of the cave to be infinite; around were numbers of Eagle-like men, who built palaces in the immense cliffs.

In the fourth chamber were Lions of flaming fire, raging around & melting the metals into living fluids.

In the fifth chamber were Unnam'd forms, which cast the metals into the expanse.

There they were receiv'd by Men who occupied the sixth chamber, and took the forms of books & were arranged in libraries . . .

An Angel came to me and said: "O pitiable foolish young man! O horrible! O dreadful state! consider the hot burning dungeon thou art preparing for thyself to all eternity, to which thou art going in such career."

I said: "perhaps you will be willing to shew me my eternal lot & we will contemplate together upon it and see whether your lot or mine is most desirable."

So he took me thro' a stable & thro' a church & down into the church vault, at the end of which was a mill: thro' the mill we went, and came to a cave: down the winding cavern we groped our tedious way, till a void boundless as a nether sky appear'd beneath us, & we held by the roots of trees and hung over this immensity; but I said: "if you please, we will commit ourselves to this void, and see whether providence is here also: if you will not, I will?" but he answer'd: "do not presume, O young-man, but as we here remain, behold thy lot which will soon appear when the darkness passes away."

So I remain'd with him, sitting in the twisted root of an oak; he was suspended in a fungus, which hung with the head downward into the deep.

By degrees we beheld the infinite Abyss, fiery as the smoke of a burning city; beneath us, at an immense distance, was the sun, black but shining; round it were fiery tracks on which revolv'd vast spiders, crawling after their prey, which flew, or rather swum, in the infinite deep, in the most terrific shapes of animals sprung from corruption; & the air was full of them, & seem'd composed of them: these are Devils, and are called Powers of the air . . .

My friend the Angel climb'd up from his station into the mill; I remain'd alone; & then this appearance was no more, but I found myself sitting on a pleasant bank beside a river by moonlight, hearing a harper, who sung to the harp; & his theme was: "The man who never alters his opinion is like standing water, & breeds reptiles of the mind."

But I arose and sought for the mill, & there I found my Angel, who, surprised, asked me how I escaped?

I answer'd: "All that we saw was owing to your metaphysics; for when you ran away, I found myself on a bank by moonlight hearing a harper. But now we have seen my eternal lot, shall I shew you yours?" he laugh'd at my proposal; but I by force suddenly caught him in my arms, & flew westerly thro' the night, till we were elevated above the earth's shadow; then I flung myself with him directly into the body of the sun; here I clothed myself in white, & taking in my hand Swedenborg's volumes, sunk from the glorious clime, and passed all the planets till we came to saturn: here I staid to rest, & then leap'd into the void between saturn & the fixed stars.

"Here," said I, "is your lot, in this space, if space it may be call'd." Soon we saw the stable and the church, & I took him to the altar and open'd the Bible, and lo! it was a deep pit, into which I descended, driving the Angel before me; soon we saw seven houses of brick; one we enter'd; in it were a number of monkeys, baboons, & all of that species, chain'd by the middle, grinning and snatching at one another, but witheld by the shortness of their chains: however, I saw that they sometimes grew numerous, and then the weak were caught by the strong, and with a grinning aspect, first coupled with, & then devour'd, by plucking off first one limb and then another, till the body was left a helpless trunk; this, after grinning & kissing it with seeming fondness, they devour'd too; and here & there I saw one savourily picking the flesh off of his own tail; as the stench terribly annoy'd us both, we went into the mill, & I in my hand brought the skeleton of a body, which in the mill was Aristotle's Analytics.

So the Angel said: "thy phantasy has imposed upon me, & thou oughtest to be ashamed."

I answer'd: "we impose on one another, & it is but lost time to converse with you whose works are only Analytics."

Opposition is true Friendship.

Once I saw a Devil in a flame of fire, who arose before an Angel that sat on a cloud, and the Devil utter'd these words:

"The worship of God is: Honouring his gifts in other men, each according to his genius, and loving the greatest men best: those who envy or calumniate great men hate God; for there is no other God."

The Angel hearing this became almost blue, but mastering himself he grew yellow, & at last white, pink, & smiling, and then replied:

"Thou Idolater. is not God One? & is not he visible in Jesus Christ? and has not Jesus Christ given his sanction to the law of ten commandments, and are not all other men fools, sinners, & nothings?"

The Devil answer'd: "bray a fool in a morter with wheat, yet shall not his folly be beaten out of him; if Jesus Christ is the greatest man, you ought to love him in the greatest degree; now hear how he has given his sanction to the law of ten commandments: did he not mock at the sabbath, and so mock the sabbath's God? murder those who were murder'd because of him? turn away the law from the woman taken in adultery? steal the labor of others to support him? bear false witness when he omitted making a defence before Pilate? covet when he pray'd for his disciples, and when he bid them shake off the dust of their feet against such as refused to lodge them? I tell you, no virtue can exist without breaking these ten commandments. Jesus was all virtue, and acted from impulse, not from rules."

When he had so spoken, I beheld the Angel, who stretched out his arms, embracing the flame of fire, & he was consumed and arose as Elijah.

Note: This Angel, who is now become a Devil, is my particular friend; we often read the Bible together in its infernal or diabolical sense, which the world shall have if they behave well.

I have also The Bible of Hell, which the world shall have whether they will or no.

One Law for the Lion & Ox is Oppression.

A song of liberty

For every thing that lives is Holy.

30

NATHANIEL
HAWTHORNE

Dreams of evil

Young Goodman Brown came forth at sunset into the street at Salem village; but put his head back, after crossing the threshold, to exchange a parting kiss with his young wife. And Faith, as the wife was aptly named, thrust her own pretty head into the street, letting the wind play with the pink ribbons of her cap while she called to Goodman Brown.

"Dearest heart," whispered she, softly and rather sadly, when her lips were close to his ear, "prithee put off your journey until sunrise and sleep in your own bed to-night. A lone woman is troubled with such dreams and such thoughts that she's afeared of herself sometimes. Pray tarry with me this night, dear husband, of all nights in the year."

"My love and my Faith," replied young Goodman Brown, "of all nights in the year, this one night must I tarry away from thee. My journey, as thou callest it, forth and back again, must needs be done 'twixt now and sunrise. What, my sweet, pretty wife, dost thou doubt me already, and we but three months married?"

"Then God bless you!" said Faith, with the pink ribbons; "and may you find all well when you come back."

"Amen!" cried Goodman Brown. "Say thy prayers, dear Faith, and go to bed at dusk, and no harm will come to thee."

So they parted; and the young man pursued his way until, being about to turn the corner by the meeting-house, he looked back and saw the head of Faith still peeping after him with a melancholy air, in spite of her pink ribbons.

"Poor little Faith!" thought he, for his heart smote him. "What a wretch am I to leave her on such an errand! She talks of dreams, too. Methought as she spoke there was trouble in her face, as if a dream had warned her what work is to be done to-night. But no, no; 't would kill her to think it. Well, she's a blessed angel on earth; and after this one night I'll cling to her skirts and follow her to heaven."

Source: *Young Goodman Brown*, Section 2.

206

With this excellent resolve for the future, Goodman Brown felt himself justified in making more haste on his present evil purpose. He had taken a dreary road, darkened by all the gloomiest trees of the forest, which barely stood aside to let the narrow path creep through, and closed immediately behind. It was all as lonely as could be; and there is this peculiarity in such a solitude, that the traveller knows not who may be concealed by the innumerable trunks and the thick boughs overhead; so that with lonely footsteps he may yet be passing through an unseen multitude.

"There may be a devilish Indian behind every tree," said Goodman Brown to himself; and he glanced fearfully behind him as he added, "What if the devil himself should be at my very elbow!"

His head being turned back, he passed a crook of the road, and, looking forward again, beheld the figure of a man, in grave and decent attire, seated at the foot of an old tree. He arose at Goodman Brown's approach and walked onward side by side with him.

"You are late, Goodman Brown," said he. "The clock of the Old South was striking as I came through Boston, and that is full fifteen minutes agone."

"Faith kept me back a while," replied the young man, with a tremor in his voice, caused by the sudden appearance of his companion, though not wholly unexpected.

It was now deep dusk in the forest, and deepest in that part of it where these two were journeying. As nearly as could be discerned, the second traveller was about fifty years old, apparently in the same rank of life as Goodman Brown, and bearing a considerable resemblance to him, though perhaps more in expression than features. Still they might have been taken for father and son. And yet, though the elder person was as simply clad as the younger, and as simple in manner too, he had an indescribable air of one who knew the world, and who would not have felt abashed at the governor's dinner table or in King William's court, were it possible that his affairs should call him thither. But the only thing about him that could be fixed upon as remarkable was his staff, which bore the likeness of a great black snake, so curiously wrought that it might almost be seen to twist and wriggle itself like a living serpent. This, of course, must have been an ocular deception, assisted by the uncertain light.

"Come, Goodman Brown," cried his fellow-traveller, "this is a dull pace for the beginning of a journey. Take my staff, if you are so soon weary."

"Friend," said the other, exchanging his slow pace for a full stop, "having kept covenant by meeting thee here, it is my purpose now to return whence I came. I have scruples touching the matter thou wot'st of."

"Sayest thou so?" replied he of the serpent, smiling apart. "Let us walk on, nevertheless, reasoning as we go; and if I convince thee not thou shalt turn back. We are but a little way in the forest yet."

"Too far! too far!" exclaimed the goodman, unconsciously resuming his walk. "My father never went into the woods on such an errand, nor his father before him. We have been a race of honest men and good Christians since the days of the martyrs; and shall I be the first of the name of Brown that ever took this path and kept —"

"Such company, thou wouldst say," observed the elder person, interpreting his pause. "Well said, Goodman Brown! I have been as well acquainted with your family as with ever a one among the Puritans; and that's no trifle to say. I helped your grandfather, the constable, when he lashed the Quaker woman so smartly through the streets of Salem; and it was I that brought your father a pitch-pine knot, kindled at my own hearth, to set fire to an Indian village, in King Philip's war. They were my good friends, both; and many a pleasant walk have we had along this path, and returned merrily after midnight. I would fain be friends with you for their sake."

"If it be as thou sayest," replied Goodman Brown, "I marvel they never spoke of these matters; or, verily, I marvel not, seeing that the least rumor of the sort would have driven them from New England. We are a people of prayer, and good works to boot, and abide no such wickedness."

"Wickedness or not," said the traveller with the twisted staff, "I have a very general acquaintance here in New England. The deacons of many a church have drunk the communion wine with me; the selectmen of divers towns make me their chairman; and a majority of the Great and General Court are firm supporters of my interest. The governor and I, too – But these are state secrets."

"Can this be so?" cried Goodman Brown, with a stare of amazement at his undisturbed companion. "Howbeit, I have nothing to do with the governor and council; they have their own ways, and are no rule for a simple husbandman like me. But, were I to go on with thee, how should I meet the eye of that good old man, our minister, at Salem village? Oh, his voice would make me tremble both Sabbath day and lecture day."

Thus far the elder traveller had listened with due gravity; but now burst into a fit of irrepressible mirth, shaking himself so violently that his snake-like staff actually seemed to wriggle in sympathy.

"Ha! ha! ha!" shouted he again and again; then composing himself, "Well, go on, Goodman Brown, go on; but, prithee, don't kill me with laughing."

"Well, then, to end the matter at once," said Goodman Brown, considerably nettled, "there is my wife, Faith. It would break her dear little heart; and I'd rather break my own."

"Nay, if that be the case," answered the other, "e'en go thy ways, Goodman Brown. I would not for twenty old women like the one hobbling before us that Faith should come to any harm."

As he spoke he pointed his staff at a female figure on the path, in whom Goodman Brown recognized a very pious and exemplary dame, who had taught him his catechism in youth, and was still his moral and spiritual adviser, jointly with the minister and Deacon Gookin.

"A marvel, truly that Goody Cloyse should be so far in the wilderness at nightfall," said he. "But with your leave, friend, I shall take a cut through the woods until we have left this Christian woman behind. Being a stranger to you, she might ask whom I was consorting with and whither I was going."

"Be it so," said his fellow-traveller. "Betake you to the woods, and let me keep the path."

Accordingly the young man turned aside, but took care to watch his companion, who advanced softly along the road until he had come within a staff's length of the old dame. She meanwhile, was making the best of her way, with singular speed for so aged a woman, and mumbling some indistinct words – a prayer, doubtless – as she went. The traveller put forth his staff and touched her withered neck with what seemed the serpent's tail.

"The devil!" screamed the pious old lady.

"Then Goody Cloyse knows her old friend?" observed the traveller, confronting her and leaning on his writhing stick.

"Ah, forsooth, and is it your worship indeed?" cried the good dame. "Yea, truly is it, and in the very image of my old gossip, Goodman Brown, the grandfather of the silly fellow that now is. But – would your worship believe it? – my broomstick hath strangely disappeared, stolen, as I suspect, by that unhanged witch, Goody Cory, and that, too, when I was all anointed with the juice of smallage, and cinquefoil, and wolf's bane —"

"Mingled with fine wheat and the fat of a new-born babe," said the shape of old Goodman Brown.

"Ah, your worship knows the recipe," cried the old lady, cackling aloud. "So, as I was saying, being all ready for the meeting, and no horse to ride on, I made up my mind to foot it; for they tell me there is a nice young man to be taken into communion to-night. But now your good worship will lend me your arm, and we shall be there in a twinkling."

"That can hardly be," answered her friend. "I may not spare you my arm, Goody Cloyse; but here is my staff, if you will."

So saying, he threw it down at her feet, where, perhaps, it assumed life, being one of the rods which its owner had formerly lent to the Egyptian magi. Of this fact, however, Goodman Brown could not take cognizance. He had cast up his eyes in astonishment, and, looking down again, beheld neither Goody Cloyse nor the serpentine staff, but his fellow-traveller alone, who waited for him as calmly as if nothing had happened.

"That old woman taught me my catechism," said the young man; and there was a world of meaning in this simple comment.

They continued to walk onward, while the elder traveller exhorted his companion to make good speed and persevere in the path, discoursing so aptly that his arguments seemed rather to spring up in the bosom of his auditor than to be suggested by himself. As they went, he plucked a branch of maple to serve for a walking stick, and began to strip it of the twigs and little boughs, which were wet with evening dew. The moment his fingers touched them they became withered and dried up as with a week's sunshine. Thus the pair proceeded, at a good free pace, until suddenly, in a gloomy hollow of the road, Goodman Brown sat himself down on the stump of a tree and refused to go any farther.

"Friend," he said, stubbornly, "my mind is made up. Not another step will I budge on this errand. What if a wretched old woman do choose to go to the devil when I thought she was going to heaven: is that any reason why I should quit my dear Faith and go after her?"

"You will think better of this by and by," said his acquaintance, composedly. "Sit here and rest yourself a while; and when you feel like moving again, there is my staff to help you along."

Without more words, he threw his companion the maple stick, and was as speedily out of sight as if he had vanished into the deepening gloom. The young man sat a few moments by the roadside, applauding himself greatly, and thinking with how clear a conscience he should meet the minister in his morning walk, nor shrink from the eye of good old Deacon Gookin. And what calm sleep would be his that very night, which was to have been spent so wickedly, but so purely and sweetly now, in the arms of Faith! Amidst these pleasant and praiseworthy meditations, Goodman Brown heard the tramp of horses along the road, and deemed it advisable to conceal himself within the verge of the forest, conscious of the guilty purpose that had brought him thither, though now so happily turned from it.

On came the hoof tramps and the voices of the riders, two grave old voices, conversing soberly as they drew near. These mingled sounds appeared to pass along the road, within a few yards of the young man's hiding-place; but, owing doubtless to the depth of the gloom at that particular spot, neither the travellers nor their steeds were visible. Though their figures brushed the small boughs by the wayside, it could not be seen that they intercepted, even for a moment, the faint gleam from the strip of bright sky athwart which they must have passed. Goodman Brown alternately crouched and stood on tiptoe, pulling aside the branches and thrusting forth his head as far as he durst without discerning so much as a shadow. It vexed him the more, because he could have sworn, were such a thing possible, that he recognized the voices of the minister and Deacon Gookin, jogging along quietly, as they were wont to do, when bound to some ordination or ecclesiastical council. While yet within hearing, one of the riders stopped to pluck a switch.

"Of the two, reverend sir," said the voice like the deacon's, "I had rather miss an ordination dinner than to-night's meeting. They tell me that some of our community are to be here from Falmouth and beyond, and others from Connecticut and Rhode Island, besides several of the Indian powwows, who, after their fashion, know almost as much deviltry as the best of us. Moreover, there is a goodly young woman to be taken into communion."

"Mighty well, Deacon Gookin!" replied the solemn old tones of the minister. "Spur up, or we shall be late. Nothing can be done, you know, until I get on the ground."

The hoofs clattered again; and the voices, talking so strangely in the empty air, passed on through the forest, where no church had ever been gathered or solitary Christian prayed. Whither, then, could these holy men be journeying so deep into the heathen wilderness? Young Goodman Brown caught hold of a tree for support, being ready to sink down on the ground, faint and overburdened with the heavy sickness of his heart. He looked up to the sky, doubting whether there really was a heaven above him. Yet there was the blue arch, and the stars brightening in it.

"With heaven above and Faith below, I will yet stand firm against the devil!" cried Goodman Brown.

While he still gazed upward into the deep arch of the firmament and had lifted his hands to pray, a cloud, though no wind was stirring, hurried across the zenith and hid the brightening stars. The blue sky was still visible, except directly overhead, where this black mass of cloud was sweeping swiftly northward. Aloft in the air, as if from the depths of the cloud, came a confused and doubtful sound of voices. Once the listener fancied that he could distinguish the accounts of towns-people of his own, men and women, both pious and ungodly, many of whom he had met at the communion table, and had seen others rioting at the tavern. The next moment, so indistinct were the sounds, he doubted whether he had heard aught but the murmur of the old forest, whispering without a wind. Then came a stronger swell of those familiar tones, heard daily in the sunshine at Salem village, but never until now from a cloud of night. There was one voice, of a young woman, uttering lamentations, yet with an uncertain sorrow, and entreating for some favor, which, perhaps, it would grieve her to obtain; and all the unseen multitude, both saints and sinners, seemed to encourage her onward.

"Faith!" shouted Goodman Brown, in a voice of agony and desperation; and the echoes of the forest mocked him, crying, "Faith! Faith!" as if bewildered wretches were seeking her all through the wilderness.

The cry of grief, rage, and terror was yet piercing the night, when the unhappy husband held his breath for a response. There was a scream, drowned immediately in a louder murmur of voices, fading into far-off laughter, as the dark cloud swept away, leaving the clear and silent sky above Goodman Brown. But something fluttered lightly down through the air and caught on a branch of a tree. The young man seized it, and beheld a pink ribbon.

"My Faith is gone!" cried he after one stupefied moment. "There is no good on earth; and sin is but a name. Come, devil; for to thee is this world given."

And, maddened with despair, so that he laughed loud and long, did Goodman Brown grasp his staff and set forth again, at such a rate that he seemed to fly along the forest path rather than to walk or run. The road grew wilder and drearier and more faintly traced, and vanished at length, leaving him in the heart of the dark wilderness, still rushing onward with the instinct that guides mortal man to evil. The whole forest was peopled with frightful sounds – the creaking of the trees, the howling of wild beasts, and the yell of Indians; while sometimes the wind tolled like a distant church bell, and sometimes gave a broad roar around the traveller, as if all Nature were laughing him to scorn. But he was himself the chief horror of the scene, and shrank not from its other horrors.

"Ha! ha! ha!" roared Goodman Brown when the wind laughed at him. "Let us hear which will laugh loudest. Think not to frighten me with your deviltry. Come witch, come wizard, come Indian powwow, come devil himself, and here comes Goodman Brown. You may as well fear him as he fear you."

In truth, all through the haunted forest there could be nothing more frightful than the figure of Goodman Brown. On he flew among the black pines, brandishing his staff with frenzied gestures, now giving vent to an inspiration of horrid blasphemy, and now shouting forth such laughter as set all the echoes of the forest laughing like demons around him. The fiend in his own shape is less hideous than when he rages in the breast of man. Thus sped the demoniac on his course, until, quivering among the trees, he saw a red light before him, as when the felled trunks and branches of a clearing have been set on fire, and throw up their lurid blaze against the sky, at the hour of midnight. He paused, in a lull of the tempest that had driven him onward, and heard the swell of what seemed a hymn, rolling solemnly from a distance with the weight of many voices. He knew the tune; it was a familiar one in the choir of the village meeting-house. The verse died heavily away, and was lengthened by a chorus, not of human voices, but of all the sounds of the benighted wilderness pealing in awful harmony together. Goodman Brown cried out, and his cry was lost to his own ear by its unison with the cry of the desert.

In the interval of silence he stole forward until the light glared full upon his eyes. At one extremity of an open space, hemmed in by the dark wall of the forest, arose a rock, bearing some rude, natural resemblance either to an altar or a pulpit, and surrounded by four blazing pines, their tops aflame, their stems untouched, like candles at an evening meeting. The mass of foliage that had overgrown the summit of the rock was all on fire, blazing high into the night and fitfully illuminating the whole field. Each pendent twig and leafy festoon was in a blaze. As the red light arose and fell, a numerous congregation alternately shone forth, then disappeared in shadow, and again grew, as it were, out of the darkness, peopling the heart of the solitary woods at once.

"A grave and dark-clad company," quoth Goodman Brown.

In truth they were such. Among them, quivering to and fro between gloom and splendor, appeared faces that would be seen next day at the council board of the province, and others which, Sabbath after Sabbath, looked devoutly heavenward, and benignantly over the crowded pews, from the holiest pulpits in the land. Some affirm that the lady of the governor was there. At least there were high dames well known to her, and wives of honored husbands, and widows, a great multitude, and ancient maidens, all of excellent repute, and fair young girls, who trembled lest their mothers should espy them. Either the sudden gleams of light flashing over the obscure field bedazzled Goodman Brown, or he recognized a score of the church members of Salem village famous for their especial sanctity. Good old Deacon Gooking had arrived, and waited at the skirt of that venerable saint, his revered pastor. But, irreverently consorting with these grave, reputable, and pious people, these elders of the church, these chaste dames and dewy virgins, there were men of dissolute lives and women of spotted fame, wretches given over to all mean and filthy vice, and suspected even of horrid crimes. It was strange to see that the good shrank not from the wicked, nor were the sinners abashed by the saints. Scattered also among their palefaced enemies were the Indian priests, or powwows, who had often scared their native forest with more hideous incantations than any known to English witchcraft.

"But where is Faith?" though Goodman Brown; and, as hope came into his heart, he trembled.

Another verse of the hymn arose, a slow and mournful strain, such as the pious love, but joined to words which expressed all that our nature can conceive of sin, and darkly hinted at far more. Unfathomable to mere mortals is the lore of fiends. Verse after verse was sung; and still the chorus of the desert swelled between like the deepest tone of a mighty organ; and with the final peal of that dreadful anthem there came a sound, as if the roaring wind, the rushing streams, the howling beasts, and every other voice of the unconcerted wilderness were mingling and according with the voice of guilty man in homage to the prince of all. The four blazing pines threw up a loftier flame, and obscurely discovered shapes and visages of horror on the smoke wreaths above the impious assembly. At the same moment the fire on the rock shot redly forth and formed a glowing arch above its base, where now appeared a figure. With reverence be it spoken, the figure bore no slight similitude, both in garb and manner, to some grave divine of the New England churches.

"Bring forth the converts!" cried a voice that echoed through the field and rolled into the forest.

At the word, Goodman Brown stepped forth from the shadow of the trees and approached the congregation, with whom he felt a loathful brotherhood by the sympathy of all that was wicked in his heart. He could have well-nigh sworn that the shape of his own dead father beckoned him to advance, looking downward from a smoke wreath, while a woman, with dim features of despair, threw out her hand to warn him back. Was it his mother? But he had no power to retreat one step, nor to resist, even in thought, when the minister and good old Deacon Gooking seized his arms and led him to the blazing rock. Thither came also the slender form of a veiled female, led between Goody Cloyse, that pious teacher of the catechism, and Martha Carrier, who had received the devil's promise to be queen of hell. A rampant hag was she. And there stood the proselytes beneath the canopy of fire.

"Welcome, my children," said the dark figure, "to the communion of your race. Ye have found thus young your nature and your destiny. My children, look behind you!"

They turned; and flashing forth, as it were, in a sheet of flame, the fiend worshippers were seen; the smile of welcome gleamed darkly on every visage.

"There," resumed the sable form, "are all whom ye have reverenced from youth. Ye deemed them holier than yourselves and shrank from your own sin, contrasting it with their lives of righteousness and prayerful aspirations heavenward. Yet here are they all in my worshipping assembly. This night it shall be granted you to know their secret deeds: how hoary-bearded elders of the church have whispered wanton words to the young maids of their households; how many a woman, eager for widows' weeds, has given her husband a drink at bedtime and let him sleep his last sleep in her bosom; how beard-less youths have made haste to inherit their fathers' wealth; and how fair damsels – blush not, sweet ones – have dug little graves in the garden, and bidden me, the sole guest, to an infant's funeral. By the sympathy of your human hearts for sin ye shall scent out all the places – whether in church, bedchamber, street, field, or forest – where crime has been committed, and shall exult to behold the whole earth one stain of guilt, one mighty blood spot. Far more than this. It shall be yours to penetrate, in every bosom, the deep mystery of sin, the fountain of all wicked arts, and which inexhaustibly supplies more evil impulses than human power – than my power at its utmost – can make manifest in deeds. And now, my children, look upon each other."

They did so; and, by the blaze of the hell-kindled torches, the wretched man beheld his Faith, and the wife her husband, trembling before that unhallowed altar.

"Lo, there ye stand, my children," said the figure, in a deep and solemn tone, almost sad with its despairing awfulness, as if his once angelic nature could yet mourn for our miserable race. "Depending upon one another's hearts, ye had still hoped that virtue were not all a dream. Now are ye undeceived. Evil is the nature of mankind. Evil must be your only happiness. Welcome again, my children, to the communion of your race."

"Welcome," repeated the fiend worshippers, in one cry of despair and triumph.

And there they stood, the only pair, as it seemed, who were yet hesitating on the verge of wickedness in this dark world. A basin was hollowed, naturally, in the rock. Did it contain water, reddened by the lurid light? or was it blood? or, perchance, a liquid flame? Herein did the shape of evil dip his hand and prepare to lay the mark of baptism upon their foreheads, that they might be partakers of the mystery of sin, more conscious of the secret guilt of others, both in deed and thought, than they could now be of their own. The husband cast one look at his pale wife, and Faith at him. What polluted wretches would the next glance show them to each other, shuddering alike at what they disclosed and what they saw!

"Faith! Faith!" cried the husband, "look up to heaven, and resist the wicked one."

Whether Faith obeyed he knew not. Hardly had he spoken when he found himself amid calm night and solitude, listening to a roar of the wind which died heavily away through the forest. He staggered against the rock, and felt it chill and damp; while a hanging twig, that had been all on fire, besprinkled his cheek with the coldest dew.

The next morning young Goodman Brown came slowly into the street of Salem village, staring around him like a bewildered man. The good old minister was taking a walk along the graveyard to get an appetite for breakfast and meditate his sermon, and bestowed a blessing, as he passed, on Goodman Brown. He shrank from the venerable saint as if to avoid an anathema. Old Deacon Gooking was at domestic worship, and the holy words of his prayer were heard through the open window. "What God doth the wizard pray to?" quoth Goodman Brown. Goody Gloyse, that excellent old Christian, stood in the early sunshine at her own lattice, catechizing a little girl who had brought her a pint of morning's milk. Goodman Brown snatched away the child as from the grasp of the fiend himself. Turning the corner by the meeting-house, he spied the head of Faith, with the pink ribbons, gazing anxiously forth, and bursting into such joy at sight of him that she skipped along the street and almost kissed her husband before the whole village. But Goodman Brown looked sternly and sadly into her face, and passed on without a greeting.

Had Goodman Brown fallen asleep in the forest and only dreamed a wild dream of a witch-meeting?

Be it so if you will; but, alas! it was a dream of evil omen for young Goodman Brown. A stern, a sad, a darkly meditative, a distrustful, if not a desperate man did he become from the night of that fearful dream. On the Sabbath day, when the congregation were singing a holy psalm, he could not listen because an anthem of sin rushed loudly upon his ear and drowned all the blessed strain. When the minister spoke from the pulpit with power and fervid eloquence, and, with his hand on the open Bible, of the sacred truths of our religion, and of saint-like lives and triumphant deaths, and of future bliss or misery unutterable, then did Goodman Brown turn pale, dreading lest the roof should thunder down upon the gray blasphemer and his hearers. Often, awaking suddenly at midnight, he shrank from the bosom of Faith; and at morning or eventide, when the family knelt down at prayer, he scowled and muttered to himself, and gazed sternly at his wife, and turned away. And when he had lived long, and was borne to his grave a hoary corpse, followed by Faith, an aged woman, and children and grandchildren, a goodly procession, besides neighbors not a few, they carved no hopeful verse upon his tombstone, for his dying hour was gloom.

31

CHARLES BAUDELAIRE

The sweetness of evil

The Flowers of Evil

Infatuation, sadism, lust, avarice
possess our souls and drain the body's force;
we spoonfeed our adorable remorse,
like whores or beggars nourishing their lice.

Our sins are mulish, our confessions lies;
we play to the grandstand with our promises,
we pray for tears to wash our filthiness,
importantly pissing hogwash through our styes.

The devil, watching by our sickbeds, hissed
old smut and folk-songs to our soul, until
the soft and precious metal of our will
boiled off in vapor for this scientist.

Each day his flattery makes us eat a toad,
and each step forward is a step to hell,
unmoved, though previous corpses and their smell
asphyxiate our progress on this road.

Like the poor lush who cannot satisfy,
we try to force our sex with counterfeits,
die drooling on the deliquescent tits,
mouthing the rotten orange we suck dry.

Source: *The Flowers of Evil*, translated by Robert Lowell.

Gangs of demons are boozing in our brain –
ranked, swarming, like a million warrior-ants,
they drown and choke the cistern of our wants;
each time we breathe, we tear our lungs with pain.

If poison, arson, sex, narcotics, knives
have not yet ruined us and stitched their quick,
loud patterns on the canvas of our lives,
it is because our souls are still too sick.

Among the vermin, jackals, panthers, lice,
gorillas and tarantulas that suck
and snatch and scratch and defecate and fuck
in the disorderly circus of our vice,

there's one more ugly and abortive birth.
It makes no gestures, never beats its breast,
yet it would murder for a moment's rest,
and willingly annihilate the earth.

It's BOREDOM. Tears have glued its eyes together.
You know it well, my Reader. This obscene
beast chain-smokes yawning for the guillotine –
you – hypocrite Reader – my double – my brother!

32

ARTHUR SCHOPENHAUER

On the vanity and suffering of life

Awakened to life out of the night of unconsciousness, the will finds itself an individual, in an endless and boundless world, among innumerable individuals, all striving, suffering, erring; and as if through a troubled dream it hurries back to its old unconsciousness. Yet till then its desires are limitless, its claims inexhaustible, and every satisfied desire gives rise to a new one. No possible satisfaction in the world could suffice to still its longings, set a goal to its infinite cravings, and fill the bottomless abyss of its heart. Then let one consider what as a rule are the satisfactions of any kind that a man obtains. For the most part nothing more than the bare maintenance of this existence itself, extorted day by day with unceasing trouble and constant care in the conflict with want, and with death in prospect. Everything in life shows that earthly happiness is destined to be frustrated or recognised as an illusion. The grounds of this lie deep in the nature of things. Accordingly the life of most men is troubled and short. Those who are comparatively happy are so, for the most part, only apparently, or else, like men of long life, they are the rare exceptions, a possibility of which there had to be, – as decoy-birds. Life presents itself as a continual deception in small things as in great. If it has promised, it does not keep its word, unless to show how little worth desiring were the things desired: thus we are deluded now by hope, now by what was hoped for. If it has given, it did so in order to take. The enchantment of distance shows us paradises which vanish like optical illusions when we have allowed ourselves to be mocked by them. Happiness accordingly always lies in the future, or else in the past, and the present may be compared to a small dark cloud which the wind drives over the sunny plain: before and behind it all is bright, only it itself always casts a shadow. The present is therefore always insufficient; but the future is uncertain, and the past irrevocable. Life with its hourly, daily, weekly, yearly,

"On the vanity and suffering of life" (source: *The World as Will and Idea*, trans. R.B. Haldane and J. Kemp, London: Kegan Paul, Trench, Trubner & Co., 1909); "On the sufferings of the world" (source: *The Pessimist's Handbook: A Collection of Popular Essays*, trans. T. Bailey Saunders, Lincoln, Nebr.: University of Nebraska Press, 1964).

little, greater, and great misfortunes, with its deluded hopes and its accidents destroying all our calculations, bears so distinctly the impression of something with which we must become disgusted, that it is hard to conceive how one has been able to mistake this and allow oneself to be persuaded that life is there in order to be thankfully enjoyed, and that man exists in order to be happy. Rather that continual illusion and disillusion, and also the nature of life throughout, presents itself to us as intended and calculated to awaken the conviction that nothing at all is worth our striving, our efforts and struggles, that all good things are vanity, the world in all its ends bankrupt, and life a business which does not cover its expenses; – so that our will may turn away from it.

We feel pain, but not painlessness; we feel care, but not the absence of care; fear, but not security. We feel the wish as we feel hunger and thirst; but as soon as it has been fulfilled, it is like the mouthful that has been taken, which ceases to exist for our feeling the moment it is swallowed. Pleasures and joys we miss painfully whenever they are wanting; but pains, even when they cease after having long been present, are not directly missed, but at the most are intentionally thought of by means of reflection. For only pain and want can be felt positively, and therefore announce themselves; well-being, on the other hand, is merely negative. Therefore we do not become conscious of the three greatest blessings of life, health, youth, and freedom, so long as we possess them, but only after we have lost them; for they also are negations. We only observe that days of our life were happy after they have given place to unhappy ones. In proportion as pleasures increase, the susceptibility for them decreases: what is customary is no longer felt as a pleasure. Just in this way, however, is the susceptibility for suffering increased, for the loss of what we are accustomed to is painfully felt. Thus the measure of what is necessary increases through possession, and thereby the capacity for feeling pain. The hours pass the quicker the more agreeably they are spent, and the slower the more painfully they are spent; because pain, not pleasure, is the positive, the presence of which makes itself felt. In the same way we become conscious of time when we are bored, not when we are diverted. Both these cases prove that our existence is most happy when we perceive it least, from which it follows that it would be better not to have it. Great and lively joy can only be conceived as the consequence of great misery, which has preceded it; for nothing can be added to a state of permanent satisfaction but some amusement, or the satisfaction of vanity.

In general, however, the conduct of men towards each other is characterised as a rule by injustice, extreme unfairness, hardness, nay, cruelty: an opposite course of conduct appears only as an exception. Upon this depends the necessity of the State and legislation, and upon none of your false pretences. But in all cases which do not lie within the reach of the law, that regardlessness of his like, peculiar to man, shows itself at once; a regardlessness which springs from his boundless egoism, and sometimes also from wickedness. How man deals with man is shown, for example, by negro slavery, the final end of which is sugar and coffee. But we do not need to go so far: at the age of five years to enter a cotton-spinning or other factory, and from that time forth to sit there daily, first ten, then twelve, and ultimately fourteen hours, performing the same mechanical labour, is to purchase dearly the satisfaction of drawing breath. But this is the fate of millions, and that of millions more is analogous to it.

We others, however, can be made perfectly miserable by trifling misfortunes; perfectly happy, not by the world. Whatever one may say, the happiest moment of the happy man is the moment of his falling asleep, and the unhappiest moment of the unhappy that of his awakening. An indirect but certain proof of the fact that men feel themselves unhappy, and consequently are so, is also abundantly afforded by the fearful envy which dwells in us all, and which in all relations of life, on the occasion of any superiority, of whatever kind it may be, is excited, and cannot contain its poison. Because they feel themselves unhappy, men cannot endure the sight of one whom they imagine happy . . .

On the sufferings of the world

Unless *suffering* is the direct and immediate object of life, our existence must entirely fail of its aim. It is absurd to look upon the enormous amount of pain that abounds everywhere in the world, and originates in needs and necessities inseparable from life itself, as serving no purpose at all and the result of mere chance. Each separate misfortune, as it comes, seems, no doubt, to be something exceptional; but misfortune in general is the rule.

I know of no greater absurdity than that propounded by most systems of philosophy in declaring evil to be negative in its character. Evil is just what is positive; it makes its own existence felt. . . . It is the good which is negative; in other words, happiness and satisfaction always imply some desire fulfilled, some state of pain brought to an end.

This explains the fact that we generally find pleasure to be not nearly so pleasant as we expected, and pain very much more painful.

The pleasure in this world, it has been said, outweighs the pain; or, at any rate, there is an even balance between the two. If the reader wishes to see shortly whether this statement is true, let him compare the respective feelings of two animals, one of which is engaged in eating the other.

The best consolation in misfortune or affliction of any kind will be the thought of other people who are in a still worse plight than yourself; and this is a form of consolation open to every one. But what an awful fate this means for mankind as a whole!

There are two things which make it impossible to believe that this world is the successful work of an all-wise, all-good, and, at the same time, all-powerful Being; firstly, the misery which abounds in it everywhere; and secondly, the obvious imperfection of its highest product, man, who is a burlesque of what he should be. These things cannot be reconciled with any such belief. On the contrary, they are just the facts which support what I have been saying; they are our authority for viewing the world as the outcome of our own misdeeds, and therefore, as something that had better not have been. Whilst, under the former hypothesis, they amount to a bitter accusation against the Creator, and supply material for sarcasm; under the latter they form an indictment against our own nature, our own will, and teach us a lesson of humility. They lead us to see that, like the children of a libertine, we come into the world with the burden of sin upon us; and that it is only through having continually to atone for this sin that our existence is so miserable, and that its end is death.

There is nothing more certain than the general truth that it is the grievous *sin of the world* which has produced the grievous *suffering of the world*. I am not referring here to the physical connection between these two things lying in the realm of experience; my meaning is metaphysical. Accordingly, the sole thing that reconciles me to the Old Testament is the story of the Fall. In my eyes, it is the only metaphysical truth in that book, even though it appears in the form of an allegory. There seems to me no better explanation of our existence than that it is the result of some false step, some sin of which we are paying the penalty.

33

FRIEDRICH NIETZSCHE

Beyond good and evil

All psychology so far has got stuck in moral prejudices and fears; it has not dared to descend into the depths. To understand it as morphology and *the doctrine of the development of the will to power*, as I do – nobody has yet come close to doing this even in thought – insofar as it is permissible to recognize in what has been written so far a symptom of what has so far been kept silent. The power of moral prejudices has penetrated deeply into the most spiritual world, which would seem to be the coldest and most devoid of presuppositions, and has obviously operated in an injurious, inhibiting, blinding, and distorting manner. A proper physio-psychology has to contend with unconscious resistance in the heart of the investigator, it has "the heart" against it: even a doctrine of the reciprocal dependence of the "good" and the "wicked" drives, causes (as refined immorality) distress and aversion in a still hale and hearty conscience – still more so, a doctrine of the derivation of all good impulses from wicked ones. If, however, a person should regard even the affects of hatred, envy, covetousness, and the lust to rule as conditions of life, as factors which, fundamentally and essentially, must be present in the general economy of life (and must, therefore, be further enhanced if life is to be further enhanced) – he will suffer from such a view of things as from seasickness. And yet even this hypothesis is far from being the strangest and most painful in this immense and almost new domain of dangerous insights; and there are in fact a hundred good reasons why everyone should keep away from it who – *can*.

On the other hand, if one has once drifted there with one's bark, well! all right! let us clench our teeth! let us open our eyes and keep our hand firm on the helm! We sail right *over* morality, we crush, we destroy perhaps the remains of our own morality by daring to make our voyage there – but what matter are *we*! Never yet did a *profounder* world of insight reveal itself to daring travelers and adventurers, and the psychologist who thus "makes a sacrifice" – it is *not* the *sacrifizio dell' intelletto*, on the contrary! – will

Source: *The Basic Writings of Nietzsche*, "Beyond good and evil," "Genealogy of morals," translated by Walter Kaufman, New York: The Modern Library, 1966.

at least be entitled to demand in return that psychology shall be recognized again as the queen of the sciences, for whose service and preparation the other sciences exist. For psychology is now again the path to the fundamental problems.

[. . .]

Love one's enemies? I think this has been learned well: it is done thousands of times today, in small ways and big ways. Indeed, at times something higher and more sublime is done: we learn to *despise* when we love, and precisely when we love best – but all of this unconsciously, without noise, without pomp, with that modesty and concealed good-ness which forbids the mouth solemn words and virtue formulas. Morality as a pose – offends our taste today. That, too, is progress – just as it was progress when religion as a pose finally offended our fathers' taste, including hostility and Voltairian bitterness against religion (and everything that formerly belonged to the gestures of free-thinkers). It is the music in our conscience, the dance in our spirit, with which the sound of all puritan litanies, all moral homilies and old-fashioned respectability won't go.

Beware of those who attach great value to being credited with moral tact and subtlety in making moral distinctions. They never forgive us once they have made a mistake *in front of* us (or, worse, *against* us): inevitably they become our instinctive slanderers and detractors, even if they should still remain our "friends."
   Blessed are the forgetful: for they get over their stupidities, too.

The psychologists of France – and where else are any psychologists left today? – still have not exhausted their bitter and manifold delight in the *bêtise bourgeoise*, just as if – enough, this betrays something. Flaubert, for example, that solid citizen of Rouen, in the end no longer saw, heard, or tasted anything else any more: this was his kind of self-torture and subtler cruelty. Now, for a change – since this is becoming boring – I propose another source of amusement: the unconscious craftiness with which all good, fat, solid, mediocre spirits react to higher spirits and their tasks – that subtle, involved, Jesuitical craftiness which is a thousand times more subtle than not only the understanding and taste of this middle class is at its best moments, but even the understanding of its victims – which proves once again that "instinct" is of all the kinds of intelligence that have been discov-ered so far – the most intelligent. In short, my dear psychologists, study the philosophy of the "norm" in its fight against the "exception": there you have a spectacle that is good enough for gods and godlike malice! Or, still more clearly: vivisect the "good man," the "*homo bonae voluntatis*" – *yourselves!*

[. . .]

Refraining mutually from injury, violence, and exploitation and placing one's will on a par with that of someone else – this may become, in a certain rough sense, good manners among individuals if the appropriate conditions are present (namely, if these men are actually similar in strength and value standards and belong together in *one* body). But as soon as this principle is extended, and possibly even accepted as the *fundamental principle of society*, it immediately proves to be what it really is – a will to the *denial* of life, a principle of disintegration and decay.

Here we must be aware of superficiality and get to the bottom of the matter, resisting all sentimental weakness: life itself is *essentially* appropriation, injury, overpowering of what is alien and weaker; suppression, hardness, imposition of one's own forms, incorporation and at least, at its mildest, exploitation – but why should one always use those words in which a slanderous intent has been imprinted for ages?

Even the body within which individuals treat each other as equals, as suggested before – and this happens in every healthy aristocracy – if it is a living and not a dying body, has to do to other bodies what the individuals within it refrain from doing to each other: it will have to be an incarnate will to power, it will strive to grow, spread, seize, become predominant – not from any morality or immorality but because it is *living* and because life simply *is* will to power. But there is no point on which the ordinary consciousness of Europeans resists instruction as on this: everywhere people are now raving, even under scientific disguises, about coming conditions of society in which "the exploitative aspect" will be removed – which sounds to me as if they promised to invent a way of life that would dispense with all organic functions. "Exploitation" does not belong to a corrupt or imperfect and primitive society: it belongs to the *essence* of what lives, as a basic organic function; it is a consequence of the will to power, which is after all the will of life.

If this should be an innovation as a theory – as a reality it is the *primordial fact* of all history: people ought to be honest with themselves as least that far.

Wandering through the many subtler and coarser moralities which have so far been prevalent on earth, or still are prevalent, I found that certain features recurred regularly together and were closely associated – until I finally discovered two basic types and one basic difference.

There are *master morality* and *slave morality* – I add immediately that in all the higher and more mixed cultures there also appear attempts at mediation between these two moralities, and yet more often the interpenetration and mutual misunderstanding of both, and at times they occur directly alongside each other – even in the same human being, within a *single* soul. The moral discrimination of values has originated either among a ruling group whose consciousness of its difference from the ruled group was accompanied by delight – or among the ruled, the slaves and dependents of every degree.

In the first case, when the ruling group determines what is "good," the exalted, proud states of the soul are experienced as conferring distinction and determining the order of rank. The noble human being separates from himself those in whom the opposite of such exalted, proud states finds expression: he despises them. It should be noted immediately that in this first type of morality the opposition of "good" and *"bad"* means approximately the same as "noble" and "contemptible." (The opposition of "good" and *"evil"* has a different origin.) One feels contempt for the cowardly, the anxious, the petty, those intent on narrow utility; also for the suspicious with their unfree glances, those who humble themselves, the doglike people who allow themselves to be maltreated, the begging flatterers, above all the liars: it is part of the fundamental faith of all aristocrats that the common people lie. "We truthful ones" – thus the nobility of ancient Greece referred to itself.

It is obvious that moral designations were everywhere first applied to *human beings* and only later, derivatively, to actions. Therefore it is a gross mistake when historians of morality start from such questions as: why was the compassionate act praised? The noble type of man experiences *itself* as determining values; it does not need approval; it judges, "what is harmful to me is harmful in itself"; it knows itself to be that which first accords honor to things; it is *value-creating*. Everything it knows as part of itself it honors: such a morality is self-glorification. In the foreground there is the feeling of fullness, of power that seeks to overflow, the happiness of high tension, the consciousness of wealth that would give and bestow: the noble human being, too, helps the unfortunate, but not, or almost not, from pity, but prompted more by an urge begotten by excess of power. The noble human being honors himself as one who is powerful, also as one who has power over himself, who knows how to speak and be silent, who delights in being severe and hard with himself and respects all severity and hardness. "A hard heart Wotan put into my breast," says an old Scandinavian saga: a fitting poetic expression, seeing that it comes from the soul of a proud Viking. Such a type of man is actually proud of the fact that he is *not* made for pity, and the hero of the saga therefore adds as a warning: "If the heart is not hard in youth it will never harden." Noble and courageous human beings who think that way are furthest removed from that morality which finds the distinction of morality precisely in pity, or in acting for others, or in *désintéressement*; faith in oneself, pride in oneself, a fundamental hostility and irony against "selflessness" belong just as definitely to noble morality as does a slight disdain and caution regarding compassionate feelings and a "warm heart."

It is the powerful who *understand* how to honor; this is their art, their realm of invention. The profound reverence for age and tradition – all law rests on this double reverence – the faith and prejudice in favor of ancestors and disfavor of those yet to come are typical of the morality of the powerful; and when the men of "modern ideas," conversely, believe almost instinctively in "progress" and "the future" and more and more lack respect for age, this in itself would sufficiently betray the ignoble origin of these "ideas."

A morality of the ruling group, however, is most alien and embarrassing to the present taste in the severity of its principle that one has duties only to one's peers; that against beings of a lower rank, against everything alien, one may behave as one pleases or "as the heart desires," and in any case "beyond good and evil" – here pity and like feelings may find their place. The capacity for, and the duty of, long gratitude and long revenge – both only among one's peers – refinement in repaying, the sophisticated concept of friendship, a certain necessity for having enemies (as it were, as drainage ditches for the affects of envy, quarrelsomeness, exuberance – at bottom, in order to be capable of being good *friends*): all these are typical characteristics of noble morality which, as suggested, is not the morality of "modern ideas" and therefore is hard to empathize with today, also hard to dig up and uncover.

It is different with the second type of morality, *slave morality*. Suppose the violated, oppressed, suffering, unfree, who are uncertain of themselves and weary, moralize: what will their moral valuations have in common? Probably, a pessimistic suspicion about the whole condition of man will find expression, perhaps a condemnation of man along with his condition. The slave's eye is not favorable to the virtues of the powerful: he is skeptical and suspicious, *subtly* suspicious, of all the "good" that is honored there – he would like to persuade himself that even their happiness is not genuine. Conversely, those qualities are brought out and flooded with light which serve to ease existence for those who suffer: here pity, the complaisant and obliging hand, the warm heart, patience, industry, humility, and friendliness are honored – for here these are the most useful qualities and almost the only means for enduring the pressure of existence. Slave morality is essentially a morality of utility.

Here is the place for the origin of that famous opposition of "good" and "evil": into evil one's feelings project power and dangerousness, a certain terribleness, subtlety, and strength that does not permit contempt to develop. According to slave morality, those who are "evil" thus inspire fear; according to master morality it is precisely those who are "good" that inspire, and wish to inspire, fear, while the "bad" are felt to be contemptible.

The opposition reaches its climax when, as a logical consequence of slave morality, a touch of disdain is associated also with the "good" of this morality – this may be slight and benevolent – because the good human being has to be *undangerous* in the slaves' way of thinking: he is good-natured, easy to deceive, a little stupid perhaps, *un bonhomme*. Wherever slave morality becomes preponderant, language tends to bring the words "good" and "stupid" closer together.

One last fundamental difference: the longing for *freedom* the instinct for happiness and the subtleties of the feeling of freedom belong just as necessarily to slave morality and morals as artful and enthusiastic reverence and devotion are the regular symptom of an aristocratic way of thinking and evaluating . . .

Genealogy of morals

Quite apart from the historical untenability of this hypothesis regarding the origin of the value judgment "good," it suffers from an inherent psychological absurdity. The utility of the unegoistic action is supposed to be the source of the approval accorded it, and this source is supposed to have been *forgotten* – but how is this forgetting *possible*? Has the utility of such actions come to an end at some time or other? The opposite is the case: this utility has rather been an everyday experience at all times, therefore something that has been underlined again and again: consequently, instead of fading from consciousness, instead of becoming easily forgotten, it must have been impressed on the consciousness more and more clearly. How much more reasonable is that opposing theory (it is not for that reason more true –) which Herbert Spencer, for example, espoused: that the concept "good" is essentially identical with the concept "useful," "practical," so that in the judgments "good" and "bad" mankind has summed up and sanctioned precisely its *unforgotten* and *unforgettable* experiences regarding what is useful–practical and what is harmful–impractical. According to this theory, that which has always proved itself useful is good: therefore it may claim to be "valuable in the highest degree," "valuable in itself." This road to an explanation is, as aforesaid, also a wrong one, but at least the explanation is in itself reasonable and psychologically tenable.

The signpost to the *right* road was for me the question: what was the real etymological significance of the designations for "good" coined in the various languages? I found they all led back to the *same conceptual transformation* – that everywhere "noble," "aristocratic" in the social sense, is the basic concept from which "good" in the sense of "with aristocratic soul," "noble," "with a soul of a high order," "with a privileged soul" necessarily developed: a development which always runs parallel with that other in which "common," "plebeian," "low" are finally transformed into the concept "bad." The most convincing example of the latter is the German word *schlecht* [bad] itself: which is identical with *schlicht* [plain, simple] – compare *schlechtweg* [plainly], *schlechterdings* [simply] – and originally designated the plain, the common man, as yet with no inculpatory implication and simply in contradistinction to the nobility. About the time of the Thirty Years War, late enough therefore, this meaning changed into the one now customary.

With regard to a moral genealogy this seems to me a *fundamental* insight; that it has been arrived at so late is the fault of the retarding influence exercised by the democratic prejudice in the modern world toward all questions of origin. And this is so even in the apparently quite objective domain of natural science and physiology, as I shall merely hint here. But what mischief this prejudice is capable of doing, especially to morality and history, once it has been unbridled to the point of hatred is shown by the *plebeianism* of the modern spirit, which is of English origin, [that] erupted once again on its native soil, as violently as a mud volcano and with that salty, noisy, vulgar eloquence with which all volcanos have spoken hitherto.—

[. . .]

One will have divined already how easily the priestly mode of valuation can branch off from the knightly–aristocratic and then develop into its opposite; this is particularly likely when the priestly caste and the warrior caste are in jealous opposition to one another and are unwilling to comes to terms. The knightly–aristocratic value judgments presupposed a powerful physicality, a flourishing, abundant, even overflowing health, together with that which serves to preserve it: war, adventure, hunting, dancing, war games, and in general all that involves vigorous, free, joyful activity. The priestly–noble mode of valuation presupposes, as we have seen, other things: it is disadvantageous for it when it comes to war! As is well known, the priests are the *most evil enemies* – but why? Because they are the most impotent. It is because of their impotence that in them hatred grows to monstrous and uncanny proportions, to the most spiritual and poisonous kind of hatred. The truly great haters in world history have always been priests; likewise the most ingenious haters: other kinds of spirit hardly come into consideration when compared with the spirit of priestly vengefulness. Human history would be altogether too stupid a thing without the spirit that the impotent have introduced into it – let us take at once the most notable example. All that has been done on earth against "the noble," "the powerful," "the masters," "the rulers," fades into nothing compared with what the *Jews* have done against them; the Jews, that priestly people, who in opposing their enemies and conquerors were ultimately satisfied with nothing less than a radical revaluation of their enemies' values, that is to say, an act of the *most spiritual revenge.* For this alone was appropriate to a priestly people, the people embodying the most deeply repressed priestly vengefulness. It was the Jews who, with awe-inspiring consistency, dared to invert the aristocratic value-equation (good = noble = powerful = beautiful = happy = beloved of God) and to hang on to this inversion with their teeth, the teeth of the most abysmal hatred (the hatred of impotence), saying "the wretched alone are the good; the poor, impotent, lowly alone are the good; the suffering, deprived, sick, ugly alone are pious, alone are blessed by God, blessedness is for them alone – and you, the powerful and noble, are on the contrary the evil, the cruel, the lustful, the insatiable, the godless to all eternity; and you shall be in all eternity the unblessed, accursed, and damned!" . . . One knows *who* inherited this Jewish revaluation . . . In connection with the tremendous and immeasurably fateful initiative provided by the Jews through this most fundamental of all declarations of war, I recall the proposition I arrived at on a previous occasion . . . that with the Jews there begins *the slave revolt in morality*: that revolt which has a history of two thousand years behind it and which we no longer see because it has been victorious.

But you do not comprehend this? You are incapable of seeing something that required two thousand years to achieve victory? – There is nothing to wonder at in that: all *protracted* things are hard to see, to see whole. *That*, however, is what has happened: from the trunk of that tree of vengefulness and hatred, Jewish hatred – the profoundest and sublimest kind of hatred, capable of creating ideals and reversing values, the like of which has never existed on earth before – there grew something equally incomparable, a *new love*, the profoundest and sublimest kind of love – and from what other trunk could it have grown? [. . .]

This is the epilogue of a "free spirit" to my speech; an honest animal, as he has abundantly revealed, and a democrat, moreover; he had been listening to me till then and could not endure to listen to my silence. For at this point I have much to be silent about.

The slave revolt in morality begins when *ressentiment* itself becomes creative and gives birth to values: the *ressentiment* of natures that are denied the true reaction, that of deeds, and compensate themselves with an imaginary revenge. While every noble morality develops from a triumphant affirmation of itself, slave morality from the outset says No to what is "outside," what is "different," what is "not itself"; and *this* No is its creative deed. This inversion of the value-positing eye – this *need* to direct one's view outward instead of back to oneself – is of the essence of *ressentiment*: in order to exist, slave morality always first needs a hostile external world; it needs, physiologically speaking, external stimuli in order to act at all – its action is fundamentally reaction.

The reverse is the case with the noble mode of valuation: it acts and grows spontaneously, it seeks its opposite only so as to affirm itself more gratefully and triumphantly – its negative concept "low," "common," "bad" is only a subsequently-invented pale, contrasting image in relation to its positive basic concept – filled with life and passion through and through – "we noble ones, we good, beautiful, happy ones!" When the noble mode of valuation blunders and sins against reality, it does so in respect to the sphere with which it is *not* sufficiently familiar, against a real knowledge of which it has indeed inflexibly guarded itself: in some circumstances it misunderstands the sphere it despises, that of the common man, of the lower orders; on the other hand, one should remember that, even supposing that the affect of contempt, of looking down from a superior height, *falsifies* the image of that which it despises, it will at any rate still be a much less serious falsification than that perpetrated on its opponent – *in effigie* of course – by the submerged hatred, the vengefulness of the impotent. There is indeed too much carelessness, too much taking lightly, too much looking away and impatience involved in contempt, even too much joyfulness, for it to be able to transform its object into a real caricature and monster.

[. . .]

But let us return: the problem of the *other* origin of the "good," of the good as conceived by the man of *ressentiment*, demands its solution.

That lambs dislike great birds of prey does not seem strange: only it gives no ground for reproaching these birds of prey for bearing off little lambs. And if the lambs say among themselves: "these birds of prey are evil; and whoever is least like a bird of prey, but rather its opposite, a lamb – would he not be good?" there is no reason to find fault with this institution of an ideal, except perhaps that the birds of prey might view it a little ironically and say: "*we* don't dislike them at all, these good little lambs; we even love them: nothing is more tasty than a tender lamb."

To demand of strength that it should *not* express itself as strength, that it should *not* be a desire to overcome, a desire to throw down, a desire to become master, a thirst for enemies and resistances and triumphs, is just as absurd as to demand of weakness that it should express itself as strength. A quantum of force is equivalent to a quantum of drive, will, effect – more, it is nothing other than precisely this very driving, willing, effecting, and only owing to the seduction of language (and of the fundamental errors of reason that are petrified in it) which conceives and misconceives all effects as conditioned by something that causes effects, by a "subject," can it appear otherwise. For just as the popular mind separates the lightning from its flash and takes the latter for an *action*, for the operation of a subject called lightning, so popular morality also separates strength from expressions of strength, as if there were a neutral substratum behind the strong man, which was *free* to express strength or not to do so. But there is no such substratum; there is no "being" behind doing, effecting, becoming; "the doer" is merely a fiction added to the deed – the deed is everything. The popular mind in fact doubles the deed; when it sees the lightning flash, it is the deed of a deed: it posits the same event first as cause and then a second time as its effect. Scientists do no better when they say "force moves," "force causes," and the like – all its coolness, its freedom from emotion notwithstanding, our entire science still lies under the misleading influence of language and has not disposed of that little changeling, the "subject" (the atom, for example, is such a changeling, as is the Kantian "thing-in-itself"); no wonder if the submerged, darkly glowering emotions of vengefulness and hatred exploit this belief for their own ends and in fact maintain no belief more ardently than the belief that *the strong man is free* to be weak and the bird of prey to be a lamb – for thus they gain the right to make the bird of prey *accountable* for being a bird of pray.

When the oppressed, downtrodden, outraged exhort one another with the vengeful cunning of impotence: "let us be different from the evil, namely good! And he is good who does not outrage, who harms nobody, who does not attack, who does not requite, who leaves revenge to God, who keeps himself hidden as we do, who avoids evil and desires little from life, like us, the patient, humble, and just" – this, listened to calmly and without previous bias, really amounts to no more than: "we weak ones are, after all, weak; it would be good if we did nothing *for which we are not strong enough*"; but this dry matter of fact, this prudence of the lowest order which even insects possess (posing as dead, when in great danger, so as not to do "too much"), has, thanks to the counterfeit and self-deception of impotence, clad itself in the ostentatious garb of the virtue of quiet, calm resignation, just as if the weakness of the weak – that is to say, their *essence*, their effects, their sole ineluctable, irremovable reality – were a voluntary achievement, willed, chosen, a *deed*, a *meritorious* act. This type of man *needs* to believe in a neutral independent "subject," prompted by an instinct for self-preservation and self-affirmation in which every lie is sanctified. The subject (or, to use a more popular expression, the *soul*) has perhaps been believed in hitherto more firmly than anything else on earth because it makes possible to the majority of mortals, the weak and oppressed of every kind, the sublime self-deception that interprets weakness as freedom, and their being thus-and-thus as a *merit*.

[. . .]

Let us conclude. The two *opposing* values "good and bad," "good and evil" have been engaged in a fearful struggle on earth for thousands of years; and though the latter value has certainly been on top for a long time, there are still places where the struggle is as yet undecided. One might even say that it has risen ever higher and thus become more and more profound and spiritual: so that today there is perhaps no more decisive mark of a "*higher nature*," a more spiritual nature, than that of being divided in this sense and a genuine battleground of these opposed values.

The symbol of this struggle, inscribed in letters legible across all human history, is "Rome against Judea. Judea against Rome": – there has hitherto been no greater event than *this* struggle, *this* question, *this* deadly contradiction. Rome felt the Jew to be something like anti-nature itself, its antipodal monstrosity as it were: in Rome the Jew stood "*convicted* of hatred for the whole human race"; and rightly, provided one has a right to link the salvation and future of the human race with the unconditional dominance of aristocratic values, Roman values.

How, on the other hand, did the Jews feel about Rome? A thousand signs tell us; but it suffices to recall the Apocalypse of John, the most wanton of all literary outbursts that vengefulness has on its conscience. (One should not underestimate the profound consistency of the Christian instinct when it signed this book of hate with the name of the disciple of love, the same disciple to whom it attributed that amorous-enthusiastic Gospel: there is a piece of truth in this, however much literary counterfeiting might have been required to produce it.) For the Romans were the strong and noble, and nobody stronger and nobler has yet existed on earth or even been dreamed of: every remnant of them, every inscription gives delight, if only one divines *what* it was that was there at work. The Jews, on the contrary, were the priestly nation of *ressentiment par excellence*, in whom there dwelt an unequaled popular-moral genius: one only has to compare similarly gifted nations – the Chinese or the Germans, for instance – with the Jews, to sense which is of the first and which of the fifth rank.

Which of them has won *for the present*, Rome or Judea? But there can be no doubt: consider to whom one bows down in Rome itself today, as if they were the epitome of all the highest values – and not only in Rome but over almost half the earth, everywhere that man has become tame or desires to become tame: *three Jews*, as is known, and *one Jewess* (Jesus of Nazareth, the fisherman Peter, the rug weaver Paul, and the mother of the aforementioned Jesus, named Mary). This is very remarkable: Rome has been defeated beyond all doubt.

There was, to be sure, in the Renaissance an uncanny and glittering reawakening of the classical ideal, of the noble mode of evaluating all things; Rome itself, oppressed by the new superimposed Judaized Rome that presented the aspect of an ecumenical synagogue and was called the "church," stirred like one awakened from seeming death: but Judea immediately triumphed again, thanks to that thoroughly plebeian (German and English) *ressentiment* movement called the Reformation, and to that which was bound to arise from it, the restoration of the church – the restoration too of the ancient sepulchral repose of classical Rome.

With the French Revolution, Judea once again triumphed over the classical ideal, and this time in an even more profound and decisive sense: the last political noblesse in Europe, that of the *French* seventeenth and eighteenth century, collapsed beneath the popular instincts of *ressentiment* – greater rejoicing, more uproarious enthusiasm had never been heard on earth! To be sure, in the midst of it there occurred the most tremendous, the most unexpected thing: the ideal of antiquity itself stepped *incarnate* and in unheard-of splendor before the eyes and conscience of mankind – and once again, in opposition to the mendacious slogan of *ressentiment*, "supreme rights of the majority," in opposition to the will to the lowering, the abasement, the leveling and the decline and twilight of mankind, there sounded stronger, simpler, and more insistently than ever the terrible and rapturous counterslogan "supreme rights of the few"! Like a last signpost to the *other* path, Napoleon appeared, the most isolated and late-born man there has ever been, and in him the problem of the *noble ideal as such* made flesh – one might well ponder *what* kind of problem it is: Napolean, this synthesis of the *inhuman* and *superhuman*.

[. . .]

But how did that other "somber thing," the consciousness of guilt, the "bad conscience," come into the world? – And at this point we return to the genealogists of morals. To say it again – or haven't I said it yet? – they are worthless. A brief span of experience that is merely one's own, merely modern; no knowledge or will to knowledge of the past; even less of historical instinct, of that "second sight" needed here above all – and yet they undertake history of morality: it stands to reason that their results stay at a more than respectful distance from the truth. Have these genealogists of morals had even the remotest suspicion that, for example, the major moral concept *Schuld* [guilt] has its origin in the very material concept *Schulden* [debts]? Or that punishment, as requital, evolved quite independently of any presupposition concerning freedom or non-freedom of the will? – to such an extent, indeed, that a *high* degree of humanity had to be attained before the animal "man" began even to make the much more primitive distinctions between "intentional," "negligent," "accidental," "accountable," and their opposites and to take them into account when determining punishments. The idea, now so obvious, apparently so natural, even unavoidable, that had to serve as the explanation of how the sense of justice ever appeared on earth – "the criminal deserves punishment *because* he could have acted differently" – is in fact an extremely late and subtle form of human judgment and inference: whoever transposes it to the beginning is guilty of a crude misunderstanding of the psychology of more primitive mankind. Throughout the greater part of human history punishment was *not* imposed *because* one held the wrong-doer responsible for his deed, thus *not* on the presupposition that only the guilty one should be punished: rather, as parents still punish their children, from anger at some harm or injury, vented on the one who caused it – but this anger is held in check and modified by the idea that every injury has its *equivalent* and can actually be paid back, even if only through the *pain* of the culprit. And whence did this primeval, deeply rooted, perhaps by now ineradicable idea draw its power – this idea of an equivalence between injury and pain? I have already divulged it: in the contractual relationship between *creditor* and *debtor*, which is as old as the idea of "legal subjects" and in turn points back to the fundamental forms of buying, selling, barter, trade, and traffic.

[. . .]

To return to our investigation: the feeling of guilt, of personal obligation, had its origin, as we saw, in the oldest and most primitive personal relationship, that between buyer and seller, creditor and debtor: it was here that one person first encountered another person, that one person first *measured himself* against another. No grade of civilization, however low, has yet been discovered in which something of this relationship has not been noticeable. Setting prices, determining values, contriving equivalences, exchanging – these preoccupied the earliest thinking of man to so great an extent that in a certain sense they constitute thinking *as such*: here it was that the oldest kind of astuteness developed; here likewise, we may suppose, did human pride, the feeling of superiority in relation to other animals, have its first beginnings. Perhaps our word "man" (*manas*) still expresses something of precisely *this* feeling of self-satisfaction: man designated himself as the creature that measures values, evaluates and measures, as the "valuating animal as such."

Buying and selling, together with their psychological appurtenances, are older even than the beginnings of any kind of social forms of organization and alliances: it was rather out of the most rudimentary form of personal legal rights that the budding sense of exchange, contract, guilt, right, obligation, settlement, first *transferred* itself to the coarsest and most elementary social complexes (in their relations with other similar complexes), together with the custom of comparing, measuring, and calculating power against power. The eye was now focused on this perspective; and with that blunt consistency characteristic of the thinking of primitive mankind, which is hard to set in motion but then proceeds inexorably in the same direction, one forthwith arrived at the great generalization, "everything has its price; *all* things can be paid for" – the oldest and naïvest moral canon of *justice*, the beginning of all "good-naturedness," all "fairness," all "good will," all "objectivity" of earth. Justice on this elementary level is the good will among parties of approximately equal power to come to terms with one another, to reach an "understanding" by means of a settlement – and to *compel* parties of lesser power to reach a settlement among themselves.

[. . .]

At this point I can no longer avoid giving a first, provisional statement of my own hypothesis concerning the origin of the "bad conscience": it may sound rather strange and needs to be pondered, lived with, and slept on for a long time. I regard the bad conscience as the serious illness that man was bound to contract under the stress of the most fundamental change he ever experienced – that change which occurred when he found himself finally enclosed within the walls of society and of peace. The situation that faced sea animals when they were compelled to become land animals or perish was the same as that which faced these semi-animals, well adapted to the wilderness, to war, to prowling, to adventure: suddenly all their instincts were disvalued and "suspended." From now on they had to walk on their feet and "bear themselves" whereas hitherto they had been borne by the water: a dreadful heaviness lay upon them. They felt unable to cope with the simplest undertakings; in this new world they no longer possessed their former guides, their regulating, unconscious and infallible drives: they were reduced to thinking, inferring, reckoning, co-ordinating cause and effect, these unfortunate creatures; they were reduced to their "consciousness," their weakest and most fallible organ! I believe there has never been such a feeling of misery on earth, such a leaden discomfort – and at the same time the old instincts had not suddenly ceased to make their usual demands! Only it was hardly or rarely possible to humor them: as a rule they had to seek new and, as it were, subterranean gratifications.

All instincts that do not discharge themselves outwardly *turn inward* – this is what I call the *internalization* of man: thus it was that man first developed what was later called his "soul." The entire inner world, originally as thin as if it were stretched between two membranes, expanded and extended itself, acquired depth, breadth, and height, in the same measure as outward discharge was *inhibited*. Those fearful bulwarks with which the political organization protected itself against the old instincts of freedom – punishments belong among these bulwarks – brought about that all those instincts of wild, free, prowling man turned backward *against man himself*. Hostility, cruelty, joy in persecuting, in attacking, in change, in destruction – all this turned against the possessors of such instincts: *that* is the origin of the "bad conscience."

The man who, from lack of external enemies and resistances and forcibly confined to the oppressive narrowness and punctiliousness of custom, impatiently lacerated, persecuted, gnawed at, assaulted, and maltreated himself; this animal that rubbed itself raw against the bars of its cage as one tried to "tame" it; this deprived creature, racked with homesickness for the wild, who had to turn himself into an adventure, a torture chamber, an uncertain and dangerous wilderness – this fool, this yearning and desperate prisoner became the inventor of the "bad conscience." But thus began the gravest and uncanniest illness, from which humanity has not yet recovered, man's suffering *of man, of himself* – the result of a forcible sundering from his animal past, as it were a leap and plunge into new surroundings and conditions of existence, a declaration of war against the old instincts upon which his strength, joy, and terribleness had rested hitherto.

Let us add at once that, on the other hand, the existence on earth of an animal soul turned against itself, taking sides against itself, was something so new, profound, unheard of, enigmatic, contradictory, *and pregnant with a future* that the aspect of the earth was essentially altered. Indeed, divine spectators were needed to do justice to the spectacle that thus began and the end of which is not yet in sight – a spectacle too subtle, too marvelous, too paradoxical to be played senselessly unobserved on some ludicrous planet! From now on, man is *included* among the most unexpected and exciting lucky throws in the dice game of Heraclitus' "great child," be he called Zeus or chance; he gives rise to an interest, a tension, a hope, almost a certainty, as if with him something were announcing and preparing itself, as if man were not a goal but only a way, an episode, a bridge, a great promise.

Part 7

THE BANALITY
OF EVIL

The cruelty of everyday life

George Grosz: "Human Paths."

Many post-Romantic authors vividly and graphically describe the evils of human suffering and decry the mindless – and sometimes willful – cruelty that brings it about. "If the Devil doesn't exist, man has created him, and created him in his own image," Ivan Karamazov says in Dostoevsky's (1821–1881) *The Brothers Karamazov*. "If the suffering of children is necessary to pay for the truth, then I protest that truth is not worth such a price. . . . Too high a price is asked for harmony; it is beyond our means to pay so much to enter on it." Ivan shares Schopenhauer's view of the world, its depravity and suffering; and Dostoevsky has him condemn a divinity who created such a world. It is a cry of outrage against Leibniz's theodicy, against the assurance that a benign divinity created the best of all possible worlds.

Writing as a journalist, Friedrich Engels (1820–1895) describes the suffering of the working classes in industrial England in terms very similar to those expressed by Dostoevsky's Ivan. He sees Hobbes's "war of each against all," continued within a political system that elevates avarice and greed as engines of an imagined progress, a progress that cannot touch the "nameless misery" of the poor. The indifference exemplified in "shamelessly barefaced . . . barbarous . . . egotism" is protected and promoted by a political system whose claim to provide fair and equal legal protection is a sham. The show of charitable institutions heaps insult upon injury: it adds hypocrisy and self-deception to the mass of vices that perpetuate the system. Mandeville's fantasy that private vices issue in public benefits is a delusion.

In 1932, Einstein (1879–1955) writes Freud, asking "Is it possible to control man's mental evolution so as to make him proof against the psychosis of hate and destructiveness?" Freud (1856–1939) replies darkly. It is impossible to bypass the instincts for aggression and destruction: they are embedded in dynamics of psychological development. Hobbes's hope of securing peace through a Sovereign state is unattainable: as long as power remains unequally distributed within a human community, there will be oppression and conflict. Ideally, destructive aggression can be checked and redirected by other instincts, and – under benign conditions – by sociability, by solid and just institutions, and by the gradual development of civilization and culture. It is an irony of human psychology that the tenacious pursuit of the checks on human aggression is itself the expression of aggression.

Writing after the second world war, Hannah Arendt (1900–1975) asks how so civilized and cultured a nation as Germany could have engaged in the horrors, the barbarous genocide of the concentration camps? How could an apparently decent citizen like Eichmann become a murderous butcher? Her answer is that the steps to evil are banal, common and almost unnoticeable. They follow the standard ordinary motions of the mind: the redirection of attention, the ability to redescribe one's actions in clichés that fall under acceptable standards. Mass slaughter is called racial purification; carnage is described as patriotism. Cruelty need not be an obvious lapse into insanity: it can be discriminating, delicate . . . and mindlessly inattentive.

Contemporary authors – Michael Stocker, Amélie Rorty and Amos Oz – develop the view that many vices are ordinary, virtually unnoticed failures of attention. Stocker goes further: he attacks the fundamental psychological assumption that all motivation is directed *sub specie boni*, that actions are directed towards what is believed to be good or desirable. The good may fail to attract; the bad may have its own attractions. He argues that men sometimes choose what they believe to be bad, that they do so with open eyes, choosing it as bad, because it is bad, without the justification of an over-arching end. Dostoevsky's Raskolnikov may have murdered an old pawnbroker to prove that he was radically free; but Camus' Meursault killed a man mindlessly, absent-mindedly, on impulse.

Amélie Rorty chronicles some stages in the banal slide towards corruption. They are, she argues, ordinary psychological habits, standardly adaptively exercised in virtually all our activities. They involve focusing attention on what is subjectively present, blocking imaginative foresight to the larger consequences of what we do, a tendency to generalize and entrench successful action patterns, imitating charismatic figures. The kinds of corrective moves that can block the slide to corruption – identifying with admirable figures and ideal causes – can themselves be perverted. As long as corruption brings personal success and social approval, it is unlikely that they will be reversed.

Amos Oz argues that we cannot classify villains and heroes into separate categories. Every man, even every admirable moral witness, combines nobility with ruthless cruelty. Responsible writers have a double moral task: they must expose the evils hidden within the virtues and they must diagnose evils with care and precision, calling them by their proper names.

34

FYODOR DOSTOEVSKY

Ivan speaks of human cruelty

"You speak with a strange air," observed Alyosha uneasily, "as though you were not quite yourself."

"By the way, a Bulgarian I met lately in Moscow," Ivan went on, seeming not to hear his brother's words, "told me about the crimes committed by Turks and Circassians in all parts of Bulgaria through fear of a general rising of the Slavs. They burn villages, murder, outrage women and children; they nail their prisoners by the ears to the fences, leave them so till morning, and in the morning they hang them – all sorts of things you can't imagine. People talk sometimes of bestial cruelty, but that's a great injustice and insult to the beasts; a beast can never be so cruel as a man, so artistically cruel. The tiger only tears and gnaws, that's all he can do. He would never think of nailing people by the ears, even if he were able to do it. [Soldiers take] pleasure in torturing children, too; cutting the unborn child from the mother's womb, and tossing babies up in the air, and catching them on the points of their bayonets before their mother's eyes. Doing it before the mother's eyes was what gave zest to the amusement. Here is another scene that I thought very interesting. Imagine a trembling mother with her baby in her arms, a circle of invaders around her. They've planned a diversion; they pet the baby, laugh to make it laugh. They succeed; the baby laughs. At that moment, a [soldier] points a pistol four inches from the baby's face. The baby laughs with glee, holds out its little hands to the pistol, and he pulls the trigger by the baby's face and blows out its brains . . .

"[I]f the devil doesn't exist, but man has created him, he has created him in his own image and likeness.

"Yours must be a fine God, if man created Him in His image and likeness. You asked just now what I was driving at. You see, I am fond of collecting certain facts, and would you believe it, I even copy anecdotes of a certain sort from newspapers and books, and I've already got a fine collection. . . . You know we prefer beating – rods and scourges – that's

Source: *The Grand Inquisitor*, translated by Charles B. Guignon, Indianapolis, Ind.: Hackett Publishing Company, 1993.

our national institution. Nailing ears is unthinkable for us, for we are, after all, Europeans. But the rod and scourge we have always with us, and they cannot be taken from us. Abroad now they scarcely do any beating. Manners are more humane, or laws have been passed so that they don't dare to flog men now. But they make up for it in another way just as national as ours. And so national that it would be practically impossible among us, though I believe we are being inoculated with it, since the religious movement began in our aristocracy. I have a charming pamphlet, translated from the French, describing how, quite recently, five years ago, a murderer, Richard, was executed – a young man, I believe, of twenty-three, who repented and was converted to the Christian faith at the very scaffold. This Richard was an illegitimate child who was given as a child of six by his parents to some shepherds on the Swiss mountains. They brought him up to work for them. He grew up like a little wild beast among them. The shepherds taught him nothing, and scarcely fed or clothed him, but sent him out at seven to herd the flock in the cold and wet, and no one hesitated or scrupled to treat him so. Quite the contrary; they thought they had every right, for Richard had been given to them as a chattel, and they did not even see the necessity of feeding him. Richard himself describes how in those years, like the Prodigal Son in the Gospel, he longed to eat of the mash given to the pigs, which were fattened for sale. But they wouldn't even given him that, and beat him when he stole from the pigs. And that was how he spent all his childhood and his youth, till he grew up and was strong enough to go away and be a thief. The savage began to earn his living as a day laborer in Geneva. He drank what he earned, he lived like a brute, and finished by killing and robbing an old man. He was caught, tried, and condemned to death. They are not sentimentalists there. And in prison he was immediately surrounded by pastors, members of Christian brotherhoods, philanthropic ladies, and the like. They taught him to read and write in prison, and expounded the Gospel to him. They exhorted him, worked upon him, drummed at him incessantly, till at last he solemnly confessed his crime. He was converted. He wrote to the court himself that he was a monster, but that in the end God had vouchsafed him light and shown grace. All Geneva was in excitement about him – all philanthropic and religious Geneva. All the aristocratic and wellbred society of the town rushed to the prison, kissed Richard and embraced him; 'You are our brother; you have found grace.' And Richard does nothing but weep with emotion. 'Yes, I've found grace! All my youth and childhood I was glad of pigs' food, but now even I have found grace; I am dying in the Lord.' 'Yes, Richard, die in the Lord; you have shed blood and must die. Though it's not your fault that you knew not the Lord, when you coveted the pigs' food and were beaten for stealing it (which was very wrong of you, for stealing is forbidden). But you've shed blood and you must die.' And on the last day, Richard, perfectly limp, did nothing but cry and repeat every minute, 'This is my happiest day. I am going to the Lord.' 'Yes,' cry the pastors and the judges and philanthropic ladies. 'This is the happiest day of your life, for you are going to the Lord!' They all walk or drive to the scaffold in procession behind the prison van. At the scaffold they call to Richard, 'Die, brother, die in the Lord, for even thou has found grace!' And so, covered with his brothers' kisses, Richard is dragged on to the scaffold, and led to the guillotine. And they chopped off his head in brotherly fashion, because he had found grace. Yes, that's characteristic. That pamphlet is translated into Russian by some Russian philanthropists of aristocratic rank and evangelical aspirations, and has been distributed gratis for the enlightenment of the people. The case of Richard is interesting because it's national. Though to us it's absurd to cut off a man's head because he had become our brother and has found grace, yet we have our own specialty, which is all but worse. Our historical pastime is the direct satisfaction of inflicting pain. There are lines in Nekrassov describing how a peasant lashes a horse on the eyes, 'on its meek eyes.' Everyone must have seen it; it's peculiarly Russian. He describes how a feeble little nag has foundered under too heavy a load and cannot move. The peasant beats it, beats it savagely, beats it at last not knowing what he is doing in the intoxication of cruelty, thrashes it mercilessly over and over again. 'However weak you are, you must pull, even if you die for it.' The nag strains. And then he begins lashing the poor defenceless creature on its weeping, on its 'meek eyes.' The frantic beast tugs and draws the load, trembling all over, gasping for breath, moving sideways, with a sort of unnatural spasmodic action – it's awful in Nekrassov. But that's only a horse, and God has given horses to be beaten. . . . [M]en, too, can be beaten. A well-educated, cultured gentleman and his wife beat their own child with a birch rod, a girl of seven. I have an exact account of it. The papa was glad that the birch was covered with twigs. 'It stings more,' said he, and so he began stinging his daughter. I know for a fact there are people who at every blow are worked up to sensuality, to literal sensuality, which increases progressively at every blow they inflict. They beat for a minute, for five minutes, for ten minutes, more often and more savagely. The child screams. At last the child cannot scream; it gasps, 'Daddy! daddy!' By some diabolical, unseemly chance the case was brought into court. A counsel is engaged. The Russian people have long called a barrister 'a conscience for hire.' The counsel protests in his client's defence. 'It's such a simple thing,' he says, 'an everyday domestic event. A father corrects his child. To our shame be it said, it is brought into court.' The jury, convinced by him, gives a favorable verdict. The public roars with delight that the torturer is acquitted. Ah, pity I wasn't there! I would have proposed to raise a subscription in his honor! . . . Charming pictures.

"But I've still better things about children. . . . There was a little girl of five who was hated by her father and mother, 'most worthy and respectable people, of good education and breeding.' You see, I must repeat again, it is a peculiar characteristic of many people, this love of torturing children, and children only. To all other types of humanity these torturers behave mildly and benevolently, like cultivated and humane Europeans; but they are very fond of tormenting children, even fond of children themselves in that sense. It's just their defencelessness that tempts the tormentor, just the angelic confidence of the child who has no refuge and no appeal, that sets his vile blood on fire. In every man, of course, a demon lies hidden – the demon of rage, the demon of lustful heat at the screams of the tortured victim, the demon of lawlessness let off the chain, the demon of diseases that follow on vice, gout, kidney disease, and so on.

"This poor child of five was subjected to every possible torture by those cultivated parents. They beat her, thrashed her, kicked her for no reason till her body was one bruise. Then, they went to greater refinements of cruelty – shut her up all night in the cold and frost in a privy, and because she didn't ask to be taken up at night (as though a child of five sleeping its angelic, sound sleep could be trained to wake and ask) they smeared her face and filled her mouth with excrement, and it was her mother, her mother who did this. And that mother could sleep, hearing the poor child's groans! Can you understand why a little creature, who can't even understand what's done to her, should beat her little aching heart with her tiny fist in the dark and the cold, and weep her meek unresentful tears to dear, kind God to protect her? Do you understand that, friend and brother, you pious and humble novice? Do you understand why this infamy must be and is permitted? Without it, I am told, man could not have existed on earth, for he could not have known good and evil. Why should he know that diabolical good and evil when it costs so much? Why, the whole world of knowledge is not worth that child's prayer to 'dear, kind God'! I say nothing of the sufferings of grownup people; they have eaten the apple, damn them, and the devil take them all! But these little ones! . . .

"One picture, only one more, because it's so curious, so characteristic, and I have only just read it in some collection of Russian antiquities. I've forgotten the name. I must look it up. It was in the darkest days of serfdom at the beginning of the century, and long live the Liberator of the People! There was in those days a general of aristocratic connections, the owner of great estates, one of those men – somewhat exceptional, I believe, even then – who, retiring from the service into a life of leisure, are convinced that they've earned absolute power over the lives of their subjects. There were such men then. So our general, settled on his property of two thousand souls, lives in pomp, and domineers over his poor neighbors as though they were dependants and buffoons. He has kennels of hundreds of hounds and near a hundred dog boys – all mounted and in uniform. One day a serf boy, a little child of eight, threw a stone in play and hurt the paw of the general's favourite hound. 'Why is my favorite dog lame?' He is told that the boy threw a stone that hurt the dog's paw. 'So you did it.' The general looked the child up and down. 'Take him.' He was taken – taken from his mother and kept shut up all night. Early that morning the general comes out on horseback, with the hounds, his dependants, dog boys, and huntsmen, all mounted around him in full hunting parade. The servants are summoned for their edification, and in front of them all stands the mother of the child. The child is brought from the lockup. It's a gloomy, cold, foggy autumn day, a capital day for hunting. The general orders the child to be undressed; the child is stripped naked. He shivers, numb with terror, not daring to cry. . . . 'Make him run,' commands the general. 'Run! run!' shout the dog boys. The boy runs. . . . 'At him!' yells the general, and he sets the whole pack of hounds on the child. The hounds catch

244

him, and tear him to pieces before his mother's eyes! . . . I believe the general was afterwards declared incapable of administering his estates . . .

"[T]he absurd is only too necessary on earth. The world stands on absurdities, and perhaps nothing would have come to pass in it without them . . .

"Listen! I took the case of children only to make my case clearer. Of the other tears of humanity with which the earth is soaked from its crust to its center, I will say nothing. I have narrowed my subject on purpose. I am a bug, and I recognize in all humility that I cannot understand why the world is arranged as it is. Men are themselves to blame, I suppose; they were given paradise, they wanted freedom, and stole fire from heaven, though they knew they would become unhappy, so there is no need to pity them. With my pitiful, earthly, Euclidian understanding, all I know is that there is suffering and that there are none guilty; that effect follows cause, simply and directly; that everything flows and finds its level — but that's only Euclidian nonsense, I know that, and I can't consent to live by it! What comfort is it to me that there are none guilty and that effect follows cause simply and directly, and that I know it — I must have justice, or I will destroy myself. And not justice in some remote infinite time and space, but here on earth, and that I could see myself. I have believed in it. I want to see it, and if I am dead by then, let me rise again, for if it all happens without me, it will be too unfair. Surely I haven't suffered, simply that I, my crimes and my sufferings, may manure the soil of the future harmony for somebody else. I want to see with my own eyes the hind lie down with the lion and the victim rise up and embrace his murderer. I want to be there when everyone suddenly understands what it has all been for. All the religions of the world are built on this longing, and I am a believer. But then there are the children, and what am I to do about them? That's a question I can't answer. For the hundredth time I repeat, there are numbers of questions, but I've only taken the children, because in their case what I mean is so unanswerably clear. Listen! If all must suffer to pay for the eternal harmony, what have children to do with it, tell me, please? It's beyond all comprehension why they should suffer, and why they should pay for the harmony. Why should they, too, furnish material to enrich the soil for the harmony of the future? I understand solidarity in sin among men. I understand solidarity in retribution, too; but there can be no such solidarity with children. And if it is really true that they must share responsibility for all their fathers' crimes, such a truth is not of this world and is beyond my comprehension. Some jester will say, perhaps, that the child would have grown up and have sinned, but you see he didn't grow up, he was torn to pieces by the dogs, at eight years old. Oh, Alyosha, I am not blaspheming! I understand, of course, what an upheaval of the universe it will be, when everything in heaven and earth blends in one hymn of praise and everything that lives and has lived cries aloud: 'Thou art just, O Lord, for Thy ways are revealed.' When the mother embraces the fiend who threw her child to the dogs, and all three cry aloud with tears, 'Thou are just, O Lord!' then, of course, the crown of knowledge will be reached and all will be made clear. But what pulls me up here is that I can't accept that harmony. And while I am on earth, I make haste to take my own measures. You see, Alyosha, perhaps it really may happen that if I live to that moment, or rise again to see it, I, too, perhaps, may cry aloud with the rest, looking at the mother embracing the child's torturer, 'Thou art just, O Lord!' But I don't want to cry aloud then. While there is still time, I hasten to protect myself, and so I renounce the higher harmony altogether. It's not worth the tears of that one tortured child who beat itself on the breast with its little fist and prayed in its stinking outhouse, with its unexpiated tears to 'dear, kind God'! It's not worth it, because those tears are unatoned for. They must be atoned for, or there can be no harmony. But how? How are you going to atone for them? Is it possible? By their being avenged? But what do I care for avenging them? What do I care for a hell for oppressors? What good can hell do, since those children have already been tortured? And what becomes of harmony, if there is hell? I want to forgive. I want to embrace. I don't want more suffering. And if the sufferings of children go to swell the sum of sufferings which was necessary to pay for truth, then I protest that the truth is not worth such a price. I don't want the mother to embrace the oppressor who threw her son to the dogs! She dare not forgive him! Let her forgive him for herself, if she will, let her forgive the torturer for the immeasurable suffering of her mother's heart. But the sufferings of her tortured child she has no right to forgive; she dare not forgive the torturer, even if the child were to forgive him! And if that is so, if they dare not forgive, what becomes of harmony? Is there in the whole world a being who would have the right to forgive and could forgive? I don't want harmony. From love for humanity I don't want it. I would rather be left with the unavenged suffering. I would rather remain with my unavenged suffering and unsatisfied indignation, *even if I were wrong*. Besides, too high a price is asked for harmony; it's beyond our means to pay so much to enter on it. And so I hasten to give back my entrance ticket, and if I am an honest man I am bound to give it back as soon as possible. And that I am doing. It's not God that I don't accept . . . only I most respectfully return Him the ticket . . .

"Imagine that you are creating a fabric of human destiny with the object of making men happy in the end, giving them peace and rest at last, but that it was essential and inevitable to torture to death only one tiny creature – that baby beating its breast with its fist, for instance – and to found that edifice on its unavenged tears, would you consent to be the architect on those conditions? Tell me, and tell the truth . . .

"And can you admit the idea that men for whom you are building it would agree to accept their happiness on the foundation of the unexpiated blood of a little victim? And accepting it would remain happy for ever?" . . .

"You said just now, is there a being in the whole world who would have the right to forgive and could forgive? But there is such a Being, and He can forgive everything, all and for all, because He gave His innocent blood for all and everything. You have forgotten Him, and on Him is built the edifice, and it is to Him they cry aloud, 'Thou art just, O Lord, for Thy ways are revealed!'"

"Ah! the One without sin and His blood! No, I have not forgotten Him; on the contrary I've been wondering all the time how it was you did not bring Him in before, for usually all arguments on your side put Him in the foreground.

35

FRIEDRICH ENGELS

Barbarous indifference

The great towns

A town, such as London, where a man may wander for hours together without reaching the beginning of the end, without meeting the slightest hint which could lead to the inference that there is open country within reach, is a strange thing. This colossal centralization, this heaping together of two and a half millions of human beings at one point, has multiplied the power of this two and a half millions a hundredfold; has raised London to the commercial capital of the world, created the giant docks and assembled the thousand vessels that continually cover the Thames. I know nothing more imposing than the view which the Thames offers during the ascent from the sea to London Bridge. The masses of buildings, the wharves on both sides, especially from Woolwich upwards, the countless ships along both shores, crowding ever closer and closer together, until, at last, only a narrow passage remains in the middle of the river, a passage through which hundreds of steamers shoot by one another; all this is so vast, so impressive, that a man cannot collect himself, but is lost in the marvel of England's greatness before he sets foot upon English soil.

But the sacrifices which all this has cost become apparent later. After roaming the streets of the capital a day or two, making headway with difficulty through the human turmoil and the endless lines of vehicles, after visiting the slums of the metropolis, one realizes for the first time that these Londoners have been forced to sacrifice the best qualities of their human nature, to bring to pass all the marvels of civilization which crowd their city; that a hundred powers which slumbered within them have remained inactive, have been suppressed in order that a few might be developed more fully and multiply through union with those of others. The very turmoil of the streets has something

Source: *The Condition of the Working Class in England*, translated by Florence Wischbewetzky, New York: Penguin (1886 translation).

repulsive, something against which human nature rebels. The hundreds of thousands of all classes and ranks crowding past each other, are they not all human beings with the same qualities and powers, and with the same interest in being happy? And have they not, in the end, to seek happiness in the same way, by the same means? And still they crowd by one another as though they had nothing in common, nothing to do with one another, and their only agreement is the tacit one, that each keep to his own side of the pavement, so as not to delay the opposing streams of the crowd, which it occurs to no man to honour another with so much as a glance. The brutal indifference, the unfeeling isolation of each in his private interest becomes the more repellent and offensive, the more these individuals are crowded together, within a limited space. And, however much one may be aware that this isolation of the individual, this narrow self-seeking, is the fundamental principle of our society everywhere, it is nowhere so shamelessly barefaced, so self-conscious as just here in the crowding of the great city. The dissolution of mankind into monads, of which each one has a separate essence, and a separate purpose, the world of atoms, is here carried out to its utmost extreme.

Hence it comes, too, that the social war, the war of each against all, is here openly declared. . . . [P]eople regard each other only as useful objects; each exploits the other, and the end of it all is, that the stronger treads the weaker under foot, and that the powerful few, the capitalists, seize everything for themselves, while to the weak many, the poor, scarcely a bare existence remains . . .

Everywhere barbarous indifference, hard egotism on one hand, and nameless misery on the other, everywhere social warfare, every man's house in a state of siege, everywhere reciprocal plundering under the protection of the law, and all so shameless, so openly avowed that one shrinks before the consequences of our social state as they manifest themselves here undisguised, and can only wonder that the whole crazy fabric still hangs together . . .

The attitude of the bourgeoisie towards the proletariat

I have never seen a class so deeply demoralized, so incurably debased by selfishness, so corroded within, so incapable of progress, as the English bourgeoisie. . . . For it nothing exists in this world, except for the sake of money, itself not excluded. It knows no bliss save that of rapid gain, no pain save that of losing gold. In the presence of this avarice and lust of gain, it is not possible for a single human sentiment or opinion to remain untainted. True, these English bourgeois are good husbands and family men, and have all sorts of other private virtues, and appear, in ordinary intercourse, as decent and respectable as all other bourgeois; even in business they are better to deal with than the Germans; they do not higgle and haggle so much as our own pettifogging merchants; but how does this help matters? Ultimately it is self-interest, and especially money gain, which alone determines them. I once went into Manchester with such a bourgeois, and spoke to him of the bad, unwholesome method of building, the frightful condition of the working people's quarters, and asserted that I had never seen so ill-built a city. The man listened quietly to the end, and said at the corner where we parted: 'And yet there is a great deal of money made here; good morning, sir.' It is utterly indifferent to the English bourgeois whether his working men starve or not, if only he makes money. All the conditions of life are measured by money, and what brings no money is nonsense, unpractical, idealistic bosh. Hence, political economy, the science of wealth, is the favourite study of these bartering Jews. Every one of them is a political economist. The relation of the manufacturer to his operatives has nothing human in it; it is purely economic. The manufacturer is capital, the operative labour. And if the operative will not be forced into this abstraction, if he insists that he is not labour, but a man, who possesses, among other things, the attribute of labour-force, if he takes it into his head that he need not allow himself to be sold and bought in the market, as the commodity 'labour', the bourgeois reason comes to a standstill. He cannot comprehend that he holds any other relation to the operatives than that of purchase and sale; he sees in them not human beings, but hands, as he constantly calls them to their faces; he insists, as Carlyle says, that 'cash payment is the only nexus between man and man'. Even the relation between himself and his wife is, in ninety-nine cases out of a hundred, mere 'cash payment'. Money determines the worth of the man; he is 'worth ten thousand pounds'. He who has money is of 'the better sort of people', is 'influential', and what *he* does counts for something in his social circle. The huckstering spirit penetrates the whole language, all relations are expressed in business terms, in economic categories. Supply and demand are the formulas according to which the logic of the English bourgeois judges all human life. Hence free competition in every respect, hence the *régime* of *laissez-faire, laissez-aller* in government, in medicine, in education, and before long in religion, too, as the State Church collapses more and more. Free competition will suffer no limitation, no State supervision; the whole State is but a burden to it. It would reach its highest perfection in a wholly ungoverned anarchic society, where each might exploit the other to his heart's content. Since, however, the bourgeoisie cannot dispense with government, but must have it to hold the equally indispensable proletariat in check, it turns the power of government against the proletariat and keeps out of its way as far as possible.

Let no one believe, however, that the 'cultivated' Englishman openly brags of his egotism. On the contrary, he conceals it under the vilest hypocrisy. What? The wealthy English fail to remember the poor? They who have founded philanthropic institutions such as no other country can boast of! Philanthropic institutions forsooth! As though you rendered the proletarians a service in first sucking out their very life-blood and then practising your self-complacent, Pharisaic philanthropy upon them, putting yourselves before the world as mighty benefactors of humanity when you give back to the plundered victims the hundredth part of what belongs to them! Charity which degrades him who gives more than him who takes; charity which treads the downtrodden still deeper in the dust, which demands that the degraded, the pariah cast out by society, shall first surrender the last that remains to him, his very claim to manhood, shall first beg for mercy before your mercy deigns to press, in the shape of an alms, the brand of degradation upon his brow. But let us hear the English bourgeoisie's own words. It is not yet a year since I read in the *Manchester Guardian* the following letter to the editor, which was published without comment as a perfectly natural, reasonable thing:

> MR EDITOR, – For some time past our main streets are haunted by swarms of beggars, who try to awaken the pity of the passers-by in a most shameless and annoying manner, by exposing their tattered clothing, sickly aspect, and disgusting wounds and deformities. I should think that when one not only pays the poor-rate, but also contributes largely to the charitable institutions, one had done enough to earn a right to be spared such disagreeable and impertinent molestations. And why else do we pay such high rates for the maintenance of the municipal police, if they do not even protect us so far as to make it possible to go to or out of town in peace? I hope the publication of these lines in your widely-circulated paper may induce the authorities to remove this nuisance; and I remain, – Your obedient servant.
>
> A LADY

There you have it! The English bourgeoisie is charitable out of self-interest; it gives nothing outright, but regards its gifts as a business matter, makes a bargain with the poor, saying: 'If I spend this much upon benevolent institutions, I thereby purchase the right not to be troubled any further, and you are bound thereby to stay in your dusky holes and not to irritate my tender nerves by exposing your misery. You shall despair as before, but you shall despair unseen; this I require, this I purchase with my subscription of twenty pounds for the infirmary!' It is infamous, this charity of a Christian bourgeois! And so writes 'A Lady'; she does well to sign herself such, it is well that she has lost the courage to call herself a woman! But if the 'ladies' are such as this, what must the 'gentlemen' be? It will be said that this is a single case; but no, the foregoing letter expresses the temper of the great majority of the English bourgeoisie, or the editor would not have accepted it, and some reply would have been made to it, which I watched for in vain in the succeeding numbers. And as to the efficiency of this philanthropy . . . the poor are relieved much more by the poor than by the bourgeoisie; and such relief given by an honest proletarian who knows himself what it is to be hungry, for whom sharing his scanty meal is really a sacrifice, but a sacrifice borne with pleasure, such help has a wholly different ring to it from the carelessly-tossed alms of the luxurious bourgeois . . .

But rightly to measure the hypocrisy of these promises, the practice of the bourgeoisie must be taken into account. We have seen in the course of our report how the bourgeoisie exploits the proletariat in every conceivable way for its own benefit! We have, however, hitherto seen only how the single bourgeois maltreats the proletariat upon his own account. Let us turn now to the manner in which the bourgeoisie as a party, as the power of the State, conducts itself toward the proletariat. It is quite obvious that all legislation is calculated to protect those who possess property against those who do not. Laws are necessary only because there are persons in existence who own nothing; and although this is directly expressed in but few laws, as, for instance, those against vagabonds and tramps, in which the proletariat as such is outlawed, yet enmity to the proletariat is so emphatically the basis of the law that the judges, and especially the Justices of the Peace, who are bourgeois themselves, and with whom the proletariat comes most in contact, find this meaning in the laws without further consideration. If a rich man is brought up, or rather summoned, to appear before the court, the Justice regrets that he is obliged to cause him so much trouble, treats the matter as favourably as possible, and if he is forced to condemn the accused, does so with extreme regret, etc., etc., and the end of it all is a miserable fine, which the bourgeois throws upon the table with contempt and then departs. But if a poor devil gets into such a position as involves appearing before the Justice of the Peace — he has almost always spent the night in the police-station with a crowd of his peers — he is regarded from the beginning as guilty; his defence is set aside with a contemptuous 'Oh! we know the excuse', and a fine imposed which he cannot pay and must work out with several months on the treadmill. And if nothing can be proved against him, he is sent to the treadmill, none the less, 'as a rogue and a vagabond'. The partisanship of the Justices of the Peace, especially in the country, surpasses all description, and it is so much the order of the day that all cases which are not too utterly flagrant are quietly reported by the newspapers, without comment. Nor is anything else to be expected. For on the one hand, these [Justices] merely construe the law according to the intent of the farmers, and, on the other, they are themselves bourgeois, who see the foundation of all true order in the interests of their class. And the conduct of the police corresponds to that of the Justices of the Peace. The bourgeois may do what he will and the police remain ever polite, adhering strictly to the law, but the proletarian is roughly, brutally treated; his poverty both casts the suspicion of every sort of crime upon him and cuts him off from legal redress against any caprice of the administrators of the law; for him, therefore, the protecting forms of the law do not exist, the police force their way into his house without further ceremony, arrest and abuse him. . . .[I]t [is] evident how little the protective side of the law exists for the working man, how frequently he has to bear all the burdens of the law without enjoying its benefits . . .

36

ALBERT EINSTEIN
AND
SIGMUND FREUD

Why are there wars?

Caputh near Potsdam, 30th July, 1932

Dear Professor Freud,

The proposal of the League of Nations and its International Institute of Intellectual Co-operation at Paris that I should invite a person, to be chosen by myself, to a frank exchange of views on any problem that I might select affords me a very welcome opportunity of conferring with you upon a question which, as things now are, seems the most insistent of all the problems civilization has to face. This is the problem: Is there any way of delivering mankind from the menace of war? It is common knowledge that, with the advance of modern science, this issue has come to mean a matter of life and death for civilization as we know it; nevertheless, for all the zeal displayed, every attempt at its solution has ended in a lamentable breakdown.

I believe, moreover, that those whose duty it is to tackle the problem professionally and practically are growing only too aware of their impotence to deal with it, and have now a very lively desire to learn the views of men who, absorbed in the pursuit of science, can see world-problems in the perspective distance lends. As for me, the normal objective of my thought affords no insight into the dark places of human will and feeling. Thus, in the enquiry now proposed, I can do little more than seek to clarify the question at issue and, clearing the ground of the more obvious solutions, enable you to bring the light of your far-reaching knowledge of man's instinctive life to bear upon the problem. There are certain psychological obstacles whose existence a layman in the mental sciences may dimly surmise, but whose interrelations and vagaries he is incompetent to fathom; you, I am convinced, will be able to suggest educative methods, lying more or less outside the scope of politics, which will eliminate these obstacles.

Source: *The Standard Edition of the Complete Psychological Works of Sigmund Freud, Vol. XXII*, London: Hogarth Press and Institute of Psycho-analysis, 1975.

As one immune from nationalist bias, I personally see a simple way of dealing with the superficial (i.e. administrative) aspect of the problem: the setting up, by international consent, of a legislative and judicial body to settle every conflict arising between nations. Each nation would undertake to abide by the orders issued by this legislative body, to invoke its decision in every dispute, to accept its judgements unreservedly and to carry out every measure the tribunal deems necessary for the execution of its decrees. But here, at the outset, I come up against a difficulty; a tribunal is a human institution which, in proportion as the power at its disposal is inadequate to enforce its verdicts, is all the more prone to suffer these to be deflected by extrajudicial pressure. This is a fact with which we have to reckon; law and might inevitably go hand in hand, and juridical decisions approach more nearly the ideal justice demanded by the community (in whose name and interests these verdicts are pronounced) in so far as the community has effective power to compel respect of its juridical ideal. But at present we are far from possessing any supranational organization competent to render verdicts of incontestable authority and enforce absolute submission to the execution of its verdicts. Thus I am led to my first axiom: the quest of international security involves the unconditional surrender by every nation, in a certain measure, of its liberty of action, its sovereignty that is to say, and it is clear beyond all doubt that no other road can lead to such security.

The ill-success, despite their obvious sincerity, of all the efforts made during the last decade to reach this goal leaves us no room to doubt that strong psychological factors are at work, which paralyse these efforts. Some of these factors are not far to seek. The craving for power which characterizes the governing class in every nation is hostile to any limitation of the national sovereignty. This political power-hunger is wont to batten on the activities of another group, whose aspirations are on purely mercenary, economic lines. I have specially in mind that small but determined group, active in every nation, composed of individuals who, indifferent to social considerations and restraints, regard warfare, the manufacture and sale of arms, simply as an occasion to advance their personal interests and enlarge their personal authority.

But recognition of this obvious fact is merely the first step towards an appreciation of the actual state of affairs. Another question follows hard upon it: How is it possible for this small clique to bend the will of the majority, who stand to lose and suffer by a state of war, to the service of their ambitions? (In speaking of the majority, I do not exclude soldiers of every rank who have chosen war as their profession, in the belief that they are serving to defend the highest interests of their race, and that attack is often the best method of defence.) An obvious answer to this question would seem to be that the minority, the ruling class at present, has the schools and press, usually the Church as well, under its thumb. This enables it to organize and sway the motions of the masses, and make its tool of them.

Yet even this answer does not provide a complete solution. Another question arises from it: How is it these devices succeed so well in rousing men to such wild enthusiasm, even to sacrifice their lives? Only one answer is possible. Because man has within him a lust for hatred and destruction. In normal times this passion exists in a latent state, it emerges only in unusual circumstances; but it is a comparatively easy task to call it into play and raise it to the power of a collective psychosis. Here lies, perhaps, the crux of all the complex of factors we are considering, an enigma that only the expert in the lore of human instincts can resolve.

And so we come to our last question. Is it possible to control man's mental evolution so as to make him proof against the psychoses of hate and destructiveness? Here I am thinking by no means only of the so-called uncultured masses. Experience proves that it is rather the so-called 'Intelligentsia' that is most apt to yield to these disastrous collective suggestions, since the intellectual has no direct contact with life in the raw, but encounters it in its easiest synthetic form – upon the printed page.

To conclude: I have so far been speaking only of wars between nations; what are known as international conflicts. But I am well aware that the aggressive instinct operates under other forms and in other circumstances. (I am thinking of civil wars, for instance, due in earlier days to religious zeal, but nowadays to social factors; or, again, the persecution of racial minorities.) But my insistence on what is the most typical, most cruel and extravagant form of conflict between man and man was deliberate, for here we have the best occasion of discovering ways and means to render all armed conflicts impossible.

I know that in your writings we may find answers, explicit or implied, to all the issues of this urgent and absorbing problem. But it would be of the greatest service to us all were you to present the problem of world peace in the light of your most recent discoveries, for such a presentation well might blaze the trail for new and fruitful modes of action.

Yours very sincerely,

A. EINSTEIN

Vienna, September, 1932

Dear Professor Einstein,

When I heard that you intended to invite me to an exchange of views on some subject that interested you and that seemed to deserve the interest of others besides yourself, I readily agreed. I expected you to choose a problem on the frontiers of what is knowable to-day, a problem to which each of us, a physicist and a psychologist, might have our own particular angle of approach and where we might come together from different directions upon the same ground. You have taken me by surprise, however, by posing the question of what can be done to protect mankind from the curse of war. I was scared at first by the thought of my – I had almost written 'our' – incapacity for dealing with what seemed to be a practical problem, a concern for statesmen. But I then realized that you had raised the question not as a natural scientist and physicist but as a philanthropist: you were following the promptings of the League of Nations just as Fridtjof

Nansen, the polar explorer, took on the work of bringing help to the starving and home-less victims of the World War. I reflected, moreover, that I was not being asked to make practical proposals but only to set out the problem of avoiding war as it appears to a psychological observer. Here again you yourself have said almost all there is to say on the subject. But though you have taken the wind out of my sails I shall be glad to follow in your wake and content myself with confirming all you have said by amplifying it to the best of my knowledge – or conjecture.

You begin with the relation between Right and Might. There can be no doubt that that is the correct starting-point for our investigation. But may I replace the world 'might' by the balder and harsher world 'violence'? To-day right and violence appear to us as antitheses. It can easily be shown, however, that the one has developed out of the other; and, if we go back to the earliest beginnings and see how that first came about, the problem is easily solved. You must forgive me if in what follows I go over familiar and commonly accepted ground as though it were new, but the thread of my argument requires it.

It is a general principle, then, that conflicts of interest between men are settled by the use of violence. This is true of the whole animal kingdom, from which men have no business to exclude themselves. In the case of men, no doubt, conflicts of *opinion* occur as well which may reach the highest pitch of abstraction and which seem to demand some other technique for their settlement. That, however, is a later complication. To begin with, in a small human horde, it was superior muscular strength which decided who owned things or whose will should prevail. Muscular strength was soon supple-mented and replaced by the use of tools: the winner was the one who had the better weapons or who used them the more skilfully. From the moment at which weapons were introduced, intellectual superiority already began to replace brute muscular strength; but the final purpose of the fight remained the same – one side or the other was to be compelled to abandon his claim or his objection by the damage inflicted on him and by the crippling of his strength. That purpose was most completely achieved if the victor's violence eliminated his opponent permanently – that is to say, killed him. This had two advantages: he could not renew his opposition and his fate deterred others from following his example. In addition to this, killing an enemy satisfied an instinctual inclination which I shall have to mention later. The intention to kill might be countered by a reflec-tion that the enemy could be employed in performing useful services if he were left alive in an intimidated condition. In that case the victor's violence was content with subju-gating him instead of killing him. This was a first beginning of the idea of sparing an enemy's life, but thereafter the victor had to reckon with his defeated opponent's lurking thirst for revenge and sacrificed some of his own security.

Such, then, was the original state of things: domination by whoever had the greater might – domination by brute violence or by violence supported by intellect. As we know, this regime was altered in the course of evolution. There was a path that led from violence to right or law. What was that path? It is my belief that there was only one: the path which led by way of the fact that the superior strength of a single individual could be rivalled by the union of several weak ones. *'L'union fait la force.'* Violence could be broken by union, and the power of those who were united now represented law in contrast to the violence of the single individual. Thus we see that right is the might of a community. It is still violence, ready to be directed against any individual who resists it; it works by the same methods and follows the same purposes. The only real difference lies in the fact that what prevails is no longer the violence of an individual but that of a community. But in order that the transition from violence to this new right or justice may be effected, one psychological condition must be fulfilled. The union of the majority must be a stable and lasting one. If it were only brought about for the purpose of combating a single dominant individual and were dissolved after his defeat, nothing would have been accomplished. The next person who thought himself superior in strength would once more seek to set up a dominion by violence and the game would be repeated *ad infinitum*. The community must be maintained permanently, must be organized, must draw up regulations to anticipate the risk of rebellion and must institute authorities to see that those regulations – the laws – are respected and to superintend the execution of legal acts of violence. The recognition of a community of interests such as these leads to the growth of emotional ties between the members of a united group of people – communal feelings which are the true source of its strength.

Here, I believe, we already have all the essentials: violence overcome by the transference of power to a larger unity, which is held together by emotional ties between its members. What remains to be said is no more than an expansion and a repetition of this.

The situation is simple so long as the community consists only of a number of equally strong individuals. The laws of such an association will determine the extent to which, if the security of communal life is to be guaranteed, each individual must surrender his personal liberty to turn his strength to violent uses. But a state of rest of that kind is only theoretically conceivable. In actuality the position is complicated by the fact that from its very beginning the community comprises elements of unequal strength – men and women, parents and children – and soon, as a result of war and conquest, it also comes to include victors and vanquished, who turn into masters and slaves. The justice of the community then becomes an expression of the unequal degrees of power obtaining within it; the laws are made by and for the ruling members and find little room for the rights of those in subjection. From that time forward there are two factors at work in the community which are sources of unrest over matters of law but tend at the same time to a further growth of law. First, attempts are made by certain of the rulers to set themselves above the prohibitions which apply to everyone – they seek, that is, to go back from a dominion of law to a dominion of violence. Secondly, the oppressed members of the group make constant efforts to obtain more power and to have any changes that are brought about in that direction recognized in the laws – they press forward, that is, from unequal justice to equal justice for all. This second tendency becomes especially important if a real shift of power occurs within a community, as may happen as a result of a number of historical factors. In that case right may gradually adapt itself to the new distribution of power; or, as is more frequent, the ruling class is unwilling to recognize the change, and rebellion and civil war follow, with a temporary suspension of law and new attempts at a solution by violence, ending in the establishment of a fresh rule of law. There is yet another source from which modifications of law may arise, and one of which the expression is invariably peaceful: it lies in the cultural transformation of the members of the community. This, however, belongs properly in another connection and must be considered later.

Thus we see that the violent solution of conflicts of interest is not avoided even inside a community. But the everyday necessities and common concerns that are inevitable where people live together in one place tend to bring such struggles to a swift conclusion and under such conditions there is an increasing probability that a peaceful solution will be found. Yet a glance at the history of the human race reveals an endless series of conflicts between one community and another or several others, between larger and smaller units — between cities, provinces, races, nations, empires — which have almost always been settled by force of arms. Wars of this kind end either in the spoliation or in the complete over-throw and conquest of one of the parties. It is impossible to make any sweeping judge-ment upon wars of conquest. Some, such as those waged by the Mongols and Turks, have brought nothing but evil. Others, on the contrary, have contributed to the transformation of violence into law by establishing larger units within which the use of violence was made impossible and in which a fresh system of law led to the solution of conflicts. In this way the conquests of the Romans gave the countries round the Mediterranean the priceless *pax Romana*, and the greed of the French kings to extend their dominions created a peacefully united and flourishing France. Paradoxical as it may sound, it must be admitted that war might be a far from inappropriate means of establishing the eagerly desired reign of 'ever-lasting' peace, since it is in a position to create the large units within which a powerful central government makes further wars impossible. Nevertheless it fails in this purpose, for the results of conquest are as a rule short-lived: the newly created units fall apart once again, usually owing to a lack of cohesion between the portions that have been united by violence. Hitherto, moreover, the unifications created by conquest, though of considerable extent, have only been *partial*, and the conflicts between these have called out more than ever for violent solution. Thus the result of all these warlike efforts has only been that the human race has exchanged numerous, and indeed unending, minor wars for wars on a grand scale that are rare but all the more destructive.

If we turn to our own times, we arrive at the same conclusion which you have reached by a shorter path. Wars will only be prevented with certainty if mankind unites in setting up a central authority to which the right of giving judgement upon all conflicts of interest shall be handed over. There are clearly two separate requirements involved in this: the creation of supreme agency and its endowment with the necessary power. One without the other would be useless. The League of Nations is designed as an agency of this kind, but the second condition has not been fulfilled: the League of Nations has no power of its own and can only acquire it if the members of the new union, the separate States, are ready to resign it. And at the moment there seems very little prospect of this. The institution of the League of Nations would, however, be wholly unintelligible if one ignored the fact that here was a bold attempt such as has seldom (perhaps, indeed, never on such a scale) been made before. It is an attempt to base upon an appeal to certain idealistic attitudes of mind the authority (that is, the coercive influence) which otherwise rests on the possession of power. We have seen that a community is held together by two things: the compelling force of violence and the emotional ties (identifications is the technical name) between its members. If one of the factors is absent, the community may possibly be held together by the other. The ideas that are appealed to can, of course, only have any significance if they give expression to important affinities between the members, and the question arises of how much strength such ideas can exert. History teaches us that they have been to some extent effective. For instance, the Panhellenic idea, the sense of being superior to the surrounding barbarians – an idea which was so powerfully expressed in the Amphictyonic Council, the Oracles and the Games – was sufficiently strong to mitigate the customs of war among Greeks, though evidently not sufficiently strong to prevent warlike disputes between the different sections of the Greek nation or even to restrain a city or confederation of cities from allying itself with the Persian foe in order to gain an advantage over a rival. The community of feeling among Christians, powerful though it was, was equally unable at the time of the Renaissance to deter Christian States, whether large or small, from seeking the Sultan's aid in their wars with one another. Nor does any idea exist to-day which could be expected to exert a unifying authority of the sort. Indeed it is all too clear that the national ideals by which nations are at present swayed operate in a contrary direction. Some people are inclined to prophesy that it will not be possible to make an end of war until Communist ways of thinking have found universal acceptance. But that aim is in any case a very remote one to-day, and perhaps it could only be reached after the most fearful civil wars. Thus the attempt to replace actual force by the force of ideas seems at present to be doomed to failure. We shall be making a false calculation if we disregard the fact that law was originally brute violence and that even to-day it cannot do without the support of violence.

I can now proceed to add a gloss to another of your remarks. You express astonishment at the fact that it is so easy to make men enthusiastic about a war and add your suspicions that there is something at work in them – an instinct for hatred and destruction – which goes halfway to meet the efforts of the warmongers. Once again, I can only express my entire agreement. We believe in the existence of an instinct of that kind and have in fact been occupied during the last few years in studying its manifestations. Will you allow me to take this opportunity of putting before you a portion of the theory of the instincts which, after much tentative groping and many fluctuations of opinion, has been reached by workers in the field of psycho-analysis?

According to our hypothesis human instincts are of only two kinds: those which seek to preserve and unite – which we call 'erotic', exactly in the sense in which Plato uses the word 'Eros' in his *Symposium*, or 'sexual', with a deliberate extension of the popular conception of 'sexuality' – and those which seek to destroy and kill and which we group together as the aggressive or destructive instinct. As you see, this is in fact no more than a theoretical clarification of the universally familiar opposition between Love and Hate which may perhaps have some fundamental relation to the polarity of attraction and repulsion that plays a part in your own field of knowledge. But we must not be too hasty in introducing ethical judgements of good and evil. Neither of these instincts is any less essential than the other; the phenomena of life arise from the concurrent or mutually opposing action of both. Now it seems as though an instinct of the one sort can scarcely ever operate in isolation; it is always accompanied – or, as we say, alloyed – with a certain quota from the other side, which modifies its aim or is, in some cases, what enables it to achieve that aim. Thus, for instance, the instinct of self-preservation is certainly of an erotic kind, but it must nevertheless have aggressiveness at its disposal if it is to fulfil its purpose. So, too, the instinct of love, when it is directed towards an object, stands in need of some contribution from the instinct for mastery if it is in any way to obtain possession of that object. The difficulty of isolating the two classes of instinct in their actual manifestations is indeed what has so long prevented us from recognizing them.

If you will follow me a little further, you will see that human actions are subject to another complication of a different kind. It is very rarely that an action is the work of a *single* instinctual impulse (which must in itself be compounded of Eros and destructiveness). In order to make an action possible there must be as a rule a combination of such compounded motives. . . . [W]hen human beings are incited to war they may have a whole number of motives for assenting – some noble and some base, some which are openly declared and others which are never mentioned. There is no need to enumerate them all. A lust for aggression and destruction is certainly among them: the countless cruelties in history and in our everyday lives vouch for its existence and its strength. The satisfaction of these destructive impulses is of course facilitated by their admixture with others of an erotic and idealistic kind. When we read of the atrocities of the past, it sometimes seems as though the idealistic motives served only as an excuse for the destructive appetites; and sometimes – in the case, for instance, of the cruelties of the Inquisition – it seems as though the idealistic motives had pushed themselves forward in consciousness, while the destructive ones lent them an unconscious reinforcement. Both may be true.

I fear I may be abusing your interest, which is after all concerned with the prevention of war and not with our theories. Nevertheless I should like to linger for a moment over our destructive instinct, whose popularity is by no means equal to its importance. As a result of a little speculation, we have come to suppose that this instinct is at work in every living creature and is striving to bring it to ruin and to reduce life to its original condition of inanimate matter. Thus it quite seriously deserves to be called a death instinct, while the erotic instincts represent the effort to live. The death instinct turns into the destructive instinct when, with the help of special organs, it is directed outwards, on to objects. The organism preserves its own life, so to say, by destroying an extraneous one. Some portion of the death instinct, however, remains operative *within* the organism, and we have sought to trace quite a number of normal and pathological phenomena to this internalization of the destructive instinct. We have even been guilty of the heresy of attributing the origin of conscience to this diversion inwards of aggressiveness. You will notice that it is by no means a trivial matter if this process is carried too far: it is positively unhealthy. On the other hand if these forces are turned to destruction in the external world, the organism will be relieved and the effect must be beneficial. This would serve as a biological justification for all the ugly and dangerous impulses against which we are struggling. It must be admitted that they stand nearer to Nature than does our resistance to them for which an explanation also needs to be found. It may perhaps seem to you as though our theories are a kind of mythology and, in the present case, not even an agreeable one. But does not every science come in the end to a kind of mythology like this? Cannot the same be said to-day of your own Physics?

For our immediate purpose then, this much follows from what has been said: there is no use in trying to get rid of men's aggressive inclinations. We are told that in certain happy regions of the earth, where nature provides in abundance everything that man requires, there are races whose life is passed in tranquillity and who know neither coercion nor aggression. I can scarcely believe it and I should be glad to hear more of these fortunate beings. The Russian Communists, too, hope to be able to cause human aggressiveness to disappear by guaranteeing the satisfaction of all material needs and by establishing equality in other respects among all the members of the community. That, in my opinion, is an illusion. They themselves are armed to-day with the most scrupulous care and not the least important of the methods by which they keep their supporters together is hatred of everyone beyond their frontiers. In any case, as you yourself have remarked, there is no question of getting rid entirely of human aggressive impulses; it is enough to try to divert them to such an extent that they need not find expression in war.

Our mythological theory of instincts makes it easy for us to find a formula for *indirect* methods of combating war. If willingness to engage in war is an effect of the destructive instinct, the most obvious plan will be to bring Eros, its antagonist, into play against it. Anything that encourages the growth of emotional ties between men must operate against war. These ties may be of two kinds. In the first place they may be relations resembling those towards a loved object, though without having a sexual aim. There is no need for psycho-analysis to be ashamed to speak of love in this connection, for religion itself uses the same words: 'Thou shalt love thy neighbour as thyself.' This, however, is more easily said than done. The second kind of emotional tie is by means of identification. Whatever leads men to share important interests produces this community of feeling, these identifications. And the structure of human society is to a large extent based on them.

A complaint which you make about the abuse of authority brings me to another suggestion for the indirect combating of the propensity to war. One instance of the innate and ineradicable inequality of men is their tendency to fall into the two classes of leaders and followers. The latter constitute the vast majority; they stand in need of an authority which will make decisions for them and to which they for the most part offer an unqualified submission. This suggests that more care should be taken than hitherto to educate an upper stratum of men with independent minds, not open to intimidation and eager in the pursuit of truth, whose business it would be to give direction to the dependent masses. It goes without saying that the encroachments made by the executive power of the State and the prohibition laid by the Church upon freedom of thought are far from propitious for the production of a class of this kind. The ideal condition of things would of course be a community of men who had subordinated their instinctual life to the dictatorship of reason. Nothing else could unite men so completely and so tenaciously, even if there were no emotional ties between them. But in all probability that is a Utopian expectation. No doubt the other indirect methods of preventing war are more practicable, though they promise no rapid success. An unpleasant picture comes to one's mind of mills that grind so slowly that people may starve before they get their flour.

The result, as you see, is not very fruitful when an unworldly theoretician is called in to advise on an urgent practical problem. It is a better plan to devote oneself in every particular case to meeting the danger with whatever means lie to hand. I should like, however, to discuss one more question, which you do not mention in your letter but which specially interests me. Why do you and I and so many other people rebel so violently against war? Why do we not accept it as another of the many painful calamities of life? After all, it seems to be quite a natural thing, to have a good biological basis and in practice to be scarcely avoidable. There is no need to be shocked at my raising this question. For the purpose of an investigation such as this, one may perhaps be allowed to wear a mask of assumed detachment. The answer to my question will be that we react to war in this way because everyone has a right to his own life, because war puts an end to human lives that are full of hope, because it brings individual men into humiliating situations, because it compels them against their will to murder other men, and because it destroys precious material objects which have been produced by the labours of humanity. Other reasons besides might be given, such as that in its present-day form war is no longer an opportunity for achieving the old ideals of heroism and that owing to the perfection of instruments of destruction a future war might involve the extermination of one or perhaps both of the antagonists. All this is true, and so incontestably true that one can only feel astonished that the waging of war has not yet been unanimously repudiated. No doubt debate is possible upon one or two of these points. It may be questioned whether a community ought not to have a right to dispose of individual lives; every war is not open to condemnation to an equal degree; so long as there exist countries and nations that are prepared for the ruthless destruction of others, those others must be armed for war. But I will not linger over any of these issues; they are not what you want to discuss with me, and I have something different in mind. It is my opinion that the main reason why we rebel against war is that we cannot help doing so. We are pacifists because we are obliged to be for organic reasons. And we then find no difficulty in producing arguments to justify our attitude.

No doubt this requires some explanation. My belief is this. For incalculable ages mankind has been passing through a process of evolution of culture. (Some people, I know, prefer to use the term 'civilization'.) We owe to that process the best of what we have become, as well as a good part of what we suffer from. Though its causes and beginnings are obscure and its outcome uncertain, some of its characteristics are easy to perceive. It may perhaps be leading to the extinction of the human race, for in more than one way it impairs the sexual function; uncultivated races and backward strata of the population are already multiplying more rapidly than highly cultivated ones. The process is perhaps comparable to the domestication of certain species of animals and it is undoubtedly accompanied by physical alterations; but we are still unfamiliar with the notion that the evolution of civilization is an organic process of this kind. The *psychical* modifications that go along with the process of civilization are striking and unambiguous. They consist in a progressive displacement of instinctual aims and a restriction of instinctual impulses. Sensations which were pleasurable to our ancestors have become indifferent or even intolerable to ourselves; there are organic grounds for the changes in our ethical and aesthetic ideals. Of the psychological characteristics of civilization two appear to be the most important: a strengthening of the intellect, which is beginning to govern instinctual life, and an internalization of the aggressive impulses, with all its consequent advantages and perils. Now war is in the crassest opposition to the psychical attitude imposed on us by the process of civilization, and for that reason we are bound to rebel against it; we simply cannot any longer put up with it. This is not merely an intellectual and emotional repudiation; we pacifists have a *constitutional* intolerance of war, an idiosyncrasy magnified, as it were, to the highest degree. It seems, indeed, as though the lowering of aesthetic standards in war plays a scarcely smaller part in our rebellion than do its cruelties.

And how long shall we have to wait before the rest of mankind become pacifists too? There is no telling. But it may not be Utopian to hope that these two factors, the cultural attitude and the justified dread of the consequences of a future war, may result within a measurable time in putting an end to the waging of war. By what paths or by what side-tracks this will come about we cannot guess. But one thing we *can* say: whatever fosters the growth of civilization works at the same time against war.

I trust you will forgive me if what I have said has disappointed you, and I remain, with kindest regards,

Sincerely yours,

SIGM. FREUD

37

HANNAH ARENDT

The banality of evil: failing to think

Thinking and moral considerations

To [write] about thinking seems to me so presumptuous that I feel I owe you a justification. Some years ago, reporting the trial of Eichmann in Jerusalem, I spoke of "the banality of evil" and meant with this no theory or doctrine but something quite factual, the phenomenon of evil deeds, committed on a gigantic scale, which could not be traced to any particularity of wickedness, pathology, or ideological conviction in the doer, whose only personal distinction was a perhaps extraordinary shallowness. However monstrous the deeds were, the doer was neither monstrous nor demonic, and the only specific characteristic one could detect in his past as well as in his behavior during the trial and the preceding police examination was something entirely negative: it was not stupidity but a curious, quite authentic inability to think. He functioned in the role of prominent war criminal as well as he had under the Nazi regime; he had not the slightest difficulty in accepting an entirely different set of rules. He knew that what he had once considered his duty was now called a crime, and he accepted this new code of judgment as though it were nothing but another language rule. To his rather limited supply of stock phrases he had added a few new ones, and he was utterly helpless only when he was confronted with a situation to which none of them would apply, as in the most grotesque instance when he had to make a speech under the gallows and was forced to rely on clichés used in funeral oratory which were inapplicable in his case because he was not the survivor. Considering what his last words should be in case of a death sentence, which he had expected all along, this simple fact had not occurred to him, just as inconsistencies and flagrant contradictions in examination and cross-examinations during the trial had not bothered him. Clichés, stock phrases, adherence to conventional, standardized codes of expression and conduct have the socially recognized function of protecting us against

Source: "Thinking and Moral Considerations: A Lecture," *Social Research*, vol. 38, no. 3, Autumn 1971.

reality, that is, against the claim on our thinking attention which all events and facts arouse by virtue of their existence. If we were responsive to this claim all the time, we would soon be exhausted; the difference in Eichmann was only that he clearly knew of no such claim at all.

This total absence of thinking attracted my interest. Is evildoing, not just the sins of omission but the sins of commission, possible in the absence of not merely "base motives" (as the law calls it) but of any motives at all, any particular prompting of interest or volition? Is wickedness, however we may define it, this being "determined to prove a villain," *not* a necessary condition for evildoing? Is our ability to judge, to tell right from wrong, beautiful from ugly, dependent upon our faculty of thought? Do the inability to think and a disastrous failure of what we commonly call conscience coincide? The question that imposed itself was: Could the activity of thinking as such, the habit of examining and reflecting upon whatever happens to come to pass, regardless of specific content and quite independent of results, could this activity be of such a nature that it "conditions" men against evildoing? (The very world *conscience*, at any rate, points in this direction insofar as it means "to know with and by myself," a kind of knowledge that is actualized in every thinking process.) Finally, is not the urgency of these questions enforced by the well-known and rather alarming fact that only good people are ever bothered by a bad conscience whereas it is a very rare phenomenon among real criminals? A good conscience does not exist except as the absence of a bad one.

Such were the questions. To put it differently and use Kantian language, after having been struck by a phenomenon – the *quaestio facti* – which willy-nilly "put me into the possession of a concept" (the banality of evil), I could not help raising the *quaestio juris* and asked myself "with what right did I possess and use it."

To raise such questions as "What is thinking?," "What is evil?" has its difficulties. They belong to philosophy or metaphysics, terms that designate a field of inquiry which, as we all know, has fallen into disrepute. If this were merely a matter of positivist and neopositivist assaults, we need perhaps not be concerned. Our difficulty with raising such questions is caused less by those to whom they are "meaningless" anyhow than by those who are under attack. Just as the crisis in religion reached its climax when theologians, as distinguished from the old crowd of nonbelievers, began to talk about the "God is dead" propositions, the crisis in philosophy and metaphysics came into the open when philosophers themselves began to declare the end of philosophy and metaphysics. Now, this could have its advantage; I trust it will once it has been understood what these "ends" actually mean, not that God has "died" – an obvious absurdity in every respect – but that the way God has been thought of for thousands of years is no longer convincing; and not that the old questions which are coeval with the appearance of men on earth have become "meaningless," but that the way they were framed and answered has lost plausibility.

What has come to an end is the basic distinction between the sensual and the super-sensual, together with the notion, at least as old as Parmenides, that whatever is not given to the senses – God or Being or the First Principles and Causes (*archai*) or the Ideas – is more real, more truthful, more meaningful than what appears, that it is not just *beyond* sense perception but *above* the world of the senses. What is "dead" is not only the localization of such "eternal truths" but the distinction itself. Meanwhile, in increasingly strident voices the few defenders of metaphysics have warned us of the danger of nihilism inherent in this development; and although they themselves seldom invoke it, they have an important argument in their favor: it is indeed true that once the suprasensual realm is discarded, its opposite, the world of appearances as understood for so many centuries, is also annihilated. The sensual, as still understood by the positivists, cannot survive the death of the supersensual. No one knew this better than Nietzsche, who, with his poetic and metaphoric description of the assassination of God in *Zarathustra*, has caused so much confusion in these matters. In a significant passage in *The Twilight of Idols*, he clarifies what the word *God* meant in *Zarathustra*. It was merely a symbol for the suprasensual realm, as understood by metaphysics; he now uses instead of *God* the [expression] *true world* and says: "We have abolished the true world. What has remained? The apparent one perhaps? Oh no! With the true world we have also abolished the apparent one."

These modern "deaths" of God, of metaphysics, of philosophy, and, by implication, of positivism may be events of great importance, but they are after all thought events, and though they concern most intimately our ways of thinking, they do not concern our ability to think, the sheer fact that man is a thinking being. By this, I mean that man has an inclination and, unless pressed by more urgent needs of living, even a need (Kant's "need of reason") to think beyond the limitations of knowledge, to do more with his intellectual abilities, his brain power, than to use them as instruments for knowing and doing. Our desire to know, whether arising out of practical necessities, theoretical perplexities, or sheer curiosity, can be fulfilled by reaching its intended goal; and while our thirst for knowledge may be unquenchable because of the immensity of the unknown, so that every region of knowledge opens up further horizons of knowables, the activity itself leaves behind a growing treasure of knowledge that is retained and kept in store by every civilization as part and parcel of its world. The activity of knowing is no less a world-building activity than the building of houses. The inclination or the need to think, on the contrary, even if aroused by none of the time-honored metaphysical, unanswerable "ultimate questions," leaves nothing so tangible behind, nor can it be stilled by allegedly definite insights of "wise men." The need to think can be satisfied only through thinking, and the thoughts which I had yesterday will be satisfying this need today only to the extent that I can think them anew.

We owe to Kant the distinction between thinking and knowing, between reason, the urge to think and to understand, and the intellect, which desires and is capable of certain, verifiable knowledge. Kant himself believed that the need to think beyond the limitations of knowledge was aroused only by the old metaphysical questions of God, freedom, and immorality and that he had "found it necessary to deny knowledge to make room for faith"; by doing so he had thrown the foundations of a future "systematic metaphysics" as a "bequest to posterity." But this shows only that Kant, still bound by the tradition of metaphysics, never became fully aware of what he had done, and his "bequest to posterity" turned out to be the destruction of all possible foundations of metaphysical systems. For the ability and the need to think are by no means restricted to any specific subject matter, such as the questions which reason raises and knows it will never be able to answer. Kant has not "denied knowledge" but separated knowing from thinking, and he has made room not for faith but for thought. He has indeed, as he once suggested, "eliminated the obstacles by which reason hinders itself."

In our context and for our purposes, this distinction between knowing and thinking is crucial. If the ability to tell right from wrong should have anything to do with the ability to think, then we must be able to "demand" its exercise in every sane person no matter how erudite or ignorant, how intelligent or stupid he may prove to be. Kant, in this respect almost alone among the philosophers, was much bothered by the common opinion that philosophy is only for the few precisely because of this opinion's moral implications. In this vein, he once remarked, "Stupidity is caused by a wicked heart," a statement which in this form is not true. Inability to think is not stupidity; it can be found in highly intelligent people, and wickedness is hardly its cause, if only because thoughtlessness as well as stupidity are much more frequent phenomena than wickedness. The trouble is precisely that no wicked heart, a relatively rare phenomenon, is necessary to cause great evil. Hence, in Kantian terms, one would need philosophy, the exercise of reason as the faculty of thought, to prevent evil.

And this is demanding a great deal, even if we assume and welcome the decline of those disciplines, philosophy and metaphysics, which for so many centuries have monopolized this faculty. For thinking's chief characteristic is that it interrupts all doing, all ordinary activities no matter what they happen to be. Whatever the fallacies of the two-world theories might have been, they arose out of genuine experiences. For it is true that the moment we start thinking on no matter what issue we stop everything else, and this everything else, again whatever it may happen to be, interrupts the thinking process; it is as though we moved into a different world. Doing and living in the most general sense of *inter homines esse*, "being among my fellowmen" – the Latin equivalent for being alive – positively prevents thinking. As Valéry once put it: "*Tantôt je suis, tantôt je pense*," now I am, now I think.

38

MICHAEL STOCKER

On desiring the bad

Desiring the bad and not desiring the good are ordinary features of our everyday life. Because of their solutions to the problem of weakness of will, many philosophers disagree with this, thinking it very problematic, if not incoherent. But such solutions pose at least as large a question about philosophy as that problem poses in philosophy.

Important questions have been conflated, and important and all too common psychological phenomena have been misunderstood or ignored. As Amélie Rorty argues,[1] typical discussions of that problem conflate the question of (i) how people can "fail" to do or even try to do what they decide/d or intend/ed to do, and the question of (ii) how people can "fail" to decide or intend to do what they believe good or best or right or. . . . Rorty deals illuminatingly with (i), explaining how such "weakness" is all too common, not merely possible.

In this paper, I examine (ii), explaining how this "weakness," also, is all too common, not merely possible, and that if such weakness, desiring the bad, is problematic, then so is the corresponding strength, desiring the good. I shall argue that motivation and evaluation do not stand in a simple and direct relation to each other, as so often supposed. Rather, they are interrelated in various and complex ways, and their interrelations are mediated by large arrays of complex psychic structures, such as mood, energy, and interest. Philosophical theories have ignored or misunderstood these structures and the corresponding all too common psychological phenomena. They have depicted the psyche, especially the interrelations between motivation and evaluation, as far too simple, far too unified, and far too rational.

Source: "Desiring the Bad: An Essay in Moral Psychology," *Journal of Philosophy*, vol. LXXVI, no. 12, December 1979.

Some traditional linkings of motivation and evaluation

Since my main concern is working toward an adequate moral psychology, I shall ignore questions of exactly how and why so many philosophers have held that, of necessity, the good or only the good attracts us. It should be sufficient merely to list some exponents and allude to various theories.

Socrates, Plato, Aristotle, and such followers as Aquinas hold this because of their "metaphysics" of psychology. Spinoza, Perry, Sartre, many contemporary social scientists, and want-satisfaction utilitarians hold this since they hold that the good is constituted by attraction. Hare and various internalists hold it since they hold that to assent to a moral principle or judgment involves being attracted to the relevant act. Various action theorists hold that this view is analytic of acting: to act involves preferring, one prefers the preferable, and "preferable" is another name for "better". Leibniz holds that such a connection is a principle of reason of a normative sort:

> If the will of God did not have for a rule the principle of the best, it would either tend toward evil which would be the worst of all, or else it would be in some fashion indifferent to good and evil and guided by chance.[2]

Other philosophers see the connection between values and desires or choices as essential underpinnings to liberalism, for respect for individuals and individual moral freedom.[3]

To be sure, the psychological phenomena and structures I shall discuss have not gone entirely unnoticed by other philosophers, not even by all those mentioned above.[4] Nonetheless, it is hardly unfair, if unfair at all, to suggest that the philosophical view is overwhelmingly that the good or only the good attracts. At the least, this is how I am forced to interpret so many philosophers. This affords me no pleasure, since that view, as argued below, is clearly and simply false. I would welcome contrary interpretations.

Some terms of my claim

For some purposes it will be important to specify what sorts of good or bad are involved in the claims that the good or only the good attracts. It may, for example, be important to determine whose good is involved, the agent's or someone else's; whether the good is an important good or not; whether "good" would better be replaced by "best" or "right"; whether what is supposedly desired is a good thing or the thing-as-good or its goodness; whether in all or some cases believed goodness, not goodness, is in question. When it is important, I shall so specify.

I shall not, however, offer an account of goodness and badness, nor of what it is to believe something good or bad, nor of the nature of motivation. My reasons for not attempting these vital tasks are, first, that my arguments are meant to be very general: to apply to any plausible accounts of evaluation and motivation, especially but not only as these figure in practical or moral reasoning and action as engaged in by us and as studied by philosophers.

Second, in order to give an adequate account of these notions, we need an adequate moral psychology. And there seem good heuristic reasons for arguments like those below to precede that psychology or those accounts. For it is unclear how successful they could be until those notions are freed from their traditional misunderstandings.

How are we to understand the relation between the good and attraction? It is too weak to require only that the attractive act or act-feature is, e.g., (believed) good in some respect or over-all or even best.[5] For unless such acts or features are (believed) absolutely good – i.e., with no aspects that are (believed) bad or neutral in any respect – they can attract because or only because they are (believed) bad or neutral in some respect or other. Thus this requirement does not give an interesting version of the thesis that the good always attracts or that only the good attracts, that we always act *sub specie boni*. These require that the (believed) goodness or the (believed) good qua good is somehow essential to the attraction: e.g., that acts or features attract because or only because they are (believed) good. It remains problematic exactly how to specify this requirement.

However, in order to show that we can "fail" to be attracted to the (believed) good and that we can be attracted to the (believed) bad, not only to the (believed) good, it is unnecessary to sort out this problem. It will be sufficient to show that there are clear and unproblematic cases where what attracts us to do an act is attractive because it is (believed) bad or in spite of its being (believed) bad, where the act or feature is not attractive because or only because it or some other relevant act or feature is (believed) good. Showing this shows neither, first, that we ever perform an act that is in no way (believed) good; nor, second, that we ever perform an act that does not attract us at least in part because it is (believed) good.[6] It is not, however, necessary to show either in order to establish that the (believed) good need not attract, that not only the (believed) good, but also the (believed) bad, can attract, and that the interrelations between motivation and evaluation are various and complex.

That the good must attract

Recently, I read a story of what might be taken as typical of one course of life. It was said of this political figure that, in his youth, he cared a lot about the suffering of people in all parts of the world and devoted himself to making their lives better. But now he concerns himself only with the lives and fortunes of his close family and friends. He remembers his past, and he knows that there is still a lot he could do to help others. But he no longer has any desire so to do.

We can fill out this story in any number of ways. Perhaps he calculated that he could do the most good close to him. This completion of the story need pose no problem for the thesis that the (believed) good must attract: it must allow for choices between various goods. Variants of the thesis deal differently with such choices. For example, some hold that it is always the (believed) best that attracts or attracts most.[7] Others hold that it is merely some (believed) good or other, whether or not it is (believed) best, that must attract.[8]

Perhaps the politician is not attracted to helping those people now because he believes he has already done enough for them or because he plans to help them a very great deal in the near-enough future. Such a completion of the story does confute many variants of the thesis that the (believed) good must attract. But just as we previously allowed for synchronic choices between goods, perhaps we should allow for diachronic choices. If we do not, that thesis would require far too rigorous a dedication to the good and its increase for it to be part of a plausible moral psychology of all people at all times.

It may not be clear exactly how to state the thesis to avoid such excessive dedication – e.g., how to include a principle that allows considerations of justice to explain, and justify, non-attraction to a (believed) good. But this internal problem of the thesis need not detain us. For the thesis is clearly wrong for reasons entirely unconnected with such, or other, choices between goods.

Suppose it is because of bitterness at the way the politician was treated that he does not desire to help those people. He has ceased caring about or for them. Perhaps he dislikes them. His non-attraction – his indifference or hostility – to the (believed) good confutes the thesis that the (believed) good must attract.

Citing the politician's bitterness or dislike or lack of care might naturally suggest two claims that sustain the thesis: First, if he does not help those people because of those feelings or moods, then his reason for not helping them must be (something like) to preserve his own peace of mind and happiness, to satisfy or at least not to displease himself. Second, these "psychic states" are (believed) good. This objection, then, is that my completion of the story involves competing (believed) goods, and thus really concedes the truth of the thesis. Discussing this objection should help both recapitulate and advance my argument.

The objection may pose a special problem for the claim that the (believed) better attracts more. Sustaining this variant of the thesis often requires imputing to the agent an implausible weighting of values. But here – because those states would have to be (believed) better than the good involved in helping the others – an implausibly egoistic weighting must be imputed.

This objection to my claim is problematic, however, whether the thesis is taken in a comparative or noncomparative form. Rejecting its first suggestion, I would argue for the following: what the politician wants can be simply that those people not be helped by him or that they not have that good. Dislike or bitterness or not caring for or about are all sufficient explanations of such non-attraction to the good of someone. They need not be supplemented by some other state or condition, in particular some egoistic state or condition, to make the non-attraction intelligible. To be sure, each of these replies needs further discussion. But for reasons concerning the second suggestion, we need not pursue them.[9]

The second suggestion must be considered. For it can be taken in a general way, independent of the first: if the attractive feature is avoiding displeasing himself, then that is (believed) good; but if the attractive feature is simply that those people not be benefited by him, then that is (believed) good. In its full generality, then, this suggestion is just what is in question: that the (believed) good must attract.

This evokes my original claim: the completion of the story in terms of dislike, bitterness, lack of care for or about does not involve competing (believed) goods; and, thus, it confutes the thesis that the (believed) good must attract. Since this objection need concern us only insofar as it raises again the question of whether the (believed) good attracts, I shall continue my argument that it need not.

I offered different explanations of the politician's indifference or hostility to the good of those people: he no longer cares for or about them, or he dislikes, is bitter toward them. Both can be expanded in various directions: e.g., to involve annoyance, hatred, fury, disgust, and the like. They can also be expanded in another direction, by considering people who are training themselves not to be affected by cares or considerations of this world. If one does not care for others, or is not interested in them, why should it be imagined that one will desire to benefit them?

Lack of this desire is commonplace. Through spiritual or physical tiredness, through accidie, through weakness of body, through illness, through general apathy, through despair, through inability to concentrate, through a feeling of uselessness or futility, and so on, one may feel less and less motivated to seek what is good. One's lessened desire need not signal, much less be the product of, the fact that, or one's belief that, there is less good to be obtained or produced, as in the case of a universal Weltschmertz. Indeed, a frequent added defect of being in such "depressions" is that one sees all the good to be won or saved and one lacks the will, interest, desire, or strength.

Let us note another consideration that shows that the (believed) good need not attract. The concept of selfishness may encompass the "metaphysical" egoist who believes that something is good only if it is good for, or a good of, him/herself. Selfishness may also encompass the "evaluative" egoist who recognizes that things can be good even insofar as they affect only others, but who ignores or discounts (his/her beliefs about) what is good for, or a good of, others. Perhaps it is "lexically" discounted – i.e., any of his/her self-regarding good is desired more than any amount of others' good; perhaps it is more modestly discounted. Families, clans, friends, classes, nations, races, . . . can play the same role as the person of these egoists. A metaphysical familist would hold that if something is good, it must be good for a family member; an evaluative familist would ignore or discount the good of those not in the family.

That the believed good must attract is consistent with the metaphysically selfish, family-ish, ... Such people see no good elsewhere; nor therefore do they desire it elsewhere. But evaluative egoists, familists, . . . do see value outside their area of concern. They simply may not be attracted to it.

I have not so far discussed the egoistical claim that the agent's own (believed) good must attract. There are some special problems with this claim: e.g., we often forgo good for ourselves in order to benefit others. As well, there are problems strictly analogous to those presented above. Self-abnegation and self-denial can be successfully implemented. One can feel, and be disposed accordingly, that one is of no worth, and thus not be at all moved to benefit oneself, to get or keep self-regarding good. So, too, the various maladies of the spirit, as they might be called, such as despair, accidie, weakness, tired-ness can play their role even in regard to self-regarding good and even to the point of extinguishing all desire for good for oneself, even to the point of making such goods repulsive.

Another variant of the claim that the (believed) good must attract is that if people are not attracted to what they believe good, then they are, so far at least, irrational. I would suggest that the same objections apply here. Not all cases of selfishness, callous-ness, uncaringness, and the like are irrationalities. The case for irrationality may be stronger if the (believed) good is the agent's own. But, again, what of demands of morality requiring giving up one's own good? What of manifestations of despair, loss of will, accidie? And what of passing up innocent goods such as the goods of amusement and the like? Are all these irrationalities?

Now we may think irrational those people so sunk in despair as not even to try to get anything of value for themselves out of life. (People are, for better or worse, locked away for such.) Some care and esteem for oneself may be, *ceteris paribus*, near enough to necessary for rationality of purpose and action, at least for certain sorts of people. However, not the care suggested by any of these variants on the theme that the good attracts.

It might be suggested that some goods or great goods play one or other of the attrac-tive roles sketched above. Perhaps Plato's view was that people could not but seek the goods constitutive of self-esteem. Many medieval Christian philosophers held that God or the vision or presence of God or perhaps salvation was an irresistible good. I shall leave these claims and similar claims about more mundane goods to others.

So far, then, I have argued that (believed) goods, at least some obvious and impor-tant (believed) goods, can "fail" to attract us, at least at times. One need not forget what is (believed) good, e.g., for a person, nor that it is good that a person have health, wisdom, and the like, simply because one no longer cares for that person. More generally, some-thing can be good and one can believe it to be good without being in a mood or having an interest or energy structure which inclines one to seek or even desire it.

Let us here note a related point which sustains both my claim that the (believed) good need not attract, and my more general claim that where the (believed) good does or does not attract, this is due to complex arrays of psychic structures. It is often held that some-thing's being good or believed good – its being rational, given the agent's values and beliefs – makes intelligible (explains) why a person seeks or desires it. If what I have said above is correct, then this is mistaken. For in at least many, if not all, of the cases mentioned, just as the person may well not seek or desire the (believed) good, so, were that person to do what would produce (believed) good, that fact might well not make intelligible why the person so acted. If I am known to be sunk deeply into despair or some other depression or to have long ago ceased caring about someone's welfare, then citing the (believed) goodness of my act will not make intelligible my act which benefits that other person.[10]

To be sure, citing the (believed) good may suggest an explanation – e.g., that the despair or depression has lifted, that I now care. But this is another way of putting my point: only against a certain assumed background of agent mood and interest does citing the (believed) good make an act intelligible. We can be as mystified by a selfish person's gratuitously benefiting a stranger as by a kindly person's gratuitously harming a stranger. Given certain assumptions about the latter's moods and interests – which do not make the harm a good or a believed good – such gratuitous malice is intelligible. So too, given certain assumptions about the former's moods and interests, such gratuitous helping is unintelligible. In all cases, the relevant moods and interest structures must be understood if the desire and act are to be intelligible.

Of course, citing the (believed) good may always be a reason in the sense of being a justifying reason. But this is only to say that what serves as a justifying reason may not help make an act intelligible, and what may help make an act intelligible may be not a justifying reason, but a "dysjustifying" one.

That only the good attracts

To establish my general contentions about the interrelations between motivation and valuation, it is insufficient to establish that the (believed) good need not attract. It is necessary to show that not only the (believed) good attracts. Some of the examples mentioned above – e.g., gratuitous malice and repulsive goods – suggest this; for they involve the attractiveness of the (believed) bad. I shall now argue explicitly for this: that we have desires and appetites for the (believed) bad.

I may desire or have an appetite for this food. But it may be the wrong amount or sort of food, it may be poisoned, spoiled. . . . Thus, the actual object of attraction is bad. To this it might be replied that desires and appetites are intentional, they may aim at what could be called the "proper" object of attraction: viz., perhaps only some aspects of a concrete object, and even an object or aspects that are mistakenly believed available. Thus, it could be held, were I aware of the nature of that food, I would see that the proper object of my desire or appetite is absent, and thus not be attracted to that food.

But there seems little justification for this claim. Actual desires and appetites may not conform to the evaluative sense of "want" or "lack" found in philosophers since

Socrates and still in our language: "He was examined and found wanting." Given certain moods, interest structures, energy levels, and the like – e.g., my having ceased caring about my well-being – what I want is this food, even though, perhaps even because, I realize it is the wrong amount, the wrong sort, . . . i.e., bad for me.

But of course, it is difficult to identify the real object of attraction. I may have wanted that food because I wanted something else, e.g., pleasure, which other thing may be consistent with the view that only the (believed) good attracts, that we always act *sub specie boni*. This can be brought out by considering the following interchange between me and supporters of that view.

To confute that view, I instanced the case of a man who wanted to and did burn himself to see if he could emulate the famous Roman. I suggested that whatever (believed) good there might be in what attracted him, such (believed) good need not be the whole or even part of what attracted him. My interlocutors said that since the act was moti-vated by the desire or appetite for knowledge, perhaps self-knowledge, the feature of the actual object of attraction which attracted him – viz., the knowledge – was wholly good. But, I contend, some knowledge is bad or harmful, some is simply not worth having, the desire to know some things is shameful, and so on. (This is so even if some knowl-edge is good in itself.) Thus, it seems that we can take the desire or appetite to know as having proper objects which are (believed) good, bad, or neutral.

Consider also our desires to harm others. To save the thesis that we desire only the (believed) good, it must be maintained either that such harming is (believed) good or that it is not the direct or proper object of desire. The former is too implausible. My interlocutors maintained the latter, holding that harming others is only an intermediate desire of, say, the desire to get pleasure for oneself, power over others, showing oneself powerful, getting things to go one's way, getting revenge.

Even if they are correct, however, what reason is there to take such (instances of those) desires to be aimed at what is (believed) good – apart, that is, from saving the thesis that only the (believed) good attracts? It might be objected that, apart from my contrary thesis, I have no reason to deny that they are (believed) good. As this paper shows, that claim is false. Even if it were true, I would be content for the issue to be put: Which thesis is better able to account for important and common psychological phenomena and structures?

But I do not think they are correct. Just as helping another can be the direct and proper object of desires and appetites, so can harming others. (Arguments to the contrary are quite similar to traditional arguments for egoism.) One way to see this is that in certain loving or caring moods, helping is precisely what is desired. So too, in other moods, harming is precisely what is desired. When we feel furious, hurt, envious, jealous, threatened, frustrated, abandoned, endangered, rejected, and so on, what we often seek is precisely the harm or destruction of someone, and not always the "offending party": "If I can't have her, no one will." "So, you are leaving me after all I have done for you.

Well then, take that." "You stole her from me, now it's my turn to get even." "The whole day has gone so badly, I might as well complete it by ruining the little I did accomplish." "I let him have it with the horn; he was the millionth Sunday driver who cut in front of me." "Watch out for him today, he just had an awful fight with his wife."

Given such moods and circumstances, harming another can be the proper and direct object of attraction. There is no need to posit another object, especially not an egoistic object like pleasure, power over others, showing oneself powerful, getting things to go one's own way, getting revenge.

Just as there are desires and appetites directed at harming others, there are desires and appetites directed at harming oneself. In certain moods, such as the self-directed modes of disgust, hatred, guilt, shame, I may seek to humble, abase, or harm myself.

Agents, even in the planning and doing of such acts, and certainly afterwards, can believe or know that what is desired is bad. Moods, interest structures, and the like can make us unconcerned about achieving the (believed) good. In such moods, . . . , we not only do not care, we are filled with "uncare."

Perhaps we have such moods, . . . and thus bad-seeking desires or appetites only under certain, mainly adverse, conditions. Perhaps having such moods, . . . , desires, and appetites shows some moral or psychological defect in us or some defect in our circumstances or society. This suggests what seems correct in any case: First, desiring the (believed) bad and not desiring the (believed) good raise serious practical problems about moral education and personal and social conditions, not just conceptual problems. Second, if it is irrational to have bad-seeking desires and appetites, the relevant sense of "rational" evaluates not only the agent's means and ends and character but also the agent's situation in society and that society as well.

In conclusion, it seems at best unjustifiable optimism or complacency to accept the liberalism and relativism of values embodied in the claim that we always act *sub specie boni*, that we desire or have an appetite for only what is (believed) good.[11] "I don't know what is good, but I know what I want" contains more truth than many seem to believe. A desire for what is bad need not make it good; on the contrary, its badness may infect the desire, making it bad.

Some programmatic conclusions

I have argued that what is (believed) good can "fail" to attract us and that what is (believed) bad can attract us. This argument is about us, not about people with radically different psychologies from ours, like those portrayed in Kosinski's novels or like psychopaths or sociopaths.[12] Even we have moods, interest and energy structures, . . . which "allow" us not to be attracted to a (believed) good or to be attracted to a (believed) bad.

The argument was not intended to show that those moods, interest and energy structures, . . . could operate – could lead to desire, intention, action – without a background structure of evaluation, as hating may require desiring the bad for the hated. Rather, it was intended to show that value structures are only complexly related with those structures and other structures such as those of motivation. To what extent moods and the like could operate without such background value structures needs discussion in any adequate moral psychology. Also needing discussion is the related problem of the extent it is possible for people – and for what sort of people – not to be attracted to what is (believed) good or to be attracted to what is (believed) bad. (As Rorty argues, other reasons, roles, group encouragement, . . . also account for such attraction and non-attraction.)

My arguments, then, must be understood as having a limited purview. But within that purview, it has been argued that motivation and evaluation need not point in the same direction, that they are related only through complex structures of mood, care, energy, interest, and the like. Upon even brief reflection, we see that those complex structures are, themselves, not of one natural, psychic kind. For example, desire arising from pique is very different from desire "failing" to arise from lack of energy. But since this paper is concerned with a role played by these disparate structures – mediating between evaluation and motivation – treating those structures as if of one sort is not harmful.

My claims about such mediation can be divided into two subclaims, the first about cases that controvert, and the second about cases that might seem consistent with, the alleged necessary connection between motivation and evaluation. This paper has been concerned almost exclusively with the controverting cases. I shall now comment directly on the "consistent" ones. Even in them, I suggest, motivation and evaluation are mediated by those psychic structures. This, if correct, helps show that the controverting cases are not exceptions, aberrations, mere anomalies or mere counterexamples, but rather that they exhibit deep and general relations between motivation and evaluation.

My comments about the "consistent" cases have been and will be brief for various reasons. To establish my contention about the lack of simple, direct, or necessary connections between motivation and evaluation, the controverting cases are sufficient, and more easily handled. A discussion of the "consistent" cases requires far more psychological, sociological, and anthropological information than I have. To explain these cases requires an adequate moral psychology: a brief paper like this can at best show the inadequacies of various moral psychologies and point the way toward an adequate one.

That moods, care, interest, energy, . . . account for disconnections between motivation and evaluation would not, of course, prove that they play a similar role in accounting for connections. But it should alert us to that possibility. If we do look at cases of such connection, at least in many of them we do find moods, care, interest, energy, and the like. It is not noteworthy if a mother gives her son something (she believes) good for him. But typically, mothers stand to their sons in ways constituted by exceptionally complex arrays of mood, interest, energy, and the like. Similarly, there are complex arrays in at least many cases of a friend helping another, of people doing what they believe obligatory, and so on. (The presence of such arrays, I take it, is the subject not so much of philosophical argument as of psychological, sociological, or anthropological study.)

Of course, the mere presence of such arrays of structures does not establish that they play the same mediating role – now with a different "polarity" – between motivation and evaluation as is played by those arrays in accounting for disconnections between motivation and evaluation. But I suggest that they do, as the following related points might indicate.

It is now a truism that men and women of our culture have different motivational "orientations" to (believed) good. Men, archetypically, seek their own good and through that the good of their families; women, archetypically, are more self-sacrificing, more altruistic, directly more eager for the good of their families. To the extent that this and similar claims are correct, such differences are explained, at least in a constitutive, if not a generative, way by the very different mood, interest, energy, . . . structures of men and women in our culture.

If this is correct and if my earlier claims are correct, then both some disconnections between motivation and evaluation and also some – e.g., sex-role-linked – connections between motivation and evaluation are mediated by arrays of structures of mood, interest, energy, and the like. It would be surprising, then, if the generalized connection between motivation and evaluation were not also so mediated. Indeed, if all people who have so far lived have had arrays of such structures mediating the particular ways their motivation and evaluation were connected, what can be made of the claim that motivation and evaluation are directly and simply connected?

This raises the second point. Very frequently at least, only what is unusual or wrong is thought to need an explanation. If our cultural archetype or ideal of a person has certain arrays of such structures, they might well go unexplained, even unnoticed. Cross-cultural studies may help us recognize and understand these structures – thus, ourselves. The point can be brought out this way: When I consider people who have been defeated by life, the wretched of the earth, those who see no hope for themselves or those they care for, who lack physical and spiritual energy, I am not at all surprised that – as political and anthropological data suggest – they may not seek even what little good they do perceive. Life may be too much for them. We, on the contrary, see the world as open to us, and more importantly, open for us. We can progress. We can make it. We see ourselves out there to be won. We have self-confidence and hope. Indeed we have more than this: we have an optimistic certainty. We have energy. We know we are worthy. We know that, barring bad luck, our enterprise will be rewarded. And so on. Such an array of structures of mood, interest, energy, . . . makes it natural, almost inevitable, that we seek the (believed) good for ourselves or others. And it seems at least arguable that such an array must be posited to give an adequate account of how, at least according to our cultural ideal, motivation and evaluation are related in us.

If this is right, then, first, even in the "consistent" cases, the connection between motivation and evaluation is mediated by those complex arrays. And, second, moods and the like cannot be understood as "defections" from our normal – and mood-free – orientation to value, nor can values be understood as what we would desire were we not in a mood.

Four brief and interrelated points should be made. It might be argued that those who are unlike us in their orientation to the (believed) good suffer from some defective or pathological condition of their psyche or society. Certainly, were we to become like them, while still in our life and society, we would very likely be said to be in such a condition. (But were they to become like us, while still in their life and society, might they not, too, be said to be in such a condition?) However, for their being in such a condition to bear on whether motivation and evaluation can be connected without the mediation of those arrays, any array playing such a mediating role would have to be, as such, pathological or defective.

Second, it will not have gone unnoticed that in indicating "our" cultural ideal, what I sketched was the successful and striving man. It may well be no accident, as various critiques put it, that this psychology is presumed, perhaps unknowingly, to be the natural or healthy human psychology by philosophers. For after all, to put it far too crudely and quickly, philosophers, at least those we now read, have been successful and striving – and with few exceptions – men. Current cultural critiques – e.g., by some feminists and Marxists – argue, first, that such an array is not inevitable, nor clearly desirable; and, second, that such an array does play the mediating role I have been urging, even in our culturally ideal cases where we "naturally" desire and seek the (believed) good.

Third, even within our culture and in regard to attraction to the (believed) good, there is not just one, but rather many significantly different, though interrelated, ideals and archetypes for men, and of course also for women and children. Just as our personality does not "fit" a defeated person, even in our society "exchanges of personality" would produce strange fits. Consider such exchanges between an American and English academic, or between a successful business man and a factory worker. Thus, even for only our culture, there will not be one array, but rather many arrays, of those mediating structures. We will need not one, but many moral psychologies.

Fourth, understanding these moral psychologies requires not only philosophy, but also psychology, sociology, and anthropology. We will need typological descriptions of different human psyches and also accounts of these differences. These would involve both interrelations among various moral–psychological notions and interrelations between these and class, culture, nationality, occupation, sex, status, region, religion, and the like – the subjects of psychology, sociology, and anthropology.

The implications of these last points are very large. Let me conclude on a smaller scale, by returning to the opening themes of the paper: If weakness of will, desiring the (believed) bad, is problematic, so is strength of will, desiring the (believed) good. We must replace those moral psychologies which generate the traditional philosophical problems about weakness of will. We need moral psychologies that recognize, in general, the complexities of the psyche and, in particular, those complex arrays of psychic structures of mood, interest, energy, . . . and also the complex mediating roles played by these arrays between motivation and evaluation.

Notes

1 In her unpublished "Weakness, Imagination, and the Self." I owe her my warmest thanks for discussing these issues with me.

2 Quoted from *Theodice* in *Philosophische Schriften*, vi.§ 86 by Arthur O. Lovejoy in *the Great Chain of Being* (Cambridge, Mass.: Harvard, 1936), p. 166.

3 See e.g., Alan Montifiore "Goodness and Choice," *Proceedings of the Aristotelian Society*, suppl. vol. xxxv (1961).

4 Cf. Aristotle on spite and envy, the *Rhetoric*, II, 2 and 10; Augustine on stealing the pears; Aquinas in 2a2ae of the *Summa Theologica* on anger and hatred (34, 6), on spite (*rancor*) and malice (*malitia*) (35, 4), and on envy (36, 2); and at least implicitly, philosophers such as Butler, Hume, and Firth on the conditions of ideal observers and the like. But they often do not seem wholehearted about such phenomena and structures. For example, the moral psychology of the *Nicomachean Ethics* appears to preclude them. (But perhaps we should take seriously the first lines of ch. 2, Bk. II, which suggest that that work is concerned with the moral psychology of good men, with references to that of bad men only to illuminate the former. The *Rhetoric*, which recognizes those phenomena and structures, is concerned with men as found, both good and bad.)

5 For "good or believed good," I shall often use "(believed) good," and similarly with "(believed) bad" and the like. However, the occurrence of only the one, e.g., only "good," should be taken as signaling exclusive import only if such intent is made clear.

6 The first quickly leads to questions of absolute (believed) badness. As to the second, although the cases below do not establish such complete lack of motivation by the (believed) good, they make it extremely plausible, even if such acts would not attract were they (believed) absolutely bad, or even simply worse than they are.

7 Cf. Donald Davidson's principle P2: "If an agent judged that it would be better to do *x* than to do *y*, then he wants to do *x* more than he wants to do *y*" ["How is Weakness of the Will Possible?," in Joel Feinberg, ed., *Moral Concepts* (New York: Oxford, 1969), p. 95].

8 Cf. Alan Gewirth, *Reason and Morality* (Chicago: University Press, 1978), p. 49.

9 For a brief discussion, see my "Morally Good Intentions," *The Monist*, LIV, 1 (January 1970): 124–141, esp. pp. 125–128 and 140/1; for an extended discussion, see Roy Lawrence's important *Motive and Intention* (Evanston, Ill.: Northwestern University Press, 1972).

10 Thus, rationality in the sense of value maximization against the background of an agent's beliefs is not the form of all action, nor even all intelligible action. Nor is the correspondingly rational person the form of all people, nor even all intelligible people. Trying to understand people as if they were such rational beings involves inadequate moral psychologies and ignores or misunderstands the important and all too common psychological phenomena discussed in this paper.

11 This optimism has clear implications for social policy, education, and so on. I thank Graeme Marshall for discussing this and other issues with me.

12 Who we are is, of course, a question. But for the present purposes, we should readily enough be able to identify ourselves.

39

AMÉLIE OKSENBERG RORTY

How to harden your heart:
six easy ways to become corrupt

Nothing is easier, nothing more natural than sliding down the slippery slope to corruption, and from there to the hardened heart that allows people to redescribe their wrongdoing so that they can accept it as reasonable and confirm it as justified. This is the banal journey charted by Hannah Arendt, the journey from regretful lapses of decency to unrepentant corruption. The writers who have most graphically depicted stages in the process – Dante, Milton, Fyodor Dostoevsky, C. S. Lewis, J. R. R. Tolkien, Iris Murdoch, William Golding – have tended to locate it within a theological context, one or another version of the Fall. Although Shakespeare's villains – Lady Macbeth, Edmund, Iago, Goneril, Richard III – degenerate as their plots unfold, they are malformed from the beginning. David Hume traced the natural history of the psychological origins of (what we are pleased to call) the virtues, locating their sources in standard-issue patterns of human desires and attitudes, in what we imagine to be useful and what we find pleasant. Although he did not extend his observations to the genealogy of (what we are pleased to call) the vices, he provides a model for locating the sources of corruption in the dynamic patterns of ordinary psychological activity. He dispels the superstitious remnants of a Manichean battle: the forces of good and evil warring in the will.

There are many ways to go wrong. Corruption covers a large scope: it can be expressed in nuance of speech and gesture as well as in overt behavior. It can be a trivial local departure from what an otherwise relatively decent and civilized person normally does. It can be a single event, or it can encompass virtually the whole of a person's life. It can happen suddenly or gradually, imperceptibly over a long period. It can happen under extreme and intolerable pressure or from the slow mounting of despair. It can be a private matter: an individual can fall from his or her own ideals and standards. But it can also presage a widespread

Source: *Yale Review*, April 1998.

and sustained absorption in global and indiscriminate resentment, revenge, murder – all in the name of an ideology gone out of control. It can begin with the perception of an injury or threat; or with a vision of what seems a tantalizing good. A society can become so pervasively corrupt that its members can typically fail to recognize their viciousness.

Our story is but one of the many possible plots of such tales: we follow several stages in the gradual corruption of an individual. Let's call him Cain. Cain begins by doing something sleazy; this can happen, virtually unnoticed, to anyone, anytime. If it were brought to his attention, he'd acknowledge it wrong, and he'd be embarrassed, perhaps ashamed. But what he does solves some problem: it may deflect an enemy or secure an endangered promotion. Or it may bring some satisfaction: it may get him a better office or a desirable apartment. When similar problems and satisfactions present themselves, it's natural for him to continue his devious ways. Bit by bit the scope of what he does becomes more general; bit by bit it becomes habitual, occurring without a second thought. Bit by bit compartmentalizing self-deception helps him deflect his previous awareness of wrongdoing. And finally, he finds and fully accepts an account that justifies what he once thought shameful or wrong.

Here's what happened:

Cain is an ordinary decent-enough fellow, as these things go. He has his weaknesses: he's conniving and self-indulgent; he tends to belittle students and to be inconsiderate of secretaries. But his flaws are well within the bounds of the common ailments of his circle, and they don't on the whole get in the way of his reliably doing what passes for the right thing among his colleagues and friends. Cain has a thing about his longtime departmental colleague, Abel. At this stage, he knows perfectly well that he has no reason for his attitude: Abel hasn't done anything to harm him; he doesn't think there's anything wrong with Abel's work or his politics; Abel has not been unjustly favored by the powers above. Cain has no sense of injury or envy or fear. Although there are no doubt many explanations for his dislike – Abel may remind him of his hateful stepfather or of unwanted aspects of himself, or he may be caught up in a simple animal response – he feels no need to explain or justify himself.

But over the years, as his hopes and ambitions have diminished, Cain's original simple dislike has grown. He now can't stand the fellow, finds his manner and his presence insufferable. In the past, Cain expressed his distaste by fleeing from Abel's approaches at parties, by sneering and rolling his eyes when Abel spoke at department meetings. His aversion has grown: it is on the verge of becoming obsessive, and when it comes time for the department to choose a new member, Cain campaigns against appointing Deborah for no other reason except that Abel strongly favors her. He doesn't think she'll join Abel on the Wrong Side; he believes – but won't publicly admit – that she's probably the best candidate. He's clever and persuasive; he calls in his debts; and he brings the department around to vote with him against Abel. He's gleeful; he's triumphed; and he's gotten considerable pleasure out of exercising his talents successfully. He half knows he's in the wrong; he's half ashamed of what he's done; he knows he could use his powers of persuasion for better purposes, but the occasion has refined his skills and his pleasures in their exercise. He digs in for more of the same.

No doubt someone else, with a similar history, equally self-indulgent, equally irritated by Abel, might not have succumbed in the same way. No doubt Cain's background, his disappointments, and the profile of his particular strengths and weaknesses all contribute to what he has become. No doubt Cain would not have attempted to undermine less vulnerable colleagues: no matter the irritation, he'd have steered clear of the chairman's son-in-law. The stages from regrettable weakness and failure to wholehearted corruption nevertheless form a general pattern, though of course that pattern is not in itself sufficient to explain Cain's banal transformation from an ordinary, somewhat weak fellow to someone who is prepared to justify subjecting a colleague to attack. Here, briefly, are a few steps in that banal transformation:

1. Cain concentrates on the present moment, on his immediate strategies in the department meeting. He is so focused on his manipulations, on how to sway Martha and to bargain with Matthew, that he doesn't think about the important consequences of his maneuvers. Because his campaign engages his full concentration, he doesn't even need to avert his attention from the fact that Abel has been unjustly ill-treated and the department has lost its most promising candidate.

2. He is self-absorbed, caught up in his own attitudes and feelings: first on his initial irritation and then on savoring his ingenuity and power. Abel's frustration, his humiliation, his increased alienation from his colleagues have no purchase on Cain's imagination.

3. Although he's fairly perceptive and reflective, Cain ignores the way his actions tend to be become encrusted as habits: he began his machinations against Abel on impulse, without any long-range plans. He doesn't notice that he's moved from teasing Abel to being insulting and obstreperous and now to entertaining fantasies of actually harming him. Cain's intrigues began as idle incidents; but the habit of acting on his animus against Abel became ingrained, virtually second-nature maneuvers of which he is only marginally aware. His active antagonism becomes one of his ways in the world, a significant aspect of his character. Besides the satisfactions they bring, successful habits free attention for other and more complex activities. We depend on them, feel frustrated when they are blocked, and develop further habits to protect them against change. Such habits ramify: they become tenacious as well as entrenched.

4. Cain finds himself increasingly uncomfortable with his high-minded principled friends, preferring the company of scandalmongers who enjoy creating a theatrical flurry

just for the sake of the spectacle. Without noticing what he's doing, he begins to imitate charismatic figures in his new circle, not questioning the directions in which they are taking him. Like children, insecure newcomers tend to imitate the powerful figures in their environment. Following the leader, he now finds amusement in spreading misleading innuendoes and falsifying rumors. He remains discriminating in his misdemeanors: he does not openly attack the powerful; he does not overstep the bounds of the permissible. He is pleased that his gifts are now more widely appreciated. Indeed it was precisely his need for social support that led him to move toward acquaintances with a looser license for acceptable behavior. (Urging France's withdrawal from Algiers, General de Gaulle was challenged by a critic who remarked that he knew no one who would countenance such a decision. De Gaulle is said to have replied: "Changez vos amis.")

5. Enjoying the exercise of his powers, Cain gradually extends his focused vendetta against Abel to more general, more far-reaching ventures in disruption: disagreeing with an editorial in the student newspaper, he arranges for their funds to be severely cut, alleging the necessity of fiscal restraint. Feeling threatened by a brilliant scholar who is the leading candidate for a position in his field, he argues for downgrading the job to a junior slot, allegedly to assure a wider age-spread in the department.

6. To the extent that he is aware of the dissonance between his former good-enough-decency and his new habits, he regrets what he does and is ashamed of what he has become. That dissonance does not mark a break between his inner and outer selves or between what he says and does. Like his excursions in corruption, his regret is expressed both in action and in speech. Awkwardly, he tries to make amends; he takes steps to reform. But he becomes increasingly unpredictable, even to himself. The erratic swings between regret and glee and the conflicting actions that they engender are uncomfortable: what he does out of regret undermines his new habits (and vice versa). Lacking a settled pattern of acceptable aims and satisfactions, he begins unconsciously to readjust his attitudes, to bring them into line. Such attempts often begin with language and gesture: although he once had a taste for precision, he starts to use prefabricated clichés, avoiding specific descriptions of his actions, characterizing them in vague, vapid, and irrelevant commonplaces: "We did the sensible thing." He lifts his eyebrows, shrugs, and sneers when he speaks of opponents: "Those idiots will endanger all we've been trying to do if we don't stop them." He becomes adept in enlisting radical ambiguity and airtight compartmentalization in the aid of self-deception, and self-deception in the aid of complete denial. Although he sees that he harms his victims, he convinces himself that his strategies will in the long run benefit his colleagues; his former regret is replaced by a sense of justified righteousness. This is what happens:

> Gradually, Cain's perceptions of Abel darken: instead of seeing him as irritatingly cringing, he begins to see him as untrustworthy, someone whose views and decisions are usually mistaken and often dangerous. Abel has become a token

figure in a larger scheme of similar people whom Cain perceives as potentially dangerous to what he regards as important and valuable. He now thinks it right to prevent Abel from having his way. Originally just an ordinary erratically weak fellow, Cain has become a corrupt scum, perhaps only a contained petty slime, yet in that limited domain a slime nevertheless.

But look again: these steps in Cain's degeneration are generic standard-issue, deeply rooted functional psychological activities: it should not be surprising that they come into play relatively automatically. They serve us well, and we could not get rid of them even if we tried. (1) *Attention to the present:* Considering how frail and vulnerable the species is, the tendency to focus on the immediate and the present is protective and adaptive. (2) *Sensitivity to subjective responses:* Sensations and feelings are prima facie indications of objective states of affairs; it is realistically responsive to attend to them and – in the absence of countervailing considerations – to be presumptively guided by them. (3) *Slippage to habit:* The species' tendency to generalize and to entrench successful action-patterns as habits is deeply embedded. It is one of the ways that we learn from experience, and it enables us to acquire increasingly complex skills. (4) *Groupie attraction:* Gravitating to the company of like-minded people provides individuals with (presumptive) social protection and support, even if the cohort is dominating, intrusive, and internally divided. (5) *Imitating the leader:* Children, newcomers, and initiates of all kinds and ages gravitate to powerful figures. Without realizing it, novices emulate the behavior of those who model "how things are done." Moreover, charismatic figures sometimes enable *l'homme moyen sensuel* to extend his narrow scope, to reach beyond himself toward unexpected generosity as well as toward lower forms of life. (6) *Papering cracks:* Because a divided self tends to undo itself, we naturally, without even being aware of it, attempt to smooth over the appearance of internal conflicts. Or, equally effectively, we compartmentalize, attempting to separate different aspects of our lives. Movements toward psychological integration are Janus-faced: they can move toward integrity as well as toward corruption. And although compartmentalization is often effectively soothing, it can rot the mind.

To be sure, Cain also has powerful and deep-seated tendencies that pull in opposite directions. And he remains discriminatingly shrewd in his slide to corruption. He matches a focus on the present with foresight; besides attending to his own responses, he is alert to the moods of others, especially if he thinks them powerful; although he depends on his habits, he can monitor and change his routines; he seeks the support of a like-minded cohort but studiously avoids his mafioso twin brother. His knack of compartmentalizing is countered by movements to integration. In any case, the instruments of self-protection are not his only standard-issue equipment. Cain is evidently also inclined to admiration and idealization; he is often generous to his friends; and he has a near-instinctive disgust at what he perceives as humanly foul. But like the movements exercised in his gradual corruption, these apparently noble psychological directions are in themselves morally neutral, capable of strengthening or weakening him. The capacity for admiration is indiscriminate; courageous self-sacrifice can have disastrous consequences; and Cain's revulsion at what appears foul to him is manifestly not always trustworthy. He may project his own corruption.

Sanity and decency consist in achieving a reflectively critical balance among all these deep-seated and contrary tendencies. Any normal person is in principle notionally capable of monitoring and adjusting them. But the ability to achieve a finely attuned balance among them depends on an individual's constitution and on the vicissitudes of experience. Crucially, cultural images of power and success direct attention and ambition; and of course social and economic structures enhance or impede the slide to corruption. Cain would almost certainly not have dared to undermine Abel's support of Deborah's appointment if Abel were the senator's rich older brother and Deborah were the dean's newest trophy wife.

What, if anything, might check the worst of Cain's decline? Character disorders are like physical ailments. Because therapeutic reversal is more difficult than setting a preventive regimen, the initial formation of habits of mind and action provide the best protection. Once he's slid down the slippery slope, Cain is unlikely to reverse himself as long as his cohort supports him. In principle, there was marginal scope for a preventive regimen. Wise parents and guardians might have armed Cain against corruption. Images of behavior beneath contempt, "*we* (Chinese, Jews, English) don't do that sort of thing," set bounds. Contemptuous gossip about sleazy neighbors and politicians is useful; imaginative role-playing enlarges empathy ("How would Martha and Matthew react to this event?"); and critical evaluation refines good judgment ("Taking everything and everyone into account, what's the best way to describe what happened?"). The family's circle of friends typically present models for imitation: Are the Good People also Fun?

But none of these preventive measures provides trouble-proof security against corruption. Each carries the lively possibility of its misuse: cultural pride sets the stage for cultural bigotry; the delights of critical gossip may diminish the capacity for respect; the ability to discern his fellows' moods may serve Cain's manipulative talents; and the scoundrel's rhetorical skill in manipulating focused indignation is among his most powerful weapons. In any case, even the best psychological habits depend on the support of pervasive social influence. Whether Cain slides to corruption depends on how his larger world forms and specifies his standard-issue psychological tendencies. His culture is largely conceived to include social practices and economic arrangements that reward and entrench (or block and stunt) the directions of his natural tendencies. When corruption is widespread, home-grown prevention can at best provide only some resistance: in such circumstances, erratic, fluctuating weakness may be an advance over prevailing corruption. As long as there are no dramatic changes in the world around him, as long as his new habits bring him the kind of success he desires and the approval of new acquaintances, Cain is unlikely to reverse his slide to corruption.

40

AMOS OZ

On degrees of evil

In January 1986, the International PEN Congress convened in New York. The theme of the congress was "The Imagination of the State and the Imagination of the Writer." Many speeches were given in the spirit of romantic anarchism, namely, declaring that the state, any state, is a monster that tramples the spirit of the simple individual – who is by nature good – with wars, oppression, and the construction of ugly housing projects. Writers, on the other hand, were depicted as courageous people who come out in opposition to the monstrous state to defend the "little man." The following address was delivered in response to these speeches.

The state has no imagination. "The imagination of the state" exists only in the imagination of some writers, like those who invented the title of this congress. St George and the Dragon – something like that must have been on their minds when they contrived this title. Every writer an empty-handed Solzhenitsyn, every dragon a wicked Leonid Brezhnev or a vicious Richard Nixon. I don't like it. I think some states are relatively decent. So are some writers. And some states and some writers are corrupt in many different ways. Our title has about it a ring of romantic, simplistic anarchism. I reject the image of a saintly lot of writers marching fearlessly to combat heartless bureaucracies on behalf of all the sweet and simple human beings out there. I am not in the business of the beauties versus the beasts.

For one thing, states and governments and bureaucracies – the fair ones *and* the hideous ones; there are both – have always been inspired by all sorts of visions generating from all kinds of writers. Some of these visions are fair, some are bad, some are monstrous – visions that various rulers have or have not distorted in ways that different writers have condemned. Or praised.

For another, some writers have indeed died in jails and gulags while some others have thrived in courts and dachas. But most have neither died in martyrdom nor thrived by licking boots. None of us has ever killed a dragon. Moreover, the sweet and simple

Source: *The Slopes of Lebanon*, translated by Maurie Goldberg-Batura, San Diego, Calif.: Harcourt Brace Jovanovich, 1989.

common people out there are neither sweet nor simple. We know, most of us, better than that. Just read our books and see.

Again and again I am amazed by the gulf between what writers see when we write our poems, stories, plays, and what we do when we formulate or sign our petitions, manifestos, titles for panel discussions. It is as if we were using two contradictory pairs of eyes – present company not excluded; myself not excluded. Most of us know a thing or two about the dragons inside the human heart. Yet outside our literary works we often tend to sound as if we believe in the simplistic, dangerous, Rousseauistic assumption that governments and establishments are wicked – all of them – whereas common people are born pure and sweet in heart – all of them.

I beg to differ. The state is a necessary evil simply because many individuals are themselves capable of evil. Moreover, there are differences among states. Some are almost good, some are bad, some are lethal. And since writers are, or at least they ought to be, in the subtleties department and in the precision department, it is our job to differentiate. Whoever ignores the existence of varying degrees of evil is bound to become a servant of evil.

Precision and subtleties – we are not reporters, and yet we are. We do not necessarily collect or reflect facts; we invent, we twist, we exaggerate, we distort. We turn things inside out and upside down. But note: The moment we put things into words, our words are promoted into evidence. Hence our responsibility for precision, for nuances, for subtleties. Hence our duty to map evil, to grade it, to measure its degrees.

The tragedy of history is not the perpetual hopeless clash between saintly individuals and diabolical establishments. It is, rather, the perpetual clash between the relatively decent societies and the bloody ones. To be more precise, it is the perpetual cowardice of relatively decent societies whenever they confront the ruthlessness of oppressive ones.

How can one be humane, which means skeptical and capable of moral ambivalence, and at the same time try to combat evil? How can one stand fanatically against fanaticism? How can one fight without becoming a fighter? How can one struggle against evil without catching it? Deal with history without becoming exposed to the poisonous effect of history? Three months ago, in Vienna, I saw a street demonstration of environmentalists protesting against scientific experiments on guinea pigs. They carried placards with images of Jesus surrounded by suffering guinea pigs. The inscription read: "He loved them too." Maybe he did, but some of the protesters looked to me as if eventually they may not be above shooting hostages in order to bring an end to the sufferings of the guinea pigs. Which is, to some extent, the story of do-gooders here and there, and maybe everywhere.

Let us not ascribe a demonic imagination to the state and a redeeming imagination to ourselves. Let us not give in to the temptation of simplification. We ought to be telling the bad from the worse from the worst.

Part 8

CONFLICT, IMMORALITY AND CRIME

Francisco Goya: "Indecision."

Many contemporary moral philosophers have been concerned with the question of whether extreme circumstances can justify the violation of moral injunctions. What is permissible in war or self-defense? Can moral obligations conflict with one another? What are the lures of corruption? Can it occur unnoticed, gradually? In what do criminal culpability and psychopathology consist?

Expounding her view of the Catholic position on the ethics of conflict and war, G.E.M. Anscombe argues that the human propensity to mutual harm requires and justifies the coercive power of the state as a check against evil. The authority of the state must nevertheless be constrained by moral maxims: not even the exigencies of war can justify injustice or vice. Although some wars are just, and some killing in war is justified, there are absolute prohibitions that cannot be morally condoned by their beneficial consequences. Murder as the taking of innocent life is wrong, no matter what good it may gain, what harm it may prevent. No man's action can be justified by redescribing his intention, as if its foreseeable consequences were wholly unintended. The evil of the intention encompasses the evil of the consequences; and there is an absolute duty to consider the consequences as well as the direction of an enacted intention.

Michael Walzer analyzes what he describes as the Machiavellian dilemma: public officials, charged with promoting the civic good, face conflicts and radical choices that leave them with "morally dirty hands." Like Anscombe, Walzer argues that there are actions which are morally wrong, in and of themselves, even if they are the only available avenue to a commanding good. Unlike Anscombe, Walzer argues that a person remains culpable of having committed a wrong even when an overriding principle appears to justify what he did. (For instance, even if Truman (acting as Commander-in-Chief) had an overriding obligation to save American lives, his commanding the bombing of Hiroshima would leave him inescapably guilty.) Walzer points to a further dilemma: a person's anguished sense of guilt cannot atone — cannot "pay" — for his moral failure. Nor does the realization that such moral dilemmas are inevitable mitigate his culpability. There is no way out of dirty hands.

Jean Hampton agrees with Aquinas and Kant that immorality involves voluntarily, knowingly, defiantly placing one's own inclinations above the authority of the moral law. Unlike Aquinas and Kant, Hampton thinks that there is no mystery about this: human beings resent and defy (what they recognize as) authority when its commands seem unpleasant or hateful. Though they may act from a "natural" human trait, they are nevertheless culpable when they acted voluntarily.

The Model Penal Code (1956) distinguishes legal liability from legal culpability. The former involves an (allegedly) illegal voluntary action (or omission). Legal culpability involves acting purposely, knowingly, recklessly or negligently. It is for the courts to determine when these conditions have been met.

The *Diagnostic and Statistical Manual of Mental Disorders, IV* (1994) published by the American Psychiatric Association defines anti-social personality disorders, linking such disorders with aggression, deceitfulness, theft, violation of rules, the destruction of property. Anti-social personalities are said to be unempathic, irresponsible and irrationally impulsive about their work and their finances, and to disregard social norms. The criteria proposed are unabashedly class oriented: the "disorder appears to be associated with low socio-economic status and urban settings." There is no investigation – no discussion – of the ways in which this disorder can manifest itself among highly educated, conventional, ambitious, self-controlled persons.

41

G.E.M. ANSCOMBE

War and murder

The use of violence by rulers

Since there are always thieves, [murderers,] frauds and men who commit violent attacks on their neighbours . . . , and since without law backed by adequate force there are usually gangs of bandits; and since there are in most places laws administered by people who command violence to enforce the laws against law-breakers; the question arises: what is a just attitude to this exercise of violent coercive power on the part of rulers and their subordinate officers?

Two attitudes are possible: one, that the world is an absolute jungle and that the exercise of coercive power by rulers is only a manifestation of this; and the other, that it is both necessary and right that there should be this exercise of power, that through it the world is much less of a jungle than it could possibly be without it, so that one should in principle be glad of the existence of such power, and only take exception to its unjust exercise.

It is so clear that the world is less of a jungle because of rulers and laws, and that the exercise of coercive power is essential to these institutions as they are now – all this is so obvious, that probably only Tennysonian conceptions of progress enable people who do not wish to separate themselves from the world to think that nevertheless such violence is objectionable, that some day, in this present dispensation, we shall do without it, and that the pacifist is the man who sees and tries to follow the ideal course, which future civilization must one day pursue. It is an illusion, which would be fantastic if it were not so familiar.

In a peaceful and law abiding country such as England, it may not be immediately obvious that the rulers need to command violence to the point of fighting to the death those that would oppose it; but brief reflection shews that this is so. For those who oppose the force that backs law will not always stop short of fighting to the death and cannot always be put down short of fighting to the death.

Source: "War and Murder"*Nuclear Weapons: A Catholic Response*, ed. Walter Stein, New York: Sheed & Ward,

Then only if it is in itself evil violently to coerce resistant wills, can the exercise of coercive power by rulers be bad as such. Against such a conception, if it were true, the necessity and advantage of the exercise of such power would indeed be a useless plea. But that conception is one that makes no sense unless it is accompanied by a theory of withdrawal from the world as man's only salvation; and it is in any case a false one. We are taught that God retains the evil will of the devil within limits by violence: we are not given a picture of God permitting to the devil all that he is capable of. There is current a conception of Christianity as having revealed that the defeat of evil must always be by pure love without coercion; this at least is shewn to be false by the foregoing consideration. And without the alleged revelation there could be no reason to believe such a thing.

To think that society's coercive authority is evil is akin to thinking the flesh evil and family life evil. These things belong to the present constitution of mankind; and if the exercise of coercive power is a manifestation of evil, and not the just means of restraining it, then human nature is totally depraved in a manner never taught by Christianity. For society is essential to human good; and society without coercive power is generally impossible.

The same authority which puts down internal dissension, which promulgates laws and restrains those who break them if it can, must equally oppose external enemies. These do not merely comprise those who attack the borders of the people ruled by the authority; but also, for example, pirates and desert bandits, and, generally, those beyond the confines of the country ruled whose activities are viciously harmful to it. The Romans, once their rule in Gaul was established, were eminently justified in attacking Britain, where were nurtured the Druids whose pupils infested northern Gaul and whose practices struck the Romans themselves as "dira immanitas." Further, there being such a thing as the common good of mankind, and visible criminality against it, how can we doubt the excellence of such a proceeding as that violent suppression of the man-stealing business[1] which the British government took it into its head to engage in under Palmerston? The present-day conception of "aggression," like so many strongly influential conceptions, is a bad one. Why *must* it be wrong to strike the first blow in a struggle? The only question is, who is in the right.

Here, however, human pride, malice and cruelty are so usual that it is true to say that wars have mostly been mere wickedness on both sides. Just as an individual will constantly think himself in the right, whatever he does, and yet there is still such a thing as being in the right, so nations will constantly wrongly think themselves to be in the right – and yet there is still such a thing as their being in the right. Palmerston doubtless had no doubts in prosecuting the opium war against China, which was diabolical; just as he exulted in putting down the slavers. But there is no question but that he was a monster in the one thing, and a just man in the other.

The probability is that warfare is injustice, that a life of military service is a bad life "militia or rather malitia," as St Anselm called it. This probability is greater than the probability (which also exists) that membership of a police force will involve malice, because of the character of warfare: the extraordinary occasions it offers for viciously unjust proceedings on the part of military commanders and warring governments, which at the time attract praise and not blame from their people. It is equally the case that the life of a ruler is usually a vicious life: but that does not shew that ruling is as such a vicious activity.

The principal wickedness which is a temptation to those engaged in warfare is the killing of the innocent, which may often be done with impunity and even to the glory of those who do it. In many places and times it has been taken for granted as a natural part of waging war: the commander, and especially the conqueror, massacres people by the thousand, either because this is part of his glory, or as a terrorizing measure, or as part of his tactics.

Innocence and the right to kill intentionally

It is necessary to dwell on the notion of non-innocence here employed. Innocence is a legal notion; but here, the accused is not pronounced guilty under an existing code of law, under which he has been tried by an impartial judge, and therefore made the target of attack. There is hardly a possibility of this; for the administration of justice is something that takes place under the aegis of a sovereign authority; but in warfare – or the putting down by violence of civil disturbance – the sovereign authority is itself engaged as a party to the dispute and is not subject to a further earthly and temporal authority which can judge the issue and pronounce against the accused. The stabler the society, the rarer it will be for the sovereign authority to have to do anything but apprehend its internal enemy and have him tried: but even in the stablest society there are occasions when the authority has to fight its internal enemy to the point of killing, as happens in the struggle with external belligerent forces in international warfare; and then the characterization of its enemy as non-innocent has not been ratified by legal process.

This, however, does not mean that the notion of innocence fails in this situation. What is required, for the people attacked to be non-innocent in the relevant sense, is that they should themselves be engaged in an objectively unjust proceeding which the attacker has the right to make his concern; or – the commonest case – should be unjustly attacking him. Then he can attack them with a view to stopping them; and also their supply lines and armament factories. But people whose mere existence and activity supporting existence by growing crops, making clothes, etc. constitute an impediment to him – such people are innocent and it is murderous to attack them, or make them a target for an attack which he judges will help him towards victory. For murder is the deliberate killing of the innocent, whether for its own sake or as a means to some further end.

The right to attack with a view to killing is something that belongs only to rulers and those whom they command to do it. I have argued that it does belong to rulers precisely because of that threat of violent coercion exercised by those in authority which is essential to the existence of human societies. It ought not to be pretended that rulers and their subordinates do not choose[2] the killing of their enemies as a means, when it has come to fighting in which they are determined to win and their enemies resist to the point of killing: this holds even in internal disturbances.

When a private man struggles with an enemy he has no right to aim to kill him, unless in the circumstances of the attack on him he can be considered as endowed with the authority of the law and the struggle comes to that point. By a "private" man, I mean a man in a society; I am not speaking of men on their own, without government, in remote places; for such men are neither public servants nor "private." The plea of self-defence (or the defence of someone else) made by a private man who has killed someone else must in conscience – even if not in law – be a plea that the death of the other was not intended, but was a side effect of the measures taken to ward off the attack. To shoot to kill, to set lethal man-traps, or, say, to lay poison for some from whom one's life is in danger, are forbidden. The deliberate choice of inflicting death in a struggle is the right only of ruling authorities and their subordinates.

In saying that a private man may not choose to kill, we are touching on the principle of "double effect." The denial of this has been the corruption of non-Catholic thought, and its abuse the corruption of Catholic thought. Both have disastrous consequences which we shall see. This principle is not accepted in English law: the law is said to allow no distinction between the foreseen and the intended consequences of an action. Thus, if I push a man over a cliff when he is menacing my life, his death is considered as intended by me, but the intention to be justifiable for the sake of self-defence. Yet the lawyers would hardly find the laying of poison tolerable as an act of self-defence, but only killing by a violent action in a moment of violence. Christian moral theologians have taught that even here one may not seek the death of the assailant, but may in default of other ways of self-defence use such violence as will in fact result in his death. The distinction is evidently a fine one in some cases: what, it may be asked, can the intention be, if it can be said to be absent in this case, except a mere wish or desire?

And yet in other cases the distinction is very clear. If I go to prison rather than perform some action, no reasonable person will call the incidental consequences of my refusal – the loss of my job, for example – intentional just because I knew they must happen. And in the case of the administration of a pain-relieving drug in mortal illness, where the doctor knows the drug may very well kill the patient if the illness does not do so first, the distinction is evident; the lack of it has led an English judge to talk nonsense about the administration of the drug's not having *really* been the cause of death in such a case, even though a post mortem shews it was. For everyone understands that it is a very different thing so to administer a drug, and to administer it with the intention of killing.

The turning of counsels into precepts results in high-sounding principles. Principles that are mistakenly high and strict are a trap; they may easily lead in the end directly or indirectly to the justification of monstrous things. Thus if the evangelical counsel about poverty were turned into a precept forbidding property owning, people would pay lip service to it as the ideal, while in practice they went in for swindling. "Absolute honesty!" it would be said: "I can respect that – but of course that means having no property; and while I respect those who follow that course, I have to compromise with the sordid world myself." If then one must "compromise with evil" by owning property and engaging in trade, then the amount of swindling one does will depend on convenience. This imaginary case is paralleled by what is so commonly said: absolute pacifism is an ideal; unable to follow that, and committed to "compromise with evil," one must go the whole hog and wage war *à outrance*.

The truth about Christianity is that it is a severe and practicable religion, not a beautifully ideal but impracticable one. Its moral precepts (except for the stricter laws about marriage that Christ enacted, abrogating some of the permissions of the Old Law), are those of the Old Testament; and its God is the God of Israel . . .

Now, it is one of the most vehement and repeated teachings of the Judaeo-Christian tradition that the shedding of innocent blood is forbidden by the divine law. No man may be punished except for his own crime, and those "whose feet are swift to shed innocent blood" are always represented as God's enemies . . .

[T]hat it is terrible to kill the innocent is very obvious; the morality that so stringently forbids it must make a great appeal to mankind, especially to the poor threatened victims. Why should it need the thunder of Sinai and the suffering and preaching of the prophets to promulgate such a law? But human pride and malice are everywhere so strong that now, with the fading of Christianity from the mind of the West, this morality once more stands out as a demand which strikes pride- and fear-ridden people as too intransigent. For Knox, it seemed so obvious as to be dull; and he failed to recognize the bloody and beastly records that it accompanies for the dry truthfulness about human beings that so characterizes the Old Testament . . .

The policy of obliterating cities was adopted by the Allies in the [Second World War.] [T]hey need not have taken that step, and it was taken largely out of a villainous hatred, and as corollary to the policy, now universally denigrated, of seeking "unconditional surrender." (That policy itself was visibly wicked, and could be and was judged so at the time; it is not surprising that it led to disastrous consequences, even if no one was clever and detached enough to foresee this at the time.) . . .

The principle of double effect

So we must ask: how is it that there has been so comparatively little conscience exercised . . . ? The answer is: double-think about double effect.

The distinction between the intended, and the merely foreseen, effects of a voluntary action is indeed absolutely essential to Christian ethics. For Christianity forbids a number of things as being bad in themselves. But if I am answerable for the foreseen consequences of an action or refusal, as much as for the action itself, then those prohibitions will break down. If someone innocent will die unless I do a wicked thing, then on this view I am his murderer in refusing: so all that is left to me is to weigh up evils. Here the theologian steps in with the principle of double effect and says: "No, you are no murderer, if the man's death was neither your aim nor your chosen means, and if you had to act in the way that led to it or else do something absolutely forbidden." Without understanding of this principle, anything can be – and is wont to be – justified, and the Christian teaching that in no circumstances may one commit murder, adultery, apostasy (to give a few examples) goes by the board. These absolute prohibitions of Christianity by no means exhaust its ethic; there is a large area where what is just is determined partly by a prudent weighing up of consequences. But the prohibitions are bedrock, and without them the Christian ethic goes to pieces. Hence the necessity of the notion of double effect.

At the same time, the principle has been repeatedly abused from the seventeenth century up till now. The causes lie in the history of philosophy. From the seventeenth century till now what may be called Cartesian psychology has dominated the thought of philosophers and theologians. According to this psychology, an intention was an interior act of the mind which could be produced at will. Now if intention is all important – as it is – in determining the goodness or badness of an action, then, on this theory of what intention is, a marvellous way offered itself of making any action lawful. You only had to "direct your intention" in a suitable way. In practice, this means making a little speech to yourself: "What I mean to be doing is. . . ."

This perverse doctrine has occasioned repeated condemnations by the Holy See from the seventeenth century to the present day. Some examples will suffice to shew how the thing goes. Typical doctrines from the seventeenth century were that it is all right for a servant to hold the ladder for his criminous master so long as he is merely avoiding the sack by doing so; or that a man might wish for and rejoice at his parent's death so long as what he had in mind was the gain to himself; or that it is not simony to offer money, not *as a price* for the spiritual benefit, but only *as an inducement* to give it. A condemned doctrine from the present day is that the practice of *coitus reservatus* is permissible: such a doctrine could only arise in connexion with that "direction of intention" which sets everything right no matter what one does. A man makes a practice of withdrawing, telling himself that he *intends* not to ejaculate; of course (if that is his practice) he usually does so, but then the event is "accidental" and *praeter intentionem*: it is, in short, a case of "double effect."

This same doctrine is used to prevent any doubts about the obliteration bombing of a city. The devout Catholic bomber secures by a "direction of intention" that any shedding of innocent blood that occurs is "accidental." I know a Catholic boy who was puzzled at being told by his schoolmaster that it was an *accident* that the people of Hiroshima and Nagasaki were there to be killed; in fact, however absurd it seems, such thoughts are common among priests who know that they are forbidden by the divine law to justify the direct killing of the innocent.

It is nonsense to pretend that you do not intend to do what is the means you take to your chosen end. Otherwise there is absolutely no substance to the Pauline teaching that we may not do evil that good may come.

Some commonly heard arguments

There are a number of sophistical arguments, often or sometimes used on these topics, which need answering.

Where do you draw the line? As Dr Johnson said, the fact of twilight does not mean you cannot tell day from night. There are borderline cases, where it is difficult to distinguish, in what is done, between means and what is incidental to, yet in the circumstances inseparable from, those means. The obliteration bombing of a city is not a borderline case.

The old "conditions for a just war" are irrelevant to the conditions of modern warfare, so that must be condemned out of hand. People who say this always envisage only major wars between the Great Powers, which Powers are indeed now "in blood stepp'd in so far" that it is unimaginable for there to be a war between them which is not a set of enormous massacres of civil populations. But these are not the only wars. Why is Finland so far free? At least partly because of the "posture of military preparedness" which, considering the character of the country, would have made subjugating the Finns a difficult and unrewarding task. The offensive of the Israelis against the Egyptians in 1956 involved no plan of making civil populations the target of military attack.

In a modern war the distinction between combatants and non-combatants is meaningless, so an attack on anyone on the enemy side is justified. This is pure nonsense; even in war, a very large number of the enemy population are just engaged in maintaining the life of the country, or are sick, or aged, or children.

It must be legitimate to maintain an opinion – viz. that the destruction of cities by bombing is lawful – if this is argued by competent theologians and the Holy See has not pronounced. The argument from the silence of the Holy See has itself been condemned by the Holy See (Denzinger, 28th Edition, 1127). How could this be a sane doctrine in view of the endless twistiness of the human mind?

Whether a war is just or not is not for the private man to judge: he must obey his government. Sometimes, this may be, especially as far as concerns causes of war. But the individual who joins in destroying a city, like a Nazi massacring the inhabitants of a village, is too obviously marked out as an enemy of the human race, to shelter behind such a plea.

Finally, horrible as it is to have to notice this, we must notice that even the arguments about double effect – which at least show that a man is not willing openly to justify the killing of the innocent – are now beginning to look old-fashioned. Some Catholics are not scrupling to say that *anything* is justified in defence of the continued existence and liberty of the Church in the West. A terrible fear of communism drives people to say this sort of thing. "Our Lord told us to fear those who can destroy body and soul, not to fear the destruction of the body" was blasphemously said to a friend of mine; meaning: "so, we must fear Russian domination more than the destruction of people's bodies by obliteration bombing."

But whom did Our Lord tell us to fear, when he said: "I will tell you whom you shall fear" and "Fear not them that can destroy the body, but fear him who can destroy body and soul in hell"? He told us to fear God the Father, who can and will destroy the unrepentant disobedient, body and soul, in hell.

A Catholic who is tempted to think on the lines I have described should remember that the Church is the spiritual Israel: that is, that Catholics are what the ancient Jews were, salt for the earth and the people of God – and that what was true of some devout Jews of ancient times can equally well be true of us now: "You compass land and sea to make a convert, and when you have done so, you make him twice as much a child of hell as yourselves." Do Catholics sometimes think that they are immune from such a possibility? That the Pharisees – who sat in the seat of Moses and who were so zealous for the true religion – were bad in ways in which we cannot be bad if we are zealous? I believe they do. But our faith teaches no such immunity, it teaches the opposite. "We are in danger all our lives long." So we have to fear God and keep his commandments, and calculate what is for the best only within the limits of that obedience, knowing that the future is in God's power and that no one can snatch away those whom the Father has given to Christ.

It is not a vague faith in the triumph of "the spirit" over force (there is little enough warrant for that), but a definite faith in the divine promises, that makes us believe that the Church cannot fail. Those, therefore, who think they must be prepared to wage a war with Russia involving the deliberate massacre of cities, must be prepared to say to God: "We had to break your law, lest your Church fail. We could not obey your commandments, for we did not believe your promises."

Notes

1 It is ignorance to suppose that it takes modern liberalism to hate and condemn this. It is cursed and subject to the death penalty in the Mosaic law. Under that code, too, runaway slaves of all nations had asylum in Israel.

2 The idea that they may lawfully do what they do, but should not *intend* the death of those they attack, has been put forward and, when suitably expressed, may seem high-minded. But someone who can fool himself into this twist of thought will fool himself into justifying anything, however atrocious, by means of it.

42

MICHAEL
WALZER

Political action:
the problem of dirty hands

Can a man ever face, or ever have to face, a moral dilemma, a situation where he must choose between two courses of action both of which it would be wrong for him to undertake.[1] Thomas Nagel worriedly suggested that this could happen and that it did happen whenever someone was forced to choose between upholding an important moral principle and avoiding some looming disaster.[2] R.B. Brandt argued that it could not possibly happen, for there were guidelines we might follow and calculations we might go through which would necessarily yield the conclusion that one or the other course of action was the right one to undertake in the circumstances (or that it did not matter which we undertook). R.M. Hare explained how it was that someone might wrongly suppose that he was faced with a moral dilemma: sometimes, he suggested, the precepts and principles of an ordinary man, the products of his moral education, come into conflict with injunctions developed at a higher level of moral discourse. But this conflict is, or ought to be, resolved at the higher level; there is no real dilemma.

I am not sure that Hare's explanation is at all comforting, but the question is important even if no such explanation is possible, perhaps especially so if this is the case. The argument relates not only to the coherence and harmony of the moral universe, but also to the relative ease or difficulty – or impossibility – of living a moral life. It is not, therefore, merely a philosopher's question. If such a dilemma can arise, whether frequently or very rarely, any of us might one day face it. Indeed, many men have faced it, or think they have, especially men involved in political activity or war. The dilemma, exactly as Nagel describes it, is frequently discussed in the literature of political action – in novels and plays dealing with politics and in the work of theorists too.

Source: "Political Action: The Problem of Dirty Hands," *Philosophy & Public Affairs*, vol. 2, 1973.

In modern times the dilemma appears most often as the problem of "dirty hands," and it is typically stated by the Communist leader Hoerderer in Sartre's play of that name: "I have dirty hands right up to the elbows. I've plunged them in filth and blood. Do you think you can govern innocently?"[3] My own answer is no, I don't think I could govern innocently; nor do most of us believe that those who govern us are innocent – as I shall argue below – even the best of them. But this does not mean that it isn't possible to do the right thing while governing. It means that a particular act of government (in a political party or in the state) may be exactly the right thing to do in utilitarian terms and yet leave the man who does it guilty of a moral wrong. The innocent man, afterwards, is no longer innocent. If on the other hand he remains innocent, chooses, that is, the "absolutist" side of Nagel's dilemma, he not only fails to do the right thing (in utilitarian terms), he may also fail to measure up to the duties of his office (which imposes on him a considerable responsibility for consequences and outcomes). Most often, of course, political leaders accept the utilitarian calculation; they try to measure up. One might offer a number of sardonic comments on this fact, the most obvious being that by the calculations they usually make they demonstrate the great virtues of the "absolutist" position. Nevertheless, we would not want to be governed by men who consistently adopted that position.

The notion of dirty hands derives from an effort to refuse "absolutism" without denying the reality of the moral dilemma. Though this may appear to utilitarian philosophers to pile confusion upon confusion, I propose to take it very seriously. For the literature I shall examine is the work of serious and often wise men, and it reflects, though it may also have helped to shape, popular thinking about politics. It is important to pay attention to that too. I shall do so without assuming, as Hare suggests one might, that everyday moral and political discourse constitutes a distinct level of argument, where content is largely a matter of pedagogic expediency.[4] If popular views are resistant (as they are) to utilitarianism, there may be something to learn from that and not merely something to explain about it.

Let me begin, then, with a piece of conventional wisdom to the effect that politicians are a good deal worse, morally worse, than the rest of us (it is the wisdom of the rest of us). Without either endorsing it or pretending to disbelieve it, I am going to expound this convention. For it suggests that the dilemma of dirty hands is a central feature of political life, that it arises not merely as an occasional crisis in the career of this or that unlucky politician but systematically and frequently.

Why is the politician singled out? Isn't he like the other entrepreneurs in an open society, who hustle, lie, intrigue, wear masks, smile and are villains? He is not, no doubt for many reasons, three of which I need to consider. First of all, the politician claims to play a different part than other entrepreneurs. He doesn't merely cater to our interests; he acts on our behalf, even in our name. He has purposes in mind, causes and projects that require the support and redound to the benefit, not of each of us individually, but of all of us together. He hustles, lies, and intrigues *for us* – or so he claims. Perhaps he is right, or at least sincere, but we suspect that he acts for himself also. Indeed, he cannot serve us without serving himself, for success brings him power and glory, the greatest rewards that men can win from their fellows. The competition for these two is fierce; the risks are often great, but the temptations are greater. We imagine ourselves succumbing. Why should our representatives act differently? Even if they would like to act differently, they probably can not: for other men are all too ready to hustle and lie for power and glory, and it is the others who set the terms of the competition. Hustling and lying are necessary because power and glory are so desirable – that is, so widely desired. And so the men who act for us and in our name are necessarily hustlers and liars.

Politicians are also thought to be worse than the rest of us because they rule over us, and the pleasures of ruling are much greater than the pleasures of being ruled. The successful politician becomes the visible architect of our restraint. He taxes us, licenses us, forbids and permits us, directs us to this or that distant goal – all for our greater good. Moreover, he takes chances for our greater good that put us, or some of us, in danger. Sometimes he puts himself in danger too, but politics, after all, is his adventure. It is not always ours. There are undoubtedly times when it is good or necessary to direct the affairs of other people and to put them in danger. But we are a little frightened of the man who seeks, ordinarily and every day, the power to do so. And the fear is reasonable enough. The politician has, or pretends to have, a kind of confidence in his own judgment that the rest of us know to be presumptuous in any man.

The presumption is especially great because the victorious politician uses violence and the threat of violence – not only against foreign nations in our defense but also against us, and again ostensibly for our greater good. This is a point emphasized and perhaps overemphasized by Max Weber in his essay "Politics as a Vocation."[5] It has not, so far as I can tell, played an overt or obvious part in the development of the convention I am examining. The stock figure is the lying, not the murderous, politician – though the murderer lurks in the background, appearing most often in the form of the revolutionary or terrorist, very rarely as an ordinary magistrate or official. Nevertheless, the sheer weight of official violence in human history does suggest the kind of power to which politicians aspire, the kind of power they want to wield, and it may point to the roots of our half-conscious dislike and unease. The men who act for us and in our name are often killers, or seem to become killers too quickly and too easily.

Knowing all this or most of it, good and decent people still enter political life, aiming at some specific reform or seeking a general reformation. They are then required to learn the lesson Machiavelli first set out to teach: "how not to be good."[6] Some of them are incapable of learning; many more profess to be incapable. But they will not succeed unless they learn, for they have joined the terrible competition for power and glory; they have chosen to work and struggle as Machiavelli says, among "so many who are not good." They can do no good themselves unless they win the struggle, which they are unlikely to do unless they are willing and able to use the necessary means. So we are suspicious even of the best of winners. It is not a sign of our perversity if we think them only more clever than the rest. They have not won, after all, because they were good, or not only because of that, but also because they were not good. No one succeeds in politics without getting his hands dirty. This is conventional wisdom again, and again I don't mean to insist that it is true without qualification. I repeat it only to disclose the moral dilemma inherent in the convention. For sometimes it is right to try to succeed, and then it must also be right to get one's hands dirty. But one's hands get dirty from doing what it is wrong to do. And how can it be wrong to do what is right? Or, how can we get our hands dirty by doing what we ought to do?

It will be best to turn quickly to some examples. I have chosen two, one relating to the struggle for power and one to its exercise. I should stress that in both these cases the men who face the dilemma of dirty hands have in an important sense chosen to do so; the cases tell us nothing about what it would be like, so to speak, to fall into the dilemma; nor shall I say anything about that here. Politicians often argue that they have no right to keep their hands clean, and that may well be true of them, but it is not so clearly true of the rest of us. Probably we do have a right to avoid, if we possibly can, those positions in which we might be forced to do terrible things. This might be regarded as the moral equivalent of our legal right not to incriminate ourselves. Good men will be in no hurry to surrender it, though there are reasons for doing so sometimes, and among these are or might be the reasons good men have for entering politics. But let us imagine a politician who does not agree to that: he wants to do good only by doing good, or at least he is certain that he can stop short of the most corrupting and brutal uses of political power. Very quickly that certainty is tested. What do we think of him then?

He wants to win the election, someone says, but he doesn't want to get his hands dirty. This is meant as a disparagement, even though it also means that the man being criticized is the sort of man who will not lie, cheat, bargain behind the backs of his supporters, shout absurdities at public meetings, or manipulate other men and women. Assuming that this particular election ought to be won, it is clear, I think, that the disparagement is justified. If the candidate didn't want to get his hands dirty, he should have stayed at home; if he can't stand the heat, he should get out of the kitchen, and so on. His decision to run was a commitment (to all of us who think the election important) to try to win, that is, to do within rational limits whatever is necessary to win. But the candidate is a moral man. He has principles and a history of adherence to those principles. That is why we are supporting him. Perhaps when he refuses to dirty his hands, he is simply insisting on being the sort of man he is. And isn't that the sort of man we want?

Let us look more closely at this case. In order to win the election the candidate must make a deal with a dishonest ward boss, involving the granting of contracts for school construction over the next four years. Should he make the deal? Well, at least he shouldn't be surprised by the offer, most of us would probably say (a conventional piece of sarcasm). And he should accept it or not, depending on exactly what is at stake in the election. But that is not the candidate's view. He is extremely reluctant even to consider the deal, puts off his aides when they remind him of it, refuses to calculate its possible effects upon the campaign. Now, if he is acting this way because the very thought of bargaining with that particular ward boss makes him feel unclean, his reluctance isn't very interesting. His feelings by themselves are not important. But he may also have reasons for his reluctance. He may know, for example, that some of his supporters support him precisely because they believe he is a good man, and this means to them a man who won't make such deals. Or he may doubt his own motives for considering the deal, wondering whether it is the political campaign or his own candidacy that makes the bargain at all tempting. Or he may believe that if he makes deals of this sort now he may not be able later on to achieve those ends that make the campaign worthwhile, and he may not feel entitled to take such risks with a future that is not only his own future. Or he may simply think that the deal is dishonest and therefore wrong, corrupting not only himself but all those human relations in which he is involved.

Because he has scruples of this sort, we know him to be a good man. But we view the campaign in a certain light, estimate its importance in a certain way, and hope that he will overcome his scruples and make the deal. It is important to stress that we don't want just *anyone* to make the deal; we want *him* to make it, precisely because he has scruples about it. We know he is doing right when he makes the deal because he knows he is doing wrong. I don't mean merely that he will feel badly or even very badly after he makes the deal. If he is the good man I am imagining him to be, he will feel guilty, that is, he will believe himself to be guilty. That is what it means to have dirty hands.

All this may become clearer if we look at a more dramatic example, for we are, perhaps, a little blasé about political deals and disinclined to worry much about the man who makes one. So consider a politician who has seized upon a national crisis – a prolonged colonial war – to reach for power. He and his friends win office pledged to decolonization and peace; they are honestly committed to both, though not without some sense of the advantages of the commitment. In any case, they have no responsibility for the war; they have steadfastly opposed it. Immediately, the politician goes off to the colonial capital to open negotiations with the rebels. But the capital is in the grip of a terrorist campaign, and the first decision the new leader faces is this: he is asked to authorize the torture of a captured rebel leader who knows or probably knows the location of a number of bombs hidden in apartment buildings around the city, set to go off within the next twenty-four hours. He orders the man tortured, convinced that he must do so for the sake of the people who might otherwise die in the explosions – even though he believes that torture is wrong, indeed abominable, not just sometimes, but always.[7] He had expressed this belief often and angrily during his own campaign; the rest of us took it as a sign of his goodness. How should we regard him now? (How should he regard himself?)

Once again, it does not seem enough to say that he should feel very badly. But why not? Why shouldn't he have feelings like those of St Augustine's melancholy soldier, who understood both that his war was just and that killing, even in a just war, is a terrible thing to do?[8] The difference is that Augustine did not believe that it was wrong to kill in a just war; it was just sad, or the sort of thing a good man would be saddened by. But he might have thought it wrong to torture in a just war, and later Catholic theorists have certainly thought it wrong. Moreover, the politician I am imagining thinks it wrong, as do many of us who supported him. Surely we have a right to expect more than melancholy from him now. When he ordered the prisoner tortured, he committed a moral crime and he accepted a moral burden. Now he is a guilty man. His willingness to acknowledge and bear (and perhaps to repent and do penance for) his guilt is evidence, and it is the only evidence he can offer us, both that he is not too good for politics and that he is good enough. Here is the moral politician: it is by his dirty hands that we know him. If he were a moral man and nothing else, his hands would not be dirty; if he were a politician and nothing else, he would pretend that they were clean.

Machiavelli's argument about the need to learn how not to be good clearly implies that there are acts known to be bad quite apart from the immediate circumstances in which they are performed or not performed. He points to a distinct set of political methods and stratagems which good men must study (by reading his books), not only because their use does not come naturally, but also because they are explicitly condemned by the moral teachings good men accept – and whose acceptance serves in turn to mark men as good. These methods may be condemned because they are thought contrary to divine law or to the order of nature or to our moral sense, or because in prescribing the law to ourselves we have individually or collectively prohibited them. Machiavelli does not commit himself on such issues, and I shall not do so either if I can avoid it. The effects of these different views are, at least in one crucial sense, the same. They take out of our hands the constant business of attaching moral labels to such Machiavellian methods as deceit and betrayal. Such methods are simply bad. They are the sort of thing that good men avoid, at least until they have learned how not to be good.

Now, if there is no such class of actions, there is no dilemma of dirty hands, and the Machiavellian teaching loses what Machiavelli surely intended it to have, its disturbing and paradoxical character. He can then be understood to be saying that political actors must sometimes overcome their moral inhibitions, but not that they must sometimes commit crimes. I take it that utilitarian philosophers also want to make the first of these statements and to deny the second. From their point of view, the candidate who makes a corrupt deal and the official who authorizes the torture of a prisoner must be described as good men (given the cases as I have specified them), who ought, perhaps, to be honored for making the right decision when it was a hard decision to make. There are three ways of developing this argument. First, it might be said that every political choice ought to be made solely in terms of its particular and immediate circumstances – in terms, that is, of the reasonable alternatives, available knowledge, likely consequences, and so on. Then the good man will face difficult choices (when his knowledge of options and outcomes is radically uncertain), but it cannot happen that he will face a moral dilemma. Indeed, if he always makes decisions in this way, and has been taught from childhood to do so, he will never have to overcome his inhibitions, whatever he does, for how could he have acquired inhibitions? Assuming further that he weighs the alternatives and calculates the consequences seriously and in good faith, he cannot commit a crime, though he can certainly make a mistake, even a very serious mistake. Even when he lies and tortures, his hands will be clean, for he has done what he should do as best he can, standing alone in a moment of time, forced to choose.

This is in some ways an attractive description of moral decision-making, but it is also a very improbable one. For while any one of us may stand alone, and so on, when we make this or that decision, we are not isolated or solitary in our moral lives. Moral life is a social phenomenon, and it is constituted at least in part by rules, the knowing of which (and perhaps the making of which) we share with our fellows. The experience of coming up against these rules, challenging their prohibitions, and explaining ourselves to other men and women is so common and so obviously important that no account of moral decision-making can possibly fail to come to grips with it. Hence the second utilitarian argument: such rules do indeed exist, but they are not really prohibitions of wrongful actions (though they do, perhaps for pedagogic reasons, have that form). They are moral guidelines, summaries of previous calculations. They ease our choices in ordinary cases, for we can simply follow their injunctions and do what has been found useful in the past; in exceptional cases they serve as signals warning us against doing too quickly or without the most careful calculations what has not been found useful in the past. But they do no more than that; they have no other purpose, and so it cannot be the case that it is or even might be a crime to override them.[9] Nor is it necessary to feel guilty when one does so. Once again, if it is right to break the rule in some hard case, after conscientiously worrying about it, the man who acts (especially if he knows that many of his fellows would simply worry rather than act) may properly feel pride in his achievement.

But this view, it seems to me, captures the reality of our moral life no better than the last. It may well be right to say that moral rules ought to have the character of guidelines, but it seems that in fact they do not. Or at least, we defend ourselves when we break the rules as if they had some status entirely independent of their previous utility (and we rarely feel proud of ourselves). The defenses we normally offer are not simply justifications; they are also excuses. Now, as Austin says, these two can *seem* to come very close together – indeed, I shall suggest that they can appear side by side in the same sentence – but they are conceptually distinct, differentiated in this crucial respect: an excuse is typically an admission of fault; a justification is typically a denial of fault and an assertion of innocence.[10] Consider a well-known defense from Shakespeare's *Hamlet* that has often reappeared in political literature: "I must be cruel only to be kind."[11] The words are spoken on an occasion when Hamlet is actually being cruel to his mother. I will leave aside the possibility that she deserves to hear (to be forced to listen to) every harsh word he utters, for Hamlet himself makes no such claim – and if she did indeed deserve that, his words might not be cruel or he might not be cruel for speaking them. "I must be cruel" contains the excuse, since it both admits a fault and suggests that Hamlet has no choice but to commit it. He is doing what he has to do; he can't help himself (given the ghost's command, the rotten state of Denmark, and so on). The rest of the sentence is a justification, for it suggests that Hamlet intends and expects kindness to be the outcome of his actions – we must assume that he means greater kindness, kindness to the right persons, or some such. It is not, however, so complete a justification that hamlet is able to say that he is not *really* being cruel. "Cruel" and "kind" have exactly the same status; they both follow the verb "to be," and so they perfectly reveal the moral dilemma.[12]

When rules are overridden, we do not talk or act as if they had been set aside, canceled, or annulled. They still stand and have this much effect at least: that we know we have done something wrong even if what we have done was also the best thing to do on the whole in the circumstances.[13] Or at least we feel that way, and this feeling is itself a crucial feature of our moral life. Hence the third utilitarian argument, which recognizes the usefulness of guilt and seeks to explain it. There are, it appears, good reasons for "overvaluing" as well as for overriding the rules. For the consequences might be very bad indeed if the rules were overridden every time the moral calculation seemed to go against them. It is probably best if most men do not calculate too nicely, but simply follow the rules; they are less likely to make mistakes that way, all in all. And so a good man (or at least an ordinary good man) will respect the rules rather more than he would if he thought them merely guidelines, and he will feel guilty when he overrides them. Indeed, if he did not feel guilty, "he would not be such a good man."[14] It is by his feelings that we know him. Because of those feelings he will never be in a hurry to override the rules, but will wait until there is no choice, acting only to avoid consequences that are both imminent and almost certainly disastrous.

The obvious difficulty with this argument is that the feeling whose usefulness is being explained is most unlikely to be felt by someone who is convinced only of its usefulness. He breaks a utilitarian rule (guideline), let us say, for good utilitarian reasons: but can he then feel guilty, also for good utilitarian reasons, when he has no reason for believing that he *is* guilty? Imagine a moral philosopher expounding the third argument to a man who actually does feel guilty or to the sort of man who is likely to feel guilty. Either the man won't accept the utilitarian explanation as an account of his feeling about the rules (probably the best outcome from a utilitarian point of view) or he will accept it and then cease to feel that (useful) feeling. But I do not want to exclude the possibility of a kind of superstitious anxiety, the possibility, that is, that some men will continue to feel guilty even after they have been taught, and have agreed, that they cannot possibly *be* guilty. It is best to say only that the more fully they accept the utilitarian account, the less likely they are to feel that (useful) feeling. The utilitarian account is not at all useful, then, if political actors accept it, and that may help us to understand why it plays, as Hare has pointed out, so small a part in our moral education.[15]

One further comment on the third argument: it is worth stressing that to feel guilty is to suffer, and that the men whose guilt feelings are here called useful are themselves innocent according to the utilitarian account. So we seem to have come upon another case where the suffering of the innocent is permitted and even encouraged by utilitarian calculation.[16] But surely an innocent man who has done something painful or hard (but justified) should be helped to avoid or escape the sense of guilt; he might reasonably expect the assistance of his fellow men, even of moral philosophers, at such a time. On the other hand, if we intuitively think it true of some other man that he *should* feel guilty, then we ought to be able to specify the nature of his guilt (and if he is a good man, win his agreement). I think I can construct a case which, with only small variation, highlights what is different in these two situations.

Consider the common practice of distributing rifles loaded with blanks to some of the members of a firing squad. The individual men are not told whether their own weapons are lethal, and so though all of them look like executioners to the victim in front of them, none of them know whether they are really executioners or not. The purpose of this stratagem is to relieve each man of the sense that he is a killer. It can hardly relieve him of whatever moral responsibility he incurs by serving on a firing squad, and that is not its purpose, for the execution is not thought to be (and let us grant this to be the case) an immoral or wrongful act. But the inhibition against killing another human being is so strong that even if the men believe that what they are doing is right, they will still feel guilty. Uncertainty as to their actual role apparently reduces the intensity of these feelings. If this is so, the stratagem is perfectly justifiable, and one can only rejoice in every case where it succeeds – for every success subtracts one from the number of innocent men who suffer.

But we would feel differently, I think, if we imagine a man who believes (and let us assume here that we believe also) either that capital punishment is wrong or that this particular victim is innocent, but who nevertheless agrees to participate in the firing squad for some overriding political or moral reason – I won't try to suggest what that reason might be. If he is comforted by the trick with the rifles, then we can be reasonably certain that his opposition to capital punishment or his belief in the victim's innocence is not morally serious. And if it is serious, he will not merely feel guilty, he will know that he is guilty (and we will know it too), though he may also believe (and we may agree) that he has good reasons for incurring the guilt. Our guilt feelings can be tricked away when they are isolated from our moral beliefs, as in the first case, but not when they are allied with them, as in the second. The beliefs themselves and the rules which are believed in can only be *overridden*, a painful process which forces a man to weigh the wrong he is willing to do in order to do right, and which leaves pain behind, and should do so, even after the decision has been made.

That is the dilemma of dirty hands as it has been experienced by political actors and written about in the literature of political action. I don't want to argue that it is only a political dilemma. No doubt we can get our hands dirty in private life also, and some-times, no doubt, we should. But the issue is posed most dramatically in politics for the three reasons that make political life the kind of life it is, because we claim to act for others but also serve ourselves, rule over others, and use violence against them. It is easy to get one's hands dirty in politics and it is often right to do so. But it is not easy to teach a good man how not to be good, nor is it easy to explain such a man to himself once he has committed whatever crimes are required of him. At least, it is not easy once we have agreed to use the word "crimes" and to live with (because we have no choice) the dilemma of dirty hands. Still, the agreement is common enough, and on its basis there have developed three broad traditions of explanation, three ways of thinking about dirty hands, which derive in some very general fashion from neoclassical, Protestant, and Catholic perspectives on politics and morality. I want to try to say something very briefly about each of them, or rather about a representative example of each of them, for each seems to me partly right. But I don't think I can put together the compound view that might be wholly right.

The first tradition is best represented by Machiavelli, the first man, so far as I know, to stage the paradox that I am examining. The good man who aims to found or reform a republic must, Machiavelli tells us, do terrible things to reach his goal. Like Romulus, he must murder his brother; like Numa, he must lie to the people. Sometimes, however, "when the act accuses, the result excuses,"[17] This sentence from *The Discourses* is often taken to mean that the politician's deceit and cruelty are justified by the good results he brings about. But if they were justified, it wouldn't be necessary to learn what Machiavelli claims to teach: how not to be good. It would only be necessary to learn how to be good in a new, more difficult, perhaps roundabout way. That is not Machiavelli's argument. His political judgments are indeed consequentialist in character, but not his moral judgments. We know whether cruelty is used well or badly by its effects over time. But that it is bad to use cruelty we know in some other way. The deceitful and cruel politician is excused (if he succeeds) only in the sense that the rest of us come to agree that the results were "worth it" or, more likely, that we simply forget his crimes when we praise his success.

It is important to stress Machiavelli's own commitment to the existence of moral standards. His paradox depends upon that commitment as it depends upon the general stability of the standards – which he upholds in his consistent use of words like good and bad.[18] If he wants the standards to be disregarded by good men more often than they are, he has nothing with which to replace them and no other way of recognizing the good men except by their allegiance to those same standards. It is exceedingly rare, he writes, that a good man is willing to employ bad means to become prince.[19] Machiavelli's purpose is to persuade such a person to make the attempt, and he holds out the supreme political rewards, power and glory, to the man who does so and succeeds. The good man is not rewarded (or excused), however, merely for his willingness to get his hands dirty. He must do bad things well. There is no reward for doing bad things badly, though they are done with the best of intentions. And so political action necessarily involves taking a risk. But it should be clear that what is risked is not personal goodness – *that is thrown away* – but power and glory. If the politician succeeds, he is a hero; eternal praise is the supreme reward for not being good.

What the penalties are for not being good, Machiavelli doesn't say, and it is probably for this reason above all that his moral sensitivity has so often been questioned. He is suspect not because he tells political actors they must get their hands dirty, but because he does not specify the state of mind appropriate to a man with dirty hands. A Machiavellian hero has no inwardness. What he thinks of himself we don't know. I would guess, along with most other readers of Machiavelli, that he basks in his glory. But then it is difficult to account for the strength of his original reluctance to learn how not to be good. In any case, he is the sort of man who is unlikely to keep a diary and so we cannot find out what he thinks. Yet we do want to know; above all, we want a record of his anguish. That is a sign of our own conscientiousness and of the impact on us of the second tradition of thought that I want to examine, in which personal anguish sometimes seems the only acceptable excuse for political crimes.

The second tradition is best represented, I think, by Max Weber, who outlines its essential features with great power at the very end of his essay "Politics as a Vocation." For Weber, the good man with dirty hands is a hero still, but he is a tragic hero. In part, his tragedy is that though politics is his vocation, he has not been called by God and so cannot be justified by Him. Weber's hero is alone in a world that seems to belong to Satan, and his vocation is entirely his own choice. He still wants what Christian magistrates have always wanted, both to do good in the world and to save his soul, but now these two ends have come into sharp contradiction. They are contradictory because of the necessity for violence in a world where God has not instituted the sword. The politician takes the sword himself, and only by doing so does he measure up to his vocation. With full consciousness of what he is doing, he does bad in order to do good, and surrenders his soul. He "lets himself in," Weber says, "for the diabolic forces lurking in all violence." Perhaps Machiavelli also meant to suggest that his hero surrenders salvation in exchange for glory, but he does not explicitly say so. Weber is absolutely clear: "the genius or demon of politics lives in an inner tension with the god of love . . . [which] can at any time lead to an irreconcilable conflict."[20] His politician views this conflict when it comes with a tough realism, never pretends that it might be solved by compromise, chooses politics once again, and turns decisively away from love. Weber writes about this choice with a passionate high-mindedness that makes a concern for one's soul seem no more elevated than a concern for one's flesh. Yet the reader never doubts that his mature, superbly trained, relentless, objective, responsible, and disciplined political leader is also a suffering servant. His choices are hard and painful, and he pays the price not only while making them but forever after. A man doesn't lose his soul one day and find it the next.

The difficulties with this view will be clear to anyone who has ever met a suffering servant. Here is a man who lies, intrigues, sends other men to their death – and suffers. He does what he must do with a heavy heart. None of us can know, he tells us, how much it costs him to do his duty. Indeed, we cannot, for he himself fixes the price he pays. And that is the trouble with this view of political crime. We suspect the suffering servant of either masochism or hypocrisy or both, and while we are often wrong, we are not always wrong. Weber attempts to resolve the problem of dirty hands entirely within the confines of the individual conscience, but I am inclined to think that this is neither possible nor desirable. The self-awareness of the tragic hero is obviously of great value. We want the politician to have an inner life at least something like that which Weber describes. But sometimes the hero's suffering needs to be socially expressed (for like punishment, it confirms and reinforces our sense that certain acts are wrong). And equally important, it sometimes needs to be socially limited. We don't want to be ruled by men who have lost their souls. A politician with dirty hands needs a soul, and it is best for us all if he has some hope of personal salvation, however that is conceived. It is not the case that when he does bad in order to do good he surrenders himself forever to the demon of politics. He commits a determinate crime, and he must pay a determinate penalty. When he has done so, his hands will be clean again, or as clean as human hands can ever be. So the Catholic Church has always taught, and this teaching is central to the third tradition that I want to examine.

Once again I will take a latter-day and a lapsed representative of the tradition and consider Albert Camus' *The Just Assassins*. The heroes of this play are terrorists at work in nineteenth-century Russia. The dirt on their hands is human blood. And yet Camus' admiration for them, he tells us, is complete. We consent to being criminals, one of them says, but there is nothing with which anyone can reproach us. Here is the dilemma of dirty hands in a new form. The heroes are innocent criminals, just assassins, because, having killed, they are prepared to die – *and will die*. Only their execution, by the same despotic authorities they are attacking, will complete the action in which they are engaged: dying, they need make no excuses. That is the end of their guilt and pain. The execution is not so much punishment as self-punishment and expiation. On the scaffold they wash their hands clean and, unlike the suffering servant, they die happy.

Now the argument of the play when presented in so radically simplified a form may seem a little bizarre, and perhaps it is marred by the moral extremism of Camus' politics. "Political action has limits," he says in a preface to the volume containing *The Just Assassins*, "and there is no good and just action but what recognizes those limits and if it must go beyond them, at least accepts death."[21] I am less interested here in the violence of that "at least" – what else does he have in mind? – than in the sensible doctrine that it exaggerates. That doctrine might best be described by an analogy: just assassination, I want to suggest, is like civil disobedience. In both men violate a set of rules, go beyond a moral or legal limit, in order to do what they believe they should do. At the same time, they acknowledge their responsibility for the violation by accepting punishment or doing penance. But there is also a difference between the two, which has to do with the difference between law and morality. In most cases of civil disobedience the laws of the state are broken for moral reasons, and the state provides the punishment. In most cases of dirty hands moral rules are broken for reasons of state, and no one provides the punishment. There is rarely a Czarist executioner waiting in the wings for politicians with dirty hands, even the most deserving among them. Moral rules are not usually enforced against the sort of actor I am considering, largely because he acts in an official capacity. If they were enforced, dirty hands would be no problem. We would simply honor the man who did bad in order to do good, and at the same time we would punish him. We would honor him for the good he has done, and we would punish him for the bad he has done. We would punish him, that is, for the same reasons we punish anyone else; it is not my purpose here to defend any particular view of punishment. In any case, there seems no way to establish or enforce the punishment. Short of the priest and the confessional, there are no authorities to whom we might entrust the task.

I am nevertheless inclined to think Camus' view the most attractive of the three, if only because it requires us at least to imagine a punishment or a penance that fits the crime and so to examine closely the nature of the crime. The others do not require that. Once he has launched his career, the crimes of Machiavelli's prince seem subject only to prudential control. And the crimes of Weber's tragic hero are limited only by *his* capacity for suffering and not, as they should be, by *our* capacity for suffering. In neither case is there any explicit reference back to the moral code, once it has, at great personal cost to be sure, been set aside. The question posed by Sartre's Hoerderer (whom I suspect of being a suffering servant) is rhetorical, and the answer is obvious (I have already given it), but the characteristic sweep of both is disturbing. Since it is concerned only with those crimes that ought to be committed, the dilemma of dirty hands seems to exclude questions of degree. Wanton or excessive cruelty is not at issue, any more than is cruelty directed at bad ends. But political action is so uncertain that politicians necessarily take moral as well as political risks, committing crimes that they only think ought to be committed. They override the rules without ever being certain that they have found the best way to the results they hope to achieve, and we don't want them to do that too quickly or too often. So it is important that the moral stakes be very high – which is to say, that the rules be rightly valued. That, I suppose, is the reason for Camus' extremism. Without the executioner, however, there is no one to set the stakes or maintain the values except ourselves, and probably no way to do either except through philosophic reiteration and political activity.

"We shall not abolish lying by refusing to tell lies," says Hoerderer, "but by using every means at hand to abolish social classes."[22] I suspect we shall not abolish lying at all, but we might see to it that fewer lies were told if we contrived to deny power and glory to the greatest liars – except, of course, in the case of those lucky few whose extraordinary achievements make us forget the lies they told. If Hoerderer succeeds in abolishing social classes, perhaps he will join the lucky few. Meanwhile, he lies, manipulates, and kills, and we must make sure he pays the price. We won't be able to do that, however, without getting our own hands dirty, and then we must find some way of paying the price ourselves.

Notes

1 *Philosophy & Public Affairs* I, no. 2 (Winter 1971/72): Thomas Nagel, "War and Massacre," pp. 123–144; R.B. Brandt, "Utilitarianism and the Rules of War," pp. 145–165; and R.M. Hare, "Rules of War and Moral Reasoning," pp. 166–181.

2 For Nagel's description of a possible "moral blind alley," see "War and Massacre," pp. 142–144. Bernard Williams has made a similar suggestion, though without quite acknowledging it as his own: "many people can recognize the thought that a certain course of action is, indeed, the best thing to do on the whole in the circumstances, but that doing it involves doing something wrong" (*Morality: An Introduction to Ethics* [New York, 1972], p. 93).

3 Jean-Paul Sartre, *Dirty Hands*, in *No Exit and Three Other Plays*, trans. Lionel Abel (New York, n.d.), p. 224.

4 Hare, "Rules of War and Moral Reasoning," pp. 173–178, esp. p. 174: "the simple principles of the deontologist . . . have their place at the level of character-formation (moral education and self-education)."

5 In *From Max Weber: Essays in Sociology*, trans. and ed. Hans H. Gerth and C. Wright Mills (New York, 1946), pp. 77–128.

6 See *The Prince*, chap. XV; cf. *The Discourses*; bk. I, chaps. IX and XVIII. I quote from the Modern Library edition of the two works (New York, 1950), p. 57.

7 I leave aside the question of whether the prisoner is himself responsible for the terrorist campaign. Perhaps he opposed it in meetings of the rebel organization. In any case, whether he deserves to be punished or not, he does not deserve to be tortured.

8 Other writers argued that Christians must never kill, even in a just war; and there was also an intermediate position which suggests the origins of the idea of dirty hands. Thus Basil The Great (Bishop of Caesarea in the fourth century AD): "Killing in war was differentiated by our fathers from murder . . . nevertheless, perhaps it would be well that those whose hands are unclean abstain from communion for three years." Here dirty hands are a kind of impurity or unworthiness, which is not the same as guilt, though closely related to it. For a general

survey of these and other Christian views, see Roland H. Bainton, *Christian Attitudes Toward War and Peace* (New York, 1960), esp. chaps. 5–7.

9 Brandt's rules do not appear to be of the sort that can be overridden – except perhaps by a soldier who decides that he just *won't* kill any more civilians, no matter what cause is served – since all they require is careful calculation. But I take it that rules of a different sort, which have the form of ordinary injunctions and prohibitions, can and often do figure in what is called "rule-utilitarianism."

10 J.L. Austin, "A Plea for Excuses," in *Philosophical Papers*, ed. J.O. Urmson and G.J. Warnock (Oxford, 1961), pp. 123–152.

11 *Hamlet* 3.4.178.

12 Compare the following lines from Bertold Brecht's poem "To Posterity": "Alas, we/ Who wished to lay the foundations of kindness/ Could not ourselves be kind . . ." (*Selected Poems*, trans. H.R. Hays [New York, 1969], p. 177). This is more of an excuse, less of a justification (the poem is an *apologia*).

13 Robert Nozick discusses some of the possible effects of overriding a rule in his "Moral Complications and Moral Structures," *Natural Law Forum* 13 (1968): 34–35 and notes. Nozick suggests that what may remain after one has broken a rule (for good reasons) is a "duty to make reparations." He does not call this "guilt," though the two notions are closely connected.

14 Hare, "Rules of War and Moral Reasoning," p. 179.

15 There is another possible utilitarian position, suggested in Maurice Merleau-Ponty's *Humanism and Terror*, trans. John O'Neill (Boston, 1970). According to this view, the agony and the guilt feelings experienced by the man who makes a "dirty hands" decision derive from his radical uncertainty about the actual outcome. Perhaps the awful thing he is doing will be done in vain; the results he hopes for won't occur; the only outcome will be the pain he has caused or the deceit he has fostered. Then (and only then) he will indeed have committed a crime. On the other hand, if the expected good does come, then (and only then) he can abandon his guilt feelings; he can say, and the rest of us must agree, that he is justified. This is a kind of delayed utilitarianism, where justification is a matter of actual and not at all of predicted outcomes. It is not implausible to imagine a political actor anxiously awaiting the "verdict of history." But suppose the verdict is in his favor (assuming that there is a *final* verdict or a statute of limitations on possible verdicts): he will surely feel relieved – more so, no doubt, than the rest of us. I can see no reason, however, why he should think himself justified, if he is a good man and knows that what he did was wrong. Perhaps the victims of his crime, seeing the happy result, will absolve him, but history has no powers of absolution. Indeed, history is more likely to play tricks on our moral judgement. Predicted outcomes are at least thought to follow from our own acts (this is the prediction), but actual outcomes almost certainly have a multitude of causes, the combination of which may well be fortuitous. Merleau-Ponty stresses the risks of political decision-making so heavily that he turns politics into a gamble with time and circumstance. But the anxiety of the gambler is of no great moral interest. Nor is it much of a barrier, as Merleau-Ponty's book makes all too clear, to the commission of the most terrible crimes.

16 Cf. the cases suggested by David Ross, *The Right and the Good* (Oxford, 1930), pp. 56–57, and E.F. Carritt, *Ethical and Political Thinking* (Oxford, 1947), p. 65.

17 *The Discourses*, bk. I, chap. IX (p. 139).

18 For a very different view of Machiavelli, see Isaiah Berlin, "The Question of Machiavelli," *The New York Review of Books*, 4 November 1971.

19 *The Discourses*, bk. I, chap. XVIII (p. 171).

20 "Politics as a Vocation," pp. 125–126. But sometimes a political leader does choose the "absolutist" side of the conflict, and Weber writes (p. 127) that it is "immensely moving when a *mature* man . . . aware of a responsibility for the consequences of his conduct . . . reaches a

point where he says: 'Here I stand; I can do no other,'" Unfortunately, he does not suggest just where that point is or even where it might be.

21 *Caligula and Three Other Plays* (New York, 1958), p. x. (The preface is translated by Justin O'Brian, the plays by Stuart Gilbert.)

22 *Dirty Hands*, p. 223.

43

JEAN HAMPTON

The nature of immorality

[There are three common explanations of immorality. According to *the Manichean explanation*, immorality arises from a division within the self, with the wayward part determining the action. According to the *ignorance explanation*, immorality is due to ignorance of right and wrong. According to the *indifference explanation*, the immoral agent is unaware that his action falls within the scope of a moral injunction. A successful explanation of immorality – the *defiance explanation* – must present an adequate alternative to these three theories. It must show,] first, against the Manichean view, that the immoral action is chosen by the self, and not caused by a self-part. Second, against the ignorance explanation, [it must show that] the immoral action is not chosen in ignorance that it is morally wrong. And third, against the indifference explanation, [it must show that] the choice of the immoral action is made in the knowledge that the moral injunction against the action is supposed to apply to oneself (so that one is inside the scope of morality). Can an explanation of immorality successfully include all these features?

The difficulty with doing so is that an explanation with these three features seems to represent the agent who makes the immoral choice as irrational. Bill Cosby, in a comedy routine, says that when he confronts his errant children after their wrongdoings, they admit that when they did the bad thing they knew they shouldn't be doing it. "So why," he asks his audience, "did they do it? There is only one explanation: brain damage."

Cosby's joke turns on our inability to comprehend the rationale behind knowing what is right but choosing to do wrong. Perhaps all this means is that the phenomenon of immorality is mysterious. But those people, such as myself, who are unsympathetic to philosophical mysteries will argue that any explanation of immorality that gives rise to such a mystery is a failure, because it fails to make immoral action intelligible. Still, I think it is possible to develop further this explanation of immorality along lines that will generate an intelligible account of immoral action that actually fits with many of our considered convictions about what such action is like. The explanation I will develop

Source: "The Nature of Immorality," *Social Philosophy & Policy*, vol. 7, no. 1, 1989.

is naturally linked with the idea that the authority of moral imperatives comes from the fact that they are categorical. I call it the *defiance explanation*, and it is very old, deeply entrenched in the Judeo-Christian tradition, and implicit in the tale of Adam and Eve, which is supposed to be an explanation of the origin of human evil.

Consider that tale: God, who made heaven and earth, also made Adam, and placed him in a bountiful garden called Eden, in which there grew a tree of the knowledge of good and evil. About the latter, God specifically issues a command: "You may eat from every tree in the garden but not from the tree of knowledge of good and evil: for on the day that you eat from it, you will certainly die." Thereafter, Eve was made and although "they were both naked, the man and his wife, . . . they had no feeling of shame towards one another." Life, however, did not proceed smoothly; the story continues:

> The serpent was more crafty than any wild creature that the Lord God had made. He said to the woman, "Is it true that God has forbidden you to eat from any tree in the garden?" The woman answered the serpent, "We may eat the fruit of any tree in the garden, except for the tree in the middle of the garden: God has forbidden us either to eat or to touch the fruit of that: if we do, we shall die." The serpent said, "Of course you will not die. God knows that as soon as you eat it, your eyes will be opened and you will be like gods knowing both good and evil." When the woman saw that the fruit of the tree was good to eat, and that it was pleasing to the eye and tempting to contemplate, she took some and ate it. She also gave her husband some and he ate it. Then the eyes of both of them were opened and they discovered that they were naked: so they stitched fig-leaves together and made themselves loincloths.

When God found out what they had done he was furious; he angrily condemned the serpent, the woman, and the man, and punished all three of them for their actions.

How does this tale explain the origin of human immorality? Consider that Adam and Eve's guilt is associated with doing something which was expressly forbidden by God. The command not to eat of the fruit of the tree of knowledge is portrayed as authoritative: not in the sense of being hypothetical, but solely because it is God's command. It is authoritative in and of itself just because He made it and He is the supreme commander who *must* be obeyed (don't ask why; God doesn't have to justify himself). Nonetheless it is interesting that God links that command with what looks like a sanction – death is threatened to anyone who eats the fruit.

Why didn't Adam and Eve obey that command? Were they somehow acting out of ignorance? The author certainly proposes this explanation of their moral failure, for the knowledge of good and evil which is, as we discussed, a necessary component of culpability only comes *after* they've eaten the fruit. It would seem that before the apple was eaten, they could not be morally culpable because they did not have the requisite knowledge of right and wrong to make that guilt possible. After the apple was eaten, that knowledge was gained and they "fell into sin" . . .

But I want to argue that the Genesis author finally abandons this ignorance explanation of immorality and presents a very different account of its source. As we discussed, we generally think that if I don't know that I am doing something wrong (and if my moral ignorance is not the result of negligence), then I am thereby excused from full culpability. So if I am Eve and I have *no* moral knowledge, then all of my actions and decisions in this state – including my choice to eat the fruit – would not be subject to moral blame. But this means the ignorance explanation of Eve's fall cannot make her culpable for her fall. And if she isn't culpable for her fall, then she cannot be considered culpable for any of the immoral actions performed after, and as a result of, that fall.

There is no doubt, however, that the author of the story wants to see Eve and Adam as culpable for eating the fruit, and thus for their descent into sin, as well as for their immoral actions subsequent to that descent. God has very strong reactive attitudes towards them; not only does he blame them for eating the fruit, but he is also presented as furiously indignant with them for what they did, sentencing them to terrible punishments. Even more interesting, the story makes clear that Eve and Adam decide to eat the fruit *knowing that God forbade it*. So it seems they had at least some moral knowledge already, i.e., the knowledge that it was wrong to eat of the tree, and then *defied* the prohibition in a way that resulted in their being held culpable and, finally, punished. They did not ignorantly stumble into evil but chose it, with their eyes open, knowing they should not.

So I would argue that, in the end, the Genesis author explains the source of human immorality as, to use Milton's words in *Paradise Lost*, a "foul revolt." This defiance explanation of immorality is, despite some similarities, importantly different from both the ignorance and indifference explanations discussed earlier.

On the indifference model, the wrongdoer is presented as someone for whom the moral imperatives have no authority whatsoever. Such a person doesn't have to rebel against the authority of morality because she is already free of its rule (although, in the guise of the law, it might exercise power over her in a way that she regrets). Compare a person from one nation-state who doesn't have to rebel against the authorities of another nation-state which has no authority over her; similarly, the indifference explanation of immorality presents immoral people as citizens of a different "moral realm" from the rest of us. But on the defiance model, the wrongdoer is presented as someone who recognizes that prima facie she is supposed to be subject to the same moral commands we are. She sees herself as inside the scope of moral injunctions: she feels the claims of its authority upon her. Nonetheless she *resists* and challenges that subjugation, like a political rebel in a civil war, in an effort to make her own desires authoritative.

I want to be precise about what the defiance is. It is a certain kind of choice. But it is not the choice to do an action knowing that it is wrong (i.e., knowing that it is prohibited by a moral injunction). This choice is not even sufficient for us to consider a person culpable for an action, since she might have performed it under duress or in a situation of dire necessity. (A bank teller who hands over her money to a gunman is not culpable for her action because we do not think that the injunction against contributing to a theft is authoritative for her in the circumstances.) Instead, the defiance that makes her culpable is her choice to do an action which she knows to be wrong, i.e., prohibited by a moral injunction, and where she knows this injunction claims to be the ruling principle of her choices. The word "claims" here is important. She doesn't know that this injunction must be authoritative over her; she knows only that it claims to be authoritative (where the demands of society or family or certain styles of reasoning might be thought to generate that claim). It is this claim that she resists, repudiates, fights off, as she chooses to do otherwise than it directs. The injunction is therefore not something that she can be merely indifferent towards, because she understands that she is supposed to be governed by it, so that its rulership must be fought off. One might say that the immoral person is attempting to establish herself as *amoral*; if her rebellion succeeds, she will show herself to be outside the scope of its imperatives. But by the very act of flouting the moral injunction, she understands that she is supposed to be inside its scope and rejects its power over her.

Let us return to the Bill Cosby joke. Does this explanation of immorality give us a better account of what is happening in the mind of the immoral person than Cosby's imputation of temporary brain damage? It does, in two ways. First, it pinpoints the mental act that constitutes the guilty mind: namely, the flouting of the authoritative command. Second, it suggests a reason for the flouting. Rebels reject the rulership of commanders not only when they perceive the commander to be directing them to act in a way that harms their interests but also when they think they can "get away" with the rebellion (either because it is possible to evade the bad consequences of the rebellion, or because they believe its costs will be outweighed by its benefits). So Eve takes the fruit and flouts God's commands, both because she is confident that getting the knowledge it promises is more desirable than remaining in her present state and because she is confident that she will be able to "handle" God if he is displeased by her defiance. As the text says, she sets herself up to be a rival god, directing her own actions and taking orders from her own will. In just this way, immoral people see moral commands as the enemy of their interests (believing neither Hobbesian claims that the commands are really precepts of enlightened self-interest, nor Kantian claims that they arise from one's own rational will), and such people expect that the authority of these commands is something they can successfully defy.

This account of the nature of immorality therefore fits with the idea that moral imperatives are authoritative because they are categorical. Knowingly defying moral imperatives whose authority is hypothetical doesn't seem to make any sense;[1] why would I resist doing an action if I know I should do it, insofar as it would help me to achieve my conception of the good? But if no such connection is made between moral actions and a person's good, if, instead, moral actions are presented simply as authoritative in and of themselves and suggestive of actions which can and frequently do *conflict* with one's self-interest, then the defiance explanation suggests itself naturally. Immorality is simply a rebellion against a kind of authority which one may very well dislike, given the way if often opposes one's own interests. I would argue that Kant implicitly assumed this account in his *Religion Within the Limits of Reason Alone*, where immorality is explained as arising from "insubordination" by one who defies the Moral Law and puts the satisfaction of his own desires ahead of doing his duty.[2] And in the Judeo-Christian tradition, immoral people are frequently presented as rebels; for example, in Christian mythology the most evil person of them all is the Devil, who is also depicted as the most thoroughly rebellious of God's creatures.

Either in a secular or non-secular version, I would argue that this account of immorality fits well with the things we say and feel about immoral people. For example, it explains the way in which "selfishness" is supposed to be a reason for immorality. The immoral person is a rebel who sets herself up as the supreme authority for her actions, defying the claim which morality is supposed to exercise. It is not what morality commands but what *she* wants which will prevail. And her pursuit of what she wants frequently results in harm to other people – whom the moral commands were protecting. It also explains how immorality comes in degrees: the more extensive the rebellion against morality, the worse the rebel, and the more negative our judgement of him.

Another virtue of this account is that it explains the kinds of reactive attitudes we have towards wrongdoers. Insofar as it presents immoral actions as chosen by a person rather than caused by a motivation, it makes sense to respond negatively to the person who made the choices. We who are (supposedly) on the side of morality find the wrongdoer's rebellious choices offensive. She is not someone to be pitied, but someone to be resented, resisted, fought against, or even despised because of her allegiance. She has sided with that which is the enemy of the authority we see ourselves as respecting and serving.

This account of immorality makes our criticisms of her not external (which is all they could be on the indifference model) but internal, so that this account presupposes an internalist thesis about moral reasons. Because the wrongdoer is rebelling against the moral authority of morality, she knows that prima facie she is subject to it. Insofar as we repudiate her rebellion, we say that she should have acted otherwise not only from *our* standpoint but also from *her* standpoint, because we think that she, like us, has reason to be moral. Her action does not show her to be making any simple-minded mistake about what she ought to do; on the contrary, she knows exactly what she ought to do. Instead, we criticize her because we see her as mistaken in thinking she can successfully overthrow moral injunctions and live solely as she chooses. "She can't get away with it," we insist (a thought that often motivates retributive punishment).[3]

Note also that this account leaves room for a distinction between being immoral and being (merely) morally mistaken. If someone accepts that she should be moral (because it will enable her to realize, rather than damage, her "true nature"), but doesn't know how to be moral and makes a mistake, she is only *morally mistaken*, not immoral. She is immoral only if (as Kant suggested) she *defies* morality's claim that it offers more for her than immorality, believing that what it offers her is different from (and seemingly less satisfying than) what morality offers.

Connected to the internal sense of "should have done otherwise" are the emotions of guilt and shame, and these emotions are nicely explicated on the defiance view. Moral rebels are often defeated, as Eve and Adam were when their rebellion was discovered and punished by God. And if the moral commands really do have categorical authority, then with defeat may come the awareness that one's immoral actions were the result of an unjustified and unjustifiable rebellion against morality. This awareness can thus produce shame, a kind of misery over what one is (a traitor to the right cause) and guilt, a kind of misery over the unjustified and unjustifiable harm one has caused to others.

Finally, this account fits well with our reactive attitudes towards wrongdoers other than ourselves. Our anger at them is a function of the fact that we see them as knowingly aligning themselves against morality. We despise their allegiance. Their knowledge that they are violating an authority that is supposed to rule them is the knowledge which makes them culpable. Our anger, however, is defused if we discover that their action did not arise out of this hateful allegiance, e.g., if it was performed in ignorance of the prohibition against it, or by accident. In fact, it is striking how many of the excusing conditions seem to pick out those states of minds in which there could be no real rebellion against moral authority and, hence, no culpability. People who do wrong out of ignorance, or mental illness, or because of a mistake do not challenge morality's authority. And those who act wrongly because they are coerced into doing so do not initiate a rebellion against this authority, but are forced to act against it in a way that they despise.

The natural way in which our everyday responses to ourselves and others are explicated by the defiance account of morality suggests that these responses might be generated by that account, perhaps implicit in our culture because of our Judeo-Christian heritage. But even if this is true, it is not an argument for it. If the defiance account of immorality is the theoretical source of the things that we say and feel about immoral people, then we must ask whether or not this account is one which, upon reflection, we can rationally embrace.

There are a number of problems one can raise with it. First, does it really fit the way we want to think about the "mildly immoral," who do wrong reluctantly, neither shaking their fist at morality nor enjoying any challenge to it, perhaps beset by a bad conscience? Second, doesn't it fail to capture the way in which negligent people are immoral insofar as negligence is, by definition, immoral action that the agent doesn't intend to perform? Third, does it really do an acceptable job of representing the more evil among us, insofar as it makes their defiance something undertaken in ignorance of the fact that it cannot succeed, an ignorance that might be thought to undercut their culpability? And fourth, does it really incorporate an intelligible conception of morality's authority? Consider that in order to ensure that those who commit wrongs cannot be excused by reason of ignorance, the explanation must impute to people knowledge of morality's claim to hold authority over them. Yet it must also represent this authority as something they not only do not appreciate but want to overthrow. Now we understand how we human beings can have a human authority over us that we hate and wish to remove, but can we sensibly be said to respond to the authority of morality in this way? Interestingly, Kant did not want to impute to morality a hateful authority but an authority that all of us fully understand and are in awe of; however, if this is so, why do we defy it? It is as if, says Kant, we have a proof against the possibility of immorality when we reflect on morality's authority, and not an explanation of it:

> It is . . . *inconceivable*, therefore, how the motivating forces of the sensuous nature should be able to gain ascendancy over a reason which commands with such authority. For if all the world were to proceed in conformity with the precepts of the law, we should say that everything comes to pass according to natural order, and no one would think of so much as inquiring after the cause.[4]

Kant ends up characterizing immorality as "inscrutable." But defenders of the defiance explanation will want to insist that immorality is perfectly understandable, given the attitude all of us human beings take towards what is in fact an unpleasant, even hateful, authority that commands us to forgo what is in our interest. What defenders of the defiance account owe the skeptics is an account of how morality can still have genuine authority over us and not simply mere power – for example, psychological power – given our distaste for (perhaps even hatred of) its commands.

Unlike the difficulties plaguing the other explanations of immorality, these four difficulties plaguing the defiance account are not obviously insurmountable, and I will attempt solutions of them in a forthcoming article.[5] But all of them, particularly the last one, highlight how problematic it is to explain why, and in what way, morality is authoritative for us. If immorality is a product of a person's defiance of its purported mastery over him, then the way to stop his immorality is to convince him either that its authority over him is good rather than hateful, or that if he rebels he must always lose. However, our belief in his inevitable defeat is based more on faith than on argument, and the idea that morality's rule is always attractive and never hateful is something that all of us who are prone to immoral acts on occasion have trouble sustaining. We await proof that we must always accept morality as our master.

Notes

1   However, Aquinas seemed to think it did. Although Aquinas's natural laws were derived from God, they were nonetheless hypothetical imperatives. In considering why people do not follow them, he seemed to be struck by Aristotle's uncertainty as to whether wrongdoers were ignorant that their deeds were wrong or aware of that fact. He attempts to reconcile the Aristotelian position by maintaining that wrongdoers are ignorant, but not in a way that excuses them, for their ignorance is willful – they know they should learn what the good is, but refuse. So, in the end, Aquinas makes defiance, rather than ignorance, the ultimate source of wrongdoing. Yet why someone would defiantly refuse to learn the good is never explained. See *Summa Theologica*, first part of the second part, question 6, article 8. "Does Ignorance Render An Act Involuntary?"

2   According to Kant, a person is the author of evil deeds and his own evil character when he orders the incentives to action (*Anlagen*) incorrectly. They are ordered correctly when the moral law (which he believes can motivate us to act) is placed first, such that nothing is performed which that law does not sanction. But immorality results from an ordering in which the moral law is subordinate to the desires:

> man (even the best) is evil only in that he reverses the moral order of the incentives when he adopts them into his maxim. He adopts indeed, the Moral Law along with the law of self-love; yet when he becomes aware that they cannot remain on a par with each other but that one must be subordinated to the other as its supreme condition, he makes the incentive of self-love and its inclinations the condition of obedience to the moral law; whereas, on the contrary, the latter, as the supreme condition of the satisfaction of the former, ought to have been adopted into the universal maxim of the will. (*Religion Within the Limits of Reason Alone*, pp. 31–32).

So the immoral person is the one who *sides with* his own inclinations over morality; insofar as he reverses the proper order of the incentives, he rebels against the authority of the moral law, and it is in virtue of that rebellion that he is condemned.

3   For more on the connection between this idea and retribution. see ch. 4 of my *Forgiveness and Mercy*, written with Jeffrie Murphy (Cambridge: Cambridge University Press, 1988).

4   *Religion Within the Limits of Reason Alone*, p. 52n. My emphasis.

5   See "Mens Rea," in *Social Philosophy & Policy*, vol. 7, no. 2 (Spring 1990); this issue is forthcoming as *Crime, Culpability, and Remedy* (Oxford: Basil Blackwell, 1990).

44

THE MODEL
PENAL CODE
Criminality

Section 1.14 Definitions

In this Code unless a different meaning plainly is required: . . .

(2) "act" or "action" means a bodily movement whether voluntary or involuntary;

(3) "voluntary" has the meaning specified in Section 2.01;

(4) "omission" means a failure to act;

(5) "conduct" means an action or omission and its accompanying state of mind, or where relevant, a series of acts and omissions . . .

Article II General principles of liability

Section 2.01 Requirement of Voluntary Act; Omission as Basis of Liability; Possession as an Act

(1) A person is not guilty of an offense unless his liability is based on conduct which includes a voluntary act or the omission to perform an act which it was physically possible to perform.

(2) The following are not voluntary acts within the meaning of this section:

(a) a reflex or convulsion;

(b) a bodily movement during unconsciousness [coma?] or sleep;

(c) conduct during hypnosis or resulting from hypnotic suggestion;

(d) a bodily movement that otherwise is not a product of the effort or determination of the actor, either conscious or habitual.

(3) Liability for the commission of an offense may not be based on an omission unaccompanied by action unless:

Source: *The Model Penal Code*, Philadelphia, PA: American Law Institute, 1956.

(a) the omission is expressly made sufficient by the law defining the offense; or

(b) a duty to perform the omitted act is otherwise imposed by law.

(4) Possession is an act, within the meaning of this section, if the possessor knowingly procured or received the thing possessed or was aware of his control for a sufficient period to have been able to terminate his possession.

Comments to article II General principles of liability

Section 2.01 *Requirement of Voluntary Act; Omission as Basis of Liability; Possession as an Act*

1. Paragraph (1) requires that criminal liability be based on conduct and that the conduct which gives rise to liability include a voluntary act or the omission to perform an act which it was physically possible to have performed. This is not, of course, to say that these conditions are enough for the establishment of liability but only that they are essential elements when liability obtains.

That penal sanctions cannot be employed with justice unless these requirements are satisfied seems wholly clear. The law cannot hope to deter involuntary movement or to stimulate action that cannot physically be performed; the sense of personal security would be short-lived in a society where such movement or inactivity could lead to formal social condemnation of the sort that a conviction necessarily entails. People whose involuntary movements threaten harm to others may present a public health or safety problem, calling for therapy or even for custodial commitment; they do not present a problem of correction.

These are axioms under the present law, though dealt with only indirectly by our penal legislation in the states where legislation touches the subject at all. See, e.g., *California Penal Code* §20: "In every crime or public offense there must exist a union, or joint operation of act and intent, or criminal negligence"; *ibid*. §26: "All persons are capable of committing crimes except . . . persons who committed the act charged without being conscious thereof" and "persons who committed the act or made the omission charged through misfortune or by accident, when it appears that there was no evil design, intention or culpable negligence."

2. It will be noted that the formulation does not state that liability must be based on the voluntary act or the omission *simpliciter*, but rather upon conduct which *includes* such action or omission. The distinction has some analytical importance. If the driver of an automobile loses consciousness with the result that he runs over a pedestrian, none of the movements or omissions that accompany or follow this loss of consciousness may in themselves give rise to liability. But a prior voluntary act, such as the act of driving, or a prior omission, such as failing to stop as he felt illness approaching, may, under given circumstances, be regarded as sufficiently negligent for liability to

be imposed. In that event, however, liability is based on the entire course of conduct, including the specific conduct that resulted in the injury. It is enough, in short, that the conduct included action or omission that satisfied the requirements of paragraph (1), and the further requirements for the establishment of culpability, as to which see Section 2.02 . . .

(3) Paragraph (2) defines "voluntary" partially and indirectly by describing movements that are excluded from the meaning of the term.

Any definition must exclude a reflex or convulsion. The case of unconsciousness is equally clear when unconsciousness implies collapse, or coma, as perhaps it does in ordinary usage of the term. There are, however, states of physical activity where self-awareness is grossly impaired or even absent, as in epileptic fugue, amnesia, extreme confusion and equivalent conditions . . .

The case of hypnotic suggestion also seems to warrant explicit treatment. Hypnosis differs from both sleep and fugue but it is characterized by such dependence of the subject on the hypnotist, that it does not seem politic to treat conduct resulting from hypnotic suggestions as voluntary, despite the state of consciousness involved . . .

Paragraph 2(d) formulates a residual category of involuntary movements, describing them as those that "otherwise are not a product of the effort or determination of the actor, either conscious or habitual." The formulation seeks to express the main content of the idea of an "external manifestation of the actor's will" (*Restatement of Torts*, §2), without putting the matter as a definition of the will. The formulation would, of course, cover the classic case whether the actor is moved by force, as distinguished from threat; such motion never has been viewed as action of the victim. (See, e.g., *Hale, Pleas of the Crown*, I, 434.) In other respects it is designed to have only the marginal meaning of the Torts Restatement definition of an act. The difficult cases are dealt with specifically in paragraphs (b) and (c).

It should be added that the application of these provisions to cases of self-induced intoxication or narcosis presents a special problem which will be dealt with in detail in Section 2.08.

4. Paragraph (3) states the conventional position with respect to omission unaccompanied by action as a basis of liability. Unless the omission is expressly made sufficient by the law defining the offense, a duty to perform the omitted act must have been otherwise imposed by law for the omission to have the same standing as a voluntary act for purposes of liability. It should, of course, suffice, as the courts now hold, that the duty arises under some branch of the civil law. If it does, this minimal requirement is satisfied, though whether the omission constitutes an offense depends as well on many other factors.

Section 2.02   General Requirements of Culpability

(1) Minimum requirements of culpability.

Except as provided in Section 2.05, a person is not guilty of an offense unless he acted purposely, knowingly, recklessly, or negligently, as the law may require, with respect to each material element of the offense.

(2) Kinds of culpability defined.

(a) *Purposely*

A person acts purposely with respect to a material element of an offense when:

(1) if the element involves the nature of his conduct or a result thereof, it is his conscious object to engage in conduct of that nature or to cause such a result; and

(2) if the element involves the attendant circumstances, he knows of the existence of such circumstances.

(b) *Knowingly*

A person acts knowingly with respect to a material element of an offense when:

(1) if the element involves the nature of his conduct or the attendant circumstances, he knows that his conduct is of that nature or he knows of the existence of such circumstances; and

(2) if the element involves a result of his conduct, he knows that his conduct will necessarily cause such a result.

Comments

Section 2.02   General Requirements of Culpability

This section attempts the extremely difficult task of articulating the general *mens rea* requirements for the establishment of liability.

1. The approach is based upon the view that clear analysis requires that the question of the kind of culpability required to establish the commission of an offense be faced separately with respect to each material element of the crime; and that . . . the concept of "material element" include the facts that negative defenses on the merits as well as the facts included in the definition of the crime.

   The reason for this treatment is best stated by suggesting an example. Given a charge of murder, the prosecution normally must prove intent to kill (or at least to cause serious bodily injury) to establish the required culpability with respect to that element of the crime that involves the result of the defendant's conduct. But if self-defense is claimed as a defense, it is enough to show that the defendant's belief in the necessity of his conduct to save himself did not rest upon reasonable grounds. As to the first element, in short, purpose or knowledge is required; as to the second negligence appears to be sufficient. Failure to face the question separately with respect to each of these ingredients of the offense results in obvious confusion.

A second illustration is afforded by the law of rape. A purpose to effect the sexual relation is most certainly required. But other circumstances are also essential to establish the commission of the crime. The victim must not have been married to the defendant and her consent to sexual relations would, of course, preclude the crime. Must the defendant's purpose have encompassed the facts that he was not the husband of the victim and that she opposed his will? These are certainly entirely different questions. Recklessness, for example, on these points may be sufficient although purpose is required with respect to the sexual result which is an element of the offense.

Under the draft, therefore, the problem of the kind of culpability that is required for conviction must be faced separately with respect to each material element of the offense, although the answer may in many cases be the same with respect to each such element.

2. The draft acknowledges four different kinds of culpability: purpose, knowledge, recklessness, and negligence. It also recognizes that the material elements of offenses vary in that they may involve (1) the nature of the forbidden conduct or (2) the attendant circumstances or (3) the result of conduct. With respect to each of these three types of elements, the draft attempts to define each of the kinds of culpability that may arise. The resulting distinctions are, we think, both necessary and sufficient for the general purposes of penal legislation.

The purpose of articulating these distinctions in detail is, of course, to promote the clarity of definitions of specific crimes and to dispel the obscurity with which the culpability requirement is often treated when such concepts as "general criminal intent," "*mens rea*," "presumed intent," "malice," "willfulness," "scienter" and the like must be employed . . .

3. In defining the kinds of culpability, a narrow distinction is drawn between acting purposely and knowingly, one of the elements of ambiguity in legal usage of "intent." . . . Knowledge that the requisite external circumstances exist is a common element in both conceptions. But action is not purposive with respect to the nature or the result of the actor's conduct unless it was his conscious object to perform an action of that nature or to cause such a result. The distinction is no doubt inconsequential for most purposes of liability; acting knowingly is ordinarily sufficient . . .

45

DIAGNOSTIC
STATISTICAL
MANUAL IV

Sociopathology

Antisocial Personality Disorder

Diagnostic features

The essential feature of Antisocial Personality Disorder is a pervasive patterns of disregard for, and violation of, the rights of others that begins in childhood or early adolescence and continues into adulthood.

This pattern has also been referred to as psychopathy, sociopathy, or dyssocial personality disorder. Because deceit and manipulation are central features of Antisocial Personality Disorder, it may be especially helpful to integrate information acquired from systematic clinical assessment with information collected from collateral sources.

For this diagnosis to be given, the individual must be at least age 18 years and must have had a history of some symptoms of Conduct Disorder before age 15 years. Conduct Disorder involves a repetitive and persistent pattern of behavior in which the basic rights of others or major age-appropriate societal norms or rules are violated. The specific behaviors characteristic of Conduct Disorder fall into one of four categories: aggression to people and animals, destruction of property, deceitfulness or theft, or serious violation of rules.

The pattern of antisocial behavior continues into adulthood. Individuals with Antisocial Personality Disorder fail to conform to social norms with respect to lawful behavior. They may repeatedly perform acts that are grounds for arrest (whether they are arrested or not), such as destroying property, harassing others, stealing, or pursuing illegal occupations. Persons with this disorder disregard the wishes, rights, or feelings of others. They are frequently deceitful and manipulative in order to gain personal profit

Source: *Diagnostic and Statistical Manual of Mental Disorders*, 4th edn, Washington, DC: American Psychiatric Association, 1994.

or pleasure (e.g., to obtain money, sex, or power). They may repeatedly lie, use an alias, con others, or malinger. A pattern of impulsivity may be manifested by a failure to plan ahead. Decisions are made on the spur of the moment, without forethought, and without consideration for the consequences to self or others; they may lead to sudden changes of jobs, residences, or relationships. Individuals with Antisocial Personality Disorder tend to be irritable and aggressive and may repeatedly get into physical fights or commit acts of physical assault (including spouse beating or child beating). Aggressive acts that are required to defend oneself or someone else are not considered to be evidence for this item. These individuals also display a reckless disregard for the safety of themselves or others. This may be evidenced in their driving behavior (recurrent speeding, driving while intoxicated, multiple accidents). They may engage in sexual behavior or substance use that has a high risk for harmful consequences. They may neglect or fail to care for a child in a way that puts the child in danger.

Individuals with Antisocial Personality Disorder also tend to be consistently and extremely irresponsible. Irresponsible work behavior may be indicated by significant periods of unemployment despite available job opportunities, or by abandonment of several jobs without a realistic plan for getting another job. There may also be a pattern of repeated absences from work that are not explained by illness either in themselves or in their family. Financial irresponsibility is indicated by acts such as defaulting on debts, failing to provide child support, or failing to support other dependants on a regular basis. Individuals with Antisocial Personality Disorder show little remorse for the consequences of their acts. They may be indifferent to, or provide a superficial rationalization for, having hurt, mistreated, or stolen from someone (e.g., "life's unfair," "losers deserve to lose," or "he had it coming anyway"). These individuals may blame the victims for being foolish, helpless, or deserving their fate; they may minimize the harmful consequences of their actions; or they may simply indicate complete indifference. They generally fail to compensate or make amends for their behavior. They may believe that everyone is out to "help number one" and that one should stop at nothing to avoid being pushed around.

The antisocial behavior must not occur exclusively during the course of Schizophrenia or a Manic Episode.

Associated features and disorders

Individuals with Antisocial Personality Disorder frequently lack empathy and tend to be callous, cynical, and contemptuous of the feelings, rights, and sufferings of others. They may have an inflated and arrogant self-appraisal (e.g., feel that ordinary work is beneath them or lack a realistic concern about their current problems or their future) and may be excessively opinionated, self-assured, or cocky. They may display a glib, superficial charm and can be quite voluble and verbally facile (e.g., using technical terms or jargon that might impress someone who is unfamiliar with the topic). Lack of empathy, inflated self-appraisal, and superficial charm are features that have been commonly included in traditional conceptions of psychopathy and may be particularly distinguishing of Antisocial Personality Disorder in prison or forensic settings where criminal, delinquent, or aggressive acts are likely to be nonspecific. These individuals may also be irresponsible and exploitative in their sexual relationships. They may have a history of many sexual partners and may never have sustained a monogamous relationship. They may be irresponsible as parents, as evidenced by malnutrition of a child, an illness in the child resulting from a lack of minimal hygiene, a child's dependence on neighbors or nonresident relatives for food or shelter, a failure to arrange for a caretaker for a young child when the individual is away from home, or repeated squandering of money required for household necessities. These individuals may receive dishonorable discharges from the armed services, may fail to be self-supporting, may become impoverished or even homeless, or may spend many years in penal institutions. Individuals with Antisocial Personality Disorder are more likely than people in the general population to die prematurely by violent means (e.g., suicide, accidents, and homicides).

Individuals with this disorder may also experience dysphoria, including complaints of tension, inability to tolerate boredom, and depressed mood. They may have associated Anxiety Disorders, Depressive Disorders, Substance-Related Disorders, Somatization Disorder, Pathological Gambling, and other disorders of impulse control. Individuals with Antisocial Personality Disorder also often have personality features that meet criteria for other Personality Disorders, particularly Borderline, Histrionic, and Narcissistic Personality Disorders. The likelihood of developing Antisocial Personality Disorder in adult life is increased if the individual experienced an early onset of Conduct Disorder (before age 10 years) and accompanying Attention-Deficit/Hyperactivity Disorder. Child abuse or neglect, unstable or erratic parenting, or inconsistent parental discipline may increase the likelihood that Conduct Disorder will evolve into Antisocial Personality Disorder.

Specific culture, age, and gender features

Antisocial Personality Disorder appears to be associated with low socioeconomic status and urban settings. Concerns have been raised that the diagnosis may at time be misapplied to individuals in settings in which seemingly antisocial behavior may be part of a protective survival strategy. In assessing antisocial traits, it is helpful for the clinician to consider the social and economic context in which the behaviors occur.

By definition, Antisocial Personality cannot be diagnosed before age 18 years. Antisocial Personality Disorder is much more common in males than in females. There has been some concern that Antisocial Personality Disorder may be underdiagnosed in females, particularly because of the emphasis on aggressive items in the definition of Conduct Disorder.

Familial pattern

Antisocial Personality Disorder is more common among the first-degree biological relatives of those with the disorder than among the general population. The risk to biological relatives of females with the disorder tends to be higher than the risk to biological relatives of males with the disorder. Biological relatives of persons with this disorder are also at increased risk for Somatization Disorder and Substance-Related Disorders. Within a family that has a member with Antisocial Personality Disorder, males more often have Antisocial Personality Disorder and Substance-Related Disorders, whereas females more often have Somatization Disorder. However, in such families, there is an increase in prevalence of all of these disorders in both males and females compared with the general population. Adoption studies indicate that both genetic and environmental factors contribute to the risk of this group of disorders. Both adopted and biological children of parents with Antisocial Personality Disorder have an increased risk of developing Antisocial Personality Disorder, Somatization Disorder, and Substance-Related Disorders. Adopted-away children resemble their biological parents more than their adoptive parents, but the adoptive family environment influences the risk of developing a Personality Disorder and related psychopathology.

Differential diagnosis

The diagnosis of Antisocial Personality Disorder is not given to individuals under age 18 years and is given only if there is a history of some symptoms of Conduct Disorder before age 15 years. For individuals over age 18 years, a diagnosis of Conduct Disorder is given only if the criteria for Antisocial Personality Disorder are not met.

When antisocial behavior in an adult is associated with a *Substance-Related Disorder*, the diagnosis of Antisocial Personality Disorder is not made unless the signs of Antisocial Personality Disorder were also present in childhood and have continued into adulthood. When substance use and antisocial behavior both began in childhood and continued into adulthood, both a Substance-Related Disorder and Antisocial Personality Disorder should be diagnosed if the criteria for both are met, even though some antisocial acts may be a consequence of the Substance-Related Disorder (e.g., illegal selling of drugs or thefts to obtain money for drugs). Antisocial behavior that occurs exclusively during the course of *Schizophrenia* or a *Manic Episode* should not be diagnosed as Antisocial Personality Disorder.

Other Personality Disorders may be confused with Antisocial Personality Disorder because they have certain features in common. It is, therefore, important to distinguish among these disorders based on differences in their characteristic features. However, if an individual has personality features that meet criteria for one or more Personality Disorders in addition to Antisocial Personality Disorder, all can be diagnosed. Individuals with Antisocial Personality Disorder and *Narcissistic Personality Disorder* share a tendency to be tough-minded, glib, superficial, exploitative, and unempathic. However, Narcissistic Personality Disorder does not include characteristics of impulsivity, aggression, and deceit. In addition, individuals with Antisocial Personality Disorder may not be as needy of the admiration and envy of others, and persons with Narcissistic Personality Disorder usually lack the history of Conduct Disorder in childhood or criminal behavior in adulthood. Individuals with Antisocial Personality Disorder and *Histrionic Personality Disorder* share a tendency to be impulsive, superficial, excitement seeking, reckless, seductive, and manipulative, but persons with Histrionic Personality Disorder tend to be more exaggerated in their emotions and do not characteristically engage in antisocial behaviors. Individuals with Histrionic and *Borderline Personality Disorders* are manipulative to gain nurturance, whereas those with Antisocial Personality Disorder are manipulative to gain profit, power, or some other material gratification. Individuals with Antisocial Personality Disorder tend to be less emotionally unstable and more aggressive than those with Borderline Personality Disorder. Although antisocial behavior may be present in some individuals with *Paranoid Personality Disorder*, it is not usually motivated by a desire for personal gain or to exploit others as in Antisocial Personality Disorder, but rather is more often due to a desire for revenge.

Antisocial Personality Disorder must be distinguished from criminal behavior undertaken for gain that is not accompanied by the personality features characteristic of this disorder. *Adult Antisocial Behavior* . . . can be used to describe criminal, aggressive, or other antisocial behavior that comes to clinical attention but that does not meet the full criteria for Antisocial Personality Disorder. Only when antisocial personality traits are inflexible, maladaptive, and persistent and cause significant functional impairment or subjective distress do they constitute Antisocial Personality Disorder.

Diagnostic criteria for 301.7 Antisocial Personality Disorder

A. There is a pervasive pattern of disregard for and violation of the rights of others occurring since age 15 years, as indicated by three (or more) of the following:

    (1) failure to conform to social norms with respect to lawful behaviors as indicated by repeatedly performing acts that are grounds for arrest

    (2) deceitfulness, as indicated by repeated lying, use of aliases, or conning others for personal profit or pleasure

    (3) impulsivity or failure to plan ahead

    (4) irritability and aggressiveness, as indicated by repeated physical fights or assaults

    (5) reckless disregard for safety of self or others

    (6) consistent irresponsibility, as indicated by repeated failure to sustain consistent work behavior or honor financial obligations

(7) lack or remorse, as indicated by being indifferent to or rationalizing having hurt, mistreated, or stolen from another

B. The individual is at least age 18 years.
C. There is evidence of Conduct Disorder with onset before age 15 years.
D. The occurrence of antisocial behavior is not exclusively during the course of Schizophrenia or a Manic Episode.

ACKNOWLEDGEMENTS

We are grateful to the following publishers for permission to reprint extracts from the following:

AMERICAN LAW INSTITUTE for *The Model Penal Code*, copyright © 1956 by the American Law Institute. Reprinted with permission.

AMERICAN PSYCHIATRIC PRESS INC. for extract from the *Diagnostic and Statistical Manual of Mental Disorders*, Fourth Edition. Washington, DC, American Psychiatric Association, 1994.

BLACKWELL PUBLISHERS for 'How to Harden Your Heart: Six Easy Ways to Become Corrupt' by Amélie Rorty in *Yale Review*, April 1998.

CAMBRIDGE UNIVERSITY PRESS for 'The Nature of Immorality' by Jean Hampton, *Social Philosophy and Policy*, vol. 7, no. 1 (1984); *The Discourses and Other Early Political Writings* by J-J. Rousseau, translated by. Victor Gourevitch, 1997. Reprinted with the permission of Cambridge University Press.

T & T CLARK for *Calvin: Institutes of the Christian Religion*, edited by John T. McNeill, translated by Ford Lewis Battles. Published by The Westminster Press, 1960. Reprinted in North America by permission of Westminster John Knox Press.

HACKETT PUBLISHING COMPANY INC. for Dostoevsky, *The General Inquisitor*, edited by Guignon, 1993; Machiavelli, *The Prince*, edited and translated by Weitch, 1995; Abelard, *Ethical Writings*, translated by Spode, 1995. Reprinted by permission of Hackett Publishing Company. All rights reserved.

HARCOURT INC. for 'On Degrees of Evil' from *The Slopes of Lebanon*, copyright © 1987 by Amos Oz and Am Oved Publishers Ltd, Tel Aviv. English translation by Maurie Goldberg-Batura, copyright © 1989 by Harcourt Inc., reprinted by permission of Harcourt Inc.

THE JEWISH NATIONAL AND UNIVERSITY LIBRARY for letters from Albert Einstein to Sigmud Freud. By permission of The Albert Einstein Archives, The Jewish National and University Library, The Hebrew University of Jerusalem, Israel.

ACKNOWLEDGEMENTS

JOHNS HOPKINS UNIVERSITY PRESS for 'Political Action: The Problem of Dirty Hands' by Michael Walzer, from *Philosophy and Public Affairs*, 2 (1973). Copyright © The Johns Hopkins University Press. Reprinted with permission.

JOURNAL OF PHILOSOPHY for 'Desiring the Bad: An Essay in Moral Psychology' by Michael Stocker, LXXVI, 12 (December 1979). Reprinted by kind permission of the author and the *Journal of Philosophy*.

PERSEUS BOOKS GROUP for *Collected Papers*, Vol. 3, by Sigmund Freud, authorized translation under the supervision of Alix and James Strachey. Published by Basic Books, by arrangement with the Hogarth Press Ltd and the Institute of Psycho-Analysis, London. Reprinted by Basic Books, a member of Perseus Books L. L. C.

RANDOM HOUSE for 'Why War?' from *The Standard Edition of the Complete Psychological Works of Sigmund Freud*, translated and edited by James Strachey. Copyright The Institute of Psycho-Analysis and The Hogarth Press; *The Basic Writings of Neitzsche* by Frederich Nietzsche, translated by Walter Kaufman. Copyright © 1967 by Walter Kaufman and renewed 1994 by Mrs Hazel Kaufman. Reprinted by permission of Random House Inc.

SHEED & WARD for *The Confessions of St Augustine*, translated by F.J. Sheed. Reprinted by permission of Sheed & Ward, an Apostolate of the Priests of the Sacred Heart, 7373 South Lover's Lane Road, Franklin, Wisconsin 53132.

TAYLOR & FRANCIS for *Theodicy* by G. W. Leibniz. Published by Routledge.

UNIVERSITY OF CHICAGO PRESS FOR *The Guide of the Perplexed* by Moses Maimonides, trans. by Shlomo Pines, 1963.

We are grateful to the following for permission to reproduce the i????? in this volume:

CHARTRES CATHEDRAL for "The Devil and Greed".

DEPARTMENT OF PRINTING AND GRAPHIC ARTS, HOUGHTON LIBRARY, HARVARD COLLEGE LIBRARY, for George Grosz, "The Wilful Possessors," *The Marked Men* (Berlin: Malik-Verlag, 1929–1930). Also for Aubrey Beardsley, "Salome," (Illustrations for Oscar Wilde's *Salome*).

DOVER PUBLICATIONS for Cesare Ripa, "Justicia," in Edward Maser (ed.) *Baroque and Rococo Pictorial Imagery*, 1971.

THE METROPOLITAN MUSEUM OF ART for Francisco Goya, "The Sleep of Reason Produces Monsters," *The Marked Men* (Berlin: Malik-Verlag, 1929–1930). Gift of M. Knoedler & Co., 1918. Photograph©1994.

MUSEUM OF FINE ARTS, BOSTON for Francisco Goya, "Indecision," Bequest of Horatio G. Curh's, by exchange, and the Harvey D. Parker collection, by exchange, 1973.

Every effort has been made to contact copyright holders. The publishers will be pleased to rectify any omissions in further editions.

BIBLIOGRAPHY

We have not listed specific citations for bibliographic information: many of these works appear in numerous adequate translations and editions, while others are only published in one.

Anthropology

Walter Burkert, *Homo Necans*; *Greek Religion*.
Bishop Bartolome las Casas, *Historical and True Account of the Cruel Massacre Slaughter of the Peoples of the West Indies by the Spaniards*.
Andrew Delbanco, *The Death of Satan*.
E.R. Dodds, *The Greeks and the Irrational*.
Wendy Doniger O'Flaherty, *The Origins of Evil in Hindu Mythology*.
Mary Douglas, *Purity and Danger*.
Rene Girard, *Violence and the Sacred*.
R. Horton and R. Finegan (eds) *Modes of Thought*.
R. Klibansky, E. Panofsky and F. Saxl, *Saturn and Melancholy*.
A.C. Lehmann and James Myers, *Magic, Witchcraft and Religion*.
Bronislaw Malinowski, *Crime and Custom in Savage Society*.
Max Marwick (ed.) *Witchcraft and Sorcery*.
John Middleton (ed.) *Magic, Witchcraft and Healing*.
Rodney Needham (ed.) *Right and Left*.
Gananath Obeyeskere, *Cult of the Goddess Pattini*.
David Parkin (ed.) *The Anthropology of Evil*.
Richard Stivers, *Evil in Modern Myth and Ritual*.
Montague Summers, *The History of Witchcraft and Demonology*.
Stanley Tambiah, *Magic, Science, Religion and Rationality*.
D.P. Walker, *The Decline of Hell*; *Unclean Spirits*; *Spiritual and Demonic Magic*.

Art

Leonard Bloomfield, *The Seven Deadly Sins* (see esp. the Bibliography).
Piero di Cosimo, *Works*.
Francisco Goya, "Disasters of War," "Proverbs," "Caprichos."

George Grosz, *Love and Other Drawings.*
William Hogarth, "The Stages of Cruelty," "A Rake's Progress," "A Harlot's Progress."
Adolf Katzenellebogen, *Allegories of Virtues and Vices in the Middle Ages.*
Cesare Ripa, *Baroque and Rococo Pictorial Imagery.*
Art Spiegelman, *Maus: A Survivor's Tale.*
See representations of vices, devils, hell in the cathedrals of Albi, Autun, Chartres, Orvieto, Notre Dame; frescos by Giotto, Lorenzetti, Michelangelo; paintings and prints by Altdorf, Francis Bacon, Aubrey Beardsley, Max Beckman, Pieter Breughel, Hieronymus Bosch, Piero di Cosimo, Albrecht Dürer, Francisco Goya, Grünewaldt, William Hogarth, Klimt, Edvard Munch; caricatures by Charles Kaspar Braun, Charles Le Brun, Honore Daumier, David Low, Charles Philipon, Hjalmar Schacht, R. Topffer.

Fiction

Chinua Achebe, *Things Fall Apart.*
Dante Alighieri, *The Inferno.*
Henri Balzac, *Père Goriot, Eugénie Grandet.*
Charles Baudelaire, "The Flowers of Evil."
Stephen Vincent Benet, *The Devil and Daniel Webster.*
William Blake, "The Marriage of Heaven and Hell."
Bertolt Brecht, *Three Penny Opera.*
Emily Brontë, *Wuthering Heights.*
John Bunyan, *Pilgrim's Progress*; *A Few Sighs from Hell.*
Wilhelm Busch, *Max and Moritz.*
Samuel Butler, *Erewhon.*
Albert Camus, *The Stranger.*
Geoffrey Chaucer, *Canterbury Tales*, "The Parson's Tale."
J.M. Coetze, *Waiting for the Barbarians*; *Disgrace.*
Joseph Conrad, *Heart of Darkness*; *Nostromo.*
Pierre Choderlos de la Clos, *Liaisons Dangereuses.*
Daniel Defoe, *Moll Flanders.*
Charles Dickens, *Hard Times*; *Oliver Twist*; *Our Mutual Friend*; *Great Expectations.*
Fyodor Dostoevsky, *Crime and Punishment*; "Ivan's Preface to the Tale of the Grand Inquisitor," *Brothers Karamazov*; *Notes from the Underground.*
Euripides, *Medea*; *The Trojan Women*; *Hippolytus.*
William Faulkner, *Light in August.*
André Gide, *The Immoralist*; *The Counterfeiters.*
William Golding, *Lord of the Flies.*
Johann Wolfgang von Goethe, *Faust.*
Nicolai Gogol, *Collected Stories.*
The Brothers Grimm, *The Collected Fairy Tales.*
J.J.C. von Grimmelshausen, *Simplicissimus.*
Nathaniel Hawthorne, *The Scarlet Letter*; *Collected Short Stories.*
E.T.A. Hoffman, *Tales of Hoffman.*
Victor Hugo, *The Hunchback of Notre Dame*; *Les Miserables.*
Henry James, *The Turn of the Screw*; *Portrait of a Lady*; *The Golden Bowl*; *Washington Square.*
Franz Kafka, *The Trial*; *The Castle.*
Heinrich von Kleist, *The Collected Stories.*
Jerzi Kosinski, *The Painted Bird.*
Mikhail Lermontov, *The Demon.*

Thomas Mann, *Mario the Magician*; *Dr. Faustus*.

Christopher Marlowe, *Dr. Faustus*.

Daphne du Maurier, *Rebecca*.

Herman Melville, *Billy Budd*; *Moby Dick*.

Arthur Miller, *The Crucible*.

John Milton, *Paradise Lost*.

Toni Morrison, *Beloved*.

Flannery O'Connor, *Collected Stories*.

George Orwell, *Nineteen Eighty-Four*.

Edgar Allan Poe, "The Cask of Amontillado"; "The Imp of the Perverse."

Anne Rice, *The Vampire Chronicles*.

Katherine Ramsland, *The Vampire Companion*.

J.-J. Rousseau, *La Nouvelle Heloise*.

Salman Rushdie, *Satanic Verses*.

Bertrand Russell, "Satan in the Suburbs."

Marquis de Sade, *A Dialogue Between a Priest and a Dying Man*.

J.-P. Sartre, *No Exit*; *The Devil and the Good Lord*; "Childhood of a Leader."

Seneca, *Plays*.

William Shakespeare, *Richard III*; *Macbeth*; *Othello*; *Coriolanus*; *Titus Andronicus*.

Mary Shelley, *Frankenstein*.

Robert Louis Stevenson, *The Strange Case of Dr. Jekyll and Mr. Hyde*.

Harriet Beecher Stowe, *Uncle Tom's Cabin*.

Bram Stoker (Leslie Shephard, ed.) *The Dracula Book of Classical Vampire Stories*.

Lev Tolstoy, *The Kreutzer Sonata*; *The Death of Ivan Ilytch*.

Mark Twain, *The Mysterious Stranger*; *Letters from the Earth*.

Voltaire, *Candide*.

Oscar Wilde, *The Picture of Dorian Gray*.

Emile Zola, *Nana*.

Sample the works of Graham Greene, Patricia Highsmith, John le Carré, P.D. James, J.R.R. Tolkien, C.S. Lewis and Charles Williams.

Films

Apocalypse Now.

The Battle of Algiers.

Belle de Jour; *Un Chien Andalou*.

Bonnie and Clyde.

The Decalogue.

The Devil's Advocate.

The Devil and Daniel Webster.

Dracula.

Faustus.

Frankenstein.

The Godfather.

All Hitchcock films

Liaisons Dangereuses.

Pulp Fiction.

Schindler's List.

Shoah.

Silence of the Lambs.

The Talented Mr. Ripley.

The Third Man.

BIBLIOGRAPHY

Titus Andronicus.
To Die in Madrid.

History

Hannah Arendt, *Eichmann in Jerusalem*; "Organized Guilt," *Jewish Frontier*, Jan. 1945.
H.R. Fox Bourne, *Civilization in the Congoland: A Story of International Wrong-doing.*
Walter Burkert, *Homo Necans*; *Greek Religion.*
Bishop Bartolome las Casas, *Historical and True Account of the Cruel Massacre Slaughter of the Peoples of the West Indies by the Spaniards.*
Jean Delumeau, *Sin and Fear.*
E.R. Dodds, *The Greeks and the Irrational.*
Alfred Dreyfus, *Five Years of My Life.*
Adoph Hitler, *Mein Kampf.*
Karl Jaspers, *The Question of German Guilt.*
Szygmon Laks, *Music of Another World.*
Primo Lévi, *If This Is a Man*; *If Not Now, When?*; *Moments of Reprieve*; *The Drowned and the Saved.*
William Prescott, *The Conquest of Mexico*; *The Conquest of Peru.*
The Protocols of Zion.
Georg Simmel, *The Metropolitan Type.*
I.F. Stone, *The Killings at Kent State.*
Thucydides, *The Peloponnesian War.*
Emile Zola, *J'Accuse.*

Law

American Law Institute, *Model Penal Code.*
John Arthur and William Shaw (eds) *Readings in the Philosophy of Law*, Secs 5–6, 8–11.
Hugo Bedau (ed.) *Civil Disobedience.*
Jeremy Bentham, *The Limits of Jurisprudence*; *Panopticon Papers.*
Joel Feinberg, *Doing and Deserving.*
Joel Feinberg and Hyman Gross (eds) *Philosophy of Law*, Parts of 4 and 5.
H.L.A Hart, "Negligence, *Mens Rea* and Criminal Responsibility," A.G. Guest (ed.) *Oxford Essays on Jurisprudence.*
H.L.A. Hart and A.M. Honore, *Causation in the Law.*
Herbert Morris (ed.) *Freedom and Responsibility.*
Jeffrie Murphy (ed.) *Civil Disobedience and Violence.*
W.L. Prosser, *Handbook of the Law of Torts.*
L. Radzinowiz and Jerome Hall, *General Principles of Criminal Law*; *Studies in Jurisprudence and Criminal Law.*
D.A. Stroud, *Mens Rea.*
J.W.C. Turner, *The Modern Approach to Criminal Law.*
Royal Commision on Capital Punishment 1949–53 Report.
Glanville Williams, *Criminal Law: the General Part.*

BIBLIOGRAPHY

Philosophy and Politics

Marilyn Adams, "The Problem of Evil," *The Encyclopedia of Philosophy* (ed. Edward Craig).

Marilyn and Robert Adams (eds), *The Problem of Evil*.

Fred Alford, *What Evil Means to Us* (see bibliography).

Ruth Nanda Anschen, *Anatomy of Evil*.

Thomas Aquinas, *De Malo*.

Hannah Arendt, *Eichmann in Jerusalem*; "Organized Guilt," *Jewish Frontier*, Jan. 1945.

Cesare Beccaria, *On Crimes and Punishments*.

Jonathan Bennett, "The Conscience of Huckleberry Finn."

Robert Burton, *The Anatomy of Melancholy*.

Paul Carus, *The History of the Devil and the Ideas of Evil from the Earliest Times to the Present*.

Karl Clausewitz, *On War*.

Marshall Cohen, Thomas Nagel and Thomas Scanlon (eds), *War and Moral Responsibility*.

Jonathan Edwards, *Sinners in the Hands of an Angry God*.

Friedrich Engels, *The Condition of the Working Class in England*.

Ian Fleming, *The Seven Deadly Sins*.

Cynthia Freeland, *The Naked and the Undead: Evil and the Appeal of Horror*.

Charles Fried, "The Evil of Lying," *Right and Wrong*.

Raimond Gaita, *Good and Evil: An Absolute Conception*.

Peter Geach, *Providence and Evil*.

Jean Genet (with the introduction by J.-P. Sartre), *Thief's Journal*.

Philip Hallie, "The Evil that Men Think and Do," *Hastings Center Report*, 1985.

Jean Hampton, "The Nature of Immorality," *Social Philosophy & Policy*, vol. 7, 1989.

John Hick, "The Problem of Evil," *The Encyclopedia of Philosophy* (ed. Paul Edwards).

Adoph Hitler, *Mein Kampf*.

Albert Hofstadter, *Reflections on Evil*.

Karl Jaspers, *The Question of German Guilt*.

Immanuel Kant, *Religion Within the Limits of Reason Alone*, Books 1–2.

John Kekes, *Facing Evil*.

G.W. Leibniz, *Theodicy*, "The Justice of God . . . and the Origin of Evil."

Nicolò Machiavelli, *The Prince*; *The Discourses*.

Moses Maimonides, *The Guide for the Perplexed*, Book III, Ch. 12.

Jacques Maritain, *St. Thomas and the Problem of Evil*.

Mary Midgley, *Wickedness: A Philosophical Essay*.

Martha Minow, *Between Vengeance and Forgiveness*.

Herbert Morris, *Responsibility and the Law*; *On Guilt and Innocence*.

Steven Nadler, "Choosing a Theodicy: The Liebnitz–Malebranche–Arnauld Connection," *Journal of the History of Ideas*, 1994.

Friedrich Nietzsche, *Beyond Good and Evil*.

Daniel O'Connor, "Good and Evil Disposition," *Kant-Studien*, 1985.

Amos Oz, "Degrees of Evil," *The New Republic*, 1986.

Alvin Plantinga, *God, Freedom, and Evil*.

Prudentius, *Psychomachia*.

Amélie Rorty, "How to Harden Your Heart: Six Easy Steps to Corruption," *Yale Review*, 1998.

Josiah Royce, *Studies of Good and Evil*.

J.-P. Sartre, *Anti-Semite and Jew*; *No Exit*; "Childhood of a Leader."

Arthur Schopenhauer, "On the Sufferings of the World," translated by T.B. Saunders, *Studies in Pessimism*.

Seneca, *On Anger*.

Judith Shklar, *Ordinary Cruelty*.

BIBLIOGRAPHY

Robert Solomon (ed.) *Wicked Pleasures*.
Georges Sorel, *Reflections on Violence*.
Michael Stocker, "Desiring the Bad," *Journal of Philosophy*, 1979.
Michael Walzer, "The Problem of Dirty Hands," *Philosophy & Public Affairs*, 2, 1973.
Richard Wasserstrom (ed.), *War and Morality*.

Psychology

Ernst Becker, *The Structure of Evil: An Essay on the Unification of the Science of Man*.
Leonard Berkowitz, *Aggression: Its Causes, Consequences, and Control*.
Diagnostic Statistical Manual IV, "Sociopathology."
Sigmund Freud, *Totem and Taboo*; *Moses and Monotheism*; *Civilization and its Discontents*.
J. Groebel and Robert Hinde (ed.), *Aggression and War: Their Biological and Social Bases*.
Fred E. Katz, *Ordinary People and Extraordinary Evil: A Report on the Beguilings of Evil*.
Jack Katz, *Seductions of Crime: Moral and Sensual Attractions in Doing Evil*.
Carl Kerenyi *et al.*, *Evil: Essays*.
Konrad Lorenz, *Aggression*.
Walter Lowe, *Evil and the Unconscious*.
Stanley Milgram, *Obedience to Authority*.
Nell Noddings, *Women and Evil*.
Eli Sagan, *Freud, Women, and Morality: The Psychology of Good and Evil*.
Ervin Straub, *The Roots of Evil: The Psychological and Cultural Origins of Genocide and Other Forms of Group Violence*.

Theology

Peter Abelard, *Know Thyself*.
Marilyn and Robert Adams (eds.), *The Problem of Evil*.
Augustine, *On Free Will*; *Confessions*, Book 2, Chs. 3–6; *City of God*, XI.17; XIV.3.
Thomas Aquinas, *On Evil*.
Leonard Bloomfield, *The Seven Deadly Sins* (see esp. the bibliography).
The Book of Job.
Martin Buber, *Good and Evil: Two Interpretations*; *Images of Good and Evil*.
John Bunyan, *A Few Sighs from Hell*.
John Calvin, *Institutes of the Christian Religion*, Book II, Chs 1–2.
John Cassian, *Institutes*, Book XII.
Richard Cavendish, *The Powers of Evil in Western Religion, Magic and Folk Belief*.
Thomas J. Csordas, *The Sacred Self: A Cultural Phenomenology of Charismatic Healing*.
Evagrius of Pontus, *On the Eight Evil Thoughts*.
The Egyptian Book of the Dead.
The Gnostic Gospels.
Peter Geach, *Providence and Evil*.
Gregory the Great, *Moralia*, Book XXXI, 45.
Brian Hebblewaite, *Evil, Suffering, and Religion*.
Pope Innocent III, *On the Misery of the Human Condition*, Book I, Chs 1, 2, 18–20; Book II, Chs 1–36.
Hans Jonas, *The Gnostic Religion*.
Adolf Katzenellenbogen, *Allegories of Virtues and Vices in the Middle Ages*.
C.S. Lewis, *The Problem of Pain*.

BIBLIOGRAPHY

Martin Luther, "Of the Double Use of the Law," "Flesh Against Spirit,"; *Commentary on Galatians*; *95 Theses*.

Edward H. Madden and Peter K. Hare, *Evil and the Concept of God*.

Wendy Doniger O'Flaherty, *The Origins of Evil in Hindu Mythology*.

Elaine Pagels, *The Origin of Satan*; *The Gnostic Gospels*.

Prudentius, *Psychomachia*.

Paul Ricoeur, *The Symbolism of Evil*.

Shalom Rosenberg, *Good and Evil in Jewish Thought*.

J.-J. Rousseau, "Preface," *Narcissus*, Secs. 24–35; *Second Discourse*, Secs. 34–38.

Jeffrey Burton Russell, *The Devil: Perceptions of Evil from Antiquity to Primitive Christianity*; *Lucifer: The Devil in the Middle Ages*; *Mephistopheles: The Devil in the Modern World*; *The Prince of Darkness: Radical Evil and the Power of Good in History*; *Satan: The Early Christian Tradition*.

Fra Girolamo Savonarola, *Prison Meditations*.

Hans Schwarz, *Evil: A Historical and Theological Perspective*.

Heinrich Kramer and Jakob Sprenger (trans. Montague Summers, ed. Arrow), *Malleus Maleficarum*.

Michael Stroeber, *Evil and Mystic's God: Toward a Mystical Theodicy*.

Tertullian, *On Spectacles*.

S. Wenzel, *The Sin of Sloth*.

Printed in the USA/Agawam, MA
March 23, 2015

611180.002